# SHAKESPEARE'S
# NOISE

# SHAKESPEARE'S NOISE

## KENNETH GROSS

the university of chicago press
chicago & london

KENNETH GROSS is professor of English at the University of Rochester and the author of *Spenserian Poetics: Idolatry, Iconoclasm, and Magic* and *The Dream of the Moving Statue.*

The University of Chicago Press gratefully acknowledges the assistance of the John Simon Guggenheim Memorial Foundation in the publication of this book.

The University of Chicago Press, Chicago 60637
The University of Chicago Press, Ltd., London
© 2001 by The University of Chicago
All rights reserved. Published 2001
Printed in the United States of America

10  09  08  07  06  05  04  03  02  01      1  2  3  4  5

ISBN: 0-226-30988-6 (cloth)
ISBN: 0-226-30989-4 (paper)

Library of Congress Cataloging-in-Publication Data

Gross, Kenneth.
  Shakespeare's noise / Kenneth Gross.
    p. cm.
  Includes bibliographical references (p. ) and index.
    ISBN 0-226-30988-6 (cloth : alk. paper)—ISBN 0-226-30989-4 (pbk. : alk. paper)
      1. Shakespeare, William, 1564–1616—Language.    2. English language—Early modern, 1500–1700—Obscene words.    3. English language—Early modern, 1500–1700—Slang.    4. Shakespeare, William, 1564–1616—Technique.    5. Language and culture—England—History.    6. Blessing and cursing—England—History.    7. Invective in literature.    8. Drama—Technique.    I. Title.
PR3072.G76 2001
822.3′3—dc21                                                                    00-031656

♾ The paper used in this publication meets the minimum requirements of the American National Standard for Information Sciences—Permanence of Paper for Printed Library Materials, ANSI Z39.48-1992.

*For my students*

# CONTENTS

# ACKNOWLEDGMENTS

I am indebted in these pages to many friends and colleagues, including Tom Bishop, Joan Dayan, Irving Feldman, Lisa Fishman, Angus Fletcher, John Hollander, Herbert Marks, Gordon Teskey, Paolo Valesio, Joseph Wittreich, and Susanne Wofford. All in their different ways made writing this book part of a larger, necessary conversation. Daniel Albright kept my ear open for more various musics. Working with Rebecca Holderness and her actors let me confront more directly the strange disciplines of theater. Leslie Katz helped me early on to listen through the noise, and to understand its life. Kari Kraus, Margaret McCarney, and Kara Molway-Russell, my research assistants over the years, found in their investigations many unexpected gems. My students at the University of Rochester provided many important insights and, just as crucial, kept me in mind of what is at stake in doing this work. Bruce Smith and Susan Stewart read the manuscript for the University of Chicago Press with great candor and generosity, aiding me particularly in the final stages of revising the book. The text has also benefited from Erik Carlson's expert and nuanced editing. Lastly, my thanks to Alan Thomas for his great care in seeing this book through to print.

A senior research fellowship at the Folger Shakespeare Library was of fundamental importance at the beginning of my work, allowing me to enter more fruitfully into the complex Renaissance obsession with slander and rumor. Fellowships awarded by the John Simon Guggenheim Foundation and the National Endowment for the Humanities, as well as financial support from the University of Rochester, allowed me the time and freedom to continue this research and to complete the writing of this book. To each I would express my profound gratitude. I also want to thank the Guggenheim Foundation for a grant to underwrite the publication of this volume.

Chapter 1, "The Rumor of *Hamlet*," first appeared in *Raritan: A Quarterly Review*. My coda, "An Imaginary Theater," was first published in *The Yale Review*. Both are reprinted here by permission of the editors.

# A NOTE ON TEXTS

Quotations from the five plays discussed most at length in this book are taken from the following editions: *Hamlet,* ed. Harold Jenkins, Arden Shakespeare, 2d ser. (London: Methuen, 1982); *Measure for Measure,* ed. J. W. Lever, Arden Shakespeare, 2d ser. (London: Methuen, 1965); *Othello,* ed. E. A. J. Honigman, Arden Shakespeare, 3d ser. (Walton-on-Thames: Thomas Nelson and Sons, 1997); *Coriolanus,* ed. Phillip Brockbank, Arden Shakespeare, 2d ser. (London: Methuen, 1976); and *King Lear,* ed. R. A. Foakes, Arden Shakespeare, 3d ser. (Walton-on-Thames: Thomas Nelson and Sons, 1997). Quotations from all other plays and poems of Shakespeare are taken from *The Riverside Shakespeare,* ed. G. Blakemore Evans, 2d ed. (Boston: Houghton Mifflin, 1997).

# INTRODUCTION

This book pursues a vision of the work of words in Shakespeare's plays. I look most closely at violent or disorderly forms of speaking: slander, defamation, insult, vituperation, malediction, and curse. Rumor and gossip play a part as well. Such forms of speech are among the playwright's deepest preoccupations. His endless supply of mocks and curses is part of what continues most deeply to charm us in the plays, freed as they are from our own taboos against speaking ill. Damaging words undergo complex metamorphoses in Shakespeare. They fissure meaning. They bind souls. They abet terror and provoke insanity. They expose speakers to their own unconscious aggression, and to their often deviant intelligence. These words also reach outward into the larger natural and social world, even if only intermittently, or in secret. The plays often lend them a suspect, half-human life of their own, a life capable of shaping character and action in astonishing ways. The life of such words becomes as much a blessing as a curse; their hurt embeds an uncanny generosity, since they open up forms of thought and feeling otherwise invisible. The violence that the human tongue does to human ears is one of my subjects here. Equally crucial is the ambivalent reach of the human ear itself. "Now this ill-wresting world is grown so bad, / Mad slanderers by mad ears believed be," writes Shakespeare in sonnet 140. I use the word "noise" in characterizing the movement of language on Shakespeare's stage, because it helps suggest a theater in which the human voice takes shape from the way that language interferes with itself, assumes the power of its own disorder—especially if we recall the word's older associations with disturbance, quarrel, and scandal.[1] We are faced with words whose force depends exactly on how they are repeated, obscured, interrupted, stolen, buried, or misheard by those who hear them. To think about noise in this sense gives us access to the inner life of the plays, their ethical conversation. It gives an idiom to silence as much as to speech and lets us better apprehend those flawed words and stubborn sounds which Shakespeare makes so demanding and resonant, so ghostly in their effects.

My own investigation into these matters took its start with wondering about a group of Shakespeare's plays which are haunted by the devious power of defamatory speech and by the shifting character of the slanderer. The most obvious instances are *Much Ado about Nothing, Measure for Measure, Othello, The Winter's Tale,* and *Cymbeline,* but the list includes, with different shadings, *The Merchant of Venice, Hamlet,* and *Coriolanus.* Slander's myriad disguises make it a mortal threat in the world of these plays. Its protean nature and quasi-magical efficacy add to its allure. These works explore the power of a distorting lie to infect both public and private knowledge, to grow in secret, diffusing itself through almost invisible networks of suspicion. They dramatize the dangers that defamation poses in a world where a person's identity, his or her "fame," depends so strongly on the words and fantasies of others. Shakespeare's concern with slander calls up the matter of rumor (from the Latin for "noise," the Latin *fama* itself meaning "rumor"). It makes us consider how words about the self are heard and overheard, and how, in passing between speakers, their identity and power is transformed. The circle described by the matter of slander and rumor becomes a starting place to examine more broadly the risks of speaking and hearing in the world, a world drawn together by fragile, often corrosive networks of murmuring, news, and tale-telling, full of interruption, derangement, nonsense, and static. Through these suspect media the most potent fictions of self emerge, along with some of Shakespeare's most unsettling reasonings about the real. A curious pattern, even a music, emerges from the noise. The playwright becomes what Elias Canetti calls an "earwitness," one who listens to the troubled, often pathological ways in which others listen to the world.[2]

The English word "slander" derives from the same root as "scandal," the Greek word *skandalon,* meaning "trap" or "stumbling block."[3] One scandal explored in this book is that folded up in acts of verbal abuse are impulses which link them to language at its most revelatory, liberating, and humanizing. The study of damaging words helps us map the ambivalent springs of human identity in Shakespeare, the quality of the self's attachment to the very things that threaten it. *Othello,* for example, ruthlessly explores the dire psychological consequences, the moral snares, of secret rumor and detraction; yet the play suggests that these abuses of speech also open up a realm of fantasy otherwise unavailable to the hero; it shows us an erotic life structured around wild hopes and losses, abjections but also strange pieces of truth, that would otherwise have remained invisible. *Hamlet* shows us a prince with a particularly acute ear for the vicious rumors, the muffled din or "coil" of life at court. These are, as it were, his enemies. Yet covertly slanderous utterance is also a tool for Hamlet, a defensive mask, a risky species of theater. Rumor and slander, in fact, become privileged, if tragic, forms of knowledge in this play (curiously connected to the storytelling of ghosts). In *Measure for Measure,* the play's chief rumormonger, Lucio, provides a comic mouthpiece for both psychological and political truth, though his slanders of authority fall into exactly the wrong ear, that of the disguised Duke of Vienna. Even more important is that this ruler, whose ear is so ready to apprehend "unfathered" rumors about his person, turns out to be peculiarly deaf to a group of more extreme, psychologically demanding voices that are released in the course of the play. *Coriolanus* presents us with a civic hero for whom all public praise, all language of public "election," seems strangely equivalent to slander, nothing but empty and contaminating public wind—against which Coriolanus can only aim self-wounding vituperation, a style of rage that echoes what is for him the purer, more candid noise of the battlefield.

The violent speech that concerns me in my last chapter, on *King Lear,* is of a different order. Here I focus on the metamorphoses of curse. Curse would seem a rawer kind of utterance than defamation or rumor, less susceptible to mere guile or subterfuge. But the dramatic use of curse in Shakespeare's plays poses questions similar to those raised by the other forms of ill-speaking. *King Lear* in particular suggests that curse shares with slander the capacity to spread its violence abroad, even given its apparent impotence. Curse acquires the look of something fatal, though also painfully human. It affects both utterer and hearer in uncanny ways; the curser and the cursed can be connected by an almost erotic bond—a link of mutual need which transforms them both, often unwittingly, a shared power that passes between them, like Plato's *eros* in the *Symposium.* Curse also shows, like slander, a liberating energy. Lear's royal curses carry not just blind rage but an intenser knowledge of the world's and history's violence; they convey an awareness of the curse of history, as well as the curse of nature. His storm of curses translates prayer and blessing, even love, in a world where prayer and blessing can scarcely be offered without irony and where love is silenced by resentment.

I want to evoke the forms of life, the quickening powers, that lie within these violent forms of language. Attention to such troubled modes of speaking and hearing allows me a way into those motives which most deeply shape the plays. In Shakespeare, rumor, slander, and curse turn out to be

ways of creating a world, as well as ways of creating a character.[4] Disorderly
as these ways of speaking are, they can shape an order, even take on a quasi-
ritual form. (One might point here to the elaborately formalized contests of
verbal aggression we find in many cultures, from the savage boasting matches
of heroes in the *Iliad* to Irish legends about magician-bards whose satirical
verses have the power to kill their enemies, though it might do equally well
to recall one's own childhood games of taunt and countertaunt.) We can see
in such words the vexed bases for our interactions with others, they show us
how one's self may be found out—rifted, harrowed, released all at once—
by the play of another person's words, even as one's own words fall back on
the self in violence or distortion. They show us the storm of meanings that
we both confront and create in our negotiations with a world that is so mutable, so infinitely capable of disappointing our wishes. They show us the
shapes assumed by our doubt and suspicion, the contaminated vehicles for
our knowledge of others, as well as the dark forms of speech on which we
stake our knowledge of ourselves.[5] Shakespeare discovers a wounding and a
self-wounding energy set loose within human speaking. Yet he also he makes
such an energy essential to whatever power human language has to frame
truth, whether the truths of the historical world or the truths of the unconscious. The deep claims of the language within Shakespearean drama, including its power of reparation, are bound to its capacity for distortion and
violence, its ability to sustain itself as interference and noise. "In the beginning was the noise; the noise never stops," writes Michel Serres. "It is a little
bit of the secret thrust of our awakenings."[6]

WRITING THIS BOOK, I became increasingly aware of how Shakespeare's preoccupation with these extreme forms of human speech grows out of their
power to animate the stage. Fictions about rumor, slander, and curse just
make for good plays; as subjects for drama, they animate certain basic energies in the medium itself. I have indeed felt at times as if all proper theater
were a theater of noise. We should remind ourselves, for example, that
Shakespeare's stage was a place of scandal, both real and imaginary; his plays
gave form to the uncanny, mutable life of scandal. On this stage otherwise
forbidden sights were exposed, analyzed, and also displaced, made at once
visible and invisible. Ancient historical crises were played over again. This
theater took up endangered and abused fames, both mythical and historical;
it showed characters wrestling with forms of compromised glory, tempting
the audience's desire to see both the mask and what was behind the mask, ad-
justing degrees of shame and exposure. It was the home of actors whose work

was seen, by hostile critics, as by nature an inescapable slander of established truths, especially given the actors' power endlessly to transform their identity on stage. Most relevant here, perhaps, is the fact that the Renaissance theater provided occasions for playwrights and players to explore multiple, always shifting registers of outrageous speech, from whispered innuendo to gaudy rant, from the dextrous verbal twistings of clowns to the cursing bombast of revengers and the bitter invective of malcontents; it allowed such speech to take on a life of its own, launching these words into a space that was itself one of the noisiest in the city of London, received by an audience whose own ears could be by turns attentive, foolish, hostile, vulnerable, and dull— not to mention "ill-wresting."[7] If such freedom of speech and freedom of hearing in the theater were scarcely unmediated, especially given the complex pressures of official censorship, playwrights yet continued to develop such unsettling languages ever more relentlessly. Indeed, in a theater strong enough to feed on its own contradictions, they could take the deployment and control of verbal violence as part of their very dramatic subject matter.

I touch on the question of theater variously in what follows, sometimes speculating about the concrete particulars of Shakespeare's stagecraft, sometimes taking theater as a metaphor, a dream or figure of performance in the text, subject to more fantastic constructions. One basic aim is to find a language alive to the plays as things written for the stage, drawing their energy from the strange thing that is theater.[8] My coda, "An Imaginary Theater," takes a yet different tack, or rather, it brings to the center of its concerns something that has been a touchstone throughout this book: my own experience of live theater in the present. The coda emerges as much from the balcony as from the study; it takes up questions that ran through my head while watching, say, stagings of *The Winter's Tale* or *The Ghost Sonata, Oedipus Rex* or a Punch-and-Judy show. Here I speak more immediately about the unsettling presence of the actor in the theater, living at once in real space and time, and yet within "a dream of passion." I consider what it feels like to be a "guilty creature sitting at a play," moved, torn, bored, or baffled by what is onstage. The paradoxical nature of gesture in theater, its joinings of secrecy and exposure, visibility and invisibility, is one of my subjects here. The coda also considers why we should register theatrical presence so strongly through complex plays of sound and voice, through the gestural use of silence and music, through dramas of listening. The poetics of theater sketched in this section takes in more than Shakespeare. But it will make clear how an account of Shakespeare's preoccupation with rumor, slander, and curse can take us to the heart of his theater's power.

My questions about noise in the theater resonate within a larger historical space. Working on this book involved plunging into what one critic has
called "the culture of slander" in Renaissance England.[9] Though I had earlier
explored sixteenth-century representations of slander, particularly in writing on Spenser's *Faerie Queene,* I was not quite prepared for how saturated,
how intricate and wild, the Renaissance's talk of evil tongues could be.[10] A
single quotation, examined more closely in chapter 2, may suffice to catch
the air of this—from a letter written by the earl of Essex to Queen Elizabeth. Imprisoned on suspicion of treason in 1600, threatened by the invisible
malice of his enemies, Essex reports that he feels "as if I were throwen into a
corner like a dead carcas," finding himself gnawed at by "the vilest and
basest creatures upon earth." He becomes a thing subject to the idle chatter
of the libelers and tavern haunters, at the mercy of scandalmongering pam-
phleteers and players: "Already they print me, & make me speak to the
world; and shortly they will play me in what forme they list upon the
stage."[11] Here verbal abuse is a strange combination of cannibalism and soul
theft; in other texts it gets described variously through metaphors of murder, plague, poisoning, rebellion, rape, abortion, witchcraft, and demonic
possession. Slander seems liable to touch everyone, from the common
householder to the purest cleric. Fear of calumny is a shadow of humanism,
the dark underside of a rhetoric-obsessed and fame-obsessed vision of the
world. That fear is also a mirror of the paranoid coloring of Tudor-Stuart
politics, especially given a culture preoccupied with dangers (both real and
imagined) of civil discontent, aristocratic conspiracy, and religious faction-
alism. For Stefano Guazzo, whose *La conversazione civile* was translated into
English in the 1580s, slander was a fixed part of the atmosphere at any
court, an intimate enemy all the harder to find out because it disguised itself
as both praise and blame, as flattery, witty joking, or innocent gossip.
Lawyers like Edward Coke and Francis Bacon suggested that detractions of
a monarch or his ministers could strike at the very heart of the social order,
corroding political authority and defiling public trust in justice. Even private words of abuse could become seeds of violence, riot, and rebellion. For
theologians like John Calvin, the matter of "scandal" brought into play critical questions about the spiritual authority and freedom of the church, even
as it tested the resources of the individual conscience. For Michel de Montaigne, our anxieties about defamation reveal just how radically a person's
private sense of self can be shaped and deformed by the state of his or her
fame; we depend dangerously on the words that others speak, the "frothy
Chaos of reports and of vulgar opinions," and so may fall, strangely enough,
into an uncivil conversation with ourselves.[12] Nor is concern with slander

absent from the debates of textual scholars, who enter into the arena of publication "armed and dangerous," bristling with accounts of the calumnies launched against them by their opponents, defending the honor of their learning, and retorting with a level of ad hominem abuse that can still astonish.[13]

Contemporary legal writings about slander, including the records of actual slander trials, have been especially helpful in trying to understand the complex implications of verbal abuse. It is precisely as a legal category that slander reveals some of its crucial ambiguities, both conceptual and, as it were, dramatic. For one thing, the encounter with the problem of slander— a category under which the law accuses persons of false accusation—sheds a light on the law's own privileges and interpretive processes. Legal trials have their own dramatic shape; the voices of law and the voices of private persons interact there often in strange ways. A courtroom is a place where institutional rules, moral idealism, politic fiction, direct coercion, and local knowledge uneasily mingle and put each other to the test. Entering into a legal conflict involves putting one's stories and desires into a public space, submitting them to very specific sorts of translation. The legal attempt to define a crime of words, to see what is culpable or innocent in them, reminds us starkly that the law demands a certain sort of hearing as well as a certain kind of seeing and may thus be deaf as well as blind, or ready to hear things that no common ear would apprehend. There is something else as well. Among many who write on the law in Shakespeare's time, one finds a sense that acts of slander—judgmental, accusatory, and punitive as they are—can become a parody of legal process itself, debasing the true work of law even as they hint at more volatile energies that the law itself can never quite contain. ("Scandal" indeed shares an etymological root with the verb "to scan"—"to judge," "to examine," and "to interpret.")[14] All of this cannot but have fascinated a playwright like Shakespeare, whose characters often find in legal categories of judgment, proof, evidence, and contract a pathway to madness and violence.

THE PLAYS I have discussed at most length here are all from the middle of Shakespeare's career: *Hamlet, Measure for Measure, Othello, King Lear,* and *Coriolanus.* All are tragedies save *Measure for Measure,* in which the comic structure is nevertheless under a kind of tragic pressure. I did not choose this group ahead of time. Rather, each play seemed as I wrote to offer a particularly compelling and unpredictable turn on the questions of rumor, defamation, vituperation, and curse. The plays do not necessarily form a developmental sequence within Shakespeare's canon. But they suggest a grouping of works that will be, I hope, at once persuasive and slightly unexpected. These plays define if not a fixed constellation, then a shared gravitational field that can pull other works within it. I wish that there had been space to consider the uses of malediction and witch talk, not to mention the uncanny forms of nocturnal hearing, in *Macbeth,* or to study the harrowing, almost unanswerable invectives of Timon alongside those of Coriolanus and Lear. The curses of Queen Margaret in *2 Henry VI* and *Richard III* and of Caliban in *The Tempest* form part of the chorus as well, as do the satirical rants of Thersites in *Troilus and Cressida.* I would like to have said more about Shylock, a character whose extreme, self-destructive postures of rage, even his mysterious interiority, are partly wrested from the very anti-Semitic slanders that wound him. An account of the hallucinatory abuses of Leontes in *The Winter's Tale* would offer a useful completion to my discussion of *Othello.* Finally, there is that troubling strain in Shakespeare's later sonnets, which expose the eerie convertibility of praise and slander and the power of desire to blacken both itself and its objects. But this book aims at being suggestive rather than exhaustive. My briefer comments on these other works will at least suggest what the unwritten chapters might have looked like. [15]

I regret most not being able to give detailed attention to *Cymbeline,* a play that is less discussed than others and yet so profound and continual a surprise. What stitches this play together is not rumor or fame, malediction or vituperation; rather, it is something that *Cymbeline* repeatedly refers to as "report." In this play, words are always being reported (from the Latin for "carried back") from one place to another, often across great distances—orally or by letter, openly or secretly, often confirmed by a token (a stolen bracelet, a bloody handkerchief). Such reports deform and reinvent bonds throughout the play. Equivocal as they are, these reports divide lovers and family members, even as they create surprising, often fleeting ties of affection between those whom rank or place or desire might divide. In *Cymbeline,* private report and public embassy intertwine. Report acquires a truly hallucinatory force over the course of the play; it becomes the material of nightmare, as well as the spur for violence, both criminal and heroic. The most obvious example is Iachimo's report to Posthumus about his wife's chamber and person, and his lies about his sexual conquest; this story seduces Posthumus to believe in Imogen's betrayal, leading to his own conflicting letters back to his servant Pisanio and his wife, which provoke their troubled wanderings in turn. Reports about other arrivals and departures, about ancient kidnappings and present wars, keep these worlds in motion as well. (Think of the fate of that crucial vial of "medicine" in the play—a sleep drug mistaken for poison by the Queen and so passed in turn from the Queen to

Pisanio and then to Imogen, in whom its effects are misidentified and mistaken even further; this is itself a strange image of the motion of report.) The prophecies and oracular dreams that become so important toward the end of the play are also fed by the power of report. Of course, the authority of such reports is continually thwarted by contradictory and eccentric revelations. Imogen declares with powerful exactitude, "Experience, O, thou disprov'st report!" (4.2.34). But the shaping power of report remains haunting, all the more so for being tested by experience. Report itself becomes a form of experience. It is the sudden candor in human reporting that helps establish the astonishing clarity and peace of the final scene—where, for all the aura of something dreamlike, Shakespeare breaks the nightmare texture of error that had kept the earlier scenes in tragic motion. All of this belongs to a world in which the notions "news" and "report" are starting to acquire a bit of their modern journalistic meaning, even as they still connote things more suspect and protean. These words help create that atmosphere which just begins to form itself at the end of *King Lear*—where inquiring about "court news," "who's in, who's out," becomes a window into "the mystery of things."

# THE RUMOR OF
# «HAMLET»

n a palace in northern Italy, under the authority of an invalid duke who is concealed from sight, a party of noble men and women debates the use and cause of laughter. They explore in particular how laughter works within the anxious, competitive domain of life at court. At issue are the tools of political survival, the often harsh means by which one steals, advances, or holds a place. We are in the second book of Baldassare Castiglione's *Book of the Courtier*. The jokes are never innocent. Speakers focus prominently on forms of humor "flavored with deceit, or dissimulation, or ridicule, or censure," delicate minglings of attack and flattery.[1] Some of their examples involve elaborate stories; others are bizarre practical jokes. But what dominates the discussion is the arts of wordplay. The great trick is for each courtier to find the wittiest, most cunning response to what another courtier has said—with the aim of undermining or taking advantage of words already in play in a courtly conversation. There are many versions of the game. One can repeat another's words in an incongruous tone, or apply them to an ironically shifted circumstance; one can slyly alter the motivation, taking the words more literally or more figuratively than a speaker originally meant them. One can appropriate a mocker's own sarcasm and turn it against him, or pretend foolish incomprehension. One can answer a question that differs from that which had been asked. One can extract a dark meaning from an innocent phrase—for example, by pointing to an

unacknowledged ambiguity, calling up an ironic homonym, adding or sub-
tracting a letter—thus making a saying seem graver or funnier, more lauda-
tory or insulting, than its speaker had intended. Such verbal tricks function
by turning a speaker's words against themselves, taking his words out of his
mouth. They work most effectively insofar as they steal, rather than simply
answer, a speaker's words. The victim who suffers such a trick appears to be
dispossessed by the very words he himself has spoken; he will find himself
defeated, shamed, even unmasked, by language itself, by its contaminations,
by its uncalculated duplicities, its irrevocable patience—like that of Time—
in tripping speakers up. Unwittingly, he mouths alien senses lurking within
his own words. The witty responder, by contrast, acquires an aura of artless,
almost invisible mastery—*sprezzatura*—unstained by any shadows of envy
or aggression.

Reading Castiglione's evocation of the space of exchange at court, I get
the uncanny feeling that I am studying one of Hamlet's training manuals.[2]
Each of *The Courtier*'s twenty or more modes of word theft and word marring can be illustrated by a remark of Hamlet's; he seems to have swallowed,
indeed devoured Castiglione's advice. But Hamlet plays that advice out in
ways, and to ends, that have no place in Castiglione's manual. As a demonic
courtier, as a fool-like "corrupter of words," he employs modes of wordplay,
forms of censure, thefts of sense, strategies of dissimulation and unconceal-
ment, and styles of self-abnegating mastery that shatter the fictions of control underlying the world of *The Courtier*. Hamlet brings within the world of
the Danish court a truly corrosive network of puns and jests, a labyrinth of
fragmentary stories and allegories, mutterings, marred resonances and allusions, haunting and infectious innuendos—if we have ears to hear them, as
Claudius and Ophelia partly do.[3] His words involve risks, cruelties, vagaries
of sense, and blatant indecorums which Castiglione explicitly proscribes.
(Think of the dangerous mingling of accusation and contempt that feeds
Hamlet's riddling response to Rosencrantz, as the latter inquires about the
location of Polonius's corpse: "The body is with the King, but the King is not
with the body. The King is a thing . . . of nothing. Bring me to him" [4.2.26–
29].)[4] Hamlet's words remember more of other words; they reflect a
mournful and mocking temporal density. Hamlet's jests make him as vulnerable as his victims. His words elicit aggressive confusions in the domain
of language, provoking both ethical uncertainty and physical assaults, reminding us of dangers, doubts, and shames that are shown only guardedly,
if at all, in Castiglione's more closed world of courtly eristics.[5] Unsettling
puns and quibbles are common to all the plays, of course. In *Hamlet,* however, the prince's wordplays and opacities of response become the marks of

a particular attitude. Hamlet's clownlike humor and verbal generosity convey a stranger violence; they project a murderousness, a sullen, metaphysical rage, that made G. Wilson Knight speak of the prince as an "embassy of death."[6]

Biting as his satire can be, Hamlet's words have a cunning looseness. They gather within themselves an immense contexture of virulence and contempt, and yet they work as much by their detachment as by their focused hurt, as if their opacity made them more likely to take and harass the ear. The specific idioms of the courtier and clown have their place here, but in characterizing Hamlet's way of speaking in this world, I find it more telling to see him as a strange herald for what the Renaissance saw as the shadow world of rumor, that domain of seditious tales, malicious reports, corrosive fames, discontented "murmurings," and "news" whose danger seemed by turns public and private. It is a shifting and often unmasterable realm of verbal exchange which is mythologized in Edmund Spenser's Blatant Beast—the multitongued monster of calumny that haunts the closing book of *The Faerie Queene,* poisoning the realms of politics, love, poetry, and religion. Like the depredations of the Beast, however, Hamlet's "murmurings" are intensely overdetermined; the objects of their violence are more than usually hard to fix, while the modes in which he launches his slanders display an eerie histrionics, an open secrecy, that complicates any simple account of his intentions. For one thing, Hamlet both deploys and suffers the overdetermination of his words in a way that neither courtly nor political accounts of slander can fully contain.

A *rumor* in Latin is literally a "noise." Latin *fama* can itself be the "rumour or noyse of a thynge," as a 1565 Latin dictionary tells us.[7] Contemporary English speakers could also call a rumor a "bruit," after French *bruit,* which a 1611 French dictionary defines as "a great sound, or noise; a rumbling, clamor, cracking, creaking," or "a rumour, common tale, publike voice, fame, reputation, report, the talke of the people, the speech abroad."[8] Consider first how noisy a play *Hamlet* is, how full of sounds, of oddly troubled hearings, overhearings, and mishearings. There are, first off, the literal or nonverbal, though not inhuman, noises that accompany the action. Kettledrums and cannon shots echo at the beginning and end of the play—accompanying Claudius's "draughts of Rhenish," Hamlet's hits against Laertes, and the funeral staged by Fortinbras. We hear the footsteps of castle guards, a royal procession, a troupe of actors, a gathered army. We hear the thud of an unseen body collapsing behind an arras, and the ring or crash of colliding swords, one of them poisoned (something we cannot hear). We hear the clanking of armor, the sound of ghosts in this play. Even more striking is the crowing of the cock that dispels the ghost. (On the battlements, the sounds of the wind and sea are just audible as well, conjured up by the words of those who wait.) Noises of this sort are part of the texture of reality on-stage—decidedly material, by turns accidental and calculated, both natural and artificial—even as they remind us of how uncertain, how uncanny the domain of the stage itself will become in the course of this work.[9] For one thing, such noises are continually interrogated by those onstage, read and misread, taken as measures of a moral attitude or signs of a mysterious threat. These noises, and what makes them, creep into the play's metaphors, as when Claudius describes the rebellious murmurs that threaten his throne as "poison'd shot" that he hopes will miss his name (4.1.40–44), or when Hamlet tells Horatio that his own accusatory words are "much too light for the bore of the matter" (4.6.23–24), or when he says in dying that "the potent poison quite o'ercrows my spirit" (5.2.358). The crowd of echoes embeds Hamlet in a troubled history, in "a world filled with vibrating memory."[10]

In this play, the domain of hearing is thickened; human voices are heard variously with eagerness and reticence, affection and fear: "Nor shall you do my ear that violence / To make it truster of your own report / Against your-self" (1.2.171–73); "Sit down awhile, / And let us once again assail your ears, / That are so fortified against our story" (1.1.33–35); "Season your admiration for a while / With an attent ear" (1.2.192–93). The ear's reach is ambiguous. Horatio asks the ghost to listen and respond to human de-mands—"If thou hast any sound or use of voice, / Speak to me" (1.1.131–32)—but it is hard to know what the specter hears in Horatio's questions, what the fiction of a ghost's hearing amounts to. It is hard to know how much those onstage hear or fail to hear the darker implications of Hamlet's speeches, how fully a word of his "unkennels" an "occulted guilt" (3.2.80), or simply "sleeps in a foolish ear" (4.2.22–23). Hamlet himself hears more in the words of others than we can fully register; we cannot even be sure what he hears in his own words, those sayings that he so readily mocks. His very capaciousness of ear isolates him amid a crowd of other speakers. Claudius, too, shows a striking fear of what others will hear in certain words (even words he does not hear himself)—as when he is warned that the common people will invest a patched-up sense in Ophelia's insane "noth-ings," or when he complains that "buzzers" have "infected" the ear of Laertes after he returns to find his father dead. The multiplied ears of the play are hungry, but also vulnerable; at times strangely opened, or reopened, they are also subject to damage (by the words of the living and the words of the dead, by what is said and what is not said—hungry for the wrong words, or for noise instead of sense). Critics commonly remark the numerous images of wounded, poisoned, bound, blasted, split, and infected ears in the play. But the scope of such images is hard to measure. It is not a simple thing to say what the poisoning of an ear amounts to in *Hamlet,* how ears are opened to their own damage, what states of mind allow a certain poison to take hold, what its mode of infection is. How can a speech affect, or fail to affect, the ears that hear it? What kind of tongues speak in a world where there are such ears? What delicacy or bluntness of ear do we need in order to hear what is rotten or out of tune in the words spoken in Denmark? In *Hamlet,* the Nietzschean question "Who speaks?" is shadowed by the question "Who listens?"[11] To ask "Who listens?" is also to ask "Who poisons?"

AT BOTH THE BEGINNING and the end of the play, Hamlet manifests a peculiar solicitude about the vulnerability of his name and fame. In act 1, Hamlet waits on the battlements for his father's ghost. Caught by the shameful spectacle of the king drinking healths to the sound of cannons and kettledrums, he speaks with an uncanny prescience about the ways in which particular men, like individual nations, can be blotted by minor faults, describing how accidents of birth, vicious "moles of nature," can become monstrous, destructive, and corrupting (1.4.14–38). The drift of this speech is curiously twofold. Hamlet is anxious about the way that a contingent habit of character can overturn "the pales and forts of reason," becoming a source of madness within an individual soul, like a miner working underground, buried from view. Yet he is also troubled by the fact that an elusive "dram of evil," a small but visible blot, provokes its corruption through being taken up by "the general censure." Wounded names harm the living even more than they harm the dead. Hamlet's words imply that a person's private character can in some essential, if uncanny, way be shaped by the scandalous rumors which the world perpetuates, deformed by what Montaigne calls "this breathie confusion of bruites, and frothy Chaos of reports and of vulgar opinions."[12] Fame, in this sense, is an uncertain guarantee; at best one might think it an "outward helpe" sought by vulnerable humans caught "betweene perfection, and unblisse," as that dark plain speaker Fulke Greville writes.[13] In his last moments, as well, Hamlet turns to the question of *fama,* preventing Horatio's death so that his friend may tell his "unknown" story to the world, lest Hamlet leave behind (in the ear of the world) a "wounded name." Horatio's hypothetical tale, Hamlet hopes, will occupy the ongoing space of the historical world and feed its hunger for knowledge, supplementing his own "dying voice" on behalf of Fortinbras's kingship. At this moment, any other news of immortality or the afterlife recedes into the unknown. No ghost will return to this stage with tales from beyond the grave. Hamlet's call toward his reputation is now more muted, touched by that preternatural candor which Hamlet seems to have found at the end; it gestures toward a place beyond noise: "The rest is silence."[14]

These two moments, early and late in the play, frame the course of Hamlet's encounter with his father's ghost and his equivocal pursuit of revenge. The ghost's arrival, indeed, interrupts Hamlet exactly as he is describing the work of molelike faults. Here I quote the 1604 quarto, whose own ambiguity or corruption makes it perhaps the most scandalous crux in the canon:

> . . . the dram of eale,
> Doth all the noble substance of a doubt,
> To his own scandale.
>> *Enter Ghost*
> *Horatio.*  Looke my Lord it comes.
> *Hamlet.*  Angels and Ministers of grace defend us. [15]

Itself the "noble substance of a doubt," the ghost enters the world in a way that forces the prince into a radical rethinking of the modalities of fame. After hearing the ghost, he himself becomes remarkably prodigal of his reputation. He actively mimes the breaking down of "the pales and forts of reason"; he puts on the mask which makes him nothing but a blot, a shame, on the memory of his former self and on the court of Denmark. Hamlet as defamer gets himself endlessly, darkly talked about. And Hamlet does not just slander himself. The prince who had vowed to hold his tongue, though it should break his heart, becomes himself the play's chief slanderer and rumormonger. He converts all language—all public truth, all official utterance or ceremony, and all gestures of affection—into slander, abuse, mockery, contempt, and curse. [16] He treats other people's utterances about him as if they were slanders, deliberate misconstructions of his identity, and at the same time turns his own slanders back upon them, spreading abroad accusations variously subtle and vulgar, local and universal, just and unjust. We see this side of Hamlet in his abuses of the word, and in his violent, mocking puns; in the "slanders" against old men which he quotes to Polonius; in his rehearsal of misogynistic clichés against Ophelia and his mother; in his extravagant abuse of Claudius; in the insulting, threatening play he stages before the king and queen (the very sort of performance that Elizabethan censors feared). He cannot help but slander the entire world, it seems, aggressively converting it into a rank garden, a coercive theater, a plagued city, a cosmic vacancy. Hamlet's is a speech about the world in which, as Janet Adelman points out, even words that echo the marriage ceremony ("man and wife is one flesh") become material for a veiled and poisonous insult. [17]

I always feel in Hamlet the loomings of great, unfathomable generosity. Even in crisis he is energized by his impulse to greet the world; he wants to entertain it as a guest, to call it by name, to make it a companion rather than an enemy or a merely doubtful thing. Think of how touching his gestures of welcome can be, as when he first greets Horatio and the guards, the players, even Rosencrantz and Guildenstern.[18] His readiness to welcome the ghost is as astonishing as the ghost itself, his words resonating with a preternatural will to know and to be known, at once anarchic and reverent:

> Angels and minsters of grace defend us!
> Be thou a spirit of health or goblin damn'd,
> Bring with thee airs from heaven or blasts from hell,
> Be thy intents wicked or charitable,
> Thou com'st in such a questionable shape
> That I will speak to thee. I'll call thee Hamlet,
> King, father, royal Dane. O answer me.
> (1.4.39–45)

But how can Hamlet welcome by name a world in which the commonest names—mother, father, wife, son, king, queen, man, woman—have become obscene?[19]

———

The word "slander," one would think, barely catches the darker motivations for Hamlet's twistings of language, his verbal daggers. It seems too legalistic, too much concerned with outward and public things, as if the offense of Hamlet's mockeries were a matter of banal public lying. The play within a play, for example, at once tests the ghost's truth and Hamlet's own obscure "imaginations," strikes secretly at both Claudius's and Gertrude's conscience, insinuates a fantasy of Hamlet himself as regicide, and perhaps even provides a salve to his own sense of lost purpose. We hear a more private cruelty (as well as masochism) in Hamlet's various abuses of Ophelia and his mother; his words to them seem the utterances of a blocked or unfinished work of mourning, or expressions of displaced revenge.[20] As for the obsessive attacks on Claudius, they seem touched with some unconscious denial, as if their very rage concealed a self-wounding identification with his uncle, as Freudian tradition surmises. All of this suggests something more complex, something deeper, than would fit our common understanding of slander. But it is precisely in examining the conflicting motives for Hamlet's verbal daggers, in tracing their disguises and metamorphoses, that the word becomes peculiarly useful. For an echoing array of ambiguities emerges in the wide range of Renaissance writings on "evil words" and "false reports," their commentaries on defamation, detraction, derogation, denigration, delation, calumny, obloquy, contumely, traducement, backbiting, libeling, and "leasing."[21] Such words are seen as having the power variously to defile, infect, poison, haunt, rob, bite, rape, and usurp. My next chapter surveys this history in more detail. But I must briefly glance at some of its important facets here.

That human beings cannot escape slander is a period commonplace. In widely read courtesy manuals such as Castiglione's, or Stefano Guazzo's *Civile Conversation,* for example, this is a piece of knowledge crucial to defining one's place in the world, living in history, or inhabiting the fragile networks of dependence and public knowledge that constitute one's "fame," "honor," and "good name." Accounts of slander's origins, its peculiar mode of virulence, are various. Like many authors, Edmund Spenser sees slander as a speech possessed by an archaic, unfathered malice. It takes its origins in envy, an emotion that nourishes in the self a self-wounding hatred of others' advantages, but that can also turn such poison outward as a form of revenge.[22] It defiles the possessions and disorders the "civil conversation" of others. Slander is the product of a fallen, rebellious will, linked to failures of charity, sinful pride, anger, and despair—hence the sense of its being all but demonic in origin. (The devil in Greek is an accuser.) Self-destructive as it is, slander also feeds on a perverse kind of delight; loving his own secrecy, the slanderer is possessed by a kind of restless curiosity about other lives, a need to know "the worst" about others, and a readiness to "improve the least speck or freckle into a leprosy, which shall overspread the whole man."[23] It is this which helps lend to slanders their peculiar air of inevitability, their uncanny generality, as if they were always there, waiting to be found. The demonic air of slander lends it the sense of being an unconscious compulsion. But writers like Guazzo and Machiavelli also make it clear that slander can be a self-conscious, social art, a calculated dissimulation. It is as much a tool of the prince as of his courtiers, in fact. Disguised as flattery, hidden truth, or sober criticism, slander can work to create out of nothing a hitherto unsuspected guilt (as it does in the hands of Iago) or shift the proper blame for a crime onto the wrong agent. There is thus, in slander, a curious intertwining of passion and guile. This, I think, is what leads contemporaries to describe slander as a kind of projection, at once conscious and unconscious; the passionate abuse and certainty of slanderers is driven by their need to spit out their own internal poison onto others, to accuse in others crimes that they cannot bear to know in themselves.

If the motives of slanderers are hard to define, so are their objects; the direction or site of slander's violence tends to be ambiguous, sometimes strangely random. Too strictly motivational an account of slander is indeed limiting, since its power to harm is seen to depend so strongly on the power of those who hear the damaging words, as much as on those who speak them. Its danger lies in the ear as well as on the tongue, in what people listen to, or in what they are afraid others will listen to, believe, and repeat. Slander wounds the fame of its intended victim, but also the innocent listener who takes it in, the one in whose ear a slander begets poisonous conviction or doubt and who in turn publishes that doubt to the world. [24]

If slander scandalizes the law, it is partly because it feeds on things beyond the law's control; slander not only presents explicit public accusations, but conjures vague, unfixable suspicions, spectral fears and doubts about a person's character—especially dangerous in a world where people are represented as always hungry to hear hurtful news, where idle detractions can become oracles, guarantees of false and damaging knowledge, not to mention provocations to criminal prosecution. Anxiety about slander is part of what Kenneth Burke calls the "malaise" of hierarchy, a recognition of how much the fragile commodity "reputation" depends on the thoughts and words of others. [25] Hence the ferocious attacks in legal statutes and royal proclamations condemning open or covert slanders directed at persons in authority, living *and* dead; such texts speak as if "false reports" and "seditious libels" about the actions or policies of sovereigns, judges, and clerics had the power to bring the whole structure of authority into jeopardy. In such a context, even innocent jests or simple truths could take on the look of "evil imaginations" and "seditious" falsehoods, since they threaten to damage the ideally pure networks of consent, the institutionalized silences and monologues, which sustain the authority of the state. The situation of slander in the troubled domain of hearing is what connects it so inescapably to rumor. A "fame" (in its obsolete sense of "rumor") seems always likely to *de*fame. Tudor laws which criminalize seditious libels and slanders always bracket them with the more diffused realm of "tales," "sayings," "bruits," and "news." [26] Trying to recover the sense of threat here, we must learn to inhabit a curious threshold space—both public and ghostly—constituted as much by the fear of those who hear nothing, or who fear what others may overhear, as by words actually spoken. Rumors exist in radical separation from individual speakers; passed from mouth to mouth, ear to ear, they take on a mutable life of their own, seemingly unauthored as well as unauthorized. A slanderous word or secret, writes Guazzo, is like a coal that is too hot to be held in the mouth. [27] In such an atmosphere, ears and tongues themselves become

uncannier organs—hence those many Renaissance personifications of slander and rumor that trace their line from Virgil's ever-enlarging, earthborn
monster *Fama* in book 4 of the *Aeneid,* a creature that, feathered with innumerable tongues, ears, and eyes, sings alike of falsehood and truth.[28] From
this creature descends not only Spenser's Blatant Beast, but also his Ate, or
Discord, who owns a double tongue that speaks against itself and two deformed and defiled ears, each of which hears something different.[29] The very
difficulty of controlling rumors invests them with a fearful power. Calling out
to buried aggressions and desires, they feed a hunger for knowledge such as
almost guarantees the distortion of knowledge. Idle and yet certain, a rumor
can drive out other, more official truths from the ear or distract the ear from
the claims of the official word—whose authority may depend on means no
more certain. This idea of rumor produces the paradoxical picture of a word
that even in its way of missing its mark can effect a "palpable hit," dividing the
hearer from himself or submitting him to an alien authority.[30]

We should not take too literally the accusatory monsterings applied to
the slanderer; these may be libels of their own, after all, the figurative tools
of those committed to sustaining a competing truth. Slander is, after all, a
word that we use to describe what other people say, not what we say ourselves. One person's slander is another's true blame. Still, looking at contemporary representations of slander, one may perceive hints of a violence
and a shame that inhabit speaking and hearing in general; they point to a
perilous pleasure and a mode of knowing that are strangely beyond government, by turns fantastic and commonplace. Slander's alienated, contaminated mode of knowledge—its illicit but accusatory force—is what links
it, in turn, to the troubled knowing of Shakespeare's tragic speakers. Indeed, if the universality of reproach is itself a cliché in the period, Shakespeare's texts have a way of deepening it, allowing the "look" of calumny to
infect other powers, other realities. So, for example, slander can take on the
look of a violence sifted into the temporality of the world, into the mutability of history and fortune. Shakespeare's Ulysses thus warns Achilles that human virtue and love are "subjects all / To envious and calumniating Time"
(*Troilus and Cressida,* 3.3.173–74), that same Time which, in *The Winter's Tale,*
Shakespeare can identify as a dramatic artist who creates and overthrows
law, "makes and unfolds error" (4.1.2). Slander undergoes even wilder
metamorphoses in Shakespeare's sonnets. In the early poems of the sequence, the threat of the beloved's earthly beauty being "besmear'd with
sluttish time" (55) or infected by envy is set against a desire in the poet to
preserve him with praise, entombing him "even in the mouths of men" (81).
The poems thus promise a redeemed circulation of human breath. As we

move through the sequence, however, the contingent, impersonal defilements of Time are replaced by a more human danger; this arises from forms of love that are themselves both black and blackening, a denigrating energy that belongs as much to the poet as to his treacherous object of affection, since that denigration so infects the poet's art of praise. "But now is black beauty's successive heir, / And beauty slander'd with a bastard shame" (127).[31] It is a strange transformation, in which the powers of denigration speak at once for time, love, and the poet. All share a certain rage, in which the powers of making are bound up with defilement, misrecognition, misprision; the poet in his love is tied to a world which dispossesses him.

———

It is not only Hamlet's pointed abuse of Claudius and members of his court that calls up the question of slander. It is as much Hamlet's fashion of exposing a slanderous potential hidden within the official languages of praise and ceremony. The threat of his slanders lies in their simultaneous embrace and repudiation of the lies of desire, the lies of the world. The vexed association of slander with the work of rumor suggests why it so troubles Claudius that Hamlet spends his time poisoning official speech and conversation in the play, stealing people's words from their mouths, making their language speak more, or worse, than it should speak, making hearers hear more, or other, than they should hear. It is hard to get a concrete sense of how ordinary hearers take in Hamlet's apparently senseless utterances—what the background noise at the court of Denmark sounds like. But the dangers his words carry are reflected in what one gentleman reports of Ophelia's mad ramblings about dead fathers and treacherous lovers:

> Her speech is nothing,
> Yet the unshaped use of it doth move
> The hearers to collection. They aim at it,
> And botch the words up fit to their own thoughts,
> Which, as her winks and nods and gestures yield them,
> Indeed would make one think there might be thought,
> Though nothing sure, yet much unhappily.
> (4.5.7–13)

"'Twere good she were spoken with," Horatio insists, "for she may strew / Dangerous conjectures in ill-breeding minds" (14–15). It is not that hard to imagine what kind of seditious thoughts about royal murderousness or sexual betrayal are likely to be "botched up" by idle listeners, or even to say what is "unhappy" in a listener's thinking that there might be thought where there isn't any. It is harder to imagine what speaking with this Ophelia might sound like, what cure it might accomplish—which should remind us of just how hard it is for others to speak with Hamlet.

Thinking of Hamlet's words as slander should not reduce one's sense of their perennial mystery, their subtler violences, or the feeling of secret shame and self-accusation that haunts even his most public and politically charged vituperations.[32] His utterances, for one thing, test the differences between just and unjust blame, between plausible and irrational accusation (an issue central to *Much Ado about Nothing, Othello,* and *The Winter's Tale* as well). Self-serving, opaque, and off the mark as they sometimes appear, Hamlet's verbal attacks reflect a dangerous, if elusive, knowledge of what is hidden, a power to expose what is buried underground.[33] What binds other speakers to him, and puts them at risk, is that he seems to know what is in everybody's heart. Or so they persuade themselves. Think of Gertrude, who seems to discover in herself exactly those "black and grained spots" that Hamlet first tells her are there. It is a strange kind of game. The very veiled quality of his words tempts those who hear or overhear Hamlet to identify his hidden thoughts with their own, or to see a danger in his thoughts unknown before. Hamlet does not work by directly pointing out some hidden truth. Rather, he says things that make others think, or suspect, he has knowledge of them, especially of their implication in matters criminal or sinful. This means that Hamlet's knowledge is in part something others project onto him (by which they betray themselves, in both senses of the word). It also means that his assumed knowledge is a reflex of other people's desperate, thwarted desire to know Hamlet, to divine for themselves his dark interior. It is as if they said to themselves, if we cannot know him, at least he can know us—that's something yet.

This paradoxical impression of Hamlet's accusatory knowledge is the more telling given the violence with which Hamlet himself reacts to all attempts to know him, to pluck out the heart of his mystery, to name the source and cause of his madness. Hamlet treats all such efforts as if they were implicitly slanderous, or as if they presented abusive misconstructions of his identity—unripe, reductive reflections of so vast an interiority. Those who try to read or question Hamlet become his enemies, persons to be misled or blinded by pleas of innocence or madness, if not slandered directly (either to their face or when they move beyond hearing). Hamlet's utterances to his interlocutors reek of a kind of revenge. He seems at times offended by their presumption that he could be addressed, interrogated, read, or comforted at all. He stands ferociously ready, a dangerous sounding board. We could say that Hamlet seems to know, to have caught rumors of, both the stories people tell about him and the ambiguous purposes those stories serve. But this alone cannot explain the heightened sense of an embattled identity conveyed by his words, or account for the sly, often violent preemptiveness of the ways he turns against others his or their own words about him.

Hamlet's defensive posture recalls a more strictly professional anxiety that one finds in many of Shakespeare's fellow writers, though Shakespeare's own texts rarely give it direct voice. Often articulated in prefatory epistles, prologues, and inductions, this is a fear that among those who read a book or hear a play are numerous persons committed to misconstruing the author's words or making them speak meanings the author had not intended. One gets a sense that the audience is always suspect, its ears and tongues willful, resentful, and aggressive. Thus, Spenser explains in his prefatory letter to the 1590 edition of *The Faerie Queene* that he wants to keep at bay those "gealous opinions and misconstructions" that will inevitably dog his "continued Allegory, or darke conceit," taking his complex critical fictions as veiled attacks on authority.[34] Allegory, as Spenser knew, is a genre that tempts extreme and ironic modes of decipherment. Similarly, Ben Jonson hints in *Poetaster* that his audience is full of hearers who will "wrest, / Pervert, and poison all they hear or see / With senseless glosses and allusions," with "spylike suggestions, privy whisperings," converting a broadly satirical fiction into a particular libel.[35] Such speakers give voice to their own malicious meanings under the guise of another's words. Yet if Hamlet echoes certain anxieties attending the emergent ambitions of the Renaissance author, his extreme posturings also help us see through the mask of innocence worn by these writers. He reminds us especially of the strategic vagueness in Jonson's complaints against his audience, a crowd which would have been inhabited by official censors as well as carping critics, noble patrons as well as ineducable groundlings, not to mention rival playwrights. Hamlet's own need for such shifting masks of aggression and jealousy may help us understand why both Spenser and Jonson themselves so anxiously identify with the contaminated language of the enemy.

I take it that Hamlet's desire at once to attract suspicions to his words and to repel such slanderous glossings of his character is what provokes so many of his dark, aversive puns. This comes through in phrases like "A little more than kin, and less than kind" and "I am too much in the sun" (1.2.65, 67)—words which archly turn on Claudius's sly and flattering applications to Hamlet of the titles "cousin" and "son." A similar resistance comes through in

Hamlet's dark reiteration of Gertrude's consolatory "common," and in his emphatic repudiation of her disenchanted "seems" (1.2.72–76). Such words keep his enemies at bay, even as they tangle Hamlet himself up in his own defenses. That game is clear enough, perhaps. Yet by itself it still leaves questions about what is at stake in Hamlet's endless slandering of general and particular "others," especially as this is joined to his preemptive slandering of himself—whether through playing the role of a madman or the volleys of self-accusation offered in the presence of Ophelia or Rosencrantz and Guildenstern. For myself, I feel a double demand. On the one hand, such utterances free up a hidden aggression, they allow unassimilated doubts and fears to articulate themselves, doubts and fears which nonetheless sustain Hamlet's power to name what's wrong with the world, even if only by indirection. At the same time, such words attempt to seal away a self, or the rumor of a self, unavailable to public knowledge, to establish an opaque space of subjectivity unavailable to the world's rumorous commentary.[36] Such a space might become unavailable to Hamlet himself, at least if we follow Wittgenstein's criticisms of the idea of a private language; he never really does unpack his heart with words; rather, he loads blockage upon blockage. Hamlet, as Martin Dodsworth observes, becomes a dangerous mystery to himself.[37] But the idea of such a closed space, a "something" that others cannot know, is paradoxically important to Hamlet. It serves him as both weapon and shield. The charisma of Hamlet's interiority indeed lies as much in its aggressivity as its ambiguity. He quite publicly deploys the idea of a hidden self to challenge the knowledge and integrity of others. Thus, he faces the queen with the insistence that "there is that within" him which "passes show" (1.2.85); Claudius senses a "something settled matter in [Hamlet's] heart" (3.1.175) that he finds both obscure and dangerous; Rosencrantz and Guildenstern must confront blank hints of sourceless melancholy and hidden spaces of dream; and Laertes is told by Hamlet that he has "in me something dangerous, / Which let thy wiseness fear" (5.1.255–56). Hamlet's evasions can seem pointedly masochistic, as Rosencrantz suggests (with some dissimulation, no doubt): "You do surely bar the door upon your own liberty if you deny your griefs to your friend" (3.2.328–30). His refusal to be known may constitute one facet of his revenge against the world for having had his liberty, his own purposes and desires, stolen by the demands of the ghost. But for Hamlet to deny himself to others is also tactical; it has the paradoxical effect of denying others to themselves. In the case of his two false friends, for instance, or even the loving "bait" Ophelia, Hamlet's self-maskings deny them the liberty to serve their

own purposes and desires in speaking to him; it also denies to them, especially to Rosencrantz and Guildenstern, the liberty to serve the purposes
and desires of the king who oversees their investigations.

Facing Guildenstern with the recorder that he cannot "command to any
utterance of harmony," whose use is "as easy as lying," Hamlet cries out,
"Why, look you now, how unworthy a thing you make of me. You would play
upon me, you would seem to know my stops, you would pluck out the heart
of my mystery, you would sound me from my lowest note to the top of my
compass; and there is much music, excellent voice, in this little organ, yet
cannot you make it speak. 'Sblood, do you think I am easier to be played on
than a pipe?" (354–61). The speech strikingly recalls the induction to *2
Henry IV*, delivered by the Virgilian figure of "Rumour, painted full of
tongues"—tongues on which "continual slanders ride":

> Rumour is a pipe
> Blown by surmises, jealousies, conjectures,
> And of so easy and so plain a stop
> That the blunt monster with uncounted heads,
> The still-discordant wav'ring multitude,
> Can play upon it.
> (Induction, 15–20)

The rumors at issue in *2 Henry IV* are those of war and peace, rebellion and
tyranny, enmity and safety, rather than of madness, adultery, or regicide
(though rumors of war are rife in *Hamlet* as well). And the prince is clearly at
pains to deny that he in any way resembles such a rumorous pipe. But one
may hear in his strident protest precisely the fear that he is all too likely to
become, as Avital Ronell suggests, nothing *but* the body or pipe of rumor,
that this is what both he and the world have been making of him.[38] This fear
would distinguish Hamlet from Falstaff in *2 Henry IV*, who is exuberantly
pleased to see himself as the body of rumor, gluttonously stuffed or pregnant with public noise about himself and his imagined heroism: "I have a
whole school of tongues in this belly of mine, and not a tongue of them all
speaks any other word but my name" (4.3.18–20).[39] Hamlet's need to pro-
nounce his own inaccessibility to knowledge, to construe the encroach-
ments of other speakers as defiling rumor, finds a more extreme parallel in
Coriolanus—for whom all praise or public knowledge takes on the guise of
slander, a poisonous nourishment. Coriolanus too suffers a phantasmic
identification with the body of rumor. The composite picture of Rumour as
a figure covered with tongues and as a pipe blown upon by the mouths of a

many-headed multitude reemerges in the Roman citizens' image of Coriolanus as an exposed body whose wounds become the mouths by which the
commons must "elect" him (even against his—or their—will): "For, if he
show us his wounds and tell us his deeds, we are to put our tongues into
those wounds and speak for them" (*Coriolanus,* 2.3.5–8).

In the case of Hamlet, a fear of being subject to rumor, of being a mouthpiece for the words and knowledge of others, is not simply irrational. For
Hamlet becomes a figure whose name, character, mind, and intentions seem
endlessly in circulation in this play, the chief subject of everyone's gossip and
random reflection. He makes himself the focus of attempts at secret investigation that are anything but innocent. His awareness of being played upon by
the words and questions of others points to the dangerous uses that those in
power could have for accusatory rumors, misperceptions, or slanders (though
power in this play puts itself in danger by thinking too much about this
prince, tying its own speculations to his unfathomable activity). Yet Hamlet's
anxiety is not strictly pragmatic or legalistic; he is worried about more than
just open or covert threats to his person or public status. The object of Hamlet's fear is rather his continued dependence on the very powers that
threaten him. It is as if he recognized his mirroring debt to the empty,
shameful voices that seek so invasively to blow through him, to make him
speak, lending him a voice with which to yield up his own mystery—no less
than to lay bare the poisonous mysteries of others. Their relentless circulation implies that he is not even giving voice to his own slanders. Hamlet may
fear that even his dreams are not his own, but, like his madness, are lent to
him by others.[40]

---

Criticism has perennially tried to name a hidden doubt or fear in Hamlet.
We can call it fear of action, fear of revenge, fear of death; it is both fear of
knowing and of being known, fear and contempt of speaking a language,
most broadly, perhaps, a fear of being human. To speak of Hamlet's fear of
rumor touches all of these in some fashion. I want to enlarge on this thought
by recalling that Hamlet is not the only instance in the play of a body or person both subjected to and yet producing something that we can identify as
rumor or slander. There is also the revenant of the dead king, Hamlet's father. He is the one who lends Hamlet his dreams, his speech, his curses,
lends him, indeed, a new ear for the words of the world. Ambiguous as he is,
or exactly in his ambiguity, the ghost shows us how the matter of slander
affects our understanding of Hamlet's potent and vulnerable interiority.

Some self-consciously witty and ideologically charged words of Francis Bacon, taken from a contemporary legal record, suggest one immediate relation of the ghost to slander. We find them in the transcript of a 1615 Star Chamber trial of a knight who was accused of "slandering the King's justice"—specifically by sending a private letter to James I attacking the conduct of Chief Justice Coke in the trial of one of those accused of poisoning Sir Thomas Overbury. Bacon, in his position as attorney general, made the following remark about the danger of secret and false counselors:

> I note to your lordships, that this infusion of a slander into a king's ear, is of all forms of libels and slanders the worst. It is true, that kings may keep secret their informations; and then no man ought to enquire after them, while they are shrined in their breast. But where a king is pleased that a man shall answer for his false information; there, I say, the false information to a king exceeds in offence the false information of any other kind; being a kind (since we are in matter of poison) of impoisonment of a king's ear.[41]

The ghost in *Hamlet* presents himself as the victim of a form of murder that literalizes Bacon's commonplace trope for the work of slander.[42] Like Bacon, Shakespeare suggests the scandalous vulnerability of the sovereign ear to the treacherous falsehood of its subjects:

> And in the porches of my ears did pour
> The leperous distilment, whose effect
> Holds such an enmity with blood of man
> That swift as quicksilver it courses through
> The natural gates and alleys of the body,
> And with a sudden vigour it doth posset
> And curd, like eager droppings into milk,
> The thin and wholesome blood. So did it mine,
> And a most instant tetter bark'd about,
> Most lazar-like, with vile and loathsome crust
> All my smooth body.
> (1.5.63–73)

Translating the ghost's own literalization, we may find an implicit account of the power of defamation. The ghost's tale offers one of the drama's most extreme images of the aversive power of the word—its enmity with its hearer's blood, its way of making the body into something monstrous, something like a tomb of itself, ruining "the inward and the outward man" in a single instant.[43] This association adds a new layer to the ambiguously sexual character of the scene, something evident in the intimacy of the ghost's account of the murderer's stealing upon his passive, sleeping person, committing a kind of aural rape or castration (recalling the scenarios of self-wounding nocturnal intrusion that haunt Shakespeare's writings, beginning with *The Rape of Lucrece*), and in the ghost's remarks about the oddly "eager" or quickening power of Claudius's poison.[44] Read strictly for the allegory of slander, the ghost's speech reminds us of the complex of desire, identification, and loathing that links the words of the slanderer to his victim, the troubling way in which the victim of a slander is unconsciously possessed, reanimated, made into a ghost, by the slanderer's words. Within the metaphoric system of this play, having one's ear poisoned while lying in a garden is not unlike being played upon like a pipe. There is the same fearful passivity, the same sense of an uncanny fluid entering from the outside, infecting and possessing one, lending to one's body and blood both a death and a vicious, unselving animation. Hamlet's pipe image suggests the fear of being made to speak in a voice belonging to someone else, at once isolating him from and binding him to the world. It is not just a matter of having the heart of his mystery plucked out, but of answering to a mystery invented and imposed on him by another. The ghost's image suggests the idea of poison running through the interior of a body in a way that solidifies it and crusts it over, gives it a monstrous armor—rendering the body's death opaque and burying its life beyond knowledge or sympathy, obviating any speech but that which itself returns as a potential slander. (There is both too much mystery here, and not enough.)

The shadowy, foundational story of poisoning is taken up, concealed, rehearsed, and tested throughout the play. Restaged in "The Murder of Gonzago," it frames the tragedy's most prominent image of the power of theatricality itself (save, perhaps, for Hamlet's broader use of an "antic disposition"). The story enters and possesses Hamlet's hearing; it becomes a privileged secret of the sort that Bacon mentions, but also something that "impoisons" Hamlet's ear in turn, converting him into a version of the ghost. In the process, it suggests how the poison of a slander, its fascination, can be passed on from mouth to mouth, from ear to ear, and how it affects the world in which it is apprehended. Admittedly, the ghost—after telling Hamlet that he cannot repeat tales from beyond the world that might harrow a living ear—presents himself as one who comes to correct a public lie: "so the whole ear of Denmark / Is by a forged process of my death / Rankly abus'd" (1.5.36–38). He wishes to wipe away otherwise blotted memories, offering the true story that will cast out deceptive rumors or explanations of

his death, stories which are themselves emblems of the more ordinary failures to remember the dead that trouble Hamlet. But even if it remains a true
report, the ghost's tale is at the same time one of the play's more troubling
images of the way that scandalous rumor can circulate in the world's ear, and
of how the need to probe the source of rumors can itself become a poison.

At a basic level, the ghost's tale provides a curious mirror for the kind of
seditious gossip that would inevitably have circulated in a Renaissance court
following the sudden death of a king and the precipitous remarriage of the
king's widow to his brother. It is the open secret that everyone winks at, spoken about in whispers to which the audience is never privy—the story of an
event which the sleeping king himself could not have seen or remembered
but which he must have learned about after his death from the mouth of
some other supernatural historian. Similar noises about the mysterious
death and burial of Polonius are what Claudius fears will "infect the ear" of
Laertes on his return from France. To speculate openly about the death of a
king was a dangerous thing during this period. G. R. Elton has shown, for
example, the ruthless care that Thomas Cromwell and his agents could ex-
pend in tracking down the originators of dangerous, seditious rumors or
"prophecies" about the death of Henry VIII.[45] Equally under suspicion were
subjects who repeated rumors about a dead king's survival—stories such as
surfaced throughout the reigns of Mary and Elizabeth about the return of
Edward VI, "of his arising from death, or his return from I know not what
Jerusalem or other strange land."[46] Rumors of looming war and political violence are themselves incarnated in the terrifying, armored body of this
ghostly king. Given what the ghost's story suggests about the criminality of
Gertrude, it is useful to recall that Elizabeth herself was dogged throughout
her reign by tales of sexual misbehavior, secret marriages, and illegitimate
children, or rumors about her secret plots to murder her rivals.[47] Provocations to public disorder, such stories are all the more troubling insofar as
they can mingle real terror and volatile faith, an indulgent prurience and a
will to truth.

The ghost's story is a dead king's poisonous word about the way words
can poison kings. If this figure represents, at a broad level, an image of the
troubled, emptied body of sovereignty in Shakespeare's theater, the scene in
*Hamlet* suggests that the authority which seeks to control or correct rumor
is itself contaminated with rumor, even constituted by it. That the rumormonger is a royal ghost only points to a more deeply ironic image of the
spectral authority of rumor, an authority which lies partly in rumor's
anonymity and externality, its being spoken by no one in particular, in its becoming part of what is "commonly known" or "famous." It is as *heimlich* as it

is *unheimlich*. The danger of rumor lies in the ghostly afterlife of stories, in their way of being taken in and put out again, becoming a focus for imaginings and desires in an unknowable field of others. In many Renaissance texts, including Bacon's, we see a fear of the illusory and yet oracular authority that rumors can acquire by echoing their hearers' prior suspicions and hidden resentments or by feeding the narcissism of listeners who find in rumors the confirmation of what has been already spoken by their "prophetic souls." Rumormongers become ghosts even as they speak such stories, spreading the words that will, in turn, make ghosts of others.

The difficult task is to describe how the ghost and his story enter into Hamlet's ear, how the prince internalizes his words and gives them a second life, how they carve out an interiority not otherwise picturable. One textual clue lies in Hamlet's antic apostrophe to his father's spirit in act 1, scene 5: "Well said, old mole. Canst work i'th'earth so fast? / A worthy pioner!" (170–71). Whether by compulsion or design, Hamlet shrinks the overwhelming paternal specter into a diminutive creature working blindly underground, like a witch's familiar, out of sight and almost out of hearing, or like those kings who "go a progress through the guts of a beggar" (4.3.30–31). Such a mole is able nonetheless to extract from Hamlet and his companions promises of fidelity, remembrance, and silence; however tiny, the ghost provokes Hamlet's strange repeated flights from those places onstage to which the ghost's substage noise has followed him. (Proverbial wisdom in the Renaissance attributed to moles an especially acute sense of hearing, even a strange concern for what was said about them above ground.)[48] This phrase "old mole" links the ghost, by a strange process of recollection, to the "vicious mole of nature" described earlier, the scandalous blot or flaw that, pioneer-like, undermines a person's embattled rationality, even as it subjects him to the censorious reports of public opinion. Indeed, the climax of this speech, with its obscure evocation of that "dram of eale" which "doth all the noble substance of a doubt, / To his own scandale," seems itself to call the ghost onto the stage.[49] This quibble on "mole" is far-fetched. But it works to locate the image or memory of the father, however diminished, in the subjectivity of the son. It locates the father-mole there under the image of a flaw or evil (*mal*), a ghostly but poisonous memory, a thing which cannot be gotten rid of—something as uncertain as rumor, yet capable of disrupting the task of mourning for the dead and praising the living.[50] This questionable mole becomes the source of a word which Hamlet takes as a "commandment" to be inscribed on the "tables" of his brain, inviting him to blot out all other pieces of trust, knowledge, or wisdom. The rumor-ghost—as represented by both the armed specter and the image of his sleeping, penetrated body—becomes at once the original voice and the chief object of doubt in the play, a vision of both doubt's corrosions and its seductive authority, its power to compel wonder and stir conviction.[51] ("A mote it is to trouble the mind's eye" [1.1.115].) The spectral authority of rumor and slander inheres in, is prepossessed by, the voice of the father, preempting Hamlet's ability to make his father's ghost a sufficiently fixed object of skepticism or aggression, and further infecting Hamlet's own manifest doubts of the world.

To identify the ghost with slanderous rumor holds together both the ghost's strangeness and its secularity. It clarifies the specter's fantastic realism, its origins within rather than beyond the contingent world of human talk. In *Hamlet,* the voice of rumor gives us our best image of the voice of the dead, a voice cut off from particular living speakers yet able to command them, living a demonic life in the ears of those who listen (like a mole burrowing underground). The ghost's voice reminds us of how a living person can be seduced into miming the voice of the dead, acquiring the wished-for authority of that voice even in submitting to its alien demands and knowledge. It hints at the extreme claims that the dead can have on the life of the living, invisible or imaginary as these claims may be; the life of our inner murmurings belongs to the dead; or rather, to put it another way, those murmurings can become our death, an infectious noise that clogs the soul's ear for its own truth or the truth of the world. This identification will not catch all of the particularity and scope of Hamlet's noise. Vicious rumors of the mother haunt Hamlet as well as rumors about the father, for example. We also still need to understand more about how Hamlet, at the end of the play, discovers that mysterious candor and ferocity that silences the noises that have dogged him throughout the play, a self-possession that makes the ghost's demands seem almost irrelevant. But the comparison is sufficiently useful if it can keep us from treating the fiction of this theatrical specter too literalistically. Thinking of the ghost as rumor, that is, can prevent us from thinking too simply that the voice of the ghost has a character essentially different from that of the voices which other human beings speak and repeat and recall during the course of the play. This can help us readjust our understanding of how to appease such a ghost, or to lay him to rest. It also helps us recognize why we can never quite lay the ghost, or Hamlet, to rest.

———

Let me close with one last rumor, or figure of noise, in the play. When the prince returns to Denmark from his interrupted sea voyage, there is a kind of breathing space. He is still concealed, not yet aware of Ophelia's death or caught in the tangles of Claudius's conspiracy with Laertes. Hamlet's jests in the graveyard, morbid as they are, seem remarkably unhaunted, his puns lacking their earlier corrosive, slightly hysterical edge. Standing by an open grave, Hamlet watches the gravedigger-clown unearth a skull. This first skull is not yet Yorick's skull, the thing Hamlet will recall having kissed, that he will make into a funereal puppet which can mock the monstrous vanity of women. The first skull belongs to no one who is named. Hamlet considers that it might be the skull of an equivocating politician or an officious courtier, but his first words on glimpsing the object suggest a surprise at once more lyrical and elegiac: "That skull had a tongue in it, and could sing once" (5.1.74). The line does not suggest the image of a living tongue in a living head. Rather, it pictures a living tongue inhabiting, like a musical worm, a dead, inanimate sphere of bone. Macabre as it is, this image displays a curious, anomalous freshness in a drama where we mostly witness something different: living voices that are themselves death dealing, or living mouths that echo, that are inhabited by, the tongues of the dead. The idea of a singing skull resonates further if we recall that the only actual singing heard in the play (other than the gravedigger's rough ballads and a few notes of Hamlet's own) has come from Ophelia, the grave's future inhabitant. Chanted riddles and "snatches of old tunes" both fill her mad speeches and accompany her to her death, as she floats mermaid-like on the surface of the stream that drowns her. The skull in Hamlet's hand is Ophelia's skull, though he does not know this.

Listening to the "nothings" that sift through the mouth of Polonius's formerly passive daughter, we hear desire, bawdry, erotic rage, social protest, sly innuendo, mourning, even a tone of commanding courtesy. Her ballads point to unsettling confusions of identity—as when references to her dead father also catch up Hamlet, Claudius, and the murdered king:

> How should I your true love know
>     From another one?
> By his cockle hat and staff
>     And his sandal shoon.
> . . . . . . . . . . . . . . . .
> He is dead and gone, lady,
>     He is dead and gone,
> At his head a grass-green turf,
>     At his heels a stone.
> (4.5.23–32)

One plangent aspect of apprehending this is that Ophelia's mad utterances represent perhaps the sole form of voice given to a character in the play that Hamlet himself neither hears nor imagines, neither mimes nor mocks (although, as critics note, Ophelia's madness itself strangely mirrors Hamlet's antic impersonations). The claims of her words are, to that degree, untested. I have often wondered what difference it would have made to the play or to our sense of Hamlet if he had heard such songs from Ophelia, or from the skull in his hand, even if only to hear in them the return, the alienated echo of his own words. I try to imagine what ghosts those songs could have banished, or coerced to speak, what they could have stolen from or restored to the rotten court of Denmark. It leads me to wonder about the ways in which we are endangered as much by our failure to hear certain rumors as by our taking others too much to heart. The playwright who stole Ophelia's skull for *The Revenger's Tragedy* could imagine only poison on the silent, painted lips. But we are free to report it as something else.

# THE BOOK OF THE
# SLANDERER

he play of slander draws us into what is most mysterious about Shakespeare's theater. It can expose that
theater's most archaic ambitions; it is a clue to the
plays' power to split open speech onstage and to split
open dramatic character, not just in moments of fantastic aggression—Lear's curses, Hamlet's vicious
punning, Othello's disgusted cries against Desde-

. . . all these detractions,
stings, tuskes, clawes,
contradictions, carpings, ca-
lumniations, and cavillations
of savage people, of
*Aristarches,* of *Catoes,* of
*Momistes,* of Monsters.

WILLIAM VAUGHAN,
*The Spirit of Detraction*

mona—but within subtler inflections as well. Rumor is central to the plays because so much happens
as words move in the space between speakers and
hearers, set adrift in memory and reflection, interwoven with the background noise of the world's attention. Psyches leap out of that noise along with
slanders. The low voice of rumor also creates the
world into which flow the desires of an audience, or a
reader. In this chapter I want to make clearer the shape of the period's larger
preoccupation with damaging words. Extreme anxieties about slander
break through everywhere at this historical moment—in royal proclamations and private letters, in courtesy manuals and handbooks for lawyers, in
epic histories and emblem books. The courtier seeking preferment, the
housewife at odds with her neighbors, the scholar glossing a text, the historian drawing parallels between past and present, the queen attending her
ministers, the preacher wrestling with heresy, the poet addressing his

patron—slander encroaches closely on each of them. All risk being defamed or becoming themselves defamers, even if the decorum of insult and the means of redress shift markedly for each different situation. Slander is less a concrete way of speaking than an atmosphere, something "in the air," a coloring in which the dramatist's trade is itself thoroughly steeped, "subdu'd / To what it works in, like the dyer's hand" (sonnet 111).

The encounter with slander charges and shakes Renaissance ideas about the nature of language, the nature of human identity and interiority, the nature of political authority, and the work of the law. It also has an impact on the idea of the theater. All of these issues I will touch on here. The crisis, if that is the right word, lies not simply in the particular damages that slander does (or that it is imagined to do), but in what its workings reveal more broadly about human impulse and human making. The tensions elicited by the problem of slander are hardly unique to the Renaissance. Yet they take on a peculiar urgency within a culture that is so unsettled in its measures of value, so vexed by its own constitutive disenchantments, and so ferociously competitive in its acts of making. This discussion will make it clearer why slander stuck so closely to Shakespeare, an author for whom both the workings of time and the workings of human love could take on the look of calumny.

———

In the Book of Psalms—which Renaissance commentators always took as being authored by King David—the slanderous tongues that wound the poet and darken his voice of praise are by turns selfish, swollen, proud, and deceitful, likened variously to razors, arrows, spears, swords, and teeth.[1] Edmund Spenser's demon of slander, the Blatant Beast, is a Hydra of tongues—tongues of dogs, cats, bears, tigers, snakes, and men, that variously bark, "wrawl," "groyn," "snar," sting, and speak reproach.[2] Slander is a monster of *linguae,* like its cousin or double, Rumour, who appears at the opening of *2 Henry IV,* "painted full of tongues." Controlling slander demands what the clergyman Richard Allestree called "the government of the tongue," the tongue being, as Erasmus writes in his treatise *Lingua,* "the governor of human life," for both good and ill.[3] A rumor-monster like Rabelais's Oüi-dire, or Hearsay—one who keeps a school for witnesses and historians—has seven tongues split seven ways, babbling of various matters in "divers Languages." But one notes that Hearsay also has "as many Ears allover his head and the rest of his body, as *Argus* formerly had Eyes," and is surrounded by a crowd of men and women "gaping, list'ning, and hearing very intensely."[4] Nicholas Breton's pamphlet "A Murmurer" (1607) describes a creature with an infected heart, clawlike hands, winged feet, and a forked tongue, yet above these he displays a pair of inhuman, batlike ears—ears that are, the author tells us, ready to catch at the most fleeting doubt in the world, keeping alive the low rumbling of suspicion that threatens the sovereign's peaceful rule.[5] Period writing suggests that the art of slander lies as much in the ear as on the tongue. It is around the activity of the ear, and how contemporaries imagine the matter of hearing, that I begin to develop my picture of slander's work.

The human ear is a place of power and danger. It opens a hole in the whole of the world. That crumpled orifice becomes an uncanny vortex sucking in creation, capturing the world as a babble of stories and half-heard sounds. Through it passes the weather of reports, the network of the world's complaints, praises, jests, and just ordinary gossip. As glimpsed through the mirror of Renaissance accounts of slander, the public world starts to look like a wilderness of uncircumcised, impure, and uncontrollable ears. These ears belong to listeners dangerously eager for knowledge, however uncertain. Within such ears, the promiscuous noise of "tales, stories, songs, ballads, bruits, and news" drives out any more official narratives, any more rational harmony. To speak ill or give ear to evil is all one.[6] Ears are open to poison, and they extract poison where they find none. It is to these ears that the slanderer calls, like the pied piper of Hamelin charming children and rats. Hearers become like the ghosts that crowd around Odysseus at the mouth of Hades, needy, desperate, unable to speak unless they fill their mouths with the blood of others. The work of slander travesties the common Renaissance emblem of the ruler as a Herculean rhetorician, able to draw those who hear him by fantastic chains that radiate from his mouth to their ears.[7]

The ear of the king, the confessor, the judge, the spy, the actor, the lover—each is different. The slanderer's ear is strangely attentive, wary, even patient; it is deformed and multiplied by its very readiness to catch at sounds in the air. The slanderer's ear and tongue seem indeed just opposing ends of the same nerve; as Allestree remarks, slander depends on an "Itch of the ear which breaks out at the Tongue."[8] The slanderer's ear finds its materials among things that are lost, rejected, fragmented, or imaginary, among stories that might just as well have vanished; it depends on both knowing falsehoods and uncharitable truths. Nor is it just a passive organ: that ear is rather something like an eye that can be trained on its object or a nose that can be turned in the wind to catch a scent. The ear is a mouth from which the evil tongue emerges. It is open to contingencies, ready to catch at any uncertain hints or chances that the world throws out to it. This is why Spenser represents Occasion as a creature full of calumnies and "foule reproch."[9] Like a trap, the ear of the slanderer holds whatever rumors of love, betrayal, and loss are available, closing especially on hints about shadowy causes or hidden motives. Slanderers "do so diligently bringe all thinges that pertayneth to him whom they accuse, to sownde to the worste parte."[10] Indeed, they often "seeke a hole where no hole is, reprehending those mysteries, which they cannot apprehend nor comprehend."[11] Exposed as it is to slander, the ear shows itself possessed by a curious appetite for knowledge, a desire to know what others cannot know and what it yet insists others cannot help but know. Slander possesses and betrays secrets at once— since its secrets must be, after all, the most common knowledge, the most banal of truths (as Iago insists so sickeningly to Othello).

For a poet and scholar such as Thomas Vaughan in *The Spirit of Detraction Coniured and Convicted in Seven Circles* (1611), or the anonymous author of *A Plaine description of the Auncient Petigree of Dame Slaunder* (1573), defamation creates an eerie, triadic community of victims.[12] Slanderous words wound the absent person who is abused, most obviously; they attack that shifting entity that is his or her "fame." The language of abuse also wounds the one who utters it, or at least reinforces the wound at the root of the slanderer's tongue, the wound that *is* the slanderer's tongue.[13] But it also inflicts a wound on the ear of the innocent listener, who is never quite innocent enough.[14] The danger of defamation inheres in the fact that one inhabits a world where a person's identity can fall so fully into the hands, into the ears, and onto the tongues of others. If there is poison on the tongue of the slanderer, its efficacy depends on finding out the ear of one whose judgment can be caught by false knowledge. This process taints the very medium of transmission: language, in its passages between tongue and ear, becomes not a transparent mirror or honest transporter of sense, an *oraculum animae* or *speculum mentis,* but an infectious wind, a bearer of buried violence.[15] Hence the story represented in a legendary allegorical painting of "Calumny" by Apelles, described in an essay by Lucian well known in the Renaissance: Ignorance and Suspicion whisper into the long, asslike ears of an enthroned judge, while impulsive Calumny—attended by Malice and Deceit and led forward by red-eyed Envy—drags before the court her miserable victim, who can only protest his innocence to the heavens. Behind him follows an old woman, Repentance, and finally naked Truth.[16]

A document from a real rather than an imaginary trial—a plaintiff's brief from 1562—may make plainer the complex burden of "hearers" in a slander case, even when it involved the abuse of an ordinary citizen:

Thomas Pyckering, late of Isham in the aforesaid county, gentleman, was attached to answer John Humfrey, gentleman, in a plea why, although the same John is a good, true and faithful liegemen of the lady the queen, and has been of good name and fame from the time of his birth to the present, and was held, spoken of, known, accepted, and reputed as such among his neighbours and many men and subjects of the lady the queen; nevertheless the aforesaid Thomas, not ignorant of the foregoing, scheming without right to harm and disturb the said John and to injure, diminish, and impair his good name and fame, and in order to bring the same John into disquiet and infamy among his neighbours, did publicly and expressly, in the presence of many of his neighbours at Isham, falsely, maliciously, and slanderously speak, announce, proclaim and publish certain slanderous words and the crime of theft against the same John, in these words as follows in English, namely, 'Thou art a thief. Thou hast stolen my horse': by reason of which words the same John is not only grievously injured, harmed and impaired by his name, fame and credit, but also has been greatly oppressed and weighed down by various labours and expenses for clearing himself in this matter.

Or, to quote a fragment of the unpointed court Latin of the original, "false maliciose et scandalose dixit retulit nominavit et publicavit in hec verba ut in anglicis verbis sequiter videlicet Thowe arte a thefe Thowe haste stolen my horse."[17] Using the quite formulaic hyperboles of the common law courts, the plaintiff asserts that his good reputation and "common fame" confirm both his own innocence and the willful malice of the accused slanderer.[18] What is striking here is that the text suggests that the same "grave and wise hearers" who confirm Pyckering's good "name and fame" are themselves the ground of danger. Once the slander moves into the world, the good hearers become a community of ears ready to hear the worst of him. Memories of past virtues dissolve, and the crowd of "true knowers" all too suddenly metamorphoses into a crowd which seconds the slanderer's lies; they become, as it were, cofabricators of an infamous monster, who is thus brought into "contumeliam, abjectionem, et vituperationem." There is something paradoxical in the will to legal knowledge that such accusations define. The need accurately to place blame is inescapable, and yet the situation of slander sets accusation at odds with itself. The hearers themselves become half responsible for the damage of the criminal slander, since "all those which have an evill report . . . most men eschew their company as an infectious disease."[19] As other contemporary texts suggest, an unmeasurable danger seems to attend the scattering of slanderous stories into the common ear: it calls up uncertain appetites; it skews alliances; it mars a common history; it provokes failures of civic charity and breaches of the peace, both threatening and displacing physical violence; it "injures a man in his profession and rep-utation."[20] In a society without a regular police force, a society which depended on both public fames and private information to prosecute criminals, a slanderous utterance, however unfounded, might even land a citizen in court.[21] It is thus not only the truth or lie of the slanderer's word but the mode of its being diffused that counts here.

Despite idealized images of the prince as wisely able to distinguish good from bad counsel, slander's false knowledge seems all too liable to wind its way into the mind of those in authority. It plants a peculiarly dangerous poi-son there. The dilemma of slander in the prince's ear is typical rather than unique. In Vaughan's *Spirit of Detraction,* indeed, the image of violated sover-eignty serves to describe the way slander overtakes even ordinary minds. Joining the language of Renaissance conspiracy theory with the terms of Aristotelian faculty psychology (mixed with a touch of demonological thinking), Vaughan shows us the poisoning of the soul as a kind of court in-trigue, full of bribery, suspicion, disguise, ruthless competition, and erring preferment:

> The *spirit of Detraction* at the first by bribing of *memory & sense* hath accesse to the *braine,* which is the lodge of the *Imaginative Lady,* and by his double dili-gence insinuates himselfe into her amity. *She* a Princesse of estimation and favor with the *Heart,* commends this *spirit of Detraction* to her protection, as a minion or play-fellow to deceive the time (or rather her selfe) and to dis-cover unto her the diversities of *Spirits,* which might harme her eyther in *de-tracting* her credite, or in disposing her subiects to insurrection. Here the *spirituall Hermaphrodite* is let in at first by secret convayances as a thiefe (for as yet he dares not openly enter into the *hearts* palace for fear of the envious *No-bles*). But in process of time having throughly (like *Absolon* or *Scianus*) stolne away the good consent of the *Heart,* and now strongly befriended by her ex-traordinary favours in this *microcosme* of man, he enduceth other *humorous spirits* to regard him, and in the fine enticeth unto him in the *hearts metropoly,* the greatest number of the purer vitall *spirits,* where he besotteth them and bewitcheth them with *melancholy, rage, choler, malice,* and other disordinate *passions:* insomuch that the *Soule,* the *hearts tutrix,* is likewise enforced *nolens volens,* will she nill she, to obey this unworthy Spirit.[22]

For Vaughan, the ear offers a passageway to an unfathomable, untrustworthy appetite for knowledge. Even a soul's just and necessary attempts to know its enemies sets it in danger; our desire for protection betrays us, leads us falsely to favor an invader and upstart, a *"spirituall Hermaphrodite,"* who slyly flatters our wish for certainty. Vaughan's book often paints "the spirit of Detraction" as a decidedly satanic creature, but its originary motive remains as hard to fix as that of Satan's rebellion against God.[23] The violence of this spirit is abroad in the world, outside us, beyond our control; and yet the wounds it gives us are weirdly self-inflicted. In picturing this spirit's invasion of "the *hearts metropoly*," Vaughan leaves the very object of its harm ambiguous: one cannot easily distinguish the wound inflicted on the ear of an innocent listener from that inflicted on the soul of the person being slandered. The allegory ends by showing Detraction's talent for self-perpetuation, as the violated "spirits" are worked up into the condition of malicious melancholy that leads only to further slanders. It is no accident, perhaps, that the vapors of melancholy are said to work on the self like a slander, as John Donne writes in his *Devotions:* "That which is *fume* in us, is in a State, *Rumor,* and these *vapours* in us, which wee consider here pestilent, and infectious fumes, are in a State *infectious rumors,* detracting and dishonourable *Calumnies, Libels.*"[24]

In Vaughan's genealogy, the external or social poison of slanderous speech calls out to a troubled interiority, one that is at least partly beyond will or self-knowledge. Here we need to ask questions about, for example, the soul's equivocal attachments to a particular way of being known. Detraction binds speakers and hearers through a medium (language) at once alien to and at home in human hearts; it depends on something that lives an uncanny life outside of the mouths and ears of any individual speaker and yet becomes a bearer of the soul's knowledge, love, fear, and doubt. (The image of its power becomes a dark synecdoche for the workings of language in general.) Are we meant to see the soul contaminated with the world's errors, or the world stained by the soul's poisonous rage? The question is hard to answer, in part because, for a writer like Vaughan, the work of slander makes present an otherwise invisible specter of the mind's power and intractability. Such uncertain revelations are as much a part of the danger of slander as any more concrete damages. Shaped by the "spirit of Detraction," the world suddenly shows itself as composed of a dangerous crowd of other minds; it takes its form from the chaos of other people's suspect, unfathomable inwardness. The space of human privacy gets discovered precisely by being invaded, even as it becomes an object of fear. The very knottiness of Vaughan's language is itself a sign of this crisis.[25]

Attempts to describe the work of slander produce a peculiarly vexed image of the life and work of words. Here is Spenser's description of the monstrous hag Sclaunder, in book 4 of *The Faerie Queene* (shedding calumnies against the always vulnerable fame of Prince Arthur's squire, Timias):

Her words were not, as common words are ment
　　T'expresse the meaning of the inward mind,
　　But noysome breath, and poysnous spirit sent,
　　From inward parts, with cancred malice lind,
　　And breathed forth with blast of bitter wind;
　　Which passing through the eares, would pierce the hart,
　　And wound the soule it selfe with griefe unkind:
　　For like the stings of Aspes, that kill with smart,
Her spightfull words did pricke, and wound the inner part.
(4.8.26)

Slander here is something alien to sense or reason; it is untethered to the space of "inward mind" which ideally controls the meanings even of "common words." Yet its poisoned breath is sent from "inward parts," producing a "blast of bitter wind" which, for all its senselessness, pierces the "inner part" of its victims. Nor can one say for certain whether those interior spaces belong to the slanderer, the person slandered, or the innocent hearer—that is part of the point. It is as if the spirit of detraction makes the entire world the mirror of its own disgust, catching up all hearts and souls in its poisonous error. Hence, perhaps, while slander reads the world through a rawly personal rage, it is able to assume an eerie garb of impersonality.

There may be a kind of reassurance—as Lacey Baldwin Smith says of Renaissance accounts of treason—in finding a poisonous source to point to, even if, as in Spenser, that source remains unlocalized, something shared by both speaker and hearer.[26] Yet there is something in the mirroring structure of slander that precisely undoes the slanderer's self-knowledge. Human speakers, however malicious, are not likely to call their own speech "slander." They will rather insist on their own purity and truth. Words like "slander" and "defamation" tend to emerge, after all, as accusations directed at what others say. They point to a mode of utterance that speakers refuse to make their own. Slander, indeed, seems to feed on a strange kind of disavowal, a desire not to know one's own malice and falsehood, a refusal to hear what one's own self has said. This is also why it so difficult to truly reach the slanderer with one's accusations (assuming that one can identify him or her at all): "Let but the shadow of their own calumny reflect on themselves, let any but truly tell them that they have falsely accused others, they grow raving and impatient, like a dog at a looking glass fiercely combating the image which himself creates: and how smoothly soever the original lie slides from them, the Eccho of it grates their ears."[27] This passage from Allestree's *Government of the Tongue* depends on an idea one finds in Vaughan, Spenser, and others who write on slander, that is, that defamation depends on something like what we would call "projection," the impulse to throw outward onto the world all of the poison that one cannot bear to hold in oneself. Hence the common Renaissance idea that slanderers accuse other people of their own sins, or what their own sinful imaginations suggest to them. "They that level / At my abuses reckon up their own," writes Shakespeare in sonnet 121.[28] Given that such projections cannot totally blind the self to its own rage, or truly cure a wounded conscience, the slanderer may yet turn against the very forms which his rage takes up in the world. In particular, as the above quotation from Allestree suggests, the slanderer will fight with a mad, almost animalistic rage against those echoes of his false accusation that fall back truly on his ear, echoes which bring him, from other mouths and tongues, the accusatory rumor of his own originary malice. Such a text suggests that the ones most attentive to the inner life of slanderers are those most struggling to master their own reactive savagery. As one scholar eloquently observes in discussing the ad hominem virulence of religious controversies in sixteenth-century Europe, "commentators' obsession with slander was not devoid, I suspect, of uneasy if unconscious dismay at the taste of their own tongues."[29]

---

Slander threatens our way of being known by the world (our "nobility," etymologically speaking). It attacks our need for external witnesses of our virtue, strength, purity, obedience, and honor. Such witnesses bind a person to a group, shield him from attack, free him to work or love, give him power. They provide an armor for the self, even as they can also sustain its attachment to an ideal beyond the self. If the interest in slander becomes so heightened in the Renaissance, it is because the nature of our human attachment to "name and fame" itself becomes more urgent and vexed at this moment. What Leo Braudy calls the "frenzy of renown" comes to be a powerful, seductive, and peculiarly treacherous sort of thing. Reading, say, Petrarch's "familiar letters" to ancient politicans or philosophers, Erasmus's epistles to fellow humanists, or even Aretino's more raucous (and scandalmongering) letters to fellow poets and artists, one can still catch the echo of fame's radicality. The struggle to emulate the fame of both ancient and contemporary exemplars, to take them as a mirror of the self, feeds the desire to extend and test human powers. Fame management in such cases is not merely a matter of manipulating externals. It involves a constant labor of knowing oneself and knowing others; it can become a means of teaching, an occasion for sorting through truth and deception, both finding and inventing enlarged mirrors of the self.[30] The quest for fame feeds a fantasy of heroic self-assertion; it promises autonomy and freedom; it allows one to brave the flux of time, to defeat death, to "penetrate eternity." Fame can seem to acquire an almost daemonic force, become a form of fate.[31] "When Virtue cut off Terror, he gat Fame"—thus Ben Jonson reads the birth of Pegasus from the body of the Medusa, whose head was severed by Perseus.[32] The disciplines of fame also offer pragmatic tools for working and doing good in the world, building a community, a polity, often by service to a noble monarch or nation. It is a way of staking a claim on present as well as future history, bringing the heroic ideal within history, making it matter for memory. As poets from Dante through Milton insist, the power to celebrate and preserve human fame is what gives special glory to poets and other artists; praising others itself brings praise, increases life. The work of fame might thus acquire an all but prophetic authority.

But fame turns out to be a very unstable guarantee of power, nobility, honor, and life. The humanist dream shows fissures, reveals within itself a hidden sting. Fame might be seen as merely a human vanity triumphed over by time; it was a prize, or laurel, always shadowed by loss, a paradox that Petrarch would trouble endlessly. Like honor in *1 Henry IV,* fame could be at once a hard-won treasure and a trick, a siren, and an idol; as such, it could become the object of a rage ready to "teare it selfe asunder," in Fulke Greville's words.[33] Fame was a franchise that depended on uncertain foundations and conflicting measures—the untrustworthy support of kings, the whim of factions and institutions, the luck of finding the right poets. It might show itself all too clearly as something arbitrary, or as a strictly pragmatic thing, a tool of Machiavellian policy, or as a commodity to be bought and sold. As Rabelais's satire suggests, *fama* could be amnesia as much as memory, building both personal and collective histories on hearsay.[34] The humanist ideal of fame did indeed help to create a more relentlessly secular, historically self-conscious notion of human identity. But fame also revealed itself as a poisoned property, a gift that, ironically, put one's identity into the hand of others. Even well-deserved fame was seen as subject to the voice of popular rumor, hungry for celebrity, fed by an ever-increasing fund of cheap and hard-to-control printed words.

Michel de Montaigne is among the sharpest critics of fame. For him, the desire for fame poisons the soul, feeding an aggressive, degrading, even idolatrous madness that steals one away from more interior measures of virtue. In "Of Glory," Montaigne shows himself darkly fascinated by our appetite to have other people speak about us, yet he also laments the fact that "we call that a magnifying of our name, to extend and disperse the same in many mouthes."[35] He found it a shameful and yet unshiftable fact of human nature. "I wot not how, we are double in our selves," he writes, and hold our own deepest beliefs in contempt.[36] We not only want others to speak of us; we let their words become the way we speak about ourselves. Human beings, Montaigne ruefully reflects, hunger to take not only their judgments but their very identities from the "frothy Chaos" of other people's words; they happily allow their inner lives to be shaped by the uncertain weather of the world's empty opinions. "We are all hollow and empty, and it is not with breath and words we should fill our selves."[37] Desire for such an equivocal possession exposes the self to the (potentially shameful) knowledge of being at the mercy of stories beyond its control. Montaigne thus suggests the self-destructiveness inherent in any cult of public fame and glory: fame is merely *fama,* rumor or hearsay; it is *fames,* famine, a hunger that can never be filled. Indeed, like Ovid's Erysichthon, fame feeds on the most degraded substances and ultimately consumes itself.[38] Virtue itself turns out to be at the mercy of corruptions of public knowledge. The House of Fame stands all too close to the House of Rumor; indeed, they threaten to become identical.

Shakespeare's Cassio cries in the aftermath of his public shaming, "Reputation, reputation, reputation! O, I have lost my reputation, I have lost the immortal part of myself—and what remains is bestial. My reputation, Iago, my reputation!" (*Othello,* 2.3.258–61). This is at best the empty shell of any classicizing ideal of public virtue as a divine prize, as an indwelling spirit sustained by risk and battle. (In context, Cassio's words serve mainly to underscore the more hallucinatory losses inflicted on Othello by Iago, who destroys not only the moor's reputation but his "occupation," his sanity, and his desire.) A more poignant and visceral protest than Cassio's can be found in the letter written by the earl of Essex to Queen Elizabeth, while he was imprisoned in 1600 after his failed campaign to suppress rebellion in Ireland, accused of having disobeyed orders, made private treaties with the enemy, and abandoned his post:

> I not only . . . am subiect to their malicious informations that first envyed me for my happiness in your favor, & nowe hate me out of custom: but as if I were throwen into a corner like a dead carcas, I am gnawed on & torne by the vilest and basest creatures upon earthe. The prating tavern-haunter speaks of me what he list: the frantick libeller writes of me what he list; already they print me & make me speak to the world; and shortly they will play me in what forme they list upon the stage.[39]

For Essex, the fact of imprisonment and the displeasure of the queen are not only punishments in themselves; they also leave him undefended, vulnerable both to secret "informations" that he fears his courtly enemies are conveying to the undefended ear of the queen and to the swarm of more common noises which take up their echo. The "I" in this lament is not so much the person that is closed in prison as a self caught between private and public realities. Essex describes what it feels like for "moles of nature" to be taken up by what Hamlet calls "the general censure," even as he is harassed by imaginary voices that echo his own fears and aggressions (panic about slander underwriting what to us will sound like a kind of schizophrenia). Subjected to a fantastic kind of gnawing and tearing, this imprisoned aristocrat undergoes a frightening metamorphosis, even while the world outside becomes a more dangerous place. In Essex's vision, the certainty that the world of ancient enviers and malicious informers will dilate over his fall converts the "I" into something like an abject human corpse or animal carcass subject to dismemberment. Slanders, and fear of slanders, make Essex into an unlicensed representation of himself, a thing of words, subject to the idle prating of drunkards, torn apart in the disordered space of the Elizabethan tavern, that place where "pots walk" and where loose language becomes itself a dangerous intoxicant. "Essex" becomes a text to be printed, a voice made to speak words not his own—"they print me & make me speak to the world"; or else he is an identity stolen by opportunistic players, made the subject of a satirical farce (something which Shakespeare's Cleopatra fears as well).[40] Though Essex hesitates to be explicit about it, he may even see such horrible forms underwritten by the eye of the queen herself, who would thus play Diana to his Actaeon, watching him be torn apart by his own hounds.

In Essex's fantasy, the inhuman cadaver that he has become yet bears a kind of shameful life about it—the life inherent in its felt capacity to be shamed. If his hyperboles reflect the hypersensitivity of an old aristocrat, they yet belong to a more common fund of images. The idea of that body torn at by beasts, for example, recalls an image from Andrea Alciati's *Emblemata:* a woodcut of three hares eating the corpse of a lion, supine on the earth. The verses under the woodcut explain that the emblem translates the dying Hector's taunt against his Greek enemies, who in cowardly fashion prepare to defile his famous person only when he is almost dead: "Tear me to pieces as you will—so even cowardly hares pluck at the beards of dead lions."[41] This is what it looks like, the commentary claims, to publish libels against the famous dead; slanderers are like those cowardly hares, violating a primal taboo, not only defiling but feeding on the dead. Yet the warning to slanderers implicitly reminds their victims that no tomb will be sufficient to defend them. The Latin motto which Alciati places above the emblem complicates this thought even further, since it gives to the picture a differently edged moral: *Cum larvis non luctandum,* "Do not wrestle with ghosts." Fames *are* ghosts. If slander seems capable of converting a person into a dead thing, it is because one's fame already has a ghostly life of its own. A public name is a possession in which more than its owner has an investment, a something that evades the ordinary laws of property. We should know, Montaigne writes, that we have no name that is sufficiently our own; the violations of slander reveal this with particular sharpness.[42] To possess a name, to acquire fame—these things might seem like defenses against time, but in fact they open their owners up more fully to the depredations of time and history. Slander means that one is always an unburied corpse. Indeed, the wounds to a person's name may carry poison to others, even when the one who bore it is dead—as if slander were simultaneously an act of reanimation and necrophilia.[43]

A version of this paradox emerges in an influential law report of Edward Coke, who served as chief justice under both Elizabeth I and James I. *De libellis famosis, or of Scandalous Libels* (1605) took as its occasion the trial of a gentleman, Lewis Pyckering, for publishing crude verses that satirized John Whitgift, archbishop of Canterbury, accusing him of corruption, impiety, popery, and injustice.[44] The suit was brought not by the cleric himself, however, since Whitgift had recently died (the verses in fact being "pinned upon his herse at his Funerals . . . a barberous windinge sheete," as the judges said).[45] The action of slander was instead brought by his living heirs. Coke makes clear that it could be a crime to slander even a dead man. To begin with, he argues, a man's reputation still sustains and does honor to his descendants. Because they exist in the shadow of his good name, it is an inheritance they must protect, for both material and spiritual reasons. Defending the archbishop's family, Coke simultaneously defends another victim, arguing that the slandering of Whitgift brings into disrepute the "fame" of the monarchy itself; it impugns the crown's wisdom and good intentions in appointing its servants. The slander attacks the honor of the state, which, unlike mortal ministers, "dies not."[46] "Making the dead speak with discernment and relevance is the ruler's art," Julien Gracq writes.[47] And Whitgift was an important ghost, a minister who suppressed sectarian "prophesyings," burned thousands of Puritan pamphlets, and ruthlessly used the Court of High Commission to enforce royal supremacy. Coke's argument scarcely conceals the ideological pressures that lead him to defend Whitgift from slander and to lend a quasi-eternal virtue to his historically contingent name. To that degree the report will seem suspect to us. Nevertheless, this jurist's way of describing slander's workings is important, since it suggests how the very attempt to recognize a slander, and to bring it within the scope of public accusation, can transform its substance. In Coke's legalistic terms, as much as in the more emotionally charged rhetoric of Essex, it is not just the victimized name that takes on a ghostly form. Slanders themselves become spectral, vampire-like creatures, unkillable, liable to be resurrected in new shapes, outliving mortal persons, hiding within the histories not just of individuals but of nations and institutions.

Here we may remind ourselves of the eerie double meaning that hovers in Alciati's Latin motto, which can be read as addressing not slanderers but their victims: *Cum larvis non luctandum,* that is to say, Do not wrestle with the ghostly voices of detractors, for one may only increase their infectious strength. Slanderers live in the dark like beasts, Vaughan writes, which "makes them alive to be enrowled in the Calender of the Dead."[48] Slanders themselves are ghosts, ghostly residues, always feeding on echoes of reputation; they live in the mouths of those murmuring and gossiping souls whom the law cannot reach or even name, at once secret and common. (And yet, as Essex fears, even nameless slanders may return stamped with the imprimatur of the monarch, who turns out to be capable of sealing the speech of ghosts.) The survival of fames, supposedly able to outlive envy and malice, helps to guarantee the survival of "defames." Fame gives to personhood a substance at once preternatural and artificial; fame both creates and undoes human fate, ties identity (through language) to the world of both the living and the dead. This is a danger that characters like Hamlet, Cleopatra, and Coriolanus seem to acknowledge at the moment of their deaths, as they all try to find for themselves some last posture or story that might cut through the poisoned *fama* they fear to inhabit.

---

The finished man among his enemies?—
How in the name of Heaven can he escape
That defiling and disfigured shape
The mirror of malicious eyes
Casts upon his eyes until at last
He thinks that shape must be his shape?
(W. B. Yeats)

Slander is not a magical spell. It emerges within the folds of a social network, even as part of a "civil conversation."[49] Yet accounts of both its origins and its ends gesture toward a place in the self not subject to civilized controls, a site one might call archaic, early. The abuse that is public in the world also "pricks the inner part," a part whose nature may in that very wounding reveal its unsettled, conflicted character—both its vulnerability and (for Montaigne) its curious emptiness or capacity for self-betrayal. We can trace this further in looking at what Renaissance writers suggest about certain more private, interior therapies by which to remedy slander's wounds or to keep at bay the madness and melancholy that can be started by "the spirit of Detraction." These therapies, if they do not exclude outward means of answering a slander, respond to a world where public answers may be themselves both insufficient and dangerous, embedding the self further in the field of words that wound it. A glance at such matters, necessarily brief, will further show us how accounts of defamation in the Renaissance shape a picture of human interiority, indeed become a part of the history of that interiority.

Geffrey Whitney's 1586 collection, *A Choice of Emblemes,* contains an emblem that answers Alciati's image of rabbits tearing at a famous corpse. The emblem shows arrows breaking against a marble wall, accompanied by the motto, *Calumniam contra calumniatorem virtus repellit.*[50] As moral consolation, this works in part by reassuring the victim that he will be revenged upon his enemies without himself having to undertake the revenge. This image of virtue as a stone wall represents more than just a face one shows to the world. It is also the image of an interior defense, a stance that the mind or soul should assume toward both outward voices and it own terrors. We can see in this emblem of inward rigidity something of the decidedly Stoic strain in Renaissance ethics and ethical psychology. It suggests an idea of human virtue as essentially embattled, taking on, as Gordon Braden argues, an agonistic and autarchic shape, especially by internalizing a public image of aggressive, sovereign power.[51] It is an ethics that converts the central self into an unwoundable stone or statue, possessed of the statue's essential *apatheia.* The possession of that private statue, one might say, helps to mortify any desire for a public one, or at least sustains a sovereign doubt about the truth of public judgment, the "common rumor" of ordinary fame. There is something self-dramatizing in this, perhaps; it has an air of spiritual pride. As playwrights like Shakespeare and Calderón suggest, such self-sufficiency in the face of slander's wounds—both inner and outer—can be at best a fragile pretense, at worst a costly form of denial, or a mask for hidden violence. (Better a Falstaffian contempt for both honor and detraction, one might think.) Yet as a specific against slander, such Stoic hardness was often joined to a more Pauline or Augustinian attitude; it opened up the resources of a different sort of privacy, especially through an appeal to the private truths of conscience.[52] When attacked by calumnies, Petrarch advises in his *De remediis,* "from the stormes of thyne eare, withdrawe thy selfe into the closet of thyne heart, whiche yf it retayne its owne tranquilitie, then hast thou a place where to rest thy selfe from the weerisomenesse of chyding and brawling, and as the common saying is, *Reioyce in thyne owne bosome*" and "comfort thy selfe with the testimonie of a good conscience."[53] Montaigne's distrust of outward honors and the chaos of the world's opinions can often balance against a terribly unstable sense of our inner lives; yet he too, in his essay "Of Glory," citing Paul and Augustine, argues that "our glory is the testimony of our conscience." Conscience, he insists, is that which must refute the world's defamations, even as it "doth shroud us from the feare of death, of sorrowes and of shame" that is started by calumny.[54]

John Calvin—more studious of the soul's vulnerability to pride, more convinced of the self's impurity—gives a different turn to such appeals to conscience. The soul's real task is not to face down the wounds of defamation, but to make a better use of them. Defamation must not be silenced inside the self, as Petrarch suggests. Rather, it must be made to speak in a different voice. Thus, Calvin urges victims of abuse, however unjust it may be, to take it as an occasion to probe their consciences. One should not simply dismiss the accusations as false. Rather, one should test them before a private tribunal, weighing their possible justice, letting them serve, even if far from the truth, as reminders of those accusations of sinfulness that must be true. Thus he writes in his *Sermons on Job:*

> As soone as any man shall backbite us, or mock us, or make us as it were a tale and laughingstocke, wee must learne to acknowlege, that God putteth us in mind to make our owne accusation. . . . Our freends beare with us, and that causeth us to feede oure owne vices. . . . But our enemies do prie upon us, and seeke all the meanes that can be, to lay open all the faults that are in us. Therefore when any man findeth fault with us, and scoffeth at us, it behoveth us too thinke thus: go to, I see here that God citeth mee to make mine owne proces, and to accuse my selfe, so as I may be my owne iudge to condemne my selfe, that by so doing, my shame may be covered and buried. . . . Let us consider (I say) that by that meanes God intendeth too set secretely before our eyes the sinnes whiche wee woulde have cast behind our backe, and that is to make us too hate the evill that is in us, withoute any flattering of oure selves.[55]

Like Stoic appeals to an interior virtue, this deflects any external action, ties up the soul's reflexive rage and resentment. Rather than turning the slanderers' accusations back on themselves, Calvin's advice works, strangely enough, by metamorphosing, even purifying such accusations, making them speak in a voice at once interior and transcendent. Slanders, indeed, become the voices of conscience. Here in particular the attempt to master the wounds of slander shows us glimpses of an otherwise unseen world; this therapy warns us, indeed, about letting the secrets of that world go unexamined. In Calvin's advice, listening to the outside world is a matter of "taking soundings" of the world inside, hearing its calls, its unowned impulses, its volatile history—though still under the aegis of a spiritual discipline framed by both scripture and church authority.[56]

If such remedies as Petrarch or Calvin propose can go only so far, it is because of something that figures like Hamlet, Macbeth, Marlowe's Faustus, or the speaker of Donne's "Holy Sonnets" suggest so starkly—that conscience itself is an abyss rather than a fixed mark that assures one of consolation. It is a noisy rather than silent space, a crossing point between competing appeals to the authority of law, tradition, reason, and feeling. The sectarian conflicts of the Reformation make the space of conscience increasingly vexed, the more so given the tremendous ambition for conscience implicit in a text like Calvin's, the desire for an interior self to bear powers and values which have lost a secure grounding in the outside world. Both larger and less securely mapped, this inner world becomes a domain of trial, a purgatorial space— a faculty given to error and fantasy, to anarchic confidences, divided against itself, most certain, perhaps, in its power to accuse the soul of sinfulness (hence perhaps its readiness to echo the voices of slander).[57] Conscience itself may thus be unable to "shroud us from the feare of death, of sorrowes and of shame." Slanders can provoke a wound "deeper than any losse, danger, bodily paine, or injury whatsover," Robert Burton writes, leading in some to an unshakable, suicidal melancholy, as well as to a relentless flood of bitterness thrown outward into the world.[58] In this situation, the combined vulnerability and scope of conscience are liable to make the wounds of slander stick more deeply.

It is just possible, I think, to see a very stark recognition glimmering behind these texts, a recognition of what it is that conditions slander's ability to wound the soul. It is something one feels in the studious self-doubt of such writers, in their mournfulness, in that fearful tone which lends to defamation the look of something preternatural, like an unconscious compulsion. The dilemma they point to is this: that the barbs of slander find purchase in the soul because—however misdirected, arbitrary, or malicious the slander seems—they hook onto wounds already in place there, wounds which show us another face of the soul's desire or instinct. Slanders stick in the soul not so much because we fear that everybody else will believe them as because they feed the soul's prior, archaic attachment to images of its own weakness, division, and illness. Calumny's cries in the street answer to rumors of the soul's self-loathing. It is the wounded soul's immensity, as well as the immensity of its wounds, that provokes the slanderer to "improve the least speck or freckle into a leprosy."[59] This is why no private remedy for such wounds may suffice, even that of making our self-doubts speak with the voice of God, as Calvin proposes. It is also why the slanderer may not, after all, have to calculate his slanders so closely. Out of the myriad calumnies that run through the world—the chaotic gifts of public speech—the soul selects just the proper poison for its own uses. One runs to stand on the exact spot where the arrow shot at random can hit the heart.

Shakespeare's engagement with these dilemmas is the subject of later chapters. For now, I will close this reflection by looking at a passage in Spenser's *Faerie Queene* whose account of an inward therapy against slander's interior wounds speaks with particular subtlety to the questions I have been raising here. In book 6 of the poem, a nameless hermit tries to heal a court lady, Serena, and Timias of wounds inflicted by the Blatant Beast. They are wounds that "wranckle inwardly," mirroring the wounds of eros. Their hurt takes its source, the hermit says, not in an external poison, but rather in "fraile affection," and "stubborne rage of passion blind" (6.6.5); it is almost as if the Beast's victims had the Beast inside them. Hence, the hermit insists, the application of "outward salves"—which might include, one supposes, legal action, physical violence, counterslander, or confession—can only augment their sickness. Instead, the cure must "proceed alone / From your owne will." The therapy he proposes is a paradoxical one. It begins with a thoroughgoing ascesis. Restrain "your eies, your eares, your tongue, your talke" from "what they most affect," keeping sight and conversation "in due termes" (7):

> Abstaine from pleasure, and restraine your will,
> Subdue desire, and bridle loose delight,
> Use scanted diet, and forbeare your fill,
> Shun secresie, and talke in open sight:
> So shall you soone repaire your present evill plight.
> (6.6.14)

Shut down, he seems to say, whatever human impulses give play to need and desire, or bind one to the world of things, sights, other bodies, and hence may breed the wounds of envy. Do not give need a chance to wound you. Yet this advice does not offer any sacred vision of privacy, nor any ideal of monastic silence or contemplative withdrawal. The ascesis promises neither a profounder knowledge of sin nor access to deeper purities. The hermit's therapy is, in fact, a startlingly secular one: "Shun secresie, and talke in open sight." A cure that starts out sounding like self-mortification turns out to include a kind of ruthless candor, a way of being present to the world. Of course, such openness may be primarily a way of keeping other people's suspicions at bay, a kind of rumor management or secret management: "Don't give *other* people something to talk about, something to spark their envious curiosity." Yet the advice seems more aimed at restraining his patients' own attachments to secrecy. It is a defense against self-wounding melancholia, a means of holding back one's appetite for brooding over wounding words or turning them about in one's head, applying unjust slanders to one's own self-hatred. The hermit suggests that we need to keep up a civil conversation with ourselves, as well as with those with whom we share the world. (His hidden name, I imagine, is Ludwig Wittgenstein).

Spenser in this episode tries to acknowledge the complexity, the volatility of an inner clamor started by slander. Yet one may feel that he tries to cure that clamor by silencing it. The discipline limned here draws a cordon sanitaire around an interior space, an interior conversation, which the poet finds too dangerous to confront directly. Shakespeare, by contrast, will enter into that space and conversation more relentlessly.

---

If the workings of slander point to an unfathomable place of wounding in the individual soul, they also expose a weak place in the soul of public order. As Renaissance jurists and moralists often argue, "evil words" tear at networks of social charity and consent, or what one contemporary philosopher has called "the web of belief." The very aptness of local slanders to feed, and feed upon, the volatile, diffuse energy of rumor, makes them particularly dangerous. Rumors were seen to have, almost by nature, a corrosive, even an accusatory edge. We may relate this to what the sociologist Françoise Reumaux sees as the derealizing, deobjectifying power of rumor—an ability to submit real persons and institutions to the logic of the imaginary, to archaic fantasies such as are themselves triggered by a rumor. Just as crucial to the peculiar mana of rumors is that, in their characteristic intertwining of the banal and the fantastic, they join people together around buried antipathies. "The dominant figure is that of the scapegoat," Reumaux writes of rumor at its most paralyzing and paranoid.[60] Thus, even as they animate a will to knowledge, a desire to uncover and publish secrets, rumors bind hearers through a shared attachment to marking and knowing "the worst." It is this shared but unconscious aggression which helps to feed the odd certainty in rumors, their status as secrets that are on everyone's lips, that everyone knows, that are held for true even without evidence. Such a danger may help us understand why, in a comprehensive abstract of criminal statutes published in England in 1577 by Ferdinando Pulton, one finds (with a small shock) that laws aimed against defamatory or seditious slanders, rumors, tales, ballads, preachings, or writings are all gathered under a single rubric: "Newes."[61] News, in this sense, is noise. In a period without anything like a modern newspaper, the word carries a breadth of suspicion hard for us to catch, including as it does the promiscuous chaos of ungrounded words, stories, and signs that are liable to be taken for certainties by those who apprehend them, or that attach themselves to our minds even in spite of their uncertainty.[62]

One danger implicit in rumors is that they let people think they can know and judge the acts of those in authority; rumor feeds on the fantasy of entering secretly into the precincts of power, usurping (if only in imagination) the privilege of ministers, or that of the king himself, who keeps solitary watch over the *arcana imperii*. Consider, for example, this passage from a manuscript collection of reports of Star Chamber cases, describing the trial in 1596 of a common soldier charged with "spreading sclanderous newes" about the lord admiral and the earl of Essex:

> Smithe had confessed that he, being a pressed soldier at Dover, and the news being there that the Spaniards were on the sea (which was false, for they were Hollanders and friends of the Queen), they were "shipte," but as it turned out to be "Grave Morris" they were dismissed; and he came to London, and reported that the news was throughout the soldiers that the Lord Admiral's "shippe beinge searchte by th'erle of Essexe & openinge divers barrelles, wherein he supposed to have bene gunpowder, he fownde ashes, duste & sande, & thereupon he Called him Traitor, and so theye Came bothe to the Cowrte, & there th'erle of Essexe and th'erle of Cumberlande before the Queene tooke the Lord Admiralle by the Berde & sayde, 'ah thou Traytor.'"[63]

In this account, rumor feeds rumor, false news is propped on false news, forming ever more complex knots of insubstantial but dangerous certainty. The accused is an unwilling, pressed soldier, now out of service, his work having turned on what was itself a false rumor. The primary scandal of his story would seem to lie in the report that the admiral had waste instead of gunpowder shut up in his barrels, suggesting that the war effort is built on dust and ashes, a corpse of firepower (the implication being, presumably, that the admiral had sold the powder for his own profit). But the lure of his story lies as much in the drama of Essex himself searching the barrels, prying them open to reveal the empty stuff hidden there. It lies in Essex's reported cry of "Traitor," and even more in that cry's potent repetition at court, where one noble accuses another of treason under the eye of the queen, making use of the most insulting of gestures, plucking at the beard. If the story slanders the lord admiral with treason, it also compromises Essex in his role as noble adviser to the queen at a time when his place at court was already precarious. Essex and the earl of Cumberland are made to abet Smithe's slander by giving it voice themselves; his story steals the words, as it were, of both juridical accusation and aristocratic challenge, leaving both dangerously unmoored. What may be most scandalous here is the way in which the tale frees up the scandalous spectacle of accusation itself, making it a means of gaining imaginative purchase on this otherwise inaccessible world. Smithe's story implicates the queen herself as witness to this false scene of false accusation, even as it allows Smithe himself, in telling the tale, to identify with the monarch as both spectator and judge. To adapt the words of the Duke in *Measure for Measure,* Smithe's story makes Elizabeth "the mother of his idle dream," feeding a promiscuous play of identification that at once exalts the slanderer's knowledge and debases its objects.

Here the danger may lie not simply in the falsehood of the tale, but in the promiscuous publication of a demeaning truth—or perhaps just a possibility—about the conduct of those in power. A storyteller like Smithe takes the investigation and accusation of injustice out of the hands (and mouths) of more official entities. I find myself recalling here a suggestion of the social historian Joel Samaha. He argues that in reading the "slanders" recorded in such trial reports, we should listen for the otherwise silenced voice of social protest. In the words of a man like Smithe—or of others accused of spreading news of royal crime and scandal—we might hear not private malice or voyeurism, but a desire for truth, a way of calling those in authority to task, asking that rulers themselves be responsible to the laws they impose on their subjects.[64] That the accused speakers could not themselves be conscious of such demands and questions is, for Samaha, part of the pathos of the situation. (Neither can the state, for that matter, hear them truly.) The argument can seem sentimental, especially to the degree that it tends to purify such utterances of any more banal or less noble impulses. Yet Samaha's suggestion reminds me of an idea that is in fact much emphasized by contemporary writers themselves, that is, a sense that the danger of a slander lies precisely in its eerie legalism. The danger of slander is that it mimics the law, something that no other crime or tort quite accomplishes (even though a murderer may assume the posture of an executioner, as Othello does). Slanders, that is to say, echo the voice of blame which frames the established work of justice. And such echoes may "grate at the ear" of those who are officially part of that work.[65] Indeed, in accusing and blaming others outside the frame of law, slanderers preempt established structures of legal accusation. They both usurp and parody the work of law, calling into question the justice system's theoretically more controlled orders of suspicion, interrogation, indictment, exposure, and judgment: "Whosoever backbiteth his neighboure, hee condempneth the lawe, in that it correcteth not filthynes, the office whereof the backbyter taketh upon him"; "When slanders are presented instead of complaints [i.e., legally sanctioned petitions], that is but to set divisions between the king and his great magistrates, to discourage judges, and vilify justice in the sight and mouths of all the people"; "[Public detraction is] a process contrary to all rules of Law or equity, for the plantiff to assume the part of a Judg. . . . 'Tis indeed sad to see how many private tribunals are every where set up, where we scan and judg our neighbor's actions, but scarce ever acquit any. We take up with the most incompetent witnesses, nay often suborn our own surmises and jealousies, that we may be sure to cast the unhappy Criminal."[66] Pulton, in his legal treatise *De pace regis et regni* (1609), argues that in judging libels, especially those directed against persons in authority, "it is not material whether the Libel be true or false, or the party scandalized thereby be lyving or dead, or be of good name or evill: for though the libell be true, & the party defamed be evill, yet our good lawes be divised to punish him . . . by course of justice," so he is not to be "carped at, accused, & condemned" save in a proper court.[67] We might remember in this context the traditional definition of defamation used in the English ecclesiastical courts—not just angry or insulting words, but the imputation of an actionable crime such as theft, adultery, or murder, words that thus put their victim in legal jeopardy.[68] As the legal historian R. H. Helmholz argues, this principle continued to hold sway even in common law courts, which during the sixteenth century began to extend their competence over a civil wrong that had earlier been tried mostly in the church courts.[69]

The law thus guards its own formal and interpretive procedures, its own language and privileges, in encounters with slander. English law, for example, recognized that people could criminally abuse its own trial procedures to defamatory ends, as when a plaintiff knowingly published charges against a person in a court which had no jurisdiction over the crime in question.[70] At the same time, the law allowed that even apparently defamatory words that were uttered as part of a legal process—for example, a prosecutor's speech during a trial, private accusations whispered strictly into the ear of a justice of the peace, or a denunciation that echoed a person's preexisting condition of legal *infamia*—were not actionable as slanders.[71] Legal fiction could also accommodate certain awkward contingencies. In common law definitions of slander, for example, intention makes a difference; malicious intent is a necessary component of an actionable slander. But as if recognizing the all but impossible nature of knowing or stating intention for certain, the courts assumed a broad interpretive latitude to define intention de jure, finding malice "implied" by certain utterances in certain contexts, even if it could not otherwise be proved.[72] The law's interpretive struggle to define the scope of slander comes through in passages like the following, from John March's 1647 common law handbook, *Action for Slander:*

> Words that touch or concern a man's life may not be actionable in these cases, where the words are too general, or not positively affirmative, or of a double or indifferent meaning, or doubtful in sense, or for that they are uncertain in themselves, or the person of whom they are spoken, or else by reason of the subsequent qualification of the words, or because they do not import an act but an intent, or inclination only to it, for that they are impossible, or lastly because it doth appear that the speaking of them could be of no damage to the Plaintiff, in all these cases the words will not be actionable.[73]

I do not want to overidealize the subtleties here. Guidelines like March's, if not purely pettifogging, could provide an occasion for wildly finessing the question of intent. They recall, for example, the infamous *mitior sensus* rule, which allowed judges to dismiss actions for slander if almost any innocent sense could be wrested from the words of an alleged defamation (a strategy that justified the rules of law but also helped to limit the flood of slander litigations entering the courts during the sixteenth century).[74] It is also clear that, in certain cases, especially in cases where the words at issue touched persons in power, judges could hear just as much malice in an alleged slander as they wanted to hear. Notwithstanding, I find March's text fascinating, for all its solemn catalog of alternatives, as the representative of a larger history of real collective thinking about slander by those involved in the law. Even a common handbook like March's (or, perhaps, especially such a handbook) helps one understand why, as scholars have shown, lawyers and jurists contributed so markedly to Renaissance debates about the complexities of historical interpretation.[75] As March's text suggests, legal thinking often showed a surprisingly nuanced sense of the contingencies of intention and circumstance, the small details of grammar and syntax, that affect how words do their work in the world and cause harm. It suggests that the law is equally concerned with understanding the limits of its own power and competence, understanding not only what Coke called the law's "artificial reason" but its artificial stupidity—an effort that becomes especially urgent when defining a crime of words. The rules reflect an awareness of how law and legal interpretations, as well as slanders, hook onto the world. For one thing, they implicitly acknowledge a crucial principle articulated by Robert Cover: that in law, nuances of interpretation have consequences, in particular because they create a mandate for sanctioned violence.[76]

I need to stand back for a moment, to take a broader view of these issues, however rough the terms. The law tries to purify energies which acts of defamation reveal to be highly impure. Slander makes visible a dangerous will to accuse that the law itself can never entirely domesticate. The law may see slander as a vicious parody of its mechanisms. But we may feel that slanders can also point to foundational impulses shaping the work of law itself—the will to know sources of pain, to divide enemies from friends, to punish those who are unjust, to make criminals know their criminality, and it shows us these impulses in all of their inevitability and potential for anarchy, or simply in their nonalignment with officially sanctioned forms of justice. The crisis of slander hinges with peculiar clarity on what Cover describes as the emergence of legal judgment or *nomos* from the aberrance of private desire, the arising of the legal out of what is illegal. In pointing back to those more foundational, creative acts (by allowing their "exiled narratives" to return, in Cover's phrase), slander starkly challenges the later forms to which those acts gave rise.[77] One might call this process, appropriately enough, the backbite principle. The voices of illicit accusation, cursed as they are, show motives that echo the aspirations of justice itself. (Such an irony is one source, as George Steiner observes, of the tragic conflict in Sophocles's *Antigone*).[78] Those accused of slander may face a rational justice system with echoes of an idealism that it cannot bear to acknowledge; they are also liable to conjure up a more archaic world of anathema and chastisement, especially given that defamation takes the uncanny form of an accusation that enacts its own punishment, somewhat like a curse. Slanders pull into view a world of linguistic gestures and moral emotions—anger, shame, resentment—which sustain the work of law, even as they threaten it with unreason. Or rather, they threaten to expose the law's own unreason, its sometimes arbitrary "shaping spirit."

From both a human and a dramatistic point of view, blame is too useful, polymorphous, and energizing a thing ever to be completely isolated within law; it is too pleasurable, as well. It is too fundamental a part of how we know the world, how we mark and give a face to what threatens or baffles us, how we name its cause.[79] Blame and accusation try to clear the ground, cure the ground. Yet they also have a tendency to poison the ground, for instance by misprising the sources of harm or founding accusation on unreal occasions for offense. This is one reason why among the most fundamental struggles of human thought and imagination is the struggle to pry true accusation apart from false. This struggle involves, in its subtlest forms, the need sort out accusation's false mirrors, stupidities, mutations, and masks; it involves probing the lies all too easily wrapped up in the feelings of fear, love, loss, generosity, pride, righteousness, and loathing that feed our accusations. One ancient face of this dilemma is the endless struggle in biblical tradition to weigh the shapes of prophetic and legal accusation, and to consider where the necessary, even sacred impulse to decry spiritual error and false religion may become itself a danger—a struggle we see, for example, in Job's cursing of his pious accusers, God's chastening of Jonah's vengeful anger against Nineveh, or Jesus's denuciation of censorious Pharisees. We see another side of this struggle in early Greek ode and epic. There, as Gregory Nagy has so powerfully argued, poets are urgently concerned with freeing the heroic work of praise and blame from the contaminations of devouring, envious reproach (though poets like Archilochus also raised the performance of reproach to an art form of its own).[80] Thus, for example, Pindar's declaration in the Seventh Nemean Ode: "I am a guest-stranger, keeping away dark blame and bringing genuine glory [*kleos*], like streams of water, to a man who is beloved. I will praise him."[81] These traditions have a crucial after-life in Renaissance culture, as should be clear, and not only in legal discussions of slander. The Greek example finds echoes in humanist debates about the poetics of praise. The biblical example shapes attempts of religious reformers to think through the grounds of moral and spiritual accusation, especially during a time of massive religious change. At this period, the agon of accusation shows some of its darker volatility, a capacity for strange duplicities and betrayals. Thus, we find in reformers like Erasmus, Calvin, and Luther a fear that biblically sanctioned postures of prophetic blame can produce a blindness, a moral fanaticism, as destructive as any error they might accuse. Hence the paradox of a creature like Spenser's Blatant Beast, who is at once a prophetic image breaker and a slanderous defiler, one who both discloses and diffuses corruption in the sacred places it ravages. In the spiritual wars of the sixteenth century, the Book of the Slanderer underwrites the Book of the Iconoclast. As Shakespeare suggests, even the subtlest, most purely intellectual refinements of doubt are not free of blight; they can all too readily align themselves with the vicious, reductive honesty we see in Iago, an honesty that anticipates the envious skepticism which drives William Blake's spectral monster, "the Idiot Questioner."

One reason for the endless, inescapable quality of these struggles is that accusation is not simply a neutral gesture or speech act that we fill with different intentions, true or false, rational or irrational, selfish or altruistic. It is not just an empty linguistic counter waiting for a meaning. Rather, we seem to need some form of accusation, in all its violence and immediacy, to get meaning itself going. That is, as I understand it, one key facet of Nietzsche's argument in *The Genealogy of Morals.* The impulse to accuse can take on a life of its own; it is something that frames our laws, myths, and psyches; it helps us weave our webs of belief, our founding dichotomies of value; it helps us invent and reinvent the world. We can delicately conceal its darker motives from ourselves or turn accusation away from such objects as cost us too much. We may lend the voice of accusation to imaginary beings and let it live vicariously in propaganda, in tragedy, in gossip, and in jest. But it is hard to think entirely outside something like accusation. This derives, in part, from a peculiar doubleness in its mode of existing for us. As something we give voice to, the energy of accusation moves outward, taking shape from our pain and rage, from both our malice and our moral will, sometimes seconded and sometimes not. It reflects, that is, our intentionality, however unstable or dependent this might be. But accusation also falls back upon us; we find ourselves accused, not always with clear occasion, and without a clear source in other agents. Our actions, our simply being in the world, put us under indictment: we find ourselves accused by circumstance, by accident, by the spectacle of our own failure, by the gap between wish and power. We are caught by inchoate, sometimes sourceless feelings of contamination, shame, and guilt, by something that Paul Ricoeur speaks of as "ethical dread," a feeling prior to any specific ethical or legal interdiction.[82] These feelings are not just left alone. They give form to our imaginings. They found cosmologies. They are things that any theology will tend to build into itself, lending them a reason, a genealogy, or a divine justification. This is one of the ways that theologies build us into the world, into a larger history or system of prohibitions. Judeo-Christian myths of an originary transgression, a Fall of Man, perform this function most obviously. Such myths are among the most resilient we know, most influential (if also most costly) in their way of reading accusation and punishment into human suffering itself, reading human suffering *as* accusation, or as a symptom of transgression (though also, in some cases, a condition of trial.)[83] The need to make sense of the paradox of accusation also shapes the more wildly revisionary accounts of the Fall such as we find in Gnostic writings, accounts which refuse to credit the orthodox reading of the sources of human guilt and instead make the paternal deity himself into a false and fallen accuser. Reformation theologians struggle crucially to place this sense of being inescapably under accusation by God (caught between an infinite demand and a terribly limited power to answer that demand). This perception shapes their pictures of what self-knowledge amounts to, where conscience lies, what action is possible in the world; it shapes the terms on which believers are allowed to accuse both others and themselves of spiritual error (as is suggested in the passage from Calvin quoted above). A heightened awareness of being accused becomes a condition for adjudicating any competing, less radical accounts of human guilt and responsibility. Such struggles help to produce that complex combination of spiritual malaise and moral stringency that characterizes so much Reformation religious writing. A late version of the paradox of accusation shapes the uncanny and aberrant legalism of Kafka's *Trial,* a book which begins, famously, "Someone must have slandered Josef K., for one morning, without having done anything truly wrong, he was arrested."[84] It is a situation which depends precisely on the strange intertwining of law and calumny I have been eliciting here. Nietzsche wanted us to unbind our moral and theological judgments from what he could see only as a kind of projected resentment, a disguise for archaic hatreds, but he knew how resilient such feelings are, and what subtle, if treacherous, tools of thought they offer.

In *The Spirit of Detraction,* Vaughan reminds readers repeatedly that *diabolos* means "accuser." The demonism that blossoms in Renaissance accounts of slander will feel like a mystification, a way of masking the more concrete psychological and social causes for abusive speech. We are likely to see only a highly self-conscious play of tropes in this seventeenth-century epigram:

> It surely was in hell that slander was begun;
> The slanderer still has the devil on his tongue.
>> And he who is persuaded easily to hear
>> The slander, he must have the devil in his ear.
> But he who finally believes the false report,
> He certainly must have the devil in his heart.[85]

Yet the sense of some more uncanny, even metaphysical harm latent in verbal accusation may still be apprehensible to us—even if we filter our perceptions of it through Kafka or Freud.

THE WITCH TRIALS of fifteenth-, sixteenth-, and seventeenth-century Europe and America have been, for many scholars, the great laboratory in which to study the demonic magic of accusation, the magic of demon talk as opposed to God talk. (The history of religious persecution, especially anti-Semitism, is another such laboratory.) So many cases, after all, present us with a situation in which accusing someone of an impossible crime seems inevitably to conjure the reality of the crime. In many such cases, as Alan Macfarlane notes, people's fear of witchcraft and its malicious magic went hand in hand with fear of being accused of witchcraft.[86] In studying the trials, indeed, it is hard not be caught sometimes strongly by a sense of how law and slander collude with each other, how the carefully structured forms of official accusation serve to prop up a system of irrational libels, echoing less public rumors, suspicions, slanders, and "fames," keeping alive wilder social and spiritual antipathies.[87] The forms of proof employed in witch trials (for example, the search for hidden marks on a witch's body, confessions extracted by coercion or torture, the famous swimming test) may seem to us not simply invasive but strangely self-sustaining, not the least because they often excluded obvious means of disproof.[88] The very word "witch" thus comes to seem like a malicious spell, or a legally sustained calumny launched against innocent victims. We can understand the uses of this. At one level, pointing to the malice of a witch, to a cause at once human and demonic, might allow people to rationalize very local troubles—a child's death, a husband's impotence, the withering of crops, a wasting illness, even the persistant failure of cream to turn into butter. Shared myths about the aberrant activities of witches—including their consorting with demons, their parodies of the Mass, sexual license, bestiality, and cannibalism—could also provide an outlet for larger fears, as Norman Cohn has argued; during a time of spiritual and social crisis, the persecution of a demonized population might serve as a desperate means for European culture to keep its failing orders pure and intact.[89] The fascination of this lies partly in how the very legal and social orders which indict and execute witches start to look like the cause of the curse they purport to cure. Those orders become the true source of the witch's malicious magic. They are the very demons with whom they are at war.

This formulation is partial, and figurative. It leaves out many questions about how official and unofficial accusations might be in conflict; it also evades the question of what beliefs or practices the accused witches themselves actually embraced (something Carlo Ginzburg has taught us to take more seriously).[90] Yet this paradox starts to catch something crucial for me about the formal and dramatic logic of accusation, also about accusation as itself an object of fantasy. This is indeed something that certain Renaissance fictions can bring out with particular acuity. One can see a version of this paradox at work, for example, in *The Witch of Edmonton,* a play authored jointly by Thomas Dekker, John Ford, and William Rowley, first performed in 1621.[91] It is a work which uses a story of witchcraft to bring ideas of accusation, slander, and law into sometimes baffling interplay.

Many of the more lurid details of this drama were based on a pamphlet published the same year, reporting the deeds and confessions of an actual woman hanged for witchcraft. But it is a more obviously fictive moment in the text that interests me, specifically, some words given to the witch herself. At the opening of act 2 of the play, an old and impoverished widow, Mother Sawyer, is chased onto the stage by a mob led by a particularly vicious landowner, who loads her with abuse and cries of "witch." Left alone, she takes these words as the occasion to become the very witch she is accused of being. Somewhat like Shakespeare's Caliban, she shamelessly turns her curses back against the world whose curses had first dogged her:

> Would some power, good or bad,
> Instruct me which way I might be revenged
> Upon this churl, I'd go out of myself
> And give this fury leave to dwell within
> This ruined cottage ready to fall with age,
> Abjure all goodness, be at hate with prayer,
> And study curses, imprecations,
> Blasphemous speeches, oaths, detested oaths,
> Or anything that's ill; so I might work
> Revenge upon this miser, this black cur
> That barks and bites, and sucks the very blood
> Of me and of my credit. 'Tis all one
> To be a witch as to be counted one.
> (2.1.107–19)

This soliloquy, disenchanting as it seems, sits oddly within the dramatic fiction, which goes on to allow the "success" of Mother Sawyer's conversion. Her curses against her doglike enemies conjure a concrete, if still mysterious, black dog (a part written for a human actor), who, like Faust's Mephistopheles, magically fulfills her malicious wishes against her neighbors, even as it ultimately betrays Mother Sawyer to her accusers. The devil is thus both there and not there in the fiction, at once a projection of human slanders and a real if unstable agent in the world. The fact that the witch's crimes are interwoven with a lurid if more secular tale of romantic murder (a murder that the devilish canine both provokes and causes to be found out) also keeps evil of a human order present simultaneously. In the end, one cannot easily pry true accusation apart from illicit defamation. The motives and objects of each have a disturbing way of bleeding together. It is a game of shadows and mirrors, in which each steals its forms from the other and courts the other under disguise.

---

The dramatic analysis of defamation in *The Witch of Edmonton* is at once naked and fantastic. It demystifies witchcraft up to a point, showing us how social malice and private rage collaborate to make Mother Sawyer the very witch she is falsely accused of being. In the lines I've quoted, it is the mob's abuses that become her demonic familiars, sucking on her reputation rather than her monstrous body. Yet her choice of literalizing her neighbor's vicious indictments remains paradoxical. Abject and self dramatizing as it may seem, her choice does gain her the magical help of that demonic, untrustworthy dog (a creature who, significantly enough, also enjoys the company of the play's clown). In a very immediate fashion, *The Witch of Edmonton* lays bare the blindness of those who accuse witches. At the same time, both its realistic and its magical fictions keep the will to accuse the witch in play, sometimes mocking it but never letting it go. Keeping alive so chaotic a picture of the causes of "evil," the play's anatomy of witchcraft accusation may thus seem at odds with itself. Yet the authors do this largely because it keeps the play alive. Legalistic or ideological consistency is not quite the point here. Rather, the play keeps the energy of accusatory speech in motion onstage in order to feed the evolution of the dramatic fiction.

Contemporary plays offer few parallels to this self-creating witch and this ambiguously human dog.[92] But that characters onstage can shape themselves out of networks of damaging words shouldn't surprise us; nor should we wonder that abusive words, even in the disillusionments they carry, can give such characters a life so potent and mutable. *The Witch of Edmonton* explores a play of detraction entirely native to the Renaissance stage.

I can imagine a history of English Renaissance theater keyed to the matter of defamation. Even among those who defend the work of the players— Philip Sidney and Thomas Heywood, for example—one feels a suspicion that theatrical representation by its very nature entails an abuse or detraction of truth. To antitheatrical writers the stage inevitably slandered the real, producing abusive translations of orthodox myths, deforming true his-

tories simply by committing them to the tainted medium of fiction, fiction
performed before an audience hungry primarily for the fantastic, the scandalous, or the distracting.[93] The stage could seem nothing but a "mirror of
monsters," or a "school of abuse" teaching only idleness, contempt, folly,
pride, treason, and blasphemy.[94] For one thing, it depended on actors,
whose social status was uncertain and whose ability to change from king to
fool, from man to woman, corroded all natural orders. Almost by nature,
the actor, standing "on a scaffold, babling vaine newes to the sclander of the
world, put . . . in scoffing the vertues of honest men," as one antitheatrical
writer asserted.[95] We should not dismiss such representations as themselves
merely libelous; they register a complex truth. The theater in Renaissance
England did in fact allow actors and playwrights to explore ever more extreme and complexly motivated forms of outrageous speech, forms of satire
and invective banished from print and pulpit. Rites of insult, railing, and
rage were clearly the bread and butter of the players, from the clown's anarchic jesting to the bombast of Senecan revengers. The release of a violent,
otherwise tabooed language was one of the seductions of all public theater,
as attested to by the stunning success of Christopher Marlowe, whose gaudy
hyperboles work in part because of their violent contempt for ordinary
measures of meaning. Such violent words release in an especially blunt way
what Michael Goldman calls "the actor's freedom," that is, the actor's quality as something *sacer,* at once cursed and blessed; such freedom involves the
actor's power to make the invisible visible on stage, and a commitment to
theatrical illusion such as overcomes ordinary fears of shame and death.[96]
More generally, in plays which so often have a decidedly forensic character,
the voices of accusation and indictment are themselves more readily freed
up and allowed in all of their ambivalence to animate an entire play.[97] That
illusory human beings stood forth onstage made up of such languages, sustained by them, could only have made the situation more unsettling.

The theater tempered its anarchic or slanderous impulses, of course. The
stage's relentless will to expose scandals could be turned to more moderate
and philosophical uses (also politically safer ones). The indecent mingling of
high and low could be shaped into a more comprehensive vision of social reality. Dangerous energies of railing and satire were themselves interrogated
within the theatrical fiction, subtilized, sometimes mocked and degraded in
their own right. The actor's troubling freedom to disguise himself, the necessity of masks and metamorphosis—these could provoke subtler lessons
in disillusionment, more self-reflexive forms of wonder. Especially given its
ambitions toward legitimacy and stability, the theater was as likely to mirror
as to mock the fables of orthodoxy and the ceremonies of state (not to

mention lending its resources directly to the making of court pageantry and masque). The developing mechanisms of official censorship lent their shaping force to the stage as well, not just in what the master of the revels might explicitly require to be canceled, cut, and rewritten, but in how the presence of censors compelled some of the stage's more subversive energies to shift into disguise, in the process training the audiences to listen with a different ear.[98] Yet despite such controls, both internal and external, the business of playing remained under suspicion. Perhaps this was because the dramatic fictions of playwrights like Marlowe, Shakespeare, Jonson, and Marston made so visible the struggle for control and so amplified in their plays the ferocious and conflicted voices which that struggle could provoke. Their theater was flexible enough to take within its fictions the very voices of antitheatrical critique, making that critique its own, a feeder of more complex histrionic invention, or a parable of other forms of doubt. For these and other reasons, stage plays never lost their reputation for being the seeds of atheism, vice, perversity, rebellion, and breach of the peace; the theater remained a place that (like Essex's tavern) gave scope to looser forms of language, even as it absorbed more stable languages to that looseness. The "wooden O" became a version of Ovid's or Chaucer's House of Rumor, both chaotic gathering places for cries and murmurs arriving from all parts of the world. In addition to being a place where the plague might breed, the theater was seen itself (in ironic anticipation of Artaud) as a kind of plague.

There is no space to do more than hint at such a history of theater here. For now, I will look at only one text, which shows us just how starkly a Renaissance playwright could reflect on his work's place within this conflicted environment. Ben Jonson's *Poetaster* (1601) begins under the patronage of Envy, a decidedly less beguiling stage daemon than Shakespeare's Rumour, which I have touched on in chapter 1. Rumour beguiles its audience with a certain Puck-like sweetness, seducing listeners with an image of their own passive and wavering need for stories. Envy with its "wounded nerves" conjures more ferocious appetites. This monster rises onto the stage through a trapdoor and begins to search the audience for a dangerous community, invoking the audience's "ample faculties" to misconstrue what it sees and hears, to exercise its skill at divining secrets that are not there. We who listen must rise to the challenge of the play, Envy urges, making it speak to our imagination, piecing out its imperfections with our thoughts (as the chorus to *Henry V* suggests). Envy asks from us "wrestings, comments, applications, / Spy-like suggestions, privy whisperings" (induction, 24–25), especially such glosses as convert the author's general moral satire into a particular

calumny, a libel that may reveal itself as both shamefully self-serving and potentially criminal.[99] To this end, Envy makes a gift of his poison to the audience, inviting us to release the rage that we may, out of habit or fear,
withhold:

> Here, take my snakes among you, come and eat,
> And while the squeezed juice flows in your black jaws,
> Help me to damn the Author. Spit it forth
> Upon his lines, and show your rusty teeth
> At every word or accent; or else choose
> Out of my longest vipers, to stick down
> In your deep throats, and let the heads come forth
> At your rank mouths, that he may see you armed
> With triple malice, to hiss, sting and tear
> His work and him; to forge, and then declaim,
> Traduce, corrupt, apply, inform, suggest:
> O, these are gifts wherein your souls are blest.
>
> (44–55)

Envy projects Jonson's vision of the audience as enemy. It sums up a complex array of opponents. For one thing, he calls out to Jonson's fellow
dramatists, including John Marston, who is satirized in *Poetaster* as the
resentful and parasitical poetaster Crispinus (made to vomit up his own
fustian), and Thomas Dekker, Jonson's Demetrius, a playwright whose
*Satiromastix* accuses Jonson himself of writing out of mere envy, arrogance,
and desire for applause. (We are in the midst of that strange and revelatory
episode, "the war of the theaters.")[100] Envy addresses as well the tribe of
carping antitheatricalists. This creature also searches the audience for the
tribe of paid and unpaid listeners whose tongues pass on secret "informations" and "news" to the state, and who are eager to read into the play seditious opinions that aren't truly there. Unconscious parodists of the humanist
project of "application," such listeners, Jonson complains, "are too witty in
another mans Workes, and utter, some times, theyre owne malicious Meanings, under our Wordes."[101] Usurping the role of the censor, even as they
serve it, these delators threaten to put the play and its author in legal jeopardy; their ears threaten the ears of Jonson himself—who twice during his
career (in 1597 and 1605) was jailed for writing seditious plays. Yet it is crucial that we cannot narrowly identify Envy's agents with a particular political faction or office. The topical references are left strategically vague, and
not just out of a desire on Jonson's part to protect himself from charges of

libel. It is a testimony to Jonson's profound generality as a satirist that one feels emerging through Envy's speech an all but metaphysical anxiety, a frightening vision of the audience's inner appetite for what it sees and hears—an appetite that precludes even the witty sort of contract he offers the audience in the induction to *Bartholomew Fair.* Instead of charitable applause, or even a desire for wonder, Envy calls out to an interrogative poison. As avatar of the audience's desires, Envy offers a kind of vicious, self-sustaining communion: take and eat that poison which you will find within you, within your gravelike throats, throats which are a source of poison, more serpentine than human. The audience feeds on waste, on what should be expelled, on the corpses of snakes which they both devour and resurrect in their mouths. This histrionic Envy projects onto the audience, or discovers within it, a world of archaic wounds; in Jonson's picture, indeed, both mouth and ear are themselves wounds, violently *made* rather than natural openings in the body. They are organs through which the soul repossesses its own poison, a poison that seems to belong to the world at large. Jonson uses Envy to externalize what the audience might otherwise guiltily repress, suggesting that each member of the audience already carries within a seed of rage that is called into action by what he or she witnesses. That is the curse or blessing which they send back to the world created onstage.[102] The important thing to add is that Jonson, in his complex jointure of moral severity and wild imagination, may have known just how much this personification speaks to impulses at the heart of his own work.[103]

---

This chapter begins and ends with monsters. Slander is a monstrous thing that produces monsters. It forces a monstrous face on others, makes a monster of their minds. It shows us the monstrous mouth and ear of those who utter slanders. The difficult thing is to take the measure of slander's ordinariness. The monsters of detraction are all too often what Wordsworth called "a simple produce of the common day," a thing of "public means which public manners breeds" (sonnet 111). Slanders become the stuff of what everyone says. They emerge out of the most banal desires. They speak to our common wishes both to diminish and to inflate the shapes of what we know about the world. They depend on our common desire to shock, as well as on our shifting, duplicitous capacity to *be* shocked by what we see or hear. (How do we measure people's power to be shocked or scandalized? How does shock penetrate the soul, how does it open or harden the heart?) If slanders speak about hidden truths, they are often truths hidden in plain sight, like Poe's purloined letter. They are part of the air we breathe, an atmosphere which is full of plain, unexceptional murmurings, though sometimes also occult impressions of crime, panic, and doubt.[104] The English word "slander," as I have said, derives originally from the Greek word *skandalon,* "trap" or "stumbling block." St. Paul uses the word to describe the shocking *kerygma* of Christ crucified—"unto the Iewes, even a stombling blocke, & unto the Grecians, foolishnes" (1 Corinthians 1:23, Geneva version). (Wycliffe's translation has "to Jewis sclaundre.")[105] The anonymous English pamphlet of 1573, *A Plaine description of the Auncient Petigree of Dame Slaunder,* follows Calvin in asking how much our spiritual freedom must be purchased at the cost of offense, distinguishing "sclaunder [or scandal] *given*" from "sclaunder *taken*."[106] The first refers to sinful behavior that sets a dangerous example, causing others to fall or err, or that threatens legitimate authority; the second refers to good, often redemptive deeds which are turned into an occasion of offense by other people's malice or misperception. One burden of our moral imagination is to distinguish between these. Yet it is also a measure of Shakespeare's difficulty that "scandal given" and "scandal taken" are so intricately bound up together, even as we are relentlessly, unendingly tasked with sorting them out. The plays thus enact the dance of our soiled knowledge of the world, and of ourselves.

# chapter three

# A DISTURBANCE
# OF HEARING IN VIENNA

In my memory, the properties of the world of prisons, theatres and dreams: anxieties, falls, fevers, apparitions, inexplicable noises, singing, suspected presences.

JEAN GENET

*easure for Measure* reads like a workshop for the trag-edies written after it—in its stark pictures of human character and conflict, in its depth of political reflection, in the way that the play's comic elements leaven the darker aspects of the story (more subtly than in any play but *King Lear*). The play's interest in words that harm makes it an inescapable piece of the mosaic I am putting together here. Yet that piece remains hard to fit. There is something in the play I miss; I sense a blank spot, or something held back from expression, both a silence and a disquieting noise. Unresolved questions about the relations of Angelo, Isabella, the Duke, and Claudio are part of what accounts for this. Like many, I am struck by what William Hazlitt describes as a pattern of cross-purposes or repugnance "between the feelings of the different characters and the sympathy of the reader or the audience."[1] That sense of repugnance may hold even if one accepts that the play works partly according to the logic of romance or masque, in which case it is a mistake to ask for too much emotional consistency.[2] For the play relentlessly evokes the very emotions that it baffles; it conjures responses which it then leaves curiously mishoused or homeless, as if it had no interest in them. Another way of putting it is to say that *Measure for Measure*'s complex catastrophe never truly discharges the spiritual debt that accumulates over

the course of the play's unfolding, or else it only pays us back in false coin-
age. The form of this play takes liberties which we cannot quite forgive it for
taking (even as the Duke takes liberties we cannot forgive him for taking,
though that is not the same thing). At the same time, *Measure for Measure*
never seems to risk its comic form in the way that another dark comedy, *The
Merchant of Venice,* does. I sometimes feel that the playwright himself grew
disgusted with the dramatic machinery he deploys so ruthlessly. This answers to my sense of something peculiarly twisted and clotted about the language in this play, as if, rather than liberating meaning, the play's language
turns against its own expression. I imagine the play saying, along with that
nameless gentleman whom Lucio tricks into admitting his own disease, "I
think I have done myself wrong, have I not?" (1.2.38).[3]

The play offers us a striking image of this bafflement in something that
Angelo says to Isabella, when he warns her against reporting to the world his
attempt at sexual blackmail. If she accuses him in public, he says, both his
own reputation for virtue and her obvious interest in the case will speak
against her, transforming her person and her words in the process: "You shall
stifle in your own report, / And smell of calumny" (2.4.157–58). The image is that of a living person who strangles herself in speaking. Her own
words steal her breath, even bury her alive; her living breath becomes the
rotten air put forth by a corpse. This smell diffuses itself throughout the
play; the speaker stifled in his or her own report indeed becomes one of
*Measure for Measure*'s central images of human desire, its odor hovering even
around those acts of justice that finally do answer Isabella's accusation of Angelo. The business of this chapter is to assess this smell, and to listen to this
peculiar metamorphosis of report.

---

My focus is on what the Duke of Vienna hears and doesn't hear, what he asks
others to hear, what he silences; I want to consider how these things shape
our sense of other characters and of the energies structured into the play as
a whole. The Duke moves through the play as an isolated, occulted ear, in
flight from both public praise and slander, from the relentless murmuring
that fills his city. That hidden ear remains hungry; it listens to prayers and
confessions, listens in on conversations, arguments, and public trials—absorbed by the shapes that power and crime take in the world he has abandoned, especially the fate of those whom he has left behind as his substitutes.
The disguised ruler stumbles upon unknown secrets that he makes part of
his ironic plots, upon scandals that he will later bring to light. He can even

fabricate secrets that never existed, if that is useful to him; he is also ready to manipulate confessions that, one imagines, should have remained secret. One difficulty he encounters is that, having given his power over to his substitute Angelo and put on the disguise of a foreign monk, he runs into the very noises he has fled. He is forced to listen to what he does not want to know. He hears words that continue to baffle him, words that he both flies from and tries to cut off. Ordinary murmurings thus acquire a peculiar charge. Commonplace things strike the Duke as if he had never heard them before, yet they claim a disturbing intimacy. The Duke finds especially in Lucio—a haunter of brothels, prisons, and lawcourts—a voice that shamelessly sticks to his person, presenting the Duke with a darker but strangely endearing vision of his activity in the play. Lucio speaks for something that the Duke cannot banish from his ear, even when he is most in control, something which in turn becomes for him evidence of the world's peculiar monstrosity. The things that do not even touch his ear, however, are more disturbing.

The Duke's protest against the world of murmurers is clearest in a passage from act 4, scene 1. It occurs at the most humanly critical moment of his plot to expose the corruptions of Angelo and to save both Isabella and her brother Claudio from wrong—that is, the moment when Isabella must persuade Mariana, Angelo's abandoned betrothed, to become her substitute in Angelo's bed. The Duke arrives with Isabella at the "moated grange," and—after Mariana's embarrassment at being caught listening to a love song, and the strange news that the Duke has long been her spiritual adviser—he sends the two women off to a corner (if not offstage), so that Isabella can tell her story to Mariana. While waiting, the Duke stands apart and speaks a brief soliloquy:

> O place and greatness! Millions of false eyes
> Are stuck upon thee: volumes of report
> Run with these false, and most contrarious quest
> Upon thy doings: thousand escapes of wit
> Make thee the father of their idle dream
> And rack thee in their fancies.
> (60–65)

The anger at talkers that breaks through here is typical of the Duke's nervous pride. As much as he hates staging himself to the public eye and public love (which also stifles him), there is a kind of inadvertent exposure that is worse. Being at the mercy of those who do not see him, whom he cannot see, wounds him more strangely. Everyone, he suddenly fears, is telling wildly erring stories about him. Crowds of wandering slanders "contrarious quest" upon his known and unknown actions, as if with a will of their own.[4] A "thousand escapes of wit" want somehow to make him the father of their own empty fantasy, that is, not just reporting false surmises about his doings, but somehow making him responsible for the lies they tell. The imagery suggests, I think, that these bruits and stories are like illegitimate children, not simply running free, but somehow seeking him out, making him their father, soliciting him to acknowledge a paternity he will not own.[5] Insofar as such an image of paternity touches his life as Duke of Vienna, he suddenly sees himself as both ruling over and subjected to a kingdom of rumor, an antikingdom or purgatory of willful dreams. Unable to put these invisible, illegitimate tongues on the rack, he is himself "racked" by rumor, as Claudio will imagine himself imprisoned and blown about in the afterlife by freezing winds. The Duke feels caught by an alien, external energy which may seem at the same time to be the scattered reflection of his own thoughts.[6]

This speech is striking enough in itself, since it speaks so directly to the Duke's uneasiness at his position and his motives in hiding himself in the guise of a friar. As editors observe, however, the lines seem curiously out of place. Nothing in the context appears to provoke this harangue. There are also too few lines in the soliloquy, some argue, to give Isabella time to tell her tale. Hence, it is surmised that the passage must have come from somewhere else in the play (perhaps torn from an earlier speech about "back-wounding calumny" in 3.2.179–82) and inserted here to fill in a gap in the play text, awkwardly patching an awkward silence.[7] What the original speech of the Duke might have been, and why or how it was omitted, is hard to say in this case. The thing I want to suggest here, however, is that the passage really is in the right place. Anomalous as the lines are, they fit an anomaly in both the character who speaks them and the scene represented onstage. For having a sense of this Duke, and of the qualities of his ear, I cannot help thinking that one object of his concern is the very conversation going on offstage, where Isabella explains to Mariana an "escape of wit" of which he is undoubtedly the father. He cannot literally hear their conference. He doesn't need to hear it, one might say. And for reasons I will suggest, he doesn't want to hear it. Yet it is just this fear or distrust of the conversation that helps to provoke his outburst.

That the Duke has asked Isabella herself to explain his plot can seem strange, since he is himself the author of the plot and moreover already knows Mariana. Perhaps it should not surprise us that he is ready to instrumentalize these women—as he instrumentalizes other deputies in the course of the play, always displacing authority for his actions, disimplicating himself even as he implicates others. It is not done entirely in cold blood, of course; he does ask Mariana plainly before sending her offstage with Isabella, "Do you persuade yourself that I respect you?" (4.1.53), which suggests something more than mere pragmatism. One could even surmise that the Duke's tactic is a way of drawing out Isabella, a way of involving her sympathies for another woman as well as further testing her powers of persuasion.[8] But this does not mean that the Duke does not feel a residual uncertainty or fear of what is being said in that space apart. Even if he is being delicate toward these women—who are spared having a male cleric listen in on what must be a difficult, intimate conversation—he is equally delicate toward himself. Consider what is taking place: in telling her story, Isabella must speak about her own victimhood and double bind. Describing the shock and shame of her situation—and of her brother's situation—she may conceal her own deeper fears. But she cannot help giving Mariana some rather painful, even repellent news about a promised husband who abandoned and humiliated her yet whom she still loves. In this situation, Isabella must represent for Mariana an erotic rival as well as a potential savior. Isabella must also explain the Duke's counterplot, a plan dangerous enough in itself, a trick both illegitimate and legitimating, insofar as it both keeps Angelo's blackmail plot in play and ironically turns that plot to other uses. For one thing, even as it saves Isabella's virginity, it becomes a strange substitute for Mariana's lost wedding night, which makes sleeping with Angelo both a recompense and a kind of revenge. (This is also an act that could beget a child whom the father might later refuse to acknowledge as legitimate.) Even if we don't suppose that the Duke has doubts about the bed trick itself (which in fact turns out to be less predictable in its consequences than he had calculated), we can see a whole realm of shame, embarrassment, and unreadiness that the conversation might conjure up. It conjures up a set of spaces—Angelo's chambers and his double-gated garden—full of treachery. Having Isabella talk to Mariana alone thus allows the Duke to keep his distance from his own contrivance, from having to hear it talked about, as well as from any hesitancy or doubt we can imagine in the women themselves. What the Duke's words about "place and greatness" and "escapes of wit" suggest, however, is that, having set the two to talk out of hearing, he unconsciously thinks about what they are saying. His outburst is a displaced comment on the very process he has set in motion and cannot entirely control. It is as if, in being talked over by those women, his own plots and the questions they set in motion took on the look of the misfathered, abusive, and idle dreams, dreams that stick to him like those "millions of false eyes." There is something dangerously impure in his plots that the lines about "report" both confess and try to put away—expressing this fear through a language which mistakes its real objects, substituting those nameless "millions" for these two very particular women talking close at hand.

We will come back to the Duke's image of slanders as questing, solicitous bastards. The point for now is just to suggest that the Duke's lines respond to something of what he hears, or overhears, in the two women's otherwise inaudible conversation. His speech reflects a wholly imaginary eavesdropping, as much a revelation of his anxiety as of theirs. At the same time, the more impersonal, politicized language of the harangue drives any recognition of such doubts out of his ear; he stops his own inner ear, as it were. That is the uncanniness of the passage. The Duke's soliloquy shows us, to adapt W. H. Auden's words, not so much a private face in a public place as a public face in a private place (his own). Remember that even as the Duke contrives by his trick to purify the sexual meeting in Angelo's garden, he struggles to make the trick itself a pure contrivance. Describing it to Isabella in an earlier scene, the Duke had insisted to Isabella that "the doubleness of the benefit defends the deceit from reproof" (3.1.258–59). Later, when Mariana returns from her conversation, the Duke protests again that the plot is innocent, and accomplishes nothing but right: "the justice of your title to him / Doth flourish the deceit.—Come, let us go" (4.1.74–75). The Duke's haste to offer such justifications suggests a certain anxiety, however, a residue of guilt harassing the father of such a brilliant "escape of wit." This too reflects a readiness to silence the doubtful noise in his own and others' heads and hearts.

---

Walke as children of light. . . . And have no fellowship with the unfruteful workes of darknes, but even reprove them rather. For it is shame even to speake of the things which are done of them in secret. But all things when they are reproved of the light, are manifest: for it is light that maketh all things manifest. Wherefore he saith, Awake thou that slepest, and stand up from the dead, and Christ shall give thee light. Take hede therefore that ye walke circumspectly, not as fooles, but as wise, redeeming the time: for the dayes are evil. (St. Paul, Epistle to the Ephesians [Geneva])

That the Duke's soliloquy displaces hidden fears of the two women's conversation may or may not be plausible. A more obvious anomaly characterizes these lines, however. Their attack on "volumes of report" misses a plainer target. The lines should, after all, be directed against Lucio, the one whose "pretty tales about the Duke" the Duke elsewhere finds so offensive, so dangerous to his reputation—even though Lucio whispers them exclusively into the disguised ruler's own ear. Yet in this case, again, the anomaly may be more than just an accident of textual transmission or an ambiguous trace of playhouse practice. The absence of any reference to Lucio also suggests the curious compulsiveness of this Duke's misrecognitions. For in this brief sermon against slander, the language both catches and fails to catch something in Lucio's mode of storytelling.

Lucio haunts the Duke like a "devoted spirit," as Anne Barton says, or like an improvisational actor who intrudes into the Duke's more stylized masque of justice.[9] The idea that this mocking, interfering tale-teller bears some true light about the Duke goes back to Romantic readers like August Wilhelm Schlegel, so perhaps it does not need much elaboration here.[10] But we need to place that idea carefully. The first thing to remember is what Lucio does not get. His tales never speak of the Duke's touchy pride, his love of moralizing, his improvisatory cunning, his love of grand effects, or his confident pursuit of marred plots. Many things that Lucio suggests about the Duke's past behavior are also unconfirmed, even impossible to imagine: we never see the Duke drunk, nakedly foolish, mouthing with a beggar, or being charitable toward lechery. Nor can one quite imagine him paying for the nursing of bastards. But the uncanniness of Lucio's reports of the Duke's history lies in how his stories speak to what we see of the Duke onstage, in the present tense of performance; they gloss what we hear as the play unfolds. To speak about the "old fantastical duke of dark corners" (4.3.156), one who "would have dark deeds darkly answered: he would never bring them to light" (3.2.171–72), does catch much of his contradictory nature, his simultaneous attachment to justice and game playing, his curious kindness, his love of secrecy, his desire to become a ghost or wanderer in his own state. These words also point to the Duke's tendency to propose legitimate cures with an air of illegitimacy. To this degree, Lucio the lurking, murmuring mocker does not just interpret, he doubles the Duke's agency, conjuring up its regressive and infantile as well as its strictly illegal aspects. He may even carry, as Harry Berger, Jr., suggests, the burden of the Duke's "interior audition," insofar as Lucio's words turn a light on the thoughts and intents that "slink about in the dark corners of [the Duke's] language, unable to make themselves part of what he seems to want to say, or hear himself say, in his speech."[11] This is why, perhaps, Lucio seems content to speak to no one *but* the disguised Duke about the Duke's foibles. When Lucio says of the Duke,

"I was an inward of his," we may see him as a piece of the Duke's own inwardness. Yet that inwardness is curiously objectified; Lucio is a double who cannot just be brought back inside, since he contains so much that the Duke denies.[12] He becomes an ironic mirror who at once defends and deforms the ruler's reputation, stealing from him his sovereign right of self-description. Lucio represents the limit of the Duke's command over his own secrets, his *arcana imperii,* his own dreams, while yet retaining a suspicious, impish, harassing "interest" in the Duke's person.[13]

We might compare the situation in Shakespeare's play with that of John Marston's contemporary tragicomedy, *The Malcontent* (1604), which also focuses on the fairy-tale plot of a displaced ruler who haunts his court in disguise. Marston's Duke Altofronto, whose throne was usurped by his brother Pietro, returns to his realm in the role of a sullen, melancholiac fool named Malevolve, a comic ranter "more discontent than Lucifer," and with an appetite "insatiable as the grave . . . to procure others' vexation" (1.3.20–22).[14] Freeing up both bizarre fantasies and bitter invective, this mask allows Altofronto to voice his own resentment and violent distrust of politics. Yet remarkable as Malevolve's noise is, full of Marston's genius for wild satire, it does little to unsettle the world. His attacks on folly and vice fall mostly on deaf ears. At best, Altofronto's words make him an intimate of the usurping Duke, who thinks that Malevolve's mockery and refusal to flatter "gives me good intelligence to my spirit" (1.3.33). Shakespeare gives this plot a different twist. To begin with, he offers us the more subtly caustic picture of a ruler exiled not by a usurper but by his own will to disappear, by his decision to "usurp the beggary he was never born to" (3.2.90). And while, as in Marston, the Duke's disguise frees up his powers of observation, it does not free up in him any such satirical voice as Altofronto finds. Instead, any more skeptical, manic voice returns in the form of Lucio, the "fantastic," as the character list in the First Folio calls him. The Duke's secret disguise seems to win him his own mocker, one that intimately shadows him in his passage through the political underworld of Vienna, listening, telling him tales which strangely mingle abuse and flattery; he gains a companion whom he cannot bear, whose "intelligence" he would banish, since it speaks to impulses he can never acknowledge.[15]

Lucio sticks to the Duke and cannot be shaken away. We might wonder, for a moment, what Lucio's own motives for sticking are—even given that he sometimes seems to exist as a double or phantasm of the Duke. It is not easy to attach individual desires or personality to a figure like Lucio; he is in essence a clown figure, and like other clowns serves centrally as a theatrical tool, a means of throwing open the languages and postures of other characters, also a way of bridging the gap between the world of the audience and the world of the play. Hence his lack of any proper "office" in this office-obsessed play, his freedom to level at both criminals and judges, subjects and rulers. Still, this creature who speaks "according to the trick" (the play's word for both moral posturing and illegitimate sex) does in fact seem to speak for some peculiar desire, some signature of self.[16] The intense quality of his attachment to the Duke is part of this. For myself, I often want to take Lucio at his word: charged by the disguised Duke with ignorant malice against him, he protests, "I know him and I love him" (3.2.145). One might argue that Lucio's love is an outright lie, or stands only as a trope for such perverse attachment as slanderers have to their defiled subjects. (Or perhaps love in this play is liable to get mistaken for slander, felt to be a form of defilement.) Yet there is a candor in Lucio's attachment that is more than merely ironic or abusive, something which may itself be a reason for the Duke's excessive dislike of him.

One verbal clue to Lucio's love has always fascinated me, fragile as it is, especially because it relates to an instance of abuse that touches Shakespeare himself. Refusing to leave the Duke as he walks offstage in act 4, scene 3, Lucio offers a charming self-description: "If bawdy talk offend you, we'll have very little of it. Nay, friar, I am a kind of burr, I shall stick" (175–77). Burrs are used elsewhere in Shakespeare as figures of playful mockery, worldly accident, and romantic frustration.[17] But the clinging burr was also a common Renaissance metaphor for courtly, servile parasites. And it is this sense of the word that shows itself in a famous libel directed at *Measure for Measure*'s author. I am thinking of Robert Greene's warning to his fellow dramatists in *A Groatsworth of Wit* (1592), a warning against the treachery of upstart actors who become playwrights themselves, competing with their former masters: "Base-minded men all three of you, if by my misery you be not warned: for unto none of you (like me) sought those burrs to cleave: those puppets (I mean) that spake from our mouths, those antics garnished in our colours."[18] We have no real evidence of what Shakespeare might have thought of this posthumously published attack (whose most famous lines I omit).[19] But we can, I think, take Lucio's words as a belated and parabolic response to such an attack, and to the mingled rage and self-hatred one hears in the dying man's words. (Consider how many years an insult may stick in our memories, and even become part of our secret self-knowledge.) With ironic bravado, Lucio embraces rather than protests the slanderous label of "burr," shamelessly answering a Duke who is himself afraid of the treachery and revolt of his puppets, afraid of those substitutes who speak from his mouth, whom he had invested with the colors of his authority. ("In our remove, be thou at full ourself. / Mortality and mercy in Vienna / Live in thy tongue, and heart" [1.1.43–45].) Lucio the burr might indeed be reminding the Duke that they are both puppets and playwrights, that they both wear the same colors, even if he will not recognize the affinity. He thus reminds the disguised ruler of his own theatrical and improvisational eros, his own attachments to upstaging others, his own equivocal love of controlling plots and appearances.[20] Lucio thus becomes Shakespeare's ironic avatar at the heart of the drama, as much as anything in the loving if perverse generosity Lucio feels toward his own fictional creations, one of whom is the "duke of dark corners" himself.

THE DUKE REMAINS a vexing parable of authority. In his mode of deploying substitutes, for example, this character suggests something about the paradoxical wish of those in positions of power *not* to wield power, their wish to be at once inside and outside the exercise of their own authority. In the case of this particular ruler, the process of substitution complexly mingles pragmatism, pedagogy, malice, often in evasive or contradictory ways—as one senses, for example, when one learns that the Duke wants Angelo to do his dirty work for him, even though at the same time he wants to expose the flaws of a deputy whom he himself clearly distrusts. His strategies in the play suggest that there is a shame or guilt, as well as a merely pragmatic risk, in wielding power directly, though also a corresponding pleasure in seeing one's power run on with a life of its own.[21] The subsequent plot shows us the uses and the limits, the betrayals, implicit in such displacement of authority, such presence-in-absence.[22] One troubling thing is that the Duke contrives never to suffer the cost of self-displacement in its own right, as happens with kings like Richard III, Macbeth, or Lear (all of whom deliver themselves up to their own dark corners in a way that the Duke of Vienna never does).[23]

The political fable is deepened insofar as the Duke, especially in his efforts to control the violences of law, is also connected to the work of "equity." An ancient juridical principle, equity speaks for a demand that judges accommodate existing legal rules to particular occasions, so that a just law does not, in being applied too narrowly, produce an injustice. Equity is the mercy of law, the conscience of law. It implies a work of reason and memory, but also speculation, since equity asks that the judge seek, as Aristotle argues, to penetrate the mind of the original lawmaker, to "correct" a law which, by accident of time or circumstance, has become a stumbling block.[24] Far from undermining law's authority, equity was seen as "the sowle and spyrit of the lawe," and a "secreat sense" that can "give life to the lawe which otherwise in the letter thereof would be dead."[25] It is equity as much as mercy that Isabella asks of Angelo, for instance. These aspects of equity—as the moral conscience and historical self-consciousness of law, as a thing that defends law's purer intentions—reflect the Duke's sense of his more serious purposes as well. Through the Duke's work, we may even be reminded of equity as something at once pragmatic and idealizing; it is a principle of justice which can seem both to found and violate the law.[26] Hence its association in the Renaissance with the power of princes, as much as judges.[27] Yet even as an avatar of equity, the Duke's position is hard to fix. The difficulty lies partly in his mysterious attachment to his own game, his love of his devices for their own sake, playing them out at the expense of others, even of the health of his own state. It lies in the Duke's narcissistic circumspection and pride, his need to insist on the purity of his motives, means, and ends in the face of their decided impurity. These things may suggest, at one level, a commentary on the politics of equity, on its potential use as an ideological mask, a cover for those in power to evade or twist the established system of laws.[28] And yet, in the present case, it is not politics in a form that either Bacon or Machiavelli would recognize.[29] The Duke's work of equity rather hints at more idiosyncratic motives, forms of need or pleasure or power whose logic is harder to clarify than legal accounts of equity suggest. The play indeed sends the Duke's motives (and perhaps equity itself) more deeply into dark corners.

I will return to the Duke's work of justice further on. For the moment, to better place these questions, if not to answer them, I want to look more closely at what I have called the Duke's *not* hearing, the blank spots in his apprehension of experience, and the peculiar way in which these exist alongside his constant plot making, his staging of *other* people's words. The shadow of the Duke's deafness falls over so much of the play, just because he makes such a point of his access to secrets, hidden truths, and confessions, claiming to be the ear into which all news must, ultimately, be delivered. A taint of impotence infects all that he accomplishes, because he so conspicuously lacks the power to be affected by what he hears, even as he lacks the power to make himself the sum of his effects on others, things which for Nietzsche were essential facets of human power.[30]

---

We measure the Duke's power by considering its stumbling blocks. His inability to recognize himself in Lucio's descriptions constitutes one such blocking point. Another limiting case is shown us in the murderer Barnardine, whom the Duke cannot convince to die in place of Claudio and so help bring the plot against Angelo to a happy conclusion:

> *Barnardine.* I will not consent to die this day, that's certain. . . . I swear I will not die today for any man's persuasion.
> *Duke.* But hear you—
> *Barnardine.* Not a word. If you have anything to say to me, come to my ward: for thence will not I today. *Exit.* (4.3.54–62)

In his drunken apprehension, Barnardine's hearing makes all performative utterances "unhappy," as J. L. Austin might say. He seems for one thing to see that the threat of death here is a contingent trick, not a ducal order but "any man's persuasion." In particular, Barnardine represents a place where a specific blockage in the ear might go along with a peculiar form of knowledge; this lucid drunkard possesses a sense of occasion at once pragmatic and comic, an ecstatic disinterest in embracing any factions outside of the self.[31]

Yet comic stumbling blocks like Lucio and Barnardine only clarify by contrast a greater blockage, a more extreme sort of scandal. This relates, again, to the Duke's inability to hear. No critics I know have spoken about this issue as such. Nor does any speaker onstage confess this problem directly, or think to name it. No impatient protests break out against this deafness, nor are counterplots carefully set in motion to thwart it. What revenges are taken against it are at best oblique. Yet this peculiar deafness represents a kind of zero point within the play's picture of the Duke's knowledge, suggesting how voices can become, for this particular listener, a kind of unaccountable noise, nothing but "a thousand escapes" of falsifying wit. Making clearer what the Duke cannot hear will indeed show how this terribly self-conscious playmaker fails, with Shakespeare's own help, the test of what is most radical in Shakespeare's mimesis of human character.

It is not simply that, in a literal sense, the Duke never hears certain scandalous utterances, such as Pompey's comparison of Vienna's prison to a brothel, or that he never knows how Elbow, the "poor Duke's officer," makes such a telling babble of the language of law—taking "benefactor" for "malefactor," "suspected" for "respected," and "an action of battery" for "an action of slander." What interests me is the Duke's inaccessibility to other, more extreme voices that break through in the text. These cries speak of radical shocks within the self and within the order of justice. They speak to moments of moral derangement and spiritual impasse; they create wounds in those who utter them and occasion wounds in others. I am thinking here of Claudio's vision of life after death, part of his request that his sister yield to Angelo; of Isabella's own terrible response to this request; and of Angelo's soliloquy at the end of act 2, scene 2, when he must address the senseless "sense" that overtakes him after he listens to Isabella's pleading. Certain moments in Isabella's second exchange with Angelo are part of this group too—in particular Isabella's confrontation with the "perilous mouths" of rulers, "That bear in them one and the self-same tongue / Either of condemnation or approof, / Bidding the law make curtsey to their will, / Hooking both right and wrong to th'appetite" (2.4.171–75). Each of these cries bears the weight of a character's changed, freshly terrifying relation to ordinary words; each marks a new relation to the claims of voice in the order of the world, shattering any more balanced or temperate moral language we might look for. They are all violent reactions to something in the words of others that a speaker hears and cannot quite bear to accept or acknowledge. Or rather, they bring into play a different order of acknowledgment. Hearing such cries ourselves, we may think a speaker's language deranged because of his or her fixation on using terms that suddenly no longer work—as when Angelo confronts the obscene muddle marked out by words like "sense," "love," and "virtue," or when Claudio asks Isabella to show him "mercy," that word which she had herself so plied with Angelo and that she now finds "devilish." Yet these traumatic cries point to moments of awakening as well as blockage, moments when voices are roused which had seemed before to have been sleeping or unimaginable, voices that transform the speakers and expose them to their own words, expose them, in Harold Bloom's telling formulation, to an otherness within those words, even as those voices transform the world around them.[32]

In *Measure for Measure,* the force of these voices is harder to weigh because they break against the Duke's ear as against a stone. What these speakers say is, undoubtedly, shaped by the conflicts of desire and justice over which the Duke wants to preside. Yet for all his demanding charge of hearing, his ruthless and paranoid desire to find out hidden intentions, he fails to hear these cries of Claudio, Isabella, and Angelo. He cannot know what Hazlitt calls their "feelings and apprehensions," what they know about the world.[33] He has no power to imagine them or to let them wound him. Of course, a speech like Angelo's monologue in act 2, scene 2 ("What dost thou, or what art thou, Angelo?"), is delivered onstage while the Duke is himself out of hearing. So he perhaps cannot be blamed for not hearing it. And yet Angelo's complaint emerges in a register or idiom that, one feels, the Duke's own language could never address; it speaks of questions that his own activity entirely fails to recognize. Other cries, rumors, or noises of self do in a literal sense reach his ear—Claudio's prayer or Isabella's curse, for example. Yet they lodge there like dead counters, soundless, held in suspension, walled about. If they catch his ear at all, or affect his action or talk in the course of the play, it is only as things reduced, stripped of all their psychological weight or unsettling moral ambiguity. He makes of them only the matter for his own Machiavellian activity, an activity that silences and purifies those cries, cutting off the possibility of their proliferation, as if they were likely to add to the chorus of dangerous rumors that the Duke always fears. The Duke's hearing, like his theater, is prophylactic.[34]

The hearing of Renaissance princes is idealized, but also vexed. As Bacon suggests, the ears of kings must be protected from false information and lying accusations; these become a kind of "poisoning" of the king's ear, virulent in particular because of his power over the state and over law.[35] The king's ear must also be protected from flattery, including self-flattery (as James wrote in *Basilicon doron*).[36] Yet it is to the ear of the king that, ideally, all public and private knowledge must be referred. Both public judges and secret spies are extensions of his official ear, one might say. And it is within or behind the king's ear that all secrets are to be adjudicated—lodged within the ideologically privileged space of *arcana imperii,* not scannable by ordinary minds or courts. Of this, ordinary subjects should not even murmur, lest they seem to usurp the king's privilege, setting up "private tribunals" that lay claim to false jurisdiction. The Duke of Vienna is himself conscious of this even in disguise. Yet this makes his inability to hear—his deadness or unreadiness of ear—all the more notable. Speculative as it is (without direct acknowledgment by the language of the play), this emphatic failure to hear certain things, or to keep pace with the compulsive hearing of his subjects, deeply fissures the drama. News of what does not reach the Duke's ear plants a strange, pliant void at the center of the play. The Duke wishes to occupy the symbolic position of a star or sun, a divine eye, the shedder of light on dark secrets. Yet his ear turns out to be a black hole. Barnardine hears blankly as well, absorbing and negating the "persuasions" that the Duke offers him. Yet Barnardine's deafness speaks for a will to live, to continue his existence asleep or awake (even if only in a jail). What masters the Duke's hearing shows more fear and flight about it: onstage the Duke's not hearing equals what Freud calls the death instinct.

Perhaps it is appropriate that only when the Duke speaks on behalf of a desire for stasis and oblivion does his language acquire the uncanny eloquence that might mark it as a real self-revelation.[37] In act 3, scene 1, the friar pours into Claudio's ears a strangely Lucretian, all but pagan sermon on the art of dying well. The speech may seem skewed in its silence about grace and its eerie contempt for the shapes of human life. But it does have the effect of silencing any lament from Claudio, who takes in the Duke's words sufficiently to offer a kind of stifled, epigrammatic summary of what he has heard: "To sue to live, I find I seek to die, / And seeking death, find life" (42–43). But something different breaks out very soon, when Isabella shows him a chance for survival. Claudio's words suggest that the Duke's consolations have only penetrated the surface:

> Ay, but to die, and go we know not where;
> To lie in cold obstruction, and to rot;
> This sensible warm motion to become
> A kneaded clod; and the delighted spirit
> To bath in fiery floods, or to reside
> In thrilling region of thick-ribbed ice;
> To be imprison'd in the viewless winds
> And blown with restless violence round about
> The pendent world: or to be worse than worst
> Of those that lawless and incertain thought
> Imagine howling,—'tis too horrible.
> (117–27)

Think of this as a howl in the hole of imagination, a terrified knowing of what cannot be known, giving "to airy nothing / A local habitation and a name." A fissure opens up in the Duke's stable "heaven" of judgment. These words shatter the tone of studied consolation with the force of something not only unrevealed but unconscious. A sustained intensity is borne within this speech that we have not heard from Claudio before (and never will again). Isabella's brother may surprise even himself, carried away by his rage and fear, his love of life, but also by the "lawless and incertain" current of his fantasy. Death for Claudio has an astonishing vitality (as opposed the Duke's image of life itself as a death). In that projected afterlife, the sense of entrapment and decay joins with troubling images of continued life: the "thrilling" animation of ice, or the restless violence of "viewless winds" which—like the breath of rumor—blindly transport through the world the very things that they imprison. The speech can be read, in fact, as a half-allegorical picture of the compulsive and liberating power of fantasy itself. It is about the awful present as much as the uncertain future: about the frozen, thrilling prison of Claudio's terror, the restless violence of his desire to live, his own sudden imaginings of prohibited places. These heighten the moral struggle that confronts him as he tries to measure Isabella's situation against his own.

Earlier in this scene, Claudio had sworn his devotion to dying for the sake of honor: "If I must die, / I will encounter darkness as a bride / And hug it in mine arms" (82–84). Isabella hears in this, she says, her brother's true voice, the voice of her father speaking from the grave. But in Claudio's hell speech, a ghostly voice breaks out that no idea of honor or heaven can console, moved by a fear which exceeds the calculations of conscience. Talk of divine justice can only add terror here, feed "lawless and incertain" figures of punishment. Claudio's vision, in turn, feeds a plea that terrifies rather than persuades Isabella. His plea provokes answering fears in her, coloring her own imagination of life and survival:

> O, you beast!
> O faithless coward! O dishonest wretch!
> Wilt thou be made a man out of my vice?
> Is't not a kind of incest, to take life
> From thine own sister's shame? . . .
> . . . . . . . . . . . . . . . . . . . . . . . . .
> O fie, fie, fie!
> Thy sin's not accidental, but a trade;
> Mercy to thee would prove itself a bawd;
> 'Tis best that thou diest quickly.
> (135–49)

Here Isabella fetches up not only archaic fears, but a kind of sudden, ferocious impulse to make metaphors. Her horror of physical violation and her fear of public shame intertwine; her brother's desire to live looks like a kind of incestuous desire for *her,* something bastard-like and impure. The terror can unsettle us all the more because it catches the twisted note of disgust and self-disgust that we have heard in Angelo's speeches ("Fie, these filthy vices!" [2.4.42]), marring her own early, idealized language about the power of mercy.

Judging Isabella's outburst has challenged all commentators on the scene. Some hear cowardice and panic, or self-dramatizing hypocrisy; others hear a real moral outrage, or sense the loomings of some more impersonal scandal about the nature of human desire and relation.[38] The crucial issue for the moment, however, is the quality of the Duke's response, and what this implies about his powers of apprehension. Just after this exchange, the Duke, who has been overhearing everything, steps into the action as a kind of deus ex machina, offering a solution to Isabella's dilemma. What strikes me is that while he is thoroughly "interested" in what is being said, he himself neither says nor does anything which suggests he has caught the shock of these speeches. He leaves Claudio the information that Angelo faked his attack to test Isabella and urges him to curtail "hopes that are fallible" (3.1.168). This might serve as a canny piece of moral education, but it works only by imposing what remains a plausible lie (a probability more troubling than the consolations of any casuist). Nor does the Duke allow an interval for Claudio to reconcile himself with his sister; in fact, he leaves him with advice to "hold" to his absolute disgust with life, bred out of his sister's disgust with him and his disgust with himself. The Duke next rapidly plucks at Isabella and explains his plot to her, measuring out its measures, its reasons and benefits, and advising her on small details, and so on. To this plot she rapidly fits herself: "The image of it gives me content already" (3.1.260). The interaction unfolds so quickly that we may not notice the Duke's failure to respond to what he has overheard. Perhaps one might say that there is no answer to it. What kind of sympathy could he offer? What consolations other than action? But this becomes part of a pattern throughout the play. Such terrors as Isabella's and Angelo's are things which the Duke systematically drops out of the equation.

Let me try to put this observation in a larger context. Broadly speaking, one central impulse in *Measure for Measure* is to stage scenes of awakening. There are many things we see awakening in the characters onstage: power, desire, fear, voice, and humanity, to name a few. Here, as sleeping things are roused, or cold things get warmed, they awaken others in turn, stirring up an answering power, desire, fear, or voice. In this process, established orders shift and yield themselves to new orders. Each main character in the play (save the Duke) inhabits his or her own version of the Pygmalion myth, a fable that Lucio evokes directly, and caustically, when he speaks of Pompey's prostitutes as "Pygmalion's images newly made woman . . . for putting the hand in the pocket and extracting clutched" (3.2.44–46). Consider, for example, Angelo's insistence that "The law hath not been dead, though it hath slept. . . . Now 'tis awake" (2.2.91–94). Or Lucio's urging to Isabella: "To him again . . . you are too cold" (43–45). Or Isabella's to Angelo: "O, think on that, / And mercy then will breathe within your lips, / Like man new made" (77–79). In attempting such awakenings, characters "assay the power" they have, whether power that is native to them, like Isabella's powers of persuasion, or a power that is lent to them, like Angelo's powers to judge and condemn. This awakening is relational, dialectical; it is a power to awaken others as much as themselves. *Waking* (as both a transitive and intransitive verb) becomes one of the chief forms of *making* in the play. Waking involves the remaking of things; it reawakens or reforms what has become fixed, moribund, or unresponsive. It is improvisatory, even a little magical. Yet as the scenes I've mentioned may suggest, such awakenings, such births and rebirths, turn out to be violently unpredictable.[39] The new births are multiple or bastard. (This is a play in which one character equates illegitimate begetting with both counterfeiting and murder.) One wakes up into a new self, but it is either a sexual monster, breeding fear, or a dead abstraction to be imposed on others and on oneself; or one awakes into a compulsion rather than a form of freedom, as when Claudio's sudden desire for "sensible warm motion" wakens into his vision of that frighteningly animate life after death. "Awake and be hanged." Something dangerous breeds. New words break out, rumors of things hidden in darkness, in past and future time. There are new lights, but they are "lights that do mislead the morn." Voices break out that shock the speakers as much as those they address. Such moments of awakening re-create speakers themselves around a wound (as when Angelo feels desire or Claudio feels fear). In awakening, speakers take upon themselves alien wishes or ideas that emerge "like an unfathered vapour" from their own souls. These new voices inflict a wound on the given meaning of words; they stain a language that speakers might have imagined as pure. New life must be taken from stains, from violations of taboo, from a sacrifice that yet has no touch of atonement in it.[40] Life awakens, or reawakens, as bawdry or theft. Hence the fact that the Pygmalion pattern— an image which in the comedies or the romances might mobilize the energies of rebirth and regeneration, as happens with the reawakened statue of Hermione—here yields only something aberrant and incomplete. Richard Wheeler writes, "the play provides no effective ironic controls that can bring the longing for death into clear relation with the comic affirmation of life."[41] Rather, the longings for death or life are terribly tangled up together (as in Claudio's fantasy) or carefully and evasively separated out (as in the friar's speech on dying).

This ironic Pygmalionism shows itself in other places. The play's central model for freeing the self from false rigor and dealing justly with the world is to seek within oneself an impulse that might measure the world's wrongs. It is a form of equity, something that pits inward thought or possibility against the rigid stupidity of mere law. So Escalus asks Angelo to imagine that he himself might have sinned like Claudio, "Had time coher'd with place, or place with wishing" (2.1.11). Isabella says something similar in her turn: "Go to your bosom, / Knock there, and ask your heart what it doth know / That's like my brother's fault" (2.2.137–39). This echoes an authoritative Christian formula: "Judge not, that ye be not judged. For with what judgement ye judge, ye shall be judged, and with what measure ye mette, it

shal be measured to you againe" (Matthew 7:1–2). (A fearful enough
maxim, as Leonardo Sciascia's mafioso / priest Don Gaetano suggests in *Todo
Modo,* since it suggests that only criminals can be judges.)[42] But for Angelo,
this wisdom is treacherous; faced with Isabella, such a look inside the self, a
glimpse of something "like [her] brother's fault," breeds corrosive fear rather
than charity. It breeds a terror at the self. His attempt to master this fear
only darkens things further. Characters like Isabella and Angelo share an impulse to invoke first principles. They live in the middle of time, but something impels them to return to some moment of first creation, or to some
moment—archaic, violent, pure—that would shift the terms of the world
to fit their wishes. This is a version of the prophetic impulse; to see divine
origins break back into human history makes one a "man new made." Yet
there is a danger of acting within time as if one were outside it; it risks making people into monsters, if not idolaters and false prophets. The return to
imaginary first principles breeds pride as much as humility; it feeds an impulse to subdue the "middle" world to the contingent desires of the self, or
repress their more muddled beginnings in human sexuality. So, as Isabella
declares, Angelo's impulse to set the law up as God, his idea that he "must be
the first that gives this sentence" (2.2.107), converts him into a grotesque,
sinful giant.

This agon of making and awakening unfolds most clearly in Angelo and
Isabella's *débat* in act 2, scene 2. Lucio himself is there to warm Isabella up,
so that she can in turn warm up mercy, sympathy, and even shame in the cold
Angelo. Isabella pleads for her brother's life; Angelo argues for the justice of
his sentence. Over the course of the scene, the two speakers fit and refit
themselves; each conjures up shifting personifications of Law and Mercy, by
turns seductive and ironic. They grapple with these figures and with each
other with growing heat, as each tries in effect to upstage the other, each
bent on casting the other in a play of his or her own making, finding out a
new face, a newly ardent mask of self.[43] One of Isabella's central strategies
is to bring in "if." Taking her cue from Lucio, she asks Angelo to assay the
power that *he* has, assaulting him with a new idea of what might be done. In
response to Angelo's frigid protest, "Look what I will not, that I cannot do"
(52), Isabella offers postures of mercy that will remake his will, even as they
remake the conditions of this trial. Isabella indeed puts herself in his place,
assuming the mantle of divine justice. Angelo, however, retreats strategically to the figure of a more impersonal form of justice. In a sense, he now
puts Law in his own place, and counters her image of awakening Mercy with
an image of Law itself as newly animate, reborn, a form of prophetic knowl-

edge. "The law hath not been dead, though it hath slept. . . . Now 'tis awake, / Takes note of what is done, and like a prophet / Looks in a glass that shows what future evils, / Either new, or by remissness new conceiv'd, / And so in progress to be hatch'd and born, / Are now to have no successive degrees" (91–99). Law, in his speech, assumes the form of a prophylactic against other unlawful births in the future, a violent incarnation of pity. Isabella warms up further, however, and quickly converts his personification of the awakened Law into a piece of comic posturing. Law is no daemonic power at work in history, only a momentary human mask glimpsed within a cosmic theater:

> But man, proud man,
> Dress'd in a little brief authority,
> Most ignorant of what he's most assur'd—
> His glassy essence—like an angry ape
> Plays such fantastic tricks before high heaven
> As makes the angels weep; who, with our spleens,
> Would all themselves laugh mortal.
> (118–24)

Her grand freedom of representation at this point finally baffles him, provoking his most nakedly human and uncertain response to her (one in which he yields the terms of the debate to her): "Why do you put these sayings upon me?" (134). Isabella answers with her own sympathetic and humane image of how authority can cure itself by turning within to find the mirroring image of its own fault. "Go to your bosom, knock there."

Isabella's speeches do indeed awaken something. They cause something to breed. Angelo calls it "sense." He suddenly finds himself subjected to a passion he had thought of as alien to him. This new desire takes the form of an infectious reproduction, as of some parasite: "She speaks, and 'tis such sense / That my sense breeds with it" (142–43). The very word arrives somehow already contaminated. As William Empson suggests, Angelo is disgusted by the very pun that he himself makes, by his ability to make his own language so impure. The half-intended play on "sense" can only shock him, in turn, by what it suggests about the dependence of sense (reason or common understanding) on sense (bodily feeling, desire).[44] Isabella's virtuous appeal to the law of mercy evokes in him something that shatters the measures around which he has formed his self. It makes him read his own fascination as a kind of monstrous defilement of what is pure—in himself and, proleptically, in Isabella:

What's this, what's this? . . .
. . . . . . . . . . . . . . . . . . . . .
            . . . Having waste ground enough,
Shall we desire to raze the sanctuary
And pitch our evils there? O fie, fie, fie!
What dost thou, or what art thou, Angelo?
Dost thou desire her foully for those things
That make her good? . . .
. . . . . . . . . . . . . . . . . . . . . . . . . . . . . .
            . . . What do I love her,
That I desire to hear her speak again?
And feast upon her eyes? What is't I dream on?
(163–79)

We start to see the cost of Isabella's having given him the gift of that "if"; it creates a way of "supposing" that he will turn against her more violently during their subsequent encounter. I quote Angelo's uneasy flood of questions to help suggest that they are, at the outset, real questions—questions about the causes of desire, the substance of his fantasy, and about the relation of who he is to what he does. These questions should remain open. The scary thing is that, even as he utters them or hears himself speak them, as *we* hear them, these questions harden into rhetorical questions or else generate only vicious answers. They point only to his evident monstrosity, making a certainty out of what was at first only a suspicion.

Angelo's sudden desire for Isabella is not in itself the monstrous thing—even if we assume it emerges impurely, out of competition, mutual attack, or struggle for mastery, or from a strange fascination with a mirror of his own wished-for sanctity. What should frighten us is rather Angelo's own fright at his desire. His telling perversity is that he allows the mere thought of his desire—and its contamination of "sense"—to sully whatever image of self he has been trying to maintain. His desire is like a corrosive rumor that attacks his interiorized reputation for pure living. Moreover, having turned his emergent desire into an accomplished defilement, he masters this crisis by turning himself into a monstrous parody of the human.[45] For Angelo, intent and act become almost one: ironically, as critics have noted, he judges himself under Christ's injunction that lust of the heart is itself fornication. He defiles himself, his image of his own justice, by seeking to defile Isabella. Her image of a warmed, humanized justice is turned into the idea of her "putting on the destin'd livery" (2.4.137), and the idea of his pitching evil into the "razed" sanctuary. His determination leaves Isabella with a choice that opens her, in turn, to further shock, in particular a shock at the freshly monstrous picture of authority's duplicitous "mouths." Her newly discovered voice can only betray her now: "You shall stifle in your own report, / And smell of calumny."

Angelo's discovery of an alien life within himself, within his own language, reads as both monstrous and human. His desire not only wounds him, but provokes a kind of nameless terror, a terror that at once drives him apart from humanity and restores him to it. He tries at once to fulfill and to deny that terror—both by becoming its outward vehicle and by imposing it on others (a strategy that links him to figures like Othello, Macbeth, King Lear, and Leontes). The upshot of that discovery—his attempt on Isabella's virtue—is the motivating source for the plot that subsequently unfolds; it is the thing which the Duke tries at once to manipulate, turn against itself, expose, and requite. Yet again it is exactly Angelo's terror and its answering shocks in Isabella that the Duke neither hears nor knows. No news of these violent perturbations of soul reaches his ear or his imagination. He neither tries to measure them nor finds a place for them within his plots. Indeed, neither discovery is resolved by the end of the play; each keeps piling up debts that are never discharged. The psychological crises are, if anything, forgotten, as if relegated to some interior cell from which they will not awake, even though there is nothing strictly to repress them. (Does the Duke need to repress what he has never imagined?)

Blame here is a parabolic thing. Within the terms of the fiction, the Duke could not have heard either Angelo's self-loathing soliloquy or the violent second interview with Isabella. Nor was he standing behind a curtain to overhear Isabella's closing protest about the duplicity of human mouths. How can one criticize him for failing to hear what he could never have heard? One reason is that the play itself, as it unfolds, structures the Duke's activity so as to call attention both to the urgency of what he does not know and to his pointed lack of interest in it.[46] Given the Duke's display of his own psychic penetration, it is striking how quick he is, when speaking with Isabella, to reduce the scandal of Angelo's desire to a banal moral instance: "But that frailty hath examples for his falling, I should wonder at Angelo" (3.1.185–86). This reflects more than just ignorance. One really should, in fact, wonder at Angelo, as both Isabella and Angelo himself do. It is a central wonder of this play, the wonder of these equivocal awakenings. One had *better* wonder at such things, I would say, baffling as they are. But for the Duke to acknowledge the self-betrayals of purity might compromise his own theatrical puritanism. The Duke's readiness with his "example" serves less to sum up the truth of Angelo's crime than to banish wonder, his own wonder and that of Angelo and Isabella as well. To that degree, he is shutting down the very theater in which such wonder is made manifest—in preparation for the more manageable public astonishments he contrives at the end of the play.

The Duke aims by his bed trick to expose Angelo's hypocrisy and, in the process, do right by Mariana. But he also tells us, in an aside, that he wishes to instruct Isabella's conscience, teaching her "trust" in heavenly justice. This is why, one supposes, he does not tell her that he is the Duke in disguise. J. W. Lever goes so far as to suggest that the Duke's activity is that of a therapist: he aims at restoring Isabella to a kind of psychic integration, tempering the violent passions wrought up by both Angelo and her brother.[47] But again, in speaking to Isabella after her argument with Claudio, he keeps at bay the question of Angelo's desire, central to which is Angelo's intenser wonder and terror at that desire, the shattering disappearance of his aura of purity. The Duke rapidly praises her "fairness" and "goodness," and briefly explains the plot—in a voice that is both oddly seductive and mechanical in its consolations. In their timing, his words work primarily to intercept the contaminated rage which fills her parting words to Claudio—and which must still hang in our ears. Perhaps he can't say more for strategic reasons: he doesn't want to debate moral psychology at this moment, much less call attention to Isabella's fear and shame; he wants her to act a part in his plot, which she does with surprising alacrity. The fact of the matter is, however, that the Duke's plots ultimately commit her to lies that, as we will see, at once silence and eerily acknowledge the secrets. With uncanny precision, his designs keep her in sight of the desire that most shames her; they ask her to assume postures which reflect the history she most feared to imagine. And they demand that she stage her own impotence, her own frustration at not being heard.

---

In this play about prisons, many things go underground: criminals, innocent victims, go-betweens, spies, pregnant women, and agents of justice. Wounded consciences bury themselves as well, alongside impulses for power and knowledge. All find at least a temporary home in the Viennese lockup. The jail in this play is indeed an eerily gay place, even a comic Green World, though here folded back within the supposedly more controlled spaces of the city.[48] The jail is a place of role-playing, altered professions, and sleights of hand; the architecture of its cells, interrogation chambers, and doorways seems endlessly ambiguous, more like that one might imagine in a brothel or the backstage spaces of a theater. Even criminals can join the ranks of those who run the place, their discontented "murmurings" mingling with the whispers of priests and informers. A complex noise grows within the prison. What may surprise one, however, given the symbolic conventions of Shakespeare's later plays, is that the cries which break out in the space of the prison are denied any afterlife. They do not return to trouble the world outside, as such voices invariably do in tragedies like *Hamlet, King Lear,* or *Macbeth.* We may hear Claudio's yell about suffering, Isabella's vitriol against corrupt justice, or Lucio's muttering about the twisted intelligence of princes. But no storm catches the echo of such utterances. They do not wander abroad in the mouths of madmen, fools, or witches. No ghost brings them back from the grave of the Duke's ear or restores them to the world as ghostly noise, as rumors that wound rather than sustain the world. Both the ordinary and extraordinary transit points for such voices seem blocked— blocked by the Duke, in part, but with the complicity of the playwright. The lack of that sovereign resonance is part of what makes the play's language seem to do violence to its own deepest impulses.

Up to a point, the public trial that ends the play does allow those torn and angry voices to come to light. The trial releases the breaths of the characters and of the audience from their bonds. Here we hear Isabella's rage at a treacherous judge, Mariana's wounded demand for a husband, even Angelo's confession of his self-loathing. Necessary accusations finally get worded, suppressed claims acknowledged, and blame properly assigned. It is, in its own way, a kind of wish-fulfillment moment for Isabella, but one that turns into a nightmare. Shakespeare's play frames these cries so that they still stifle in their own report. This trial, staged at the gates of the city of Vienna, frames a subtler, virtual jail, an enclosure more troubling than Angelo's walled garden or the "moated grange" in which Mariana nurses her frustrated love.

At the climax of act 3, Isabella accepts a key role in the Duke's improvised plot, making her decision with astonishing swiftness. Perhaps the traumas occasioned by her attempts at persuading Angelo and Claudio make Isabella more ready to trust another person's game before her own. The roles that the Duke asks her to perform clearly answer to her immediate needs, both pragmatic and emotional. They allow her the hope of saving her brother without losing her chastity; she can also hope to see the false deputy tricked and shamed by his own desire, by his secret abuse of power. The Duke may calculate that Isabella would savor her part in this dramatic scheme of revenge, which takes place under cover and by proxy. He shows her forms of power and forms of agency that leave her less exposed and solitary. Hence, she says simply on hearing the plot, "the image of it gives me content already." Isabella remains partly in the dark. She does not yet know that she is acting on behalf of her disguised prince. Still, she is privy to the basic turns of the plot, free to choose her way and ready to risk abetting a crime if it achieves a more complex justice. But the degree of her knowledge changes radically after Angelo himself proves less tractable. He is not quite the automaton of cowardly vice that the Duke had thought him, as is shown when he orders Claudio executed despite Isabella's apparent yielding. After the Duke's false report to her of Claudio's beheading, the gap between what Isabella knows and what she thinks she knows widens scandalously. This report opens up yet another view of her agency in the world, of Angelo's game, and of the Duke's own intentions. He is no longer using Isabella simply as a tool to catch a corrupt "substitute." Isabella herself becomes his pupil, one whom he will, by deceit, teach "heavenly comforts of despair" (4.3.109). The lie about Claudio's death creates a wound that he will, after a time, cure by himself. But in so tying Isabella's later actions in the play to her own false knowledge, the Duke's game infects his justice.

In act 5, at the friar's instruction, Isabella encounters the returned Duke at the gates of the city. She cries out to him for justice, as if she truly had submitted her body to Angelo. This becomes the only form in which she is allowed to mourn publicly for her brother's death; the strength of her (false) protest about being violated must indeed be fed by the unassimilated energy of her shock at this death. The part she is asked to play is a striking one, calculated both to give scope to her rhetorical skills and to maximize Angelo's anxiety: suddenly, what he had thought impossible appears before him. The Duke might even think of the role as therapeutic, since Isabella gains so large a court to which she can scream her grievance. But as he sets it up, the game also keeps Isabella in earshot of her earlier fear, shame, and impotence. If anything, it must heighten them. The story she tells keeps her in view of the spectacle of Angelo's desire and asks her to report a version of her history that, however false, had terrified her. Moreover, Isabella's protest only proves true Angelo's promise that her attacks would stifle in their own report "and smell of calumny." To all around, her words take on the look of a brazen mask; she is not even allowed to retreat in silence, but is held onstage under arrest, the suspected tool of some "mightier member." I said earlier that the Duke has no ear for the moral shock that Isabella experiences when she must confront Angelo's threats. The role which the Duke shapes for her here might, after all, persuade us that he has heard some rumor of that trauma. The part he has carved for Isabella allows her to speak her rage, her sense of violation, her pained amazement at the disorder she found within the central orders of justice. Her rhetoric, moreover, shows again its mastery, strategically turning on the display of paradox and scandal, creating before us a dark theater of wonder:

> Most strange: but yet most truly will I speak.
> That Angelo's forsworn, is it not strange?
> That Angelo's a murderer, is't not strange?
> That Angelo is an adulterous thief,
> An hypocrite, a virgin-violator,
> Is it not strange, and strange?
> (5.1.39–44)

But if the Duke, in giving her occasion to speak thus, seems to acknowledge her buried pain or rage, he does so only in the way a teacher of method acting might. That is to say, as the Duke has framed (if not himself scripted) this scene, Isabella's hidden emotions mainly work as a ground for building a more persuasive public posture onstage. Isabella's trauma is framed within a lie, a lie that colors the Duke's return to the public world even as it colors how we see the postures of accusation that make up the scene of justice.

I don't want to cheapen the force of the scene, only to suggest how much Isabella's words are put in a position to twist or block themselves onstage. Playing the wronged maiden does free Isabella to "trumpet forth" accusations against the false deputy, to share her strange knowledge of him with the world. There is a persuasive truth in her reporting as real what she knows was only imagined, that is, Angelo's violation of her chastity and her own public shame at having traded with him for her brother's life. She thus illustrates the monstrosity of a world that makes possible "things unlike," unimaginable. (Indeed, her speech offers a barbed surmise that might hit the Duke himself, when she says that "'Tis not impossible / But one, the wicked'st caitiff on the ground, / May seem as shy, as grave, as just, as absolute / As Angelo" [55–58].) Yet her truth emerges only with a sting. No sooner does she speak than she faces counteraccusations of madness, perjury, conspiracy, and seditious falsehood. Even Mariana, her ally in the Duke's plot, is brought out as a faction against her. (Of course, she is *in* on this, but being in on the Duke's plots only increases the possibilities for betrayal.) Isabella is exposed to her own words and exposed by them; she is as if playing within a dumb show, held or arrested onstage. Impersonating a violated maiden puts her in almost as vexed a position as that of Hamlet impersonating a mad revenger, and it is a position considerably less under her own control. Angelo himself makes her out to be nearly the hysteric which so many critics take her to be in the earlier scene with Claudio.

The precariousness of Isabella's position increases as one follows the rapid pace of the scene. After her first thwarted accusation, she tries to leave the stage but is restrained at the Duke's order. While guards go off to search for the friar who has "set her on," Friar Peter produces another witness who will prove Isabella a liar. Mariana's paradoxical confession holds the stage for a moment, catches us with the riddle of Angelo's ignorant assumption of knowledge—which marks both his crime and his unwitting innocence. She speaks of her husband Angelo, "Who thinks he knows that he ne'er knew my body, / But knows, he thinks, that he knows Isabel's" (202–3). She removes her veil, facing Angelo with an old shame and a new demand. Angelo himself has been oddly silent up to this point in the scene; he had left the Duke to mock and challenge his deputy's accusers. It is Mariana's story, which he must understand as a lie, that brazens him to search for a hidden master behind the two women's accusations. The Duke, who has left the stage, returns in disguise, free now to defame the monstrous shape of the trial that he has himself arranged. Using his pious mask in public for the first and only time, the Duke gives voice to the starkest attack on the corruption and injustice of the state we have yet heard:

> My business in this state
> Made me a looker-on here in Vienna,
> Where I have seen corruption boil and bubble
> Till it o'errun the stew: laws for all faults,
> But faults so countenanc'd that the strong statutes
> Stand like the forfeits in a barber's shop,
> As much in mock as mark.
> (314–20)

This reminds us, as Berger observes, of a much longer history of corruption than what we have seen unfolding onstage.[49] At one level, the Duke might be offering the kind of vulnerable acknowledgment that, for rulers, is ordinarily impossible. (As Julien Gracq writes, "there's no known language . . . in which a tottering state can confess its innermost difficulties, like a sick man to his doctor. No language—and that's too bad.")[50] Yet the Duke's accusations cannot be tested, not only because they remain so terribly generalized, but because his words emerge under disguise, taking the ear of

Escalus and others as a "slander to th' state."[51] If anything, the Duke's veiled confession is his subtlest vehicle for excluding from public scrutiny any more pointed questions about his conduct as a ruler, whether in the past or present. His broad talk of faults and forfeits, for one thing, distances us from any particular images of his character and action, such as Lucio has freed up in earlier scenes.

Escalus's call for the friar to be imprisoned and tortured has little real menace at this point. The friar's assertion that the Duke "dare no more stretch this finger of mine than he / Dare rack his own" (312–13) is a bit of self-gratifying bravado. Plucking off the Duke's hood undoes entirely Lucio's power to expose the concealed ruler's more shadowy motives. The Duke is "made" onstage, given back to his kingdom in his proper form, but he takes his mask off gradually. As the scene unfolds, he keeps the action centered around his own eerily self-concealing postures of authority. Angelo confesses his crime in the face of his sovereign's "divine" knowledge, asking for rapid death; he is answered by being sent offstage to wed Mariana. The Duke apologizes to Isabella for his failure to save Claudio, offering assurance of his greater happiness in heaven. Angelo returns, blessed with his new wife, to the promise of execution. The Duke pronounces the sentence of death. Mariana pleads for mercy and—in one of the most emotionally demanding turns of the scene—persuades Isabella to kneel down in prayer beside her. Isabella herself argues for the justice of Angelo's act, despite his poisoned intent—appealing to a measure that the play as a whole has called into question (his "due sincerity"). But the Duke will hear none of this. The man whose ear seemed so strangely deaf now proclaims his special apprehension of a daemonic voice emerging from within these merely secular events, a voice that silences any other calls for kinder treatment:

> The very mercy of the law cries out
> Most audible, even from his proper tongue:
> "An Angelo for Claudio; death for death."
> (405–7)

The Duke next turns to accuse the provost of complicity in this illegal action. The provost, in turn, while acknowledging his fault, quickly produces two unexecuted prisoners to mitigate his guilt. The Duke acquits Barnardine and asks that the other—"as like almost to Claudio as himself," says the provost—be unhooded. Without missing a beat, the Duke turns the provost's paradox into occasion for what is, at once, a bargain, an acquittal, and a marriage proposal:

If he be like your brother, *for his sake*
Is he pardon'd; and *for your lovely sake*
Give me your hand and say you will be mine.
He is my brother too: but fitter time for that.

(488–91; my emphasis)

Hard upon this interrupted proposal, the Duke turns to Lucio, threatening him with torture and death, but commuting his sentence to nothing but forced marriage to a prostitute. Urging Angelo, whose "evil quits him well," to love his wife—"I have confess'd her, and I know her virtue" (524)—the Duke returns to his "motion" toward Isabel's hopefully "willing ear," leading the company offstage with the promise to "show / What's yet behind that's meet you all should know" (535–36).

I risk this compressed summary of the action partly to make clear how intricately infolded the facets of the Duke's gambit are: a blank shadow as much as a light radiates outward from his activity. The structure of the scene at once demands and leaves unvoiced crucial questions about what the Duke thinks and what his subjects make of his thinking. His very display of self-dramatizing equity calls out for our critical scrutiny; it baffles audiences' desires even in the process of meeting them. The final trial shames Angelo for his injustice and reconfirms the Duke's authority, reclaiming the world he had abandoned and purifying the corruption that had crept in while he was invisible. It is as if he were trying to re-create his city in a moment. Yet the Duke's connivances compromise all of those cries that belong to the work of justice; all accusations and counteraccusations emerge through a strange, sticky taint of falsehood, blindness, and coercion. His handling of the scene lends to the Duke's own grand gestures an air of contingent and self-gratifying theatricality; he makes these gestures up even as he seems ready to disown them, as if he can't bear their mortal responsibility. Our interest in the buried emotions at which his game tugs must be all the stronger for their being held in check, thwarted, or put to the test (as when Mariana prays that Isabella share her plea for mercy). But the Duke's involvement in the scene makes the legal forms of accusation which frame these emotions feel at once inescapable and arbitrary. Pointing blame becomes a strikingly labile gesture, a thing unowned and yet subject to unsettling struggles for possession. Accusation becomes an inflection of voice that can empty out or stifle itself, not to mention shift with strange rapidity from throat to throat, person to person. We start to feel the dangerous pleasure of placing blame itself, rightly or wrongly; we also start to feel how much the freedom of accusation exposes the accuser. Confusions about what is true accusation and what is slander are precisely mirrored in the final trial: both concern the questions of whom Angelo has known or not known, and how legitimate or illegitimate that knowing is. What we get is a defense mingled with accusation, a knowing which is undone by another sort of knowing. The Duke's game gives life to bastard accusations, fornicating accusations, calls for justice to which Mercy could only serve as a bawd. Even the act of pardon is subject to strange games, as when the Duke apologizes to the provost for abusing his office but quickly adds, "Th' offence pardons itself" (531).[52]

The Duke's game silences any idealistic voices of accusation such as Isabella's, as if her idealism were itself a contaminant at this point—not as it was for Angelo, a provocation of desire or a motive for self-disgust, but as a threat to the Duke's own theater of justice. At one level, his demands mirror the work of equity, which must look through the false purity of legal forms and acknowledge the messier, more inchoate realm of contingency and personal judgment. But here the voice of Mercy—which in the Duke's hearing calls for death—is contaminated with shaming, silencing, and pretense. The Duke's conduct thus keeps the legal forms off balance even as he gives them a weird kind of necessity or inescapability. He makes his return to the state feel as arbitrary as it is fated. The newly refurbished forms of prosecution and judgment acquire the feel of something shadowy, a kind of mortal play. That this game forms a background to his courtship of Isabella and the forced marriages of Lucio and Angelo thickens the problem: a shadow of blank coercion and ironic punishment falls across the ritual of marriage, especially as that ritual is asked to do the work of justice, to expose a truth or compensate a loss. As Marc Shell suggests, the Duke's final arranging of things plays on the more promiscuous, figurative, even commercial logic built into the system of exchanges that structure this play.[53] But the rituals of law also start to acquire the coloring of a slightly frenetic, vengeful carnival, a "one-man" carnival, if that is possible to conceive. It is a display that detracts from justice by lending to justice the feel of an infectious simulacrum. Moreover, the conduct of the trial cannot be questioned from any place on the stage, since it absorbs all points of question, preempts attack. Even for a critic, to question the Duke's conduct feels a little like punching air.

It is the silences which accumulate or break out at the end of the play that are hardest to measure. "Open, crosscutting, bleeding" as they are, it is hard to find any obvious potency in them.[54] There is something mute about these silences, even among the "unmuffled" souls that stand onstage—in part because the flood of reversals intensifies one's desire to hear their response. One listens to the silences that hang in the space between the Duke and his subjects and between those subjects themselves; one considers the array of legal, erotic, and familial bonds those silences put to the test. Claudio stands silent, rescued from death. Barnardine stands silent, forcibly freed. Angelo stands silent, stripped of the execution he had begged for. Isabella utters no word. Only Lucio is garrulous, and even he is silenced after his protest at being married to a whore as punishment for "slandering a prince." Such muteness seems contrived to task the actor and director as much as the audience.

In actual productions, there are innumerable ways of accommodating the characters' scandalous failure to speak, and so making their silence part of an articulate response. I have seen the assembled characters stand in postures of nervous obedience or back away slightly in shock. One Claudio bitterly refused his sister's embrace. I have seen a Lucio who, despite the ruler's attempt at public humiliation, kept an icy, ironic gaze on the restless Duke till the very end. One Duke showed a slight but genuine uneasiness at the desire he makes public to both Isabella and his court. One Isabella turned angrily from the Duke's first proposal, slapped him when he proposed a second time, yet followed the blow with a passionate kiss. Other productions tried to open the possibility of truer forgiveness: Angelo and Mariana holding hands or Isabella slowly smiling at the Duke. The most willful solution had the entire cast quietly, in unison, moving offstage, leaving the Duke alone to run through his final speech. He had, we were meant to feel, gone mad: left isolated onstage to describe his neat rearrangements of the world, his eyes were wild, his tone frenetic; he did not notice even that he was alone. At the end, he turned, as if hallucinating applause, to wave happily to the audience, the only subjects he had left. Literalistic and silly as this was, it didn't feel essentially less willful than more modest solutions. There is something about the end of *Measure for Measure* that seems intended to thwart us by the very flatness of its silences. Of course, it is risky to make broad pronouncements about what a Shakespearean text must compel directors to do. Part of the miracle of the plays lies in how much room they leave for a director to surprise us as well as to disappoint us. Philip McGuire describes these intervals as "open silences" which, in the hands of different directors, can freely become vehicles of wonder, reconciliation, or resistance.[55] There are no words in the text to which the silences need be "faithful," one reason why, for McGuire, they help show the limits of a purely literary approach to Shakespearean drama. Still, even in thinking about their real presence onstage, the silences here feel more closed than open; they suggest a peculiar kind of muteness, a stifling of speech, something that is not willed or owned. And it is a stifling with which the play itself seems to cooperate. Consider the resolved silence of Hamlet at his death, the exacting silence of Cordelia (living or dead), or the moving silence of the statue of

Hermione. Compared to these, the silences in *Measure for Measure* remain voiceless. They lack what Hamlet calls a "cue and motive." Ambiguous as the silences from *Hamlet, Lear,* or *The Winter's Tale* are, they are framed by a language of silence which unfolds within the play as a whole; we can read them, and measure their costs. By contrast, the silences at the end of *Measure for Measure* are abortive rather than pregnant. They lie in cold obstruction, silences silenced, eaten up, neither cursed nor blessed. There is nothing to hear. Speech is buried alive, as Antigone is buried alive. If these silences are filled with anything it is with the weight of an undischarged debt that has been accumulating since the Duke first reentered the kingdom he had pretended to leave.

Time has been eaten up, too, at the end of this play. Time, as well as the Truth which Time should unveil or give birth to, is redeemed only in appearance. At the very close, the Duke draws the crowd together by saying that there is still time to tell stories, to fill in the gaps of time, as Leontes wishes to do at the end of *The Winter's Tale*. But who, one might ask, still has an appetite for stories? And which story would matter more than another? What would they requite? What everybody already knows one could not bear to hear repeated. What remains unspoken is either blank or, if we try to imagine it, obscene or vaguely sickening—for instance, Mariana's thoughts about her wedding night or about her future with Angelo, or Barnardine's thoughts about being released from prison. (Robert Browning, in one of his darker moods, might have imagined their internal monologues.) Even the Duke's sudden desire to marry Isabella goes unexplained; I am not sure I can imagine any account of motives from the Duke that wouldn't be a fright. Coleridge thought that audiences couldn't forgive Angelo or accept his forced marriage to Mariana as anything but degrading to women, because we can't imagine Angelo repenting of crimes pursued with such cruelty.[56] Part of the difficulty is that the Duke closes off any space in which one might imagine repentance; he leaves no one an interval in which to imagine or question or answer for Angelo's conscience. Just rule is restored through the Duke's chilling grace. He is trying to reoriginate and reawaken things, to bring them back to birth, into the light. Seeing Angelo married, he tells him with unsettling irony and triumph, "your evil quits you well" (5.1.494). What future can be promised to any of those onstage in the face of such quittance, or requital?

THE END OF THE PLAY restores the city, though without quite returning Vienna to what it was before the Duke vanished. He wants to remake law and authority, which also means canceling Angelo's violent acts of reform.

But the poverty of the Duke's justice—which does too little and too much—extends itself to one's image of the city at large. The creative work of law here, its power to make a world, produces only a sense of desolation.

In a fine meditation in his book *The End of Kinship,* Marc Shell tries to answer the question of whether Juliet, Claudio's wife, should appear onstage at the end of the play carrying her newborn infant.[57] She has, after all, been in labor with this child throughout the entire drama, having been housed within the precincts of the prison itself. So it might make sense that this child, whose birth goes unremarked in the text, is put on display as ornament to the other restorations. In the end, Shell thinks it a bad idea. For any stage child—whether a cloth bundle or a real baby—would shunt our attention away from a more important metaphorical birth or rebirth. It is Claudio who appears in the place of his own fictive child. He is the creature newly born, restored from the bonds of death and from his own terror of death. Nor is he only Juliet's son. He is, as it were, the creature to which Isabella has given birth, as the result of her incestuous union with her brother; as such, Claudio's return marks the possibility that "incest" no longer begets shrinking terror and reactive curse but allows us to entertain the spiritual, yet humanizing scandal of "universal siblinghood," an implicit acknowledgment of the limits and potential dangers of our culture's frenetic attempts to enforce rules of legitimacy in love, reproduction, or commerce.

Shell's book offers one of the subtlest accounts I know of *Measure for Measure* as a kind of idealizing romance or masque. He questions any too automatic an ironization of the work of justice (though Shell trusts the Duke as little as anyone) and reminds us of the recuperative, rather than merely satirical, reasons that the play might set charitable nuns in parallel with mercenary prostitutes. His imagining of Claudio as a reborn child troubles me only because it stops too short. On the terms that Shell proposes, other solutions must proliferate, like the thousand escapes of wit that the Duke so fears. Claudio must also be the child of Angelo and Mariana, begotten during their legitimate and legitimating "wedding night," when Angelo thought he was sleeping with Isabella. Or else it is Isabella and the Duke who beget him; Claudio stands forth as proof of the potential and profit of the Duke's proposed marriage. On the other hand, perhaps Claudio represents the parthenogenic child of the Duke alone, the dramatic evidence of his solipsistic power to restore his state to life, defeating those who would slander it.[58] Claudio might also be the unowned infant, "a year and a quarter old come Philip and Jacob," whom Lucio begot on "Kate Keep-down" (3.2.195–96) and who will perhaps soon gain a legal father. One starts to wonder whose child Barnardine is or which of the newly married couples will adopt him, as they adopt Claudio.

This is more the work of fancy than of imagination. Yet it helps me to place my sense of the desolation of this particular play. Such proliferating fancies point to an implicit poverty. Shell's reading reminds one strongly that, in the logic of romance, "children" are always figures of imaginative possibility. But if Claudio stands in place of so many children, it is because, in this restored city, there are not enough children to go around. Too few rather than too many infants get born here. Likewise, there are not enough players to play all the children in this decimated troupe. At the end of *Measure for Measure,* the brothels and the theaters have been plucked down and the players prevented from playing, even exiled, due to plague, which in this drama is seen as the running rampant of venereal disease. The city of Vienna is, as Pompey had predicted to Escalus, a wasteland, nearly uninhabited, as if, in fulfillment of his fantastic prophecy, "all the youth of the city" had been gelded and "splayed," and he can now "rent the fairest house in it after three pence a bay" (2.1.228–39). So many noble fathers are dead. The monasteries, one feels, are on the verge of dissolution as well. No past nobility will carry its famous spirit ("there my father's grave / Did utter forth a voice") alive into this present, and so create a Renaissance. Yet neither is this Vienna a reformist utopia to be founded, or refounded, on first principles. Rather than being full of children whose presence redeems time, keeps love and charity alive and thriftily husbanded, the city is full of the produce of a desire which looks to the poet like emptiness, waste, shame, proliferated nothings, the detraction of desire rather than its fulfillment. Such desolation will, in the plays that follow, help the poet to frame some of his fullest characters. In *Measure for Measure* he has not yet struck the bargain that will make that possible.

# chapter four

# DENIGRATION AND HALLUCINATION IN «OTHELLO»

he brief play entitled *Desdemonum,* an "Ethiopian bur-
lesque" published in New York City in 1874, begins
with a scene of courtship, set at night: a minstrel
show moor, named Oteller, comes onstage and begins
singing below his beloved's window, accompanied by
a tambourine and banjo. It is a serenade that cunningly
inverts the street scene which begins Shakespeare's
original, in which Iago and Roderigo wake Brabantio, Desdemona's father,
and hurl up at him the slanderous news of his daughter's marriage to a monster. In the minstrel show, we have rather Oteller as a parodic Romeo, calling to Desdemonum to show her "lubly phiz," and "sing a song of welcome,
while I go troo my biz."[1] His bride comes out onto the balcony and responds
eagerly in the stage dialect of minstrelsy:

> Fotch along your ladderum, I'm de gal to wed!
> Since burnt-cork am de fashion, I'll not be behind—
> I'll see Oteller's wisage in his highfalutin' mind.

It is hard to say what the moor's "biz" would have involved. It might have
been something presented as an authentic "Negro" dance of shuffles, hops,
and strange leaps.[2] It might have been a piece of physical farce, setting up the

ladder, falling off and climbing back, and so on. One thing is clear, however: Not only Oteller, but also Desdemonum—who would have been played by a man—appears onstage already "blacked up," or "corked up," as the common phrase was (because of the burnt cork pigment in the face paint). The daughter of Venice enters in blackface onto a nocturnal stage where, Oteller reassures her, "all cullers am de same."

The minstrels translate Othello's proud, florid gesturing, his stagy exoticism, into more comic antics; his tragic nobility becomes, if anything, the risky dignity of the clown. Iagum, as he's called, is no subtle snake but a crude, bad-mouthing crony, and the murder of Desdemonum turns high melodrama into rough domestic farce. It is likely, in fact, that they were parodying the more typically romantic and noble Othello of actors like Tommaso Salvini or Edwin Booth, who would themselves have used a bowdlerized text, one that stripped away much of the play's animal imagery and fierce sexuality.[3] *Desdemonum* might thus remind audiences of a more vulgar theatrical energy in the play—its commedia dell'arte elements, its knife-edge courtship of grotesque farce (on which Thomas Rymer made his famous attack).[4] There is in fact a bizarrely democratizing quality to the minstrel show. One starts to see how, in this theater, a layer of black paint applied to white faces could release performers from certain aesthetic taboos, allowing them to make fun of the more idealized and grandiloquent version of Shakespearean theater so popular in America—even as those performers freed up, for white audiences, a grotesque, exorcistic vision of black clownishness, folly, and social pretension.[5] This work, from what Ralph Ellison described as America's first national theater, both travesties and simplifies the more complex play of blackness in *Othello,* not only by putting everyone onstage into blackface, but also by making that color merely a matter of theatrical "fashion."[6] The minstrel show thus protects its audience from having to hear its own hatred and fear echoed through the mouth of a white villain, or from having to face the possibility of identifying with its isolated black hero. The effect of blackface is to make black skin more invisible than white.

My interest in this text here is decidedly idiosyncratic; I will not be able directly to do justice to the issues it raises about nineteenth-century American theater, for example. I want rather to use it as a doorway back into the original play. For by a strange combination of parodic intelligence and historical accident, *Desdemonum* can sharply point up certain crucial aspects of Shakespeare's work that we sometimes forget. Most importantly, it reminds us that Othello's blackness was, for Shakespeare, a thoroughly theatrical thing, the part having been composed for an actor who would have worn black makeup on his face. That blackness is thus as much artificial as natural, as much a gesture as a fact. This in turn shapes how we see the play's figurative transformations of blackness—for example, the ways that blackness becomes a color for the mind as well as the face, or how this blackening of Othello is linked to other images of staining, coloring, and spotting in the play. Unlike what happens in the burlesque, the black face of Shakespeare's Othello isolates him onstage; it establishes no visible community, even one so grotesquely created as in *Desdemonum*. Yet even in the original, that blackness does not stay with Othello alone. It touches other characters, shifting place and face in often dreamlike ways. No one onstage calls Othello's blackness a "fashion," yet like other aspects of Othello's exotic nature, it moves love, emulation, and hatred. His exoticism is something that sticks close to the skin, like a perfume: volatile, but still hard to rub off, touching the whole activity of playing. At some hidden level, I would say, the tragedy itself evokes the fantasy that it should be performed by a cast made up entirely of persons in blackface (fashionable or unfashionable).[7]

Othello does not own his face. The play unfixes it, turning it into an object of desire and loathing.[8] As a stage device, one might compare this mask of blackness with the mask of maleness assumed by Viola in *Twelfth Night*. On being shipwrecked in Ilyria, Viola disguises herself as her own brother, whom she presumes drowned. The disguise at first both protects her wounded heart and lets her move more freely in an alien world; it even lets her hold onto the brother that she has lost. As the play unfolds, however, the disguise assumes a life of its own. It gives to Viola a strength she doesn't recognize as her own and cannot always control, moving the desire and suspicion of others, exposing her to both jealousy and violence. Othello's blackness is not a mask that he chooses for himself, nor does it double a lost relation. Yet it too takes on the look of a fate, something subject to an alien life, moved by both contingency and compulsion. Othello's face both frees him and subjects him. Iago's slander of Desdemona indeed leads Othello to speak of his own blackness as if it resulted from a specific *act* of blackening, one produced not by makeup, but by soot, dirt, or ashes. In his jealousy, he begins to share that idea of blackness with Desdemona. So, for example, Othello proclaims, "Her name, that was as fresh / As Dian's visage, is now begrimed and black / As mine own face" (3.3.389–91), as if Iago's lie about her infidelity had blackened both their faces. Desdemona's imaginary betrayal inherits Othello's blackness; it allows him to displace that blackness onto the object of his wounded desire. Later, even more strangely, he tells his wife that, were he to put her crimes into words, his offended modesty might blush hot enough to burn his face ash-black, mirroring her black character: "What committed! / Committed? O thou public commoner! / I should make very forges of my cheeks / That would to cinders burn up modesty / Did I but speak thy deeds" (4.2.73–77). Here Desdemona's guilt and shame threaten further to blacken Othello himself, as if his black face were produced, and also consumed, by the heat of his blush (a burning that threatens Desdemona as well). Iago's slanders thus free Othello to transform his own mask, to make it both his own and the world's in a way it had not been before.

*Othello* explores how a will to defilement and a will to purification are tangled together and contaminate each other. The moor lends the paint on his face to the world, even as he lends to the world a whiteness that similarly distorts his vision. It sometimes seems as if Othello's mask of blackness were not just unowned, but materially unstable, as if his makeup were liable to rub off onto other faces and bodies, staining clothing, bedclothes, and handkerchiefs, darkening eyes as well as objects. (I would like to see a production where the makeup of the actor playing Othello did, literally, smear onto other actors and props and costumes; where Othello and Iago used their fingers to rub from the moor's face a pigment that they in turn rubbed onto others.) Blackness thus becomes for Othello at once a mark of the real and the substance of hallucination, the color of what is both visible and invisible, of what is hidden as well as of what is shown. It is the color of his soul and of his desire. It becomes the color of a certain form of speech as well.[9]

The play's concern with blackening faces is a direct extension of the play's concern with blackening names—Othello's, Desdemona's, Cassio's. The imagery I have been describing plays on and literalizes the etymological meaning of "denigration." It helps to show how slanderous words can, as one Tudor writer put it, "mynisshe, denygrate, or derke" a person's "name and fame," wounding both a public self and a private identity.[10] It is indeed essential to the dramaturgy of this play that the fate and power of characters are so much tied to what other people say about them, and to the ways in which they both resist and embrace the masks of *fama*. At moments Othello's activity onstage can seem coextensive with his defamation, as if this character were primarily the theatrical animation of a blackened name; the denigration which Iago claims will restore Othello to the truth actually embeds him in a hallucinatory simulacrum of human life. The theme of denigration implicates the contagious, idolatrous enchantments of theater itself. In his *Anatomie of Abuses,* Phillip Stubbes complains of the power of stage plays (like that of carnivals, dances, cosmetics, even perfumes) to "denigrate, darken, and obscure the spirit and sences" of those who watch them—not unlike Brabantio's accusation that the moor had abused his daughter's mind and body by witchcraft.[11]

Two aspects of the Renaissance image of slander are of particular interest for thinking about this play. The first is the idea that defamation tends to imitate, even as it travesties, the language of legal blame, the idea that public calumnies dangerously preempt the machinery of judgment.[12] Slander, as Francis Bacon said of revenge, "is a kinde of Wilde Justice."[13] Part of the fright of Othello's jealousy is that in it a posture of judicial revenge shapes itself around the coarsest slanders, driving a deformed and deforming wish for some kind of legalistic proof.[14] "Where's that palace whereinto foul things / Sometimes intrude not?" (3.3.140–41), Iago asks. Worked on by detraction, the space of Othello's mind becomes a mental tribunal where, in Iago's words, "some uncleanly apprehensions / Keep leets and law-days and in session sit / With meditations lawful" (142–44). One other idea that this play takes up and radically transforms is the link between slander and rumor. The play reminds us that abusive stories are damaging in particular because of how they are taken up and repeated by a field of treacherous listeners; the crisis of slander reveals how much one's name and fame can become a public commodity subject to uncanny sorts of abuse and theft, especially among those hungry for accusation, for knowledge of other people's criminality. The intense investment of the self in its own reputation produces, by reflex, the specter of a world of other minds fed by hidden malice and envy. *Othello* winds the thread of this threat more closely; it explores just how vulnerable a supposedly pure, private conviction can become to the depredations of rumor, in particular rumors of another person's desire—rumors which themselves shape a language of suspicion, monstrosity, and secret accusation.[15] The work of Iago shows us why, at a psychological level, defamation might be compared variously to murder, theft, rape, poisoning, and treason. Shakespeare also suggests how the domain of a private self reshapes itself, even expands its imaginative scope, through the intrusion of the very noises that do it violence.[16]

---

The common law definition of actionable slander required that the alleged words of abuse reflect malicious intent, a will to harm, on the part of the speaker. Intention is notoriously hard to prove, however, even in cases where juries were free to consider evidence of a defendant's personal history, social relations, and prior dealings with the law. But intention could also be supplied as legal fiction. Certain words, in fact—imputations of criminality, of professional incompetence, or of the pox—were taken as implying a malice without further proof, assuming no other mitigations were offered. Malice thus existed in law, not withstanding that the court might know nothing for certain about the slanderer's motives.[17] Here the posited intention, however speculative, mainly helps to close the circle of legal knowledge; it is a way for the law to hold to its own definitions of crime, its own ideal interests, and yet make clear that certain questions cannot be answered by an earthly court. The law acknowledges thereby its own peculiar limits. In thinking about Iago's crime, however, the inescapably fictive nature of intention creates critical chaos; no legal fiction suspends our questioning. In his seductions, Iago darkens Othello's ear as well as his eye by the pretense of opening up new senses, new visions of human intention. But Iago himself provides us, as well as his victims, with simply too many motives for his practicing on Othello, Desdemona, Brabantio, Cassio, and Roderigo.[18] A demon of possibility, manipulating the currency of unseen "purses," Iago provokes jealousy exactly through speculating on its uncertain origins, even by accusing himself of a tendency to seek out foul and filthy causes.

Coleridge noted something restlessly self-regarding and evasive in the soliloquies where Iago confesses his motives to himself (though the poet's paradoxical formula, "the motive-hunting of a motiveless Malignity," seems like an evasion of its own).[19] Iago's shifting explanations of his motives "appear and disappear in the most extraordinary manner," as he stands "fingering his feelings, industriously enumerating their sources, and groping about for new ones."[20] His reasons reach the audience as merely possible truths or plausible rationalizations offered in response to some residue of a need in Iago to explain himself, or to avoid some blunter and more self-wounding explanation. He tells Roderigo that he justly envies Cassio's lieutenancy; later, in soliloquy, he adds as a motive his fear of having been cuckolded, first by Othello, then by Cassio, though both suspicions seem groundless, almost arbitrary. Later still he speaks of his hatred of being made ugly by Cassio's "daily beauty," and even insists twistedly that he himself loves Desdemona, "Not out of absolute lust—though peradventure / I stand accountant for as great a sin— / But partly led to diet my revenge" (2.1.290–92). Such shifts suggest that Iago is improvising the account of his hidden motives to fit each new occasion or to answer some new, passing scruple, testing each explanation in turn for its usefulness in persuading himself, or in persuading others. August Strindberg notes that Iago not only contradicts himself in his reports, he seems compulsively to malign himself, for example, in his way of embracing the degrading mask of a jealous cuckold, or in his way of posturing as an agent of hell.[21] It is as if the habits of a slanderer had turned back on his accounts of his own soul. One gets the strange sense that Iago's own thoughts, for all the energy with which he addresses himself to them, are composed mainly of uncertain, half-plausible rumors that circulate in his head and that he reports to himself and to us. These never suggest the power of Hamlet's mysterious, rumorous interiority, however, only an eerie combination of stupidity and guile.

Othello asks Lodovico before he dies, "Will you, I pray, demand that demi-devil / Why he hath thus ensnared my soul and body?" (5.2.298–99). Iago responds, "Demand me nothing. What you know, you know. / From this time forth I never will speak word" (300–301). This is Iago mystifying motives even at the end of things, at once provoking and thwarting any demand for knowledge. Still, there are a number of things that I think I know about Iago's motives. He clearly loves practicing on other persons; he loves standing back, looking "askance to watch the working of his lie," lowly, mischievous, yet feeding on a secret sense of superiority. This is what A. C. Bradley saw as his deep vanity, his ironic and vulnerable self-regard.[22] Perhaps for this reason, he notably entertains himself with the spectacle of his victims' *self*-betrayal; he wants to see how their own power or desire or love destroys them and those they love. This is the particular theater that enchants him, the one whose risks and improvisation entangle him almost to the point of self-destruction. This slanderer's "breaches of the peace" work mainly to poison the quiet and the delight of hearts and minds, rather than some larger social harmony. Iago, so apparently dead to feeling, knows enough of Othello's inner life to tug violently, musically, at his heartstrings—indeed, to lend Othello a version of his own interior restlessness. The disturbing paradox is that while Iago seems to know people like Othello, Brabantio, and Cassio, as it were, from the inside, he shows no trace of emotional interest in the inner lives of his victims. Despite Iago's irritable vanity, his ability to be offended by certain aspects of other people's moral nature, he never makes himself inwardly vulnerable to their feelings for *him*. Like the Duke in *Measure for Measure,* he never sets himself at risk before another's inner life or lets himself be transformed by his effects on others, save perhaps in becoming more ruthless. Iago confesses to Othello his own susceptibility to jealousy, the "green-ey'd monster, which doth mock / The meat it feeds on" (3.3.168–69). But Iago's vice, if one wants to be schematic, is not jealousy but envy. Jealousy depends on our ability to imagine another person's desire for us, and to be wounded by the loss of it (which is never Iago's problem), whereas envy, the more archaic emotion, arises out of the real or imaginary loss of some object whose desire for us is irrelevant.[23] Iago at this level represents something more primitive than Othello, for all his "modern" skepticism.[24] This distrust of other people's desires—the odd, resentful contempt for what he doesn't have (including, perhaps, jealousy)—feeds what William Empson sees as Iago's "honesty," his posture of being downright and bluff, scornful of high-mindedness and romantic self-delusion, ready to blow down all pretensions, including his own.[25] (William Hazlitt observes that "he even resents the good opinion entertained of his own integrity.")[26] Such delusions help compose the "daily beauty" of Cassio's life, a beauty which makes Iago not so much ugly to others as ugly to himself. As Empson notes, Iago's critical realism about sexual love cannot conceal either his prurience or his prudery. Othello gets it partly right when he says that Iago "hates the slime / That sticks on filthy deeds" (5.2.144–45). Iago's identification of "loathing" with knowledge indeed means that any self that Iago knows is founded on self-loathing, on a discovery of slime where there may not be any. The slime he loves is that which sticks to his own tongue, and which he can spread onto other people.

I want to focus here first on Iago's way of practicing on his own and Othello's language. Iago is a discourse monster, somehow able to nudge any language game toward the corrosive and nonsensical. Iago often means a lot less rather than a lot more than he seems to say. His signature utterance, "I am not what I am" is a complex riddle that parodies Yahweh's "I am that I am" and also suggests the ironic self-alienation that constitutes his ego, as Joel Fineman argues.[27] But those words are also a kind of disguised babble; their main effect is to make his listeners lend their ears to a meaning they do not comprehend but think of as urgent. The same goes for utterances such as "Men should be what they seem, / Or those that be not, would they might seem none" (3.3.129–30), and again, "Demand me nothing. What you know, you know." Part of the danger of this kind of language is that Iago can count on Othello's relentless desire to make sense out of that captious nonsense and in turn to take that deformed sense upon himself, to use it to read his own soul. It is through this desire that Iago can so play on his victim, and orchestrate the obscure but convulsive rhythms of the seduction scene in act 3, scene 3.

In the lines below, Iago catches Othello by a game of repetition. Or perhaps we should call it language lesson, one which shows to the much-traveled moor a "new world of words" (as John Florio, Montaigne's translator, titled his 1611 Italian-English dictionary):

| | |
|---|---|
| *Iago.* | Did Michael Cassio, when you wooed my lady, |
| | Know of your love? |
| *Othello.* | He did, from first to last |
| | Why dost thou ask? |
| *Iago.* | But for a satisfaction of my thought, |
| | No further harm. |
| *Othello.* | Why of thy thought, Iago? |
| *Iago.* | I did not think he had been acquainted with her. |
| *Othello.* | O yes, and went between us very oft. |
| *Iago.* | Indeed? |
| *Othello.* | Indeed? Ay, indeed. Discern'st thou aught in that? |
| | Is he not honest? |
| *Iago.* | Honest, my lord? |
| *Othello* | Honest? Ay, honest. |
| *Iago.* | My lord, for aught I know. |
| *Othello.* | What dost thou think? |
| *Iago.* | Think, my lord? |
| *Othello.* | Think, my lord! By heaven, thou echo'st me |
| | As if there were some monster in thy thought |
| | Too hideous to be shown. Thou dost mean something. |

(3.3.94–111)

Here, Iago conjures suspicions by precisely *not* adding hidden meanings or double entendres; that he means nothing rather than something is the one thing that Othello probably will not believe. He renders words such as "honest" and "think" at once empty and full, vacant purses burdened by the illusion that there is meaning inside them, implicating Othello himself in the game of repetitions, stopping the moor's speech with his blank questions. It is like a flattened-out but demonic version of an echo song (in which, conventionally, Echo responds to the poet by repeating and turning on the last word or phrase of a verse—for example, Poet: "Who knows when we shall die?" Echo: "I").[28] Iago's game not only makes his questions unanswerable, the words ambiguous, but leaves the words in a deep sense unutterable, unspeakable. It offers, among other things, a peculiar test for the actor playing Othello, who must repeat Iago's words in a way that conveys both their harassing interest and their absence of real meaning. The dumb chaos of this conversation, or nonconversation, both locks Othello into these words and sets him adrift within them, steals the words from him. The exchange forces Othello to speak babble, and it furthermore makes him take that babble for sense (another's sense, if not his own). Iago plays on Othello's impatience, his desire that words yield up their sense in a moment, rather than through time. Othello tries in turn to master his confusion by projecting onto Iago an inward fright, a monster-making (and meaning-making) power of mind that is properly his own.

Desdemona and Othello had formerly spoken of their generous allowance of their free and separate "minds." In this dialogue, the sharing of terms, the passing back and forth of blank verbal counters, forces Othello to confront or project a kind of interiority that he has (strangely enough) never confronted before. The seductive, abusive babble of the dialogue is the space in which that frightening inwardness first emerges, that to which it is bound; this inwardness takes its character from a structure of sourceless verbal doubt and verbal noise rather than one of fixed faith. One could say that Othello finds out that he doesn't know his own mind or trust what he himself thinks, that the sudden need to probe another's mind calls up an array of questions such as makes a horror not only of words but of other minds (Iago's mind, Desdemona's mind, even his own mind). Othello suddenly perceives the world to be full of secrets, but in a way that robs him of his privacy. After such an exchange, the very word "think" becomes a self-wounding thing in Othello's mouth: "I do not think but Desdemona's honest" (229); "I think my wife be honest, and think she is not, / I think that thou art just, and think thou art not" (387–88). "Think" itself becomes an obscenity in such lines—though of a sort that no censorship could police, because it is also a word that, however empty, Othello cannot do without.

Ludwig Wittgenstein, in his *Philosophical Investigations,* poses the enigmatic question, "What would be missing . . . if you did not feel that a word lost its meaning and became a mere sound if it was repeated ten times over?"[29] What is missing in Othello is an ability to inhabit his own bafflement; he lacks that self-trust which John Keats (thinking of Shakespeare) called negative capability, "that is when man is capable of being in uncertainties, Mysteries, doubts, without any irritable reaching after fact & reason."[30] What I find most frightening is that in grasping at reason Othello remains bound to Iago's blunter, more corrosive sort of negative capability. The moor's impossible need for satisfaction attaches him to Iago's way of keeping obscene possibility in play, even as he denies that it is possible. Thus, later, when Othello expresses his need to be "satisfied" by "ocular proof" of Desdemona's infidelity, Iago asks,

> how satisfied, my lord?
> Would you, the supervisor, grossly gape on?

> Behold her topped? . . .
>
> . . . . . . . . . . . . . . . . . . . . . . . . . . . . . . .
>
> It is impossible you should see this
> Were they as prime as goats, as hot as monkeys,
> As salt as wolves in pride, and fools as gross
> As ignorance made drunk.
>
> (397–408)

Iago, in holding back "evidence," keeps Othello's desire tied to that which most astonishes him. He keeps the moor terrified by his own "thought" as well as the putative "facts." It is not just the desire for ocular proof that is at stake here.[31] Iago's improvised bestiary—prime as goats, hot as monkeys, and so on—invites Othello to share a concrete and vicious language of moral disgust, a language whose application yet remains hypothetical. This hypothetical disgust evokes not just the lovers' unseen copulation, but their animal ignorance and folly. Iago's great trick is that, having offered to Othello such a language of disgust, he quickly takes it back, reminding Othello that, as hot or foolish as these adulterers are, they must keep some residue of wisdom that will keep their starkly pictured activities out of Othello's view—a wisdom whose necessity Iago doesn't explain, of course, but which itself becomes as much an object of horrified contempt as their putative folly. Othello's disgust becomes, I want to say, hallucinatory, because it is so bound to what is not there, to what is absent and impossible, to something at once unthinkable and stolen away by thought. This allows Iago to build up a series of proofs that further intertwine speculation and fact, proofs by which Iago becomes the sole prop of Othello's knowledge. It is a strategy that shows itself best, I think, in Iago's report that he had heard Cassio murmur to Desdemona in his sleep about needing to "hide" their love, even as he twined his leg around Iago's, kissing him "as if he plucked up kisses by the roots / That grew upon my lips" (425–26). What Iago creates by this story is, as it were, a dream within a dream, a hallucination within a lie. Othello takes the dream report as proof of a "foregone conclusion" (430). Indeed, it is proof, not of Desdemona's physical betrayal, but of her infidelity to Othello's founding illusions about his wife. Earlier in his talks with Iago, he had seemed shaken to find that Desdemona was not entirely a creature of his own stories, that the words he would use to describe her (words which help to confirm his *own* nobility) belonged to a larger world of words accessible to uncertainty, rumor, and lie.[32] Listening to the dream anecdote, strangely enough, he seems to find it monstrous that dreams can be dreamed about her by someone other than himself, dreamed by a person whose own dreams, in fact, betray themselves, spilling over into an image of ignorant coupling such as is calculated, I think, to catch Othello's picture of his own marriage with Desdemona herself—particularly dangerous if the marriage has not yet been consummated. It is as if Othello were starting to take within himself such monstrous images of human lovemaking as Iago had cast up at Desdemona's father, in order to "poison his delight" (1.1.67). Othello, as is often noted, devours these obscene suggestions with as greedy an ear as Desdemona herself had devoured Othello's own stories.

IAGO TEACHES OTHELLO about the nature of dreams, about the wanderings of sexual fantasy. Despite what Iago says to Roderigo about Othello's talent for "bragging and telling . . . fantastical lies" (2.1.221) or what the moor himself claims to know about "close delations, working from the heart" (3.3.126), Othello reacts as if he had never before felt the power of either dreams or fantasy. He takes from Iago a cluster of words and images for his own imagination to work on. The same words take away something from Othello; they corrode or mar his own mind and speech.[33] The end of this is to make Othello feel to what degree both desire and the destruction of desire are themselves tied to dream and fantasy. (Imagine a poem by Wallace Stevens entitled "The Contaminations of What Is Possible.") The viciousness of Iago here is at least twofold. Having spurred the opening of fantasy in Othello, he gets Othello's mind at once to accept and enlarge on Iago's own denigrating images of Desdemona, Cassio, and even Othello himself—the monstrous, undesirable moor. He makes Othello demand the satisfaction of the very thing that tears at him, wounds him. In addition, Iago inflects the imaginary, hallucinated evidence so as to suggest, even prove (to the eye of the mind, at least), that the shapes of human fantasy, the creations of mind and desire, can produce only monstrosities—whether those monstrosities are slanderous, foul suspicions, outright lies, or even, in the end, scandalous "deeds." That thoughts inevitably imply action is another conclusion Othello wrongly draws. The result is that not only does Iago make fantasy and desire and dream the sources of slanders, he also slanders fantasy and desire and dream themselves. An interior space opens up for Othello in his dialogues with Iago, both in Iago's words and in his own thought, but that space looks back at him with a mask of blackness. Blackness becomes the color of this frightening interior space of mind, a space full of things at once hidden and visible. It is a blackness which, in the wake of Iago's work, Othello can only associate with radical falsehood, betrayal, and contamination. This is a blackness that, inevitably, blackens. It is Othello's mis-seeing of this imaginative blackness that should trouble us here, as much as his denigrated gaze on his wife or his own skin color. Black is, after all, the color of the face of melancholia—a damaging pathology, but also a disease whose ambiguous nature spurs some of the most potent Renaissance reflections on the shape of the imagination. As Giorgio Agamben argues, it is through their investigations of melancholia that thinkers like Marsilio Ficino and Giordano Bruno start to understand the power of an imaginative faculty that is at once corporeal and spiritual and thus the key to our peculiar threshold condition as human beings in the world.[34] In Shakespeare's later sonnets, blackness becomes the face of desire itself. Black is the color of the beloved and the color of that which drives the lover toward her, though in these poems, of course, both lover and object are "dyed" in betrayal, falsehood, and lust, while love is always met with the revelation of its own slander and perjury (of the lover, and the beloved).[35] The enigma is that this blackness is also a color of disillusioned knowledge, a form of candor.

It is the violence done against this blackness in the soul, as well as against the blackness of a man's face, that chills. At the end of act 3, scene 3, Othello swears his devotion to a revenge which will never turn back, but will keep its "icy current and compulsive course" like the Pontic Sea (457). "Even so my bloody thoughts with violent pace / Shall ne'er look back, ne'er ebb to humble love / Till that a capable and wide revenge / Swallow them up" (460–63). Listening carefully, one realizes that Othello's "them" is ambiguous. It is not just the criminal lovers that he wants "swallowed up," it is also his own "bloody thoughts." He wants revenge so that he can stop thinking— a little as Macbeth wants to commit his murders to keep himself from *fantasizing* about murder. The difficulty is that the waters of his revenge cannot wash away his own thoughts any more than ordinary waters are able to "wash an Ethiop white"—that Renaissance adage or proverb for the "impossible."[36] These thoughts stick with him; if anything, he spits out the thoughts he has swallowed, only to redevour them in freshly horrible ways.

The mind thus stained by its doubt takes revenge against both public gesture and its own most intimate tokens of love.[37] It commits its desires to a hallucinatory theater of accusation, subjecting to slander and shame the outward signs of both private and public knowledge. Take, for example, the scene in which Othello conjures up before Desdemona the monstrous specter of the lost handkerchief. This piece of silk spotted with strawberries was, we are told, a first gift. Desdemona plays with it, even talks to it; at another moment she wraps it around Othello's head as a kind of therapeutic turban. Yet it is not purely private. It is a thing whose "work" can be copied, "taken out" by another; it can be held, dropped, stolen, passed from hand to hand. The cloth is a stage prop after all, like Macbeth's dagger, Lear's mirror, or Hamlet's skull. But Othello's own theater makes the most frightening use of it. The handkerchief, in its very ordinariness, changes under Othello's words into both a token of magical fidelity and a twisted sign of betrayal.[38] In act 3, scene 4, convinced she has given the handkerchief to Cassio, Othello asks from Desdemona what he knows she does not have. "I have a salt and sullen rheum offends me, / Lend me thy handkerchief" (51–52). It is a pretext, of course, but a telling one. Even if only in fantasy, Othello asks if he can blow his nose, or more probably spit, into the handkerchief—literalizing his need to project his interior offenses outward and stain his own love in the process. Othello in fact steals back his absent gift and stains it more completely by improvising a fantastic account of its magical power and origins:

> *Othello.*                                     That handkerchief
> Did an Egyptian to my mother give,
> She was a charmer and could almost read
> The thoughts of people. She told her, while she kept it
> 'Twould make her amiable and subdue my father
> Entirely to her love; but if she lost it
> Or made a gift of it, my father's eye
> Should hold her loathed and his spirits should hunt
> After new fancies. She, dying, gave it me
> And bid me, when my fate would have me wive,
> To give it her. I did so, and—take heed on't!
> Make it a darling, like your precious eye!—
> To lose't or give't away were such perdition
> As nothing else could match.
> *Desdemona.*                          Is't possible?
> *Othello.*     'Tis true, there's magic in the web of it.
> A sibyl that had numbered in the world
> The sun to course two hundred compasses,
> In her prophetic fury sewed the work;
> The worms were hallowed that did breed the silk,
> And it was dyed in mummy, which the skilful
> Conserved of maidens' hearts.
>
> (57–77)

Kenneth Burke hears within this speech "the sinister invitation to an ultimate lie, an illusion carried to the edge of metaphysical madness, as private ownership, thus projected into realms for which there are no unquestion-

ably attested securities, is seen to imply also, profoundly, ultimately, es-
trangement; hence, we may in glimpses peer over the abyss into the regions
of pure abstract loneliness."[39] Here, everything that we might want language to do, or fear that it can do, turns out to be all too possible and all too
poisonous. Othello entangles his idea of faith in the very superstitions about
magical agency he had mocked so sharply at the opening of the play. We hear
an echo of Othello the teller of tales, the one who creates himself for the
world through dilated chains of eloquent, exotic narrative.[40] In this case,
however, the sort of story with which he had won Desdemona's love is used
to mock, terrorize, and shame her.[41] One gets a sense of language or storytelling on the verge of silencing itself, acquiring a furious lack of meaning
such as drives the world away, drives memory away. A shadow of self-
loathing in Othello—who is now so uncertain about other people's
minds—can be heard in his reference to a sibyl who can "almost read" the
thoughts of people. That shadow colors his sense of the handkerchief's
power to "subdue" the heart or to convert love into hatred. The hallucinatory conviction of the moor's story attaches itself to the idea of there being
"nothing else" so absolute as this handkerchief in confirming their love. That
absoluteness in turn attaches itself to the realm of the dead, as Othello converts the love gift into an enchanted corpse, or at least something stained
with the dust of corpses, dyed in powdered "mummy," "conserved of maid-
ens' hearts." Such a form of preservation is itself mortal, like that which
Othello promises to Desdemona at the end: "Once more, once more: / Be
thus when thou art dead and I will kill thee / And love thee after" (5.2.17–
19). The cloth is, in own its way, a kind of prophecy: woven of silk "bred" by
hallowed worms, it is made of the same stuff as Desdemona's bedsheets,
sheets which Othello thinks contaminated but which he is afraid to stain
with his wife's blood, and which Desdemona herself will ask to be made her
shroud.

Othello registers the world and his own accusations of it through a haze
of dream. Onstage, it is as if he stood continually on the threshold of falling
asleep, trying in the process to put the entire world to sleep. This gets liter-
alized in act 4, scene 1, where, just before Othello collapses completely into
unconsciousness, he registers his chaotic attachment both to nonexistent,
hallucinatory proofs and to the rumorous words that frame such proofs.
Here, Iago has just told Othello that Cassio has confessed:

> *Othello.*           Hath he said anything?
> *Iago.*           He hath, my lord, but be you well assured
>                No more than he'll unswear.

| | |
|---|---|
| *Othello.* | What hath he said? |
| *Iago.* | Faith, that he did—I know not what. He did— |
| *Othello.* | What? What? |
| *Iago.* | Lie. |
| *Othello.* | With her? |
| *Iago.* | With her, on her, what you will. |

*Othello.* Lie with her? lie on her? We say lie on her when they belie her!
Lie with her, zounds, that's fulsome!—Handkerchief! confessions! handkerchief!—To confess, and be hanged for his labour! First to be hanged, and
then to confess: I tremble at it [ . . . ] It is not words that shakes me thus.
Pish! Noses, ears, and lips. Is't possible? Confess! handkerchief! O devil! *[He
falls in a trance.]*

(4.1.29–43)

For Othello, now turned into a kind of dumb deconstructor, the possibility
of Desdemona's "slipping" gets confirmed by the very slipperiness and infidelity of English syntax and word usage: "Lie with her? lie on her? We say
lie on her when they belie her. . . . Handkerchief! confessions! handkerchief!" Othello wanders into an inverted scheme of justice that recalls nothing so much as that of the Queen of Hearts in *Alice in Wonderland:* "First to be
hanged, and then to confess." In this fantasy, one glimpses the human face—
Othello's, Desdemona's, Cassio's—not so much blackened as exploded, set
adrift in condemned, bizarrely autonomous fragments—"Pish! Noses, ears,
and lips." These parts of the body are variously portals of sense, recognition,
and pleasure; they have become, for Othello, objects of fear and contempt,
fetishistic displacements of both desire and violence.[42]

Othello regains his self-possession in the next scene, where he is no
longer in direct proximity to Iago. Yet his posture and his language assume an
even creepier violence and a more unsettling commitment to the truth of
what is invisible, to making the real world disappear behind another more
fantastic and shameful. This is the scene where he most bluntly blackens
Desdemona's name with accusations of adultery, calls her "whore." He
stands with his wife in an unidentified chamber in the castle; scholars tend to
refer to it as the "brothel scene" because Othello speaks to Desdemona as if
she were a prostitute, and he her client, while Emilia becomes the bawd who
must watch the door against any intrusions: "Some of your function, mistress, / Leave procreants alone and shut the door; / Cough, or cry hem, if
anybody come" (4.2.27–29), Othello says to her, sending her offstage.
Later, Emilia will report to Iago that Othello not only called Desdemona a
whore, but he "bewhored" her. The phrase, in its common sense, refers to

the illicit sexual act itself, suggesting that Othello's slanderous certainty, his naming and knowledge of Desdemona's infidelity, itself takes the form of an imaginary fornication. In Othello's fantasy, he is not only present at but responsible for his own cuckoldry, as if his own marriage to Desdemona had made her a whore.[43]

The twisted spirit of accusation gets further heightened when, at the climax of the scene, Othello tries to localize the object of his accusation, an object that yet continues to elude him. He is for a moment freshly caught up in the stance of heroic storyteller: he talks about the array of trials he could survive—poverty, abjection, captivity, even being turned into "a fixed figure for the time of scorn / To point his slow unmoving finger at!" (55–56), a blackened statue of shame.[44] Faced with all of these, he protests, "I should have found in some place of my soul / A drop of patience":

> But there where I have garnered up my heart,
> Where either I must live or bear no life,
> The fountain from the which my current runs
> Or else dries up—to be discarded thence!
> Or keep it as a cistern for foul toads
> To knot and gender in! Turn thy complexion there,
> Patience, thou young and rose-lipped cherubin,
> Ay, here look, grim as hell!
> (58–65)

I recall a curious dream I once had, in which Roland Barthes turned to me during the interval of some play and observed, "Our theater is a double nightmare, in which our dream of attention plays itself out." Othello engages in a furious, hallucinatory species of attention here; he looks or points toward a place of loss, the origin of a betrayal, a source of shame and disgust. He points toward "the cause, the cause." The horrible room in the imaginary brothel has metamorphosed into something more frightening, a home from which he has been exiled and which he has yet been forced to keep as a place of perverse coupling. It is a chamber filled with knotted and procreating toads rather than hallowed silkworms. Othello fixes himself in a posture of pointing, turning toward a place of crime and abject survival which recedes from view the more it is pointed at. A near hysteria echoes in his reiterated markers of place: "*there* where I have garnered up my heart," "to be discarded *thence*," "turn thy complexion *there*." The very invisibility of what he is pointing at converts it into a space of monstrosity. At one level, he must be pointing at Desdemona's invisible womb or genitals—localizing there the breeding place of her treacherous desire. Her desire, in which he had found the magical source of his own life, has not only been narrowly physicalized; the place of her desire has been bound to his fantasies of tragic exile and stolen property. As a second to his accusation, Othello conjures the blackened "complexion" of an angelic figure of Patience, who here is invited to look "grim as hell." This imaginary witness doubles his own denigrated face, which now contains the eye of the slanderous accuser. The thing that turns its look on Desdemona's shame, however, also turns its face back on Othello. Whether he knows it or not, in looking into Desdemona Othello is looking into a mirror at the projected image of his own slanderous, self-exiling fantasy.

What strikes me as most horrible is the image of Othello's calling or pointing itself (whatever its object). He is frozen onstage in a posture of attention, looking for what he cannot see, what his own cry drives into the dark. Here I need to correct a generalization I made above. I suggested that it is in this scene that Othello most openly calls Desdemona a "whore," indeed makes her a whore by his very accusation. The "publishing" of that word has a peculiar shock and danger, especially in a milieu where merely to call a woman a whore was almost enough to create the reality of her crime.[45] If Desdemona is not in a position to answer Othello's words, however, it is not only because she has mistaken a private for a public accusation, or because she has aggressively stripped her marriage to Othello of any public accountability. It is as much because the word "whore," that plainest and most common label of abuse for women—indeed, a term applied promiscuously to such suspect entities as acting, theater, and false religion—never really emerges as a direct accusation from Othello's lips.[46] Emilia, reporting the scene to Iago, says this: "He called her whore. A beggar in his drink / Could not have laid such terms upon his callat. . . . Why should he call her whore?" (122–23, 139). But Emilia has heard an exchange different from the one the audience hears, something coarser, more bluntly violent, perhaps an echo of her own domestic quarrels with Iago. For Othello never does directly call Desdemona "whore." Rather, he lets the word emerge through a web of reiterated questions, vague innuendos, figurative circumlocutions, and mocked exculpations. He has learned Iago's language lessons well:

Was this fair paper, this most goodly book
Made to write "whore" upon? What committed!
Committed? O, thou public commoner!
I should make very forges of my cheeks
That would to cinders burn up modesty
Did I but speak thy deeds. What committed!

Heaven stops the nose at it, and the moon winks,
The bawdy wind that kisses all it meets
Is hushed within the hollow mine of earth
And will not hear't. What committed!
Impudent strumpet! . . .
Are you not a strumpet? . . .
· · · · · · · · · · · · · · · · · · · · · · · · · · · · · · · · · · · · ·
What; Not a whore? . . .
Is't possible? . . .
                                    . . . I cry you mercy then,
I took you for that cunning whore of Venice
That married with Othello.
(72–92)

Othello's very obliqueness keeps the word suspended in air and heightens its power to wound. The word "whore" arrives saturated with his own dream-like negativity; his utterance remains haunted and mocked by the phantasm of his own questionable certainty, his self-wounding attachment to an impossible possibility. Desdemona's whoredom becomes a rumor at once diffuse and madly closed up on itself, cutting off Othello's ability to hear from her, silencing Desdemona herself. Hence, I think, Othello's strange, disgusted image of this scandal as a promiscuous wind that yet shuts itself up in shame: "The bawdy wind that kisses all it meets / Is hushed within the hollow mine of earth / And will not hear't."

In *The Wheel of Fire,* G. Wilson Knight evokes what he calls "the *Othello* music."[47] By this he means the formal eloquence, the jewel-like precision of language in the play, and, by extension, the exacting, dancelike interaction of the four characters and their distinct voices. Chorusing with this music, however, is what I would call the *Othello* noise, or the *Othello* babble. "O, you are well tuned now," Iago says, "but I'll set down / The pegs that make this music, as honest / As I am" (2.1.198–200). By this I mean something different from the profane cacophony of abuses that Iago hurls up at Brabantio, or the incoherent fragments that Othello utters in his fit, or even the hint of bombast and fustian that one may catch in Othello's nobler speeches.[48] What concerns me is rather a kind of furious blankness of meaning that gathers around certain words and utterances in the play. It is something that arises most often around moments of iteration or repetition such as I pointed to in Othello's dialogue with Iago, where words like "honest" and "thought" become so thoroughly stripped of sense, and yet are so caught by Othello's desire to make sense of them. In Othello's mouth, especially, such repetition produces silence and confusion, rather than clear response; it spoils and dulls the sense of the uttered words, even as it disguises misprision as truth and converts vague suspicion into ruthless certainty. In this play, characters start to hear each other's words as if they were alien, unintelligible rumors, reports from enclosed worlds whose language games they did not share—yet games that become wounding rather than simply unintelligible, because the speakers remain bound in body and soul to those shared words, because they depend on them both to frame faith and to motivate violence. In the brothel scene, Othello's way of turning on "whore" makes the word madly resonant. It has all of his fear and jealous fantasy in it. But the word reverberates with the noise of a speaker who wants to be exempted from meaning, exempted from having to test the sense of what he says, and who at the same time wants to make his meaninglessness troubling to others. He wants his words especially to attack those who, like Desdemona, cannot escape either his words' meaninglessness or their hallucinations of meaning, as if he would revenge upon her his own loss of sense.

Such iteration is not invariably a sign of violence or dementia in this play. It can harass listeners to less vicious ends. Consider, for example, Desdemona's bluntly repeated response to Emilia's playful speculations about making her husband a cuckold: "Wouldst thou do such a deed for all the world? . . . Wouldst thou do such a thing for all the world? . . . Beshrew me, if I would do such a wrong, / For the whole world!" (4.3.63–78). If this doesn't exactly repudiate Emilia's vision of what she might do in her "own world," it draws a circle around Desdemona's "thinking" about Othello and the idea of marriage, suggesting that for her this thought belongs to a space apart from the chaos of the world's clichés (a chaos into which Othello has so readily thrown himself). Then there are Emilia's own astonished responses to Othello's information about Iago:

| | |
|---|---|
| *Othello.* | Thy husband knew it all. |
| *Emilia.* | My husband? |
| *Othello.* | Thy husband. |
| *Emilia.* | That she was false? |
| | To wedlock? |
| *Othello.* | Ay, with Cassio . . . |

. . . . . . . . . . . . . . . . . . . . . . . . . . . . . . . . . . .

| | |
|---|---|
| *Emilia.* | . . . My husband? |
| *Othello.* | Ay, 'twas he that told me on her first; |
| | An honest man he is, and hates the slime |
| | That sticks on filthy deeds. |

*Emilia.*                                    My husband!
*Othello.*                                                        What needs
          This iterance, woman? I say thy husband.
*Emilia.*     O mistress, villainy hath made mocks with love!
          My husband say that she was false?
*Othello.*                                                    He, woman;
          I say thy husband: dost thou understand the word?
          My friend thy husband, honest, honest Iago.
(5.2.137–50)

Far from driving meaning away, Emilia's "iterance" marks a sudden access of knowledge and salient wonder. What she recognizes is, in part, how scandalously uncertain and treacherous the word "husband" has become at this moment (like the word "wife" in Othello's "My wife, my wife! what wife? I have no wife" [96]). Her repetitions give voice to that knowledge. If her astonishment baffles Othello, he himself only confirms his own continuing dependence on, and vulnerability to, words which he merely thinks he understands, as when he answers Emilia's repetitions with his own, "thy husband, honest, honest Iago." Reading this, I get the sense that, were Othello to repeat the word "honest" a third time, he would explode, or tear himself to pieces.[49]

    Again, it comes down to a complex drama of hearing. Recall that, from the opening of the play, Desdemona's ear has been exquisitely tuned to her husband's speech, to its expansiveness and eloquence, to its shifts of tone and sudden starts of emotion.[50] But as the drama unfolds, Desdemona's ear, though it continues to apprehend Othello's words, comprehends them less and less. She mistakes the sources of his fury, the reason for certain evasions; she poses questions that only elicit further rage. In the brothel scene, Othello's blank questions and viciously suspended placing of "whore" defeat entirely her ability to make sense of what he says. His words demand that she transform herself, find some relation to a name she cannot bear, whose truth she entirely repudiates. Once Othello has left, she can only ask, half to herself, "Am I that name, Iago?" The word "whore" makes her own words alien, unbearable, even as she tries to take the word into her mouth, and self-consciously to pun on it, to make her own language reject the possibility it names: "I cannot say whore: / It does abhor me now I speak the word" (4.2.163–64). It is as if Othello had made his wife at once eat and cast up his words, filled her mouth with his sly silences and evasive questions.

    Hearing this noise of "whore" and "strumpet," Desdemona does not imagine the monster in Othello's mind. Neither does she respond with the kind of furious protest against male desire and jealousy that we hear from Emilia. This reticence may seem a kind of failure on her part (as scandalous to many readers as Desdemona's falling in love with Othello seems to her father). Yet she does find an answer to Othello, however delayed. That answer is heard, I would argue, in the willow song that she sings to herself as Emilia prepares her for bed in act 4, scene 3. The space of this scene had itself begun to emerge at the close of the earlier brothel scene, when Desdemona, "half asleep" after Othello's angry departure, had asked Emilia to lay her wedding sheets on her bed, the same sheets in which she now asks Emilia to shroud her if she should die. Desdemona—as if caught by Othello's fantasy of married love as loss and adultery, and by his unvoiced wish to murder his wife on her wedding bed—returns to the site of her husband's hallucination. It is a paradoxical form of fidelity to his infidelity. But she also tries to revise and restage that hallucination on her own terms, manipulating the stage properties—the bed, sheets, and pillows, which will all too quickly become the means of murder. The singing of the willow song itself becomes Desdemona's ambiguous, lyrical response to Othello's noise, her undoing of its (partly disguised) nonsense. It is less a response to Othello's palpable injustice than to his self-wounding, fantasy-induced grief and the madness that follows from it. Desdemona here conjures up a gentler double of the space of monstrous interiority and hallucinatory reflection that Iago's rumorous words impose on the moor. In the story she tells herself, she becomes her mother's unfortunate maid:

> My mother had a maid called Barbary,
> She was in love, and he she loved proved mad
> And did forsake her. She had a song of "willow",
> An old thing 'twas, but it expressed her fortune
> And she died singing it. That song tonight
> Will not go from my mind. I have much to do
> But to go hang my head all at one side
> And sing it like poor Barbary.
> (4.3.24–31)

Reversing the logic of her response to Othello's stories—"she wished / That heaven had made her such a man" (1.3.163–64)—Desdemona becomes now "such a woman" as she fancies her mother's maddened servant to have been. She takes upon herself the voice, almost the very posture, of Barbary, over whose song Desdemona falls asleep (and, later, falls dead). She takes on herself the slanderous label that Iago had turned on Othello ("a Barbary horse"), and makes it her own name, the sign of a gentler madness than Othello's (though a madness of which his demented jealousy is the cause). At the beginning of the play she had protested, "I saw Othello's visage in his mind." At this point it is a more private story and song, one she inherits from a mother's maid, that "will not go from my mind."

> The poor soul sat sighing by a sycamore tree,
>      Sing all a green willow:
> Her hand on her bosom, her head on her knee,
>      Sing willow, willow, willow.
> The fresh streams ran by her and murmured her moans,
>      Sing willow, willow, willow:
> Her salt tears fell from her and softened the stones,
>      Sing willow, willow, willow.
> . . . . . . . . . . . . . . . . . . . . . . . . . . . . . . . . . .
> Sing all a green willow must be my garland.
> Let nobody blame him, his scorn I approve—
> (39–51)

Desdemona's fragile ballad holds the stage for a moment, a little like Ophelia's mad songs or Lady Macbeth's somnambulistic murmurings. What should astonish us in this revery, I think, is its lucidity, its candor. However dreamlike, it has none of the blind rage and self-loathing we hear in Othello's speeches. Rather, she imagines a song that softens stone, instead of making stone of flesh, as Othello does to both his own heart and Desdemona's body. The song's refrain of "willow, willow, willow" offers another sort of "iterance," a lyrical babble that does not explain itself, that neither pretends to more sense than it has nor uses its nonsense to stop another's speech. The song makes iterance into music, rather than dumb noise. It is a music in which a kind of knowledge hovers. In that echoing "willow," she prophetically sings her own funeral dirge, as well as a mourning song for her romance and marriage. Her "willow" may also translate, as Fineman speculates, the etymological source of her husband's name, from the Greek verb *ethelō*, "to will or desire"—again as if she could repossess his fury within a gentler key and marry it to her own.[51]

The song is a very fragile, troubled sort of answer. Far from voicing a just outrage, it translates Desdemona's acceptance of Othello's accusations: "Let nobody blame him, his scorn I approve" (though this might just be a way of saying "Othello's anger is nobody's business but my own"). It also embeds a wife's protest in a cynical, mocking game more proper to Iago: "I called my love false love; but what said he then? / Sing willow, willow, willow: / If I court moe women, you'll couch with moe men" (54—56). Toward the close, Desdemona stammers over the lyrics, misses some of the words, and imagines a knock on the door. (It is nothing but the wind, Emilia reassures her, but the wind too is contaminated in this play.) Still, even as a kind of dream, the song holds out a cure for the more infectious babble of this play, a noise that does not so directly bind or blind its hearers, or turn itself into the motive for murder. Whatever knowledge the song offers to us draws a lyrical circle around itself. We need to feel it as visionary, rather than hallucinatory. Otherwise, we will mistake the nature of the tragic breach which the play shows us. One loss that it faces us with is that, in the end, Barbary's ballad cannot penetrate Othello's ears; it cannot banish the jealous, self-damaging noise that accumulates within his speech, the filth that clings to his images, or convert Othello in the way his stories had once converted Desdemona. Nor is the revery of the willow song strong enough to answer the eerie scenario conjured up by Othello as he enters the bedchamber to waken Desdemona.

THE MARRIAGE BED of Desdemona and Othello remains unseen until this last scene in the play. Previous to this, it is only something alluded to, made the subject of fantasy, suspicion, and slander, most strikingly by Othello himself. Bedchambers are important spaces in this play, but they tend to be invisible or notional. In previous scenes, we become aware of them primarily as offstage spaces into which a particular onstage noise tends to break, pulling sleepers from their unseen beds, out into the streets and into our sights, into the space of playing—as when the clamor of Cassio's brawl wakes Othello and Desdemona on their first night in Cyprus, when the shouts of conflicting messengers find Othello at the Sagitarry Inn in Venice, or when Iago and Roderigo's shouts wake Brabantio in the play's opening scene. We should remember that such public noise, contingent as it may appear, is itself orchestrated by Iago, who makes that noise serve his plots. In the final scene, when the bedroom is suddenly visible, Othello assumes the guise of a more intimate, private awakener. He enters with an uncanny softness, freed of outward rage, using again the grave, delicate language that had characterized him earlier in the play, the purest expression of "the *Othello* music." Yet as he enters this chamber, caught in his hallucinatory vision of Desdemona as a marble statue, quiet Othello also becomes the strange, covert embodiment of that more violent, intrusive noise (whose penetration into bedrooms we have not previously been in a position to witness). In this form, Othello's

entry is a revelation of how closely Iago's jealous rumors have transformed both him and his bride:

> It is the cause, it is the cause, my soul!
> Let me not name it to you, you chaste stars,
> It is the cause. Yet I'll not shed her blood
> Nor scar that whiter skin of hers than snow
> And smooth as monumental alabaster.
> (5.2.1–5)

Almost a ghost himself, Othello enters the bedchamber, the stage space, as
the hallucination of denigration, as the mouthpiece for slanderous nonsense
disguised as bitter praise and legal judgment, wrapping its own worst truths
in self-deceptive silence. It is a noise that darkens the stage, puts out a
candle, and tries to keep a sleeping woman stony white, at once pure and
contaminated, dead and alive: "Be thus when thou art dead, and I will kill
thee / And love thee after."

———

The script of a minstrel show entitled *Dar's de Money,* roughly contemporary
with *Desdemonum,* offers a more bluntly farcical, if still surreal, rendition of
the murder scene. It begins with two blackface clowns meeting on the stage,
as if by accident. Jake boasts a silk cravat and a stuffed coat with huge brass
buttons, miming prosperity. Pete is tieless, disheveled, thin; he carries an
old carpetbag and wears the broken cap of a Union soldier. The two banter,
share news, and competitively exchange stories about lost jobs and failed
dodges—Pete describing one particularly macabre scam, in which the
audience's fear and mockery of black trickery strangely combine: "I whitewashed my hands and implored persistance as a man what had been garrot-
ted . . . black in de face wid de choking."[52] That is to say, Pete convinces
people to take the artificial whiteness of his hands for his natural color, by insisting that his black face is not a fact of race (which it after all isn't), but
rather the contingent result of having been choked to death—by an assassin,
an executioner, or a lynch mob. In his eerily appropriate malapropism, he
"implored persistance" for himself as the animated corpse of a strangled
white man. It turns out that both clowns are out-of-work actors, and they
decide to set up a theater of their own. As if inspired by the story of Pete's
ghostly con game, Jake suggests that they rehearse the well-known "tablow"

of "Darsdemoney's" murder. Jake assumes the role of Othello and explains that he will put some brown soap in his mouth at the final moment to work up a mad "froth." Two chairs are pulled out, and draped with a sheet to form an improvised bridal couch, and Jake goes offstage while he waits for Pete to take his place as the sleeping victim:

> (*comic business of trying to lie down on chairs.*)
>
> *Jake.* (*without,* L.) Are you ready?
>
> *Pete.* Not yet. (*in sitting up with the sheet around him, he sits between the two chairs—they slide away from him to each side, and he falls between them, the sheet around him over his head and only off his black face.*)
>
> *Jake.* (*without,* L.) Are you ready?
>
> *Pete.* Don't put in your soap! (*wraps himself up in the sheet, and lies along on the chairs, head towards* R.)
>
> *Jake.* (*without,* L.) Ready?
>
> *Pete.* Ninny, ninny, now come!
>
> *Enter* Jake, L., *a lighted candle in left hand, a pillow on left arm.*
>
> *Jake.* "It is the caws, the caws, my crow! It is the caws! Yet I'll not shed her blood! Nor scar that whiter skin of hers than snow, and smooth as monumental alabastrum."
>
> *Pete.* How are you, alabastrum?

After a few more words, Jake smothers Pete with the pillow and then stabs himself with a wooden sword. But Pete doesn't move when the rehearsal is finished. Unsure as to whether or not Pete is merely playing dead, Jake tries unsuccessfully to rouse his partner by shaking and threats, by promises of drink, and finally by imitating the sounds of creditors approaching with their dogs. Exasperated, Jake exits stage right and returns with a large stuffed club, proceeding to pummel Pete on the head. Awakened at last, Pete rushes offstage and, with Punch-like enterprise, comes back bearing a club of his own; he beats Jake until he howls and runs off again, and then Pete follows close behind. The play ends.

Strangely enough, this parody extends a line of possibility that exists within the original play. It can remind one in particular of what Shakespeare does with a theater of slander. Othello's opaquely iterated legalism—"it is the cause, it is the cause"—comes back more literally as animal noise, the cries of predatory crows, which that are also the stuff of racial stereotype. Likewise, Pete hears in the figure of Desdemona's purity, "monumental alabastrum," only the occasion for a coarse, punning insult. Other forms of whiteness—for example, those grimly whitewashed hands and that recalcitrant bedsheet—turn out to be theatrical residua, failed disguises or comic props. The claustrophobic, dreamlike sense of menace has vanished. Yet the clowns' improvisation of Desdemona's death, even their unreadiness and impatience, take their cue from the oddly self-conscious, theatrical quality of the original. Jake and Pete catch the staginess and melodrama, even the potential for bathos, which in Shakespeare's play trouble any sense of the murder's tragic inevitability or, rather, tie that inevitability to the hallucinations which Othello has taken upon himself. Their game with the sheets, for instance, catches some of the strangeness of Desdemona's falling asleep on those overdetermined bedclothes, so soon made into the instruments of murder; they remind us that Desdemona's death and sudden reawakening are composed so as to keep us aware of the actor's task of miming both sleep and death. (Remember the death of Falstaff at the Battle of Shrewsbury.) Jake's entry, which contains the scene's one direct quotation from Shakespeare's text, also mirrors Othello's self-conscious, Senecan posturing on the threshold of murder, the odd combination of lucidity and delusion that possess him at the end. The scene in *Dar's de Money* thus catches the possibility that Othello is acting within a deformed, somewhat self-serving version of his own tragedy.[53]

The minstrels lend to Othello's victim a different sort of knowledge than in the original. Pete as Darsdemoney not only resists orders, but flatly refuses to play the game on Jack/Othello's terms. He transforms the theatrical fiction of the heroine's sleep and death by stealing back the initiative of awakening, and turning his attacker's (or awakener's) weapons back against him. Different as it is, such resistance might remind us that Desdemona herself tries to reconfigure the terms of her own murder in the eerie moment when she awakens in response to Emilia's cry, making Othello vanish and taking his violence upon herself: Emilia: "O, who hath done / This deed?" Desdemona: "Nobody. I myself" (5.2.121–22). Even more strikingly, the burlesque translates another dream or hallucination already at work in Shakespeare, the dream in which Othello's murder of Desdemona doubles as an attack on himself, an attack on the denigrated, whitened phantasm of his own purity. In the parody, that attack directs itself against a black-faced twin who clutches a shroud, while his theatrical supports slide out from under him. Pete, who had begged alms by suggesting that his blackened face was a contingency of murder, turns out in playing Darsdemoney to be his attacker's mirror image. Indeed, as in Shakespeare's play, Othello's murder doubles his suicide, just as the suicide divides Othello against himself, positioning him as both the loyal servant and the alien, turbaned traducer (Jake's club, pulled suddenly from offstage, substituting for the second sword, "the ice-brook's temper," that Othello has mysteriously hidden in his bedchamber).

The relief of *Dar's de Money* lies in the clowns' driving each other offstage, making the tragic struggle into a mere slapstick and leaving the theatrical platform bare. It mostly reassures us to find the conflict so ad hoc and evanescent, leaving us happily ready for fresh improvisation. Desdemona and Othello, by contrast, are driven to occupy the stage all the more violently at the end of their play. They reoccupy it, as it were, in order to exile us in turn. The two lie together on that bed, miming death, at once the image of a marriage and the evidence of a crime.[54] This is the utmost of what it is possible to see, yet it feels like something more impossible to see than the adultery which Iago conjures up in act 3. Recall Lodovico's terribly divided orders at the very close: he says first to Iago (and, by extension, the audience), "Look on the tragic loading of this bed: / This is thy work," and then immediately adds, perhaps when he looks himself, "The object poisons sight, / Let it be hid" (5.2.361–63). The object poisons sight by tempting one to look at it, no doubt. So Lodovico demands that the bed-curtains be shut, or pulls the sheets over the bodies. What can be hidden by cloth, however, is no greater than what these visible bodies, or the play as a whole, manage to hide or place beyond reach. It is all the more unreachable because one cannot begin to connect it with a more extended atmosphere or order of meaning, or even an order of meaninglessness—as is possible in plays like *Hamlet, King Lear,* and *Macbeth.*[55] It is unreachable because we are faced at once with the opaque forms of these particular fictive characters, with their ambiguous histories, and with the forms of waking actors, whose freedom to make the hidden visible and overcome death by miming it is here pushed to so extreme a limit. The disillusionment created by the scene must try us. Defending the last tableau against charges of gothic sensationalism or of offering a kind of moral pornography, Bradley writes, "If we fully imagine the inward tragedy in the souls of the persons as we read, the more obvious and almost physical sensations of pain or horror do not appear in their own likeness, and only serve to intensify the tragic feelings in which they are absorbed."[56] That demand to imagine an "inward tragedy" still seems to me an essential one for both readers and spectators, not to be shaken even by the play's relentless darkening of our sense of the inner lives of these characters or by our awareness of their talent for self-dramatization. Yet one shudders a bit to find that Bradley pursues this goal by making those literal, theatrical presences fade away into feeling. For he suggests that the actual bodies "not appear in their own [horrible] likeness," as if our full, imaginative knowledge of "inward tragedy" depended on a vision that (like Othello's hallucinatory jealousy) made solid, visible things disappear, or took them for monsters —rather than teaching us to bear what the forms of those creatures onstage make both visible and invisible.

# chapter five

# WAR NOISE

he war of tongues is more savage in *Coriolanus* than in any other play I know. The noise of the battlefield and the noise of the city chorus against one another throughout; they provoke each other, exchanging or usurping each other's parts, or else they run together to their own decay. These noises are the objects of desire and the objects of hatred. Coriolanus flies from the words and voices of Rome; he is exiled by "whoops" and "hoos" of its citizens. Yet he also possesses a "throat of war" that charms the ears of his fellow soldiers and makes his enemies "shake, as if the world / Were feverous and did tremble" (1.4.60–61), even as it strives against the civic noise of the world he hates. His postures of voice are radiant with loathing. They capture and sum up a human world under the mask of contempt, furiously metamorphosing it into animals, chaff, wind, even as they peel back the layers of lie and subterfuge that surround him.[1] For all their urgency and precision, however, his speeches have little claim on his Roman listeners. The hero's words serve primarily to isolate him from the world that depends upon his violent deeds. Eerily invulnerable in the face of swords, nourished rather than weakened by his physical wounds and loss of blood, his vituperation costs him most; it exposes him to a violence that he himself conjures. Public speech is for this Herculean hero a Nessus garment, a poisoned gift that burns him up, torments him in his skin, yet can only be escaped from by self-immolation.[2] He takes almost any audience for his enemy. Words are a food that starves him, a dangerous supply, a fund of desolations; he takes them into his mouth only so that he can, with pleasure, spit them out. Even the

name that memorializes his heroism—in particular his all but miraculous capture of the city of Corioles—becomes a burden. Coriolanus in fact disinherits himself of his own name and fame in the course of the play, seeking to become "a kind of nothing, titleless" (5.1.13). By the end, he recalls the name "Coriolanus" not to mark his reputation in Rome, but only to extract from it the memory of the solitary violence that gave it birth. With chilling irony, he bequeaths his heroic identity to the keeping of his enemies:

> Cut me to pieces, Volsces, men and lads,
> Stain all your edges on me. Boy! False hound!
> If you have writ your annals true, 'tis there,
> That like an eagle in a dove-cote, I
> Flutter'd your Volscians in Corioles.
> Alone I did it. Boy!
> (5.6.111–16)³

It is the shape of Coriolanus's rage that I have struggled with most here, its outward signs and its ambivalent springs. It is an emotion always in excess of its apparent ends and occasions. As William Hazlitt wrote, Coriolanus's heroism displays itself most fully in postures of anger; it is an aristocratic *furor,* always searching for fresh objects to set itself above or against, as if he accumulated around him what he destroys: "before him he carries noise, and behind him he leaves tears" (2.1.157–58).⁴ We see this rage in his contempt for the plebeians in the opening scenes, where Coriolanus "seeks their hate with greater devotion than they can render it him" (2.2.18–19), as they riot for bread and demand a share in political power. We see it equally in his anger at his fellow patricians, who accommodate the rioters and grant them tribunes. That rage takes on a more physical form when Coriolanus is pulled into the wars against the Volscians, and he risks his own bodily survival in the face of the enemy. Here too his heroic violence is fed by his loathing of the cowardice of common soldiers, the "chaff" of Rome whom he had hoped the wars would consume. After the battle, he rejects even the praise that his fellow officers heap on him. Back in the city, Coriolanus's rage directs itself not just against civil unrest, but against the very rituals of civic peace, especially that election which submits him to voices that, he sees, are both spiritually contaminated and politically malleable.⁵ Accused of treason and unable to accommodate or apologize, he wins himself only banishment. In revenge, Coriolanus tries to turn the collective rage of Rome's enemies to his own advantage, joining with his rival Aufidius to lead the armies of Volscia against his home. But it becomes clear that no collective violence can contain or enact this hero's rage, any more than a collective praise can capture his idea of nobility. In making peace with Rome, Coriolanus tries at last to disimplicate himself from any aggressivity that does not belong to him alone—even if this means yielding to dismemberment.

Despite his physical bravery and military leadership, his honoring of Roman virtue, not to mention his real political understanding, Coriolanus's rage undoes him. His commitment to the public terms of heroism is curiously fragile, at odds with itself; it radically endangers the civic order he claims to serve, so that his patrician allies find him more dangerous than the commons themselves. We may feel an aura of the tragic around Coriolanus's career, insofar as tragedy is a form that "exacts a vitality capable of going beyond the Instinct for Self-preservation."[6] But the specifically self-destructive form of that vitality can make his suffering seem more grotesque than tragic, in particular because, unlike the Herculean model that Eugene Waith describes, Coriolanus's self-created sufferings serve no larger or more ideal end.[7] Or, perhaps, his ideal is so deeply hidden, or emerges in so paradoxical a language, that we can barely trace it. Certainly, there is no moment of tragic knowledge or recognition that draws itself out of the fatal course of the action. There remains about Coriolanus, as critics remind us, the sense of something unspoken, a buried impulse; but that unspoken drive is as much infantile as heroic. For all his *Romanitas* and aristocratic stature, Coriolanus keeps about him the energy of an angry, dissatisfied child, a boy in love with the expression of his will through verbal taunt and physical violence.[8] His quickness in anger suggests a child's desperate need, as does the fact that even the grandest expressions of care only feed his dissatisfaction, and the highest praise produces only more contempt. We tend to imagine Coriolanus as his own son, tearing apart a butterfly with his teeth in revenge for a fall.[9]

The difficult thing is finding the key or register of Coriolanus's excess, as well as its shifting objects. The play's account of the hero tempts us to theorize about his unconscious aggressions and hidden resentments, especially given the text's pointed account of his violent childhood and the continuing, shaping presence of his mother. Yet any attempt to speak of this hero's psyche must balance against Coriolanus's strange opacity as a literary character. It is hard to find the cue and motive to his passion, stark as its manifestations are. The play gives us none of those flickering, fragmentary hints about the character's interiority which we get in the case of Hamlet, Othello, and Macbeth. No rumors of melancholy or wounded conscience emerge. Unlike Macbeth, there is no flood of unreal speculation both driving and thwarting his violence, nor any vulnerable calculation about his life in time. There is nothing in Coriolanus like Othello's self-wounding fantasies about his own and Desdemona's love, nor any of Hamlet's dark reflections on his own ambivalence. Never a soliloquist, Coriolanus in his vituperations lacks that interior eloquence which might serve to give a point of purchase for the audience's sense of his motives. There is a hallucinatory force to some of Coriolanus's curses, no doubt. And his violent career can readily become a source of fantasy for others, including both his mother Volumnia and his archenemy Aufidius. But in himself, Coriolanus seems to be a character that lives without fantasy, without hallucination, something that makes him more rather than less uncanny. Coriolanus lives without guilt as well, without the suspicion of interior wounds or stains such as might create the impression of a soul. It is as if Shakespeare had set out to write, after his central tragedies of mind, the tragedy of someone with no interiority. [10]

We could also say that Coriolanus is a hero who hates having to act the role of hero—hates playing to the audience, seeking its breath, or exposing his desire for its approval. But it might be better to say that Coriolanus presents us with the paradox of an actor who has only one role and one kind of stage where he knows that role, that is, the battlefield. Disabled by requests that he assume a different mask or even play the part he knows on an unfamiliar platform, Coriolanus assumes this role as a sort of alienating compulsion. He thus makes himself at once more isolated and more exposed than any other "player" among Shakespeare's line of heroes. There is something of the clown or satyr in Coriolanus, as Kenneth Burke suggests. [11] Meredith Anne Skura reminds us that Coriolanus as actor mirrors the archetypal victim of the Renaissance theater, the bear in the bearbaiting shows; he is like one of those creatures nicknamed "Sackerson" or "Harry Hunks," whom audiences watched so fervently—comic, clumsy, relentless, bellowing and striking back at the dogs who tore at them. [12] For Coriolanus's undoubtedly human rage retains about it something of the blankness and clarity of an animal's, even as his language converts his enemies into beasts. The postures of violence Coriolanus assumes through the play, the masks of blood and noise, put him almost beyond purchase by the politic and human world he serves. And yet that violence is never divine or Dionysiac—for while others in the play often figure Coriolanus as god, demon, and even idol, he himself never seeks valorization or blessing from any transcendental source. [13] Even his brand of terrorism is paradoxical, as we shall see. Indeed, if one seeks a motive for Coriolanus's activity in the play, it ends up looking negative or oppositional. Coriolanus is an actor who seeks to burn through all political and theatrical contexts, through all civic role playing, all available names. That is the true form of his "treachery." [14] He is an actor unable to remain onstage with his fellow actors, an actor moved primarily by violence against his audience—whose very applause joins the chorus of noise from which he flees. He seeks his voice in a world where all other voices have become poison or coercion, a promise of curse, where even his mother's praises limit rather than enlarge the self.

This impulse of repudiation—in itself a kind of negative capability—makes one both depend upon and distrust what others say about Coriolanus. This tension is itself basic to the play, and to its account of Coriolanus's dilemma. Part of what drives the imaginary, phantasmagoric theater of this play is the struggle over what it means to write heroic lives, to tell the history of a person for public consumption. Reading this play, one can feel the poet's immediate encounter with the Roman history which is his principal source. Shakespeare seems to rediscover Plutarch as he writes him up for the stage; his "dialectical imitations" of Roman history form part of an implicit dramatic parable about the work of storytelling, about the struggle to repeat "famous" things, to keep heroic names alive, giving them fresh bodily shape, making them address changing times and demands.[15] The stage character Coriolanus indeed seems caught up in this process himself—something that makes Shakespeare's closeness to Plutarch, as well his pointed differences, so dramatically compelling. The Coriolanus of the *Lives* is a ferociously dangerous hero—uncivil, proud, contemptuous of the plebeians, unadapted to public life—a victimizer who is himself, in the end, victimized.[16] But there is nothing in Plutarch about his resistance to public praise, nor any suggestion that Coriolanus's "eloquence" (which is mentioned in passing) realizes itself primarily in inventive vituperation against those who want to claim his name for themselves. These remarkable inventions of Shakespeare, in turn, seem exactly to respond to the problem of what it means for this man to be composed or recomposed within a heroic history; it is as if Shakespeare had imagined a character who wants to resist or revise the "name" that Plutarch made for him. Insofar as this play is the history of a name, it is also the history of an unnaming and renaming. The honorific "Coriolanus" is the only token of "praise" that he seems to accept without any audible resistance; yet he also loves to take into his mouth the sounds and syllables of that name and to spew them out or scatter them again through his invective, which is filled with words like "cur," "curses," "cry," "carcase," "corn," "kites and crows," "cockle," "choired," "coin," "corrupt," "calved." And insofar as Shakespeare himself takes a stand against Plutarch's representations, questioning the matrix of that history, examining its blank spaces, the hero's negativity finds an echo in the playwright's.

There is, perhaps, one oblique source for the scandal of Coriolanus's voice and fame to be found in Plutarch. But it is a part of the story that

Shakespeare never mentions directly. The play rather calls this passage up in bits and pieces, letting it form a ghostly mirror, or a kind of allegorical sub-text, for Coriolanus's way of being. The passage is itself, tellingly, the report of a questionable rumor. It is a story troubling enough to lead Plutarch to a digression that exposes his own mingled doubt and piety as an interpreter of ancient stories. The Romans, Plutarch writes, built a temple to the goddess Fortuna in order to honor Volumnia, Valeria, and Virgilia, after their success in preventing Coriolanus's attack on Rome. The city itself raised one image of Fortuna in the temple, but the women put up a second image of the god-dess on their own. At the ceremony of dedication, this second statue was re-ported to have uttered the words, "Ladies, ye have devoutly offered me up." Plutarch's consideration of this report leads him to a marvelous excursus about legends concerning miraculous statues. Skepticism breaks in first. If stories about speaking or bleeding statues have any truth in them, it is the re-sult of strictly material accidents:

> For, to see images that seem to sweat or weep, or to put forth any humour red or bloody, it is not a thing unpossible. For wood and stone do commonly receive certain moisture, whereof is engendered an humor, which do yield of themselves, or do take of the air, many sorts and kinds of spots and colours. . . . And it is possible, also, that these images and statues do some-times put forth sounds like unto sighs or mourning, when in the midst or bottom of the same there is made some violent separation, or breaking asun-der of things blown or devised therein.[17]

Plutarch argues first that it is irrational, almost sacrilegious, to find life or intention in such accidents, to believe that soulless objects "should have any direct or exquisite word formed in it by express voice."[18] Such thoughts tes-tify primarily to the power of human fantasy to believe in the impossible. Yet Plutarch's doubt is Pyrrhonistic, even fideistic: as in the *Moralia,* when he writes on the cults of Isis and Osiris, he worries about atheism as much as superstition, the dangers of impiety. At the end of his digression, therefore, he acknowledges that the gods might in fact use such accidental signs of life to provide true oracles about human life and fate; it is, he says, a piety to en-tertain this possibility, to believe that divine intentions are often hidden from us, even if this same piety points equally toward error.[19]

The only direct echo of the story comes in Coriolanus's own parting words after making peace with Rome: "Ladies, you deserve / To have a temple built you" (5.3.206–7). Still, Philip Brockbank is right to say that "Shakespeare seems slily to transpose into human ordeal Plutarch's marvellings about stone images that seem 'to sweat or weep' in Roman temples."[20] Brockbank is thinking of the moment when Coriolanus protests to Aufidius that it is no common thing to make him "sweat compassion," but in fact Plutarch's digression offers an ambivalent emblem for conflicting impulses that shape the entire drama. The statue story points to the imaginary fate of Coriolanus himself; he both is and is not such a noisy statue. Plutarch's hearsay statue suggests his fate as an icon of Roman heroism and piety, a civic hero subject to the shifting whims of superstition and public fantasy—a living tombstone, given life only by what amounts to noise or inhuman wind, given expression only by accidental stains. Coriolanus becomes, like that statue, a tabooed colossus without interior recognitions. Throughout the play, the hero resists attempts to make him an allegorical, daemonic tool in the world of Roman politics, an "administrative god," as Angus Fletcher calls him. He understands (as Aufidius also does) that fame destroys those it enthrones; he sees that insofar as the making of famous heroes "comprises an obsessive system, it opens itself up to fanatic interpretation."[21] The statue thus represents a fate that Coriolanus fears. Yet paradoxically he also strives throughout the play to become something close to a statue, an automaton, a thing, a machine, half human, half inhuman; he becomes a creature whose voice reflects "some violent separation, or breaking asunder" of the unknown substances within it. This more uncivil identity is a fate he embraces, if only because it offers, ironically, his best escape from the sanctioned names and fames, the civic statuary, of Rome. Hence, he becomes, in both his own eyes and those of his family, the invulnerable, inhuman thing that is Rome's enemy, a self-made monster that resists any names or titles, whose fame belongs (if anywhere) to an alien nation. As such he is a thing whose human tears, whether natural or unnatural, can only prove mortal.

This analogy helps one understand the strange kind of play that Shakespeare has written. For Plutarch, the speaking statue raises questions about religious piety and sacrilege. It pushes him to speculate about the nature of supernatural things and to consider their vulnerability to superstition, idolatry, idle fantasy, and skepticism all at once. There is little of the supernatural in *Coriolanus,* little of the shudder at things tabooed. Yet the play does probe our piety and superstition about human nature; it examines the ways in which we can lose or give over our humanity. What concerns us in the play is the human will to put certain images of human life to the test, even the quality of the human will to become inhuman—both in history and in the theater. When, the play asks, is it natural to be unnatural? The gods themselves are not the issue, unless it is a question of what it means to be an *unsuccessful* god.[22]

How simply the fictive hero becomes the real;
How gladly with proper words the soldier dies,
If he must, or lives on the bread of faithful speech.
(Wallace Stevens)

The first task is to describe the combative atmosphere surrounding words in this play. Against Plutarch's statue, consider one of the play's more explicit transfigurations of Coriolanus, at the moment when he has returned home from the Volscian wars and is proclaimed consul by the full Senate of Rome. According to custom, he must stand in the marketplace, dressed in a white garment of humility, and solicit the common people to lend their "voices" to his "election." He must also show them his wounds, those multiple scars that attest to the deeds he has done on behalf of his country. We know by now that Coriolanus hates the commons and loathes the idea of seeking their approval, standing before them as if he had received his wounds "for the hire / Of their breath only" (2.2.148–49). Three citizens who wait for him are equally uncertain about the value of their voices:

> *First citizen.* Once, if he do require our voices, we ought not to deny him.
> *Second citizen.* We may, sir, if we will.
> *Third citizen.* We have a power in ourselves to do it, but it is a power that we have no power to do. For, if he show us his wounds and tell us his deeds, we are to put our tongues into those wounds and speak for them. So if he tell us his noble deeds, we must also tell him our noble acceptance of them. (2.3.1–9)

The last speaker in particular understands that the power of their voices is not entirely their own; their will and Coriolanus's deeds are bound by the ritual form itself and by the political hierarchy it sustains. Their power can be stolen and distributed by others. What nobility they have here is tied to Coriolanus's nobility, and their very tongues are bound by his narration of his deeds. If he follows the ritual, the citizen insists, they will have no power other than to accept his consulship, no power to say other than that his wounds were won for their sake. This sense of having their will stolen, of being forced to do a deed that is not entirely their own, is no doubt the source of that combined disgust and aggression one feels in the citizen's image of placing tongues in those wounds. It is a fantasy in which their tongues reopen and reinflict those wounds, even as those wounds become mouths which steal away those tongues.

The citizen's fear is not his alone (any more than his power is). His unsettling image inadvertently translates a nightmare that haunts Coriolanus himself. (As William Blake might observe, those we hate with most devotion are also those who know us best.) The idea of depending on other tongues to speak his praise and lend him power horrifies Coriolanus throughout the play; his true and ancient enemies are not Volsces but voices. To have his person made heroic by other people's contaminated tongues is to become a monster. Coriolanus's always invisible scars—counted up so lovingly by Volumnia and Meninius, as if they were the bank of Roman nobility—are for Coriolanus himself hypersensitive ears. Or rather, those scars become ears, and fresh wounds, at moments when he must "hear my nothings monster'd" (2.2.77), when the scars are made available for public knowledge and public use. Hence, he conceals his scars from public view (another departure from Plutarch), says nothing of his deeds, and mocks the common people by literalizing their ritualized status as "voices":

> I will make much of your voices . . .
> . . . . . . . . . . . . . . . . . . . . . . . . . .
> Most sweet voices!
> Better it is to die, better to starve,
> Than crave the hire which first we do deserve.
> . . . . . . . . . . . . . . . . . . . . . . . . . . . . . . . .
> Here come moe voices.
> Your voices! For your voices I have fought,
> Watch'd for your voices; for your voices, bear
> Of wounds two dozen odd; battles thrice six
> I have seen and heard of; for your voices have
> Done many things, some less, some more: your voices!
> (2.3.108–29)

Public voice here is nothing but *fama,* rumor, or *fames,* hunger, famine, nothing but empty air, foul breath—no more proper to this hero than the stains and moisture and air that break from Plutarch's corroding statue (marks of time, rather than magical utterance). We hear in this mockery, as D. J. Gordon argues, a powerful critique of fame that runs throughout the play.[23] It is a critique fed by an extreme skepticism of public language, a distrust of what it means to let oneself be spoken of by another. No doubt Coriolanus defames the commons with his descriptions of their emptiness and folly. As the third citizen shows, these speakers are sufficiently aware of both their naked need and their limited power. They also understand something about the conflicts that drive Coriolanus's heroic violence, and even make this knowledge visible to the hero himself. But Coriolanus's way of speaking turns out to be true enough—an accurate picture of the political realities of civic life

in Rome. For these "voices" that approach him do in fact turn out to be un-
usually volatile; they are, as it were, up for grabs, readily manipulated by the
people's own tribunes, who turn the plebeians against Coriolanus and invite
their mythologized voices to cry for Coriolanus's death or banishment. ("We
are the Furies, we are the Furies," cry the vengeful citizens in one eighteenth-
century reworking of the text.)[24] What he hates in these speakers is not so
much their social lowness as that they knowingly take their power from others, and in turn claim a power which is not their own; that even in expressing their resentment of this position they subordinate their voices more fully
to another's influence. For Coriolanus, to be himself subject to such voices
looks like a double cannibalism: it is to be eaten by those who let themselves
be eaten. The third citizen's image, in fact, gives a striking turn to the idea of
Coriolanus's public person as the body of "Rumour, painted full of tongues"
(*2 Henry IV,* induction)—tongues not simply painted on a costume but night-
marishly concrete, penetrating and emerging from the hero's body. We
might even think of this image as a more grotesque, more disenchanted version of that idealized emblem of civic power that appears on the frontispiece
of Thomas Hobbes's *Leviathan,* showing the body of the ruler composed
of the faceless but calmly gathered bodies of his subjects.[25]

It is not just the ceremony of election that troubles Coriolanus, of course;
he cannot bear to hear the commons speak at any time. When he first bursts
onto the stage in act 1—following Meninius's accommodating oration
about the Senate as Rome's good belly, justly distributing nourishment to
the people—Coriolanus seems intent on devouring the people's words. He
turns their protests about the lack of corn into nothing but "shreds" and
"vents" of truth and mocks the tribunes, the "mouths of the people," that had
just been granted them.

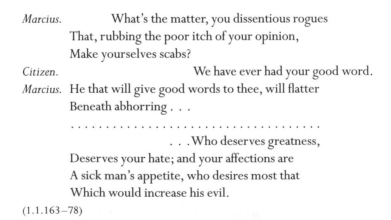

> *Marcius.*          What's the matter, you dissentious rogues
>                     That, rubbing the poor itch of your opinion,
>                     Make yourselves scabs?
> *Citizen.*                              We have ever had your good word.
> *Marcius.* He that will give good words to thee, will flatter
>            Beneath abhorring . . .
>            . . . . . . . . . . . . . . . . . . . . . . . . . . . . . . . . . . .
>                              . . . Who deserves greatness,
>            Deserves your hate; and your affections are
>            A sick man's appetite, who desires most that
>            Which would increase his evil.

(1.1.163–78)

Coriolanus, rather than feed on the people's speech, becomes what Franz Kafka calls "a hunger artist." Feeding on his own starvation, he transfigures the voices of plebeians into the sources of a love which only wastes those who desire it. But it is not only the words of the commons that Coriolanus cannot bear. Even the praise of his fellow aristocrats wounds Coriolanus. Coriolanus can scarcely stand in the same space with any words that mark his deeds, that put his heroism in other mouths. Being praised, he seems crowded out by some sickening shadow version of himself, some degraded image of his own heroism. Indeed, he treats all praise as if it were, in truth, a form of abuse or slander, or a flattery that makes its object "beneath abhoring." What Coriolanus sees, I think, is that other speakers do not know the cost of their words; they do not measure the desolation that those words can bring about. Nor is Coriolanus ever in a position to explain this to them, or to provide their ears with the power to hear his reasons.

This loathing of praise breaks in strikingly after the hero's victories in the Volscian wars, as his fellow soldiers prepare the chariot of praise that will carry Coriolanus back to the city. The general Cominius says, "If I should tell thee o'er this thy day's work, / Thou't not believe thy deeds; but I'll report it" (1.9.1–2). Coriolanus refuses to listen when they begin to praise those deeds in public. The instruments of war are, he complains, profaned in such a celebration. He not only tries to silence any telling over of his deeds, but converts his acts into a kind of empty, infantile triumph:

> No more, I say!
> For that I have not wash'd my nose that bled,
> Or foil'd some debile wretch, which without note
> Here's many else have done, you shout me forth
> In acclamations hyperbolical,
> As if I lov'd my little should be dieted
> In praises sauc'd with lies.
> (46–52)

Such delicacy of ear, such a way of being "cruel to your good report," seems evident madness to Cominius, who promises jokingly to put the hero in manacles, "like one that means his proper harm" (56). His wounds, Cominius says, must either speak their own praise, or "fester 'gainst ingratitude, / And tent themselves with death" (30–31). Those wounds, then, must be made to speak by others:

> You shall not be
> The grave of your deserving; Rome must know

The value of her own. 'Twere a concealment
Worse than a theft, no less than a traducement,
To hide your doings.
(19–23)

But again, in the face of such praise, Coriolanus's wounds develop ears that "smart / To hear themselves remember'd" (28–29). Later he will try to leave the stage itself, saying, "I had rather have my wounds to heal again / Than hear say how I got them" (2.2.69–70). It is in this scene, we should remember, that Cominius has offered one of the play's great transfiguring visions of Coriolanus, an epic recounting of his heroism that begins with his ardent childhood, and ends thus:

> his sword, death's stamp,
> Where it did mark, it took; from face to foot
> He was a thing of blood, whose every motion
> Was tim'd with dying cries: alone he enter'd
> The mortal gate of th'city, which he painted
> With shunless destiny, aidless came off,
> And with a sudden reinforcement struck
> Corioles like a planet.
> (107–114)

Yet Coriolanus will not stay "to hear my nothings monster'd," as if such public mythopoesis were nothing but distorting report, monster-making rumor.

Such flight from public praise, as if it were something tabooed or impure, has an irrational ardor about it. Coriolanus implicitly defends a private language of heroism—"mine own truth"—about which the play gives us few clues. To many critics, his attitude suggests a mad resistance to the facts of living in the world. Insofar as he refuses to share in the matrix of common speech, he refuses to become part of the community of need which that speech serves. In Janet Adelman's forceful psychoanalytic reading, this hatred is really a displaced revenge for having had human nourishment early denied him by his own mother, who pushed him so early to the wars, as if to fulfill her own thwarted hunger for violence.[26] Hence, he must nourish himself with his own spilt blood rather than with her milk, even though his "pose of self-sufficient manhood" continues to reflect his subjection to the mother who thus starves him. In this account, Adelman in fact echoes Coriolanus's own fellow aristocrats, who often treat him as a wrongheaded, dangerous, and self-destructive child. Yet in taking Coriolanus's postures as merely regressive, infantile in the opprobrious sense, one risks overlooking not only Coriolanus's eerier pictures of his virtue (where he exceeds any vision of heroism his mother offers), but also the profound political intelligence that sifts through his rages against *fama*. For Coriolanus's hearing is as acute as Hamlet's; the noise of the battlefield has not dulled his ear for the political lie, for evasive double meanings or self-flattering equivocations.[27] It is not lies merely about himself that enrage him. It is also the treachery of other ears—ears that are hungry for self-deception and falsehood, ears all too ready to believe others' words about the power of their tongues.[28] What offends him about the plebeians is not their hatred—which makes him happy—but their readiness to have their wills changed by others or to be buoyed up by a power that they possess only as part of a mob. He understands and is repelled by their *hunger* for other people's words, their appetite for empty reassurances and self-flattering rumors, their facile brandishing of words like "will" and "shall" and "must." He distrusts just as much the passive accommodations that guide his fellow patricians, which seem to him a cowardly self-betrayal. What he sees, and hates, is not simply their factional wrangling, but how they appropriate his fame for their own uses, in particular by identifying his heroism with their own merely political power. He knows that the magical substance of his heroism has become a dangerous but necessary commodity, such that even his own mother is ready to convert his pride and honor into the material for a Machiavellian public show. We might thus hear not just infantile rage, but a moral, even prophetic register in Coriolanus's contempt—something implicit in Stanley Cavell's evocative comparison of Coriolanus to Montaigne's taunting cannibal, and even to the Son of Man in Revelation, from whose mouth a prophetic sword emerges.[29] Coriolanus's words, like Christ's, ask his audience if they have "ears to hear" truths other than those which they already know.

Coriolanus cannot conceive of escaping to a speculative or interior place such as tempts Hamlet. Neither his own mind nor the kingdom of the Volscians offers a "world elsewhere," free from the labyrinth of politics. Such a world looms within this play only on the battlefield. The theater of war is the only stage on which Coriolanus can bear something like acting, or allow himself to be spoken by other voices. In the city, he is washed free of blood, garbed in white, a heroic corpus bristling with tongues of cowards that poke through his wounds. On the battlefield, that nightmare is replaced by the spectacle of his body entirely covered in blood; it is a royal robe, or rather, the one form of theatrical makeup he can readily ask others to share—as when he invites support in battle only from those of his soldiers who "love this painting / Wherein you see me smear'd" (1.6.68–69). Such painting is, as it were, a voice of blood, all the more uncanny because we cannot quite tell to whom the blood belongs, or of what particular violence it speaks. During the battle, in conversation with his general Titus Lartius—who lauds him for his courage but wishes him to rest—Coriolanus implies that the blood on his body is his own, a spillage that mysteriously gives him strength: "Sir, praise me not . . . / The blood I drop is rather physical / Than dangerous to me" (1.5.16–19). But when he faces Aufidius at the battle's climax, Coriolanus claims that the blood which mantles him belongs to his victims: " 'tis not my blood / Wherein thou seest me mask'd" (1.8.9–10). As such it becomes a badge of terror and contempt. Whosever blood he carries, however, one thing is clear: the force of that blood is confined to the battlefield alone; it cannot be enshrined, or bottled, or used to paint a public mural. After the battle, he refers to that blood itself with marked disdain, refusing to be praised, as he says, "For that I have not wash'd my nose that bled."

Coriolanus's mask of blood amplifies a peculiar voice. On the battlefield, in lieu of empty voices, stinking breath, shreds of wisdom, and political lying, we have the voice of the war itself, the *noise* of war that not only spreads around Coriolanus but gathers in his mouth.[30] As Volumnia says, "before him he carries noise, and behind him he leaves tears" (2.1.157–58). Or Cominius: "from face to foot / He was a thing of blood, whose every motion / Was tim'd with dying cries" (2.2.108–10). Coriolanus possesses what one Roman soldier calls a "throat of war," a voice that becomes the signature sound of Coriolanus himself: "The shepherd knows not thunder from a tabor, / More than I know the sound of Martius's tongue / From every meaner man" (1.6.25–27). This voice echoes the "thunder-like percussion" of his sword blows. Coriolanus also has an ear of war, so that, when "the din of war gan pierce / His ready sense" (2.2.115–16), he discovers fresh strength to fight, and finds his way to the heart of the battle through the field of noise.[31]

This deep association of war and noise is no idiosyncracy of the play. As Paul A. Jorgensen has amply shown, Shakespeare throughout his work organizes his theatrical wars very much around structures of sound—keying the battles to offstage drums or pipes, trumpet "alarums," cannon shots, and cries, filling his characters' ears with the rumors of war, true and untrue. War noise can mingle with the sound of storms (as in *King Lear*) or with the sounds of kingly carousing (as in *Hamlet*).[32] From a pragmatic, theatrical point of view, such sound play reinforces the mimesis of battle onstage, helping the audience to "piece out our imperfections with your thoughts," as the chorus to *Henry V* urges. Such stage devices also reflect the literal practice of Renaissance warfare, in which the sound of drums, trumpets, and fifes was considered essential for maintaining order and discipline on the battlefield, carrying commands over the less orderly din, signaling the position of troops, warning of changed circumstances, and so on. These martial sounds roused the energy and determination of an army at the same time as they might frighten its enemy. Here even the nonmusical clamor of war could be thought of as a kind of music, both human and inhuman, echoing the noise of oceans, tempests, or animals. As Jorgensen makes clear, Renaissance treatises on war often see it as a violent but essentially orderly, rational activity. Machiavelli, for instance, understood war as an agent and example of civilized harmony, an extreme test of the human power to keep in balance the order of kingdoms and peoples, as well as a school that trained citizen soldiers in discipline, obedience, and virtue. The bellow of ordnance, the clash of armor, and the cries of men—enraged and in pain, attacking and dying—all formed part of a complex, even strategic symphony. Giacomo Porcia, in *The Preceptes of Warre* (1544), argues that it is a good thing in battle for "al the host to make an outcrye, brefely to fyll heaven and earth with the noyse and sound of trompettes, and make all on a rore, wherewith thyne enemyes be afrayd, & thy frendes gladdened."[33]

The noise of war has a peculiar register in *Coriolanus*. The fundamental reason for this is simply that such noise appertains so closely to the person of the hero.[34] This helps us to understand the kind of war that Coriolanus makes, and hence, in the end, the kind of peace. As it is filtered through that noise, Coriolanus's warfare cannot be seen as "an extension of politics by other means" (von Clausewitz's formula). It is not "glorious war," as it is for Othello, full of pomp, pride, and circumstance, resonant with the sound of trumpets and horses; indeed, the minute that the trumpets and cries of the battle are taken over by triumphal celebration, their sounds become poisonous, flattering, and empty for Coriolanus. His war does not feed the grand, sometimes vengeful music of royal sovereignty or civic peace, as in the history plays, nor does it reinforce the noise of petty wrangling and contemptuous satire, as in *Troilus and Cressida*. Coriolanus's war noise does not echo the frantic spells of witches, as in *Macbeth*, or the shrieks of ghosts, as in *Hamlet*. His is not quite the quasi-magical, terrifying, anarchic *furor* of ancient Germanic warriors that Georges Dumézil studies (and sees as opposed to the discipline of Roman military practice).[35] Nor is it (despite

Volumnia's representations) the collective brutality of war noise that attracts this hero, much less pleasure in others' suffering; modern stage versions of Coriolanus as a Fascist strongman get it wrong. To a degree, Coriolanus's attachment to battle resembles Fulke Greville's ambivalent fascination with war as at once violent ruin and renovating purgation.[36] Yet what Coriolanus primarily takes from the noise of war is a kind of moral candor and freedom; it is a freedom associated with a realm of physical risk and violence, but also one of clear knowledge and action. Centered as it is on Coriolanus himself, that noise of war indeed suggests a private language, but one in which, paradoxically, nothing is hidden (though much may be lost, and abandoned). Such noise belongs to a domain of pure or at least purifying food, a realm where even "the blood I drop is rather physical / Than dangerous to me." It is a noise associated with his solitary heroism, especially his virtual death and rebirth within the gate of Corioles; it projects a rage that isolates him, somewhat as Turnus—the anti-Virgilian hero—is progressively isolated within the *Aeneid*.[37] For Coriolanus, the clamor of battle is something that no merely political order, no cult or social hypocrisy, can possess for itself. And unlike the sounds made by Plutarch's statue, it is a noise that no skepticism dare call in doubt, a noise that sharpens rather than dulls Coriolanus's ear for the tricks of Roman political debate. The war, in fact, gives to Coriolanus a wilder, a more capacious sense of hearing than that possessed by anyone else in the play.

This noise inhabits Coriolanus; it is at once a mythic thing and a token of the real.[38] Hence, perhaps, the strange but inevitable fact that he refuses to let that noise remain isolated on the field of battle. Coriolanus's deep risk, the fundamental shape his folly and heroism takes, is to bring his "throat of war" into the city. As such, his noise will not be ordered and domesticated; it cannot (as the first section of T. S. Eliot's "Coriolan" suggests) be made part of a triumphal march.[39] Nor is that noise translated into the grandiose, often melodramatic jargon that characterizes oratorical soldiers like Othello—mocked by Iago for his use of "bombast circumstance / Horribly stuffed with epithets of war" (1.1.12–13), echoing the Latin tradition of the *miles gloriosus*.[40] If Coriolanus disobeys the ancient Roman law against armies entering the precincts of the city, it is by carrying in a noise of war which takes the form of savage, self-destructive vituperation. That noise forms part of a "theater" that the citizens of Rome cannot abide, perhaps even recognize, since it is neither common nor elitist in any easy-to-define way. On the battlefield, such noise is the form of Coriolanus's heroic mastery. In Rome, it cuts him off from persuasion, makes his wisdom inaudible, dangerous, out of tune, mistaken for the mere blunt outbursts of a thoughtless soldier.[41] It makes him both more and less than human. (He who would live outside the city "must be either a beast or a god," wrote Aristotle in the *Politics*.[42] Coriolanus wants to bring that outsideness inside.) Powerful as it is, such war noise betokens an order which yet remains unripe, larval, childish, somewhat like Coriolanus himself; its revelations cannot face or nourish what matures, what shapes itself in time. Something that R. P. Blackmur wrote about the conceptual effect of the Second World War resonates with Coriolanus's war as well: "War with its violence and *its imposition of adventitious order* only shows us what we already lacked, or had let go, or ignored."[43] (Here Machiavelli's *virtú* would only serve the ends of *fortuna*.)

The chilling eloquence of Coriolanus's vituperation comes through most strongly at the moment of his exile. Here he indicts the people's own poisonous powers of speech and hearing, bequeathing to the city an image of its present desolation:

> You common cry of curs! whose breath I hate
> As reek o'th'rotten fens, whose loves I prize
> As the dead carcasses of unburied men
> That do corrupt my air: I banish you!
> And here remain with your uncertainty!
> Let every feeble rumour shake your hearts!
> Your enemies, with nodding of their plumes,
> Fan you into despair! Have the power still
> To banish your defenders, till at length
> Your ignorance—which finds not till it feels,
> Making but reservation of yourselves,
> Still your own foes—deliver you as most
> Abated captives to some nation
> That won you without blows! Despising
> For you the city, thus I turn my back.
> There is a world elsewhere!
> (3.3.120–35)

The metamorphic verve of this text takes on the aspect of hallucination, half accurate satire and half projection. The entire city becomes, first, a bearbaiting pit full of howling dogs—Coriolanus being, by extension, the victimized, bellowing bear. Coriolanus also projects the city as a battlefield, but a battlefield *after* the battle, filled not with living warriors, Roman or Volscian, but littered with the dead. Urban Rome, its swamps so carefully drained, becomes a fenlike wilderness full of the corpses, without burial or obsequy, of creatures whose breath is their stench, a vehicle of a plague rather than a form of life. He leaves to the Roman people the legacy of their own empty power, the power of that noise which banishes those who defend them, the force of those "feeble rumors" which terrify rather than rouse their weak hearts. Coriolanus's words are not a curse, strictly speaking, since he calls upon nothing but what, as he sees it, the Romans already suffer; their fate is something that needs neither his word nor a punishing god's to underwrite it. He gives back to the citizens what he already knows they possess—their viciousness, their suspicion, and their mutable spirit. His parting taunt, "I banish you," which appropriates to himself the sovereign power of a king or commonwealth, is not so much blind as naked, since it so plainly acknowledges the impotence of his words in the city, even as it conveys his contempt of civic words.

Turned as he is against the civic spectacles and politic disguisings of Rome, Coriolanus projects the possibility of a different kind of theater of war, neither popular nor elite, neither objective nor subjective, a theater of cruelty that must be, as Antonin Artaud thought, as cruel to the actor as it is to the audience.[44] The music or noise of this theater is more caustic, more spare in its charms than that of the central tragedies, yet in the end just as harrowing.

―――――

What power is left to Coriolanus after he exiles himself? Abandoning Rome, Coriolanus crosses over the threshold into a world not entirely elsewhere, but not yet defined. From this realm, he promises his mother, she will hear nothing but echoes of what he was like formerly. He departs uncertainly, like an "lonely dragon" (4.1.30). The city of Rome is now the truer wilderness, so the literal wilderness around it becomes "th'city of kites and crows" (4.5.43). His only possession turns out to be something his enemy has a part in: his name, and the memory of shame that goes with it. This he brings with him as he arrives, like an incarnation of the uncanny, at Aufidius's house in Antium. Provoking at first nothing but a comic, if also vaguely haunting, confusion among the servants who cannot displace this muffled intruder, Coriolanus's arrival finally calls out Aufidius himself:

> *Aufidius.*  Whence com'st thou? What wouldst thou? thy name?
> Why speak'st not? Speak, man: what's thy name?
> *Coriolanus.* [*unmuffling*]                                        If, Tullus,
> Not yet thou know'st me, and, seeing me, dost not

>                       Think me for the man I am, necessity
>                       Commands me name myself.
> *Aufidius.*                               What is thy name?
> *Coriolanus.* A name unmusical to the Volscians' ears,
>                       And harsh in sound to thine.
> *Aufidius.*                                   Say, what's thy name?
>                       Thou hast a grim appearance, and thy face
>                       Bears a command in't. Though thy tackle's torn,
>                       Thou show'st a noble vessel. What's thy name?
> *Coriolanus.* Prepare thy brow to frown: know'st thou me yet?
> *Aufidius.* I know thee not! Thy name?
> *Coriolanus.* My name is Caius Marcius, who hath done
>                       To thee particularly, and to all the Volsces,
>                       Great hurt and mischief: thereto witness may
>                       My surname, Coriolanus. The painful service,
>                       The extreme dangers, and the drops of blood
>                       Shed for my thankless country, are requited
>                       But with that surname: a good memory,
>                       And witness of the malice and displeasure
>                       Which thou should'st bear me. Only that name remains.

(4.5.54–74)

Angus Fletcher catches the intense strangeness of the encounter, the sense of something urgent yet out of phase, oddly childish: "One wonders what sort of game these grown men are playing, unless this is some kind of ritual, which, without preamble, they understand and go through, to test the sacred bond between them."[45] They are like two magicians, Fletcher thinks: Aufidius tries to find out whether his opponent's credentials are good, whereas Coriolanus holds his name back, as if to prevent himself, like Rumpelstiltskin, from falling too much into another's power. The name Coriolanus becomes the material of a fragile, latent spell—unmusical, provoking frowns. Aufidius, in the logic of romance, cannot even recognize this apparition until he is given the right name for it. We could say that Coriolanus is trying to redirect the ambivalent charge of his name, the electricity of his reputation, in a way he never could have done in his native city. At the end, he releases the "spell" of his name to Aufidius only on such terms as facilitate his revenge.

Coriolanus rehearses for the mute Aufidius his history of being "whooped" out of Rome by popular noise. With undisguised contempt, he offers himself to his former enemy, either to be killed or to be made use of.

He speaks like one of the dead, the compressed account of his history possessing the uncanny completeness of those stories offered up by souls in Dante's Inferno or Purgatory—though Coriolanus's vision of his punishment belongs entirely to the historical world, the world of names and fames. The starkness of his vision is conveyed, perhaps, by Percy Bysshe Shelley's striking echo of Coriolanus's "only that name remains" in his description of the desolate ruin of Ozymandias's statue, a thing that stands at once for the ruin of human work and for its infectious afterlife within human history: "Nothing beside remains."[46] The astonishing thing is that, despite this desolation, despite his devotion to provoking only hatred, Coriolanus starts in his enemy a different kind of devotion:

> O Martius, Martius!
> Each word thou hast spoke hath weeded from my heart
> A root of ancient envy. If Jupiter
> Should from yond cloud speak divine things
> And say, "'Tis true," I'd not believe them more
> Than thee, all-noble Martius. Let me twine
> Mine arms about that body, where against
> My grained ash an hundred times hath broke,
> And scarr'd the moon with splinters. Here I clip
> The anvil of my sword, and do contest
> As hotly and as nobly with thy love
> As ever in ambitious strength I did
> Contend against thy valour. Know thou first,
> I lov'd the maid I married; never man
> Sigh'd truer breath; but that I see thee here,
> Thou noble thing, more dances my rapt heart
> Than when I first my wedded mistress saw
> Bestride my threshold . . .
> . . . . . . . . . . . . . . . . . . . . . . . . . . . . . .
> . . . Thou hast beat me out
> Twelve several times, and I have nightly since
> Dreamt of encounters 'twixt thyself and me—
> We have been down together in my sleep,
> Unbuckling helms, fisting each other's throat—
> And wak'd half dead with nothing.
> (102–27)

What is it like to find oneself the object of an archenemy's dream? What mingling of private and public history unfolds here, and how does it answer

Coriolanus's own story—nightmarish enough, perhaps, but not a dream, since Coriolanus never dreams? The wildness of the tasks that Shakespeare sets for his actors comes through as amazingly here as anywhere else in the canon. Consider the ambiguous register of these words, even the uncertain weight of the pause that must carry Aufidius's shock; consider the astonishment of a presence which breaks open the floodgates of such love, love that strives to repossess the spell of his enemy's power (partly by refusing to use the name won from the Volscians—he calls him only "Martius"). Aufidius wonders aloud that his rage has so quickly vanished, rooted from his heart as he so fervently embraces his enemy's body. Perhaps he finds in Coriolanus's story enough of a sop for his resentment that his profound imaginative identification with his rival can finally break through. As Aufidius speaks, he becomes a kind of exotic Cleopatra, absorbing a more austere image of Roman heroism within an extravagant revery, a dream history of erotized violence. What had Aufidius seen, as he caught a glimpse of the silent moon above the noisy, nighttime battlefield? His words project a fantasy in which the memory of war's violence is translated into a mingled vision of almost inhuman strength (the spear breaking against the body) and displaced cosmic vulnerability (the moon scarred with splinters, mirroring the scarred body of Coriolanus). Aufidius speaks like a late survivor of a Marlovian theater, though with a coloring of elegy that Marlowe could never have managed. His words also suggest a competitive, homoerotic love driving this warrior's aggression. The question is, How much does Aufidius's version of things catch the truth of Coriolanus? Powerful as his words are, they may only remind us by contrast of the more opaque impulse that drives Coriolanus's violence. Perhaps the most important thing to note dramaturgically is Coriolanus's absolute muteness after he hears this speech, when Aufidius leads him away to meet the Volscian nobility. At this moment, the exiled warrior's vituperation and loathing are absorbed within the prospect of an active revenge, his noise silenced until the very close of the play.

---

All through earlier scenes, we have been made to glimpse Coriolanus through the mirrors of his friends and enemies. We see him, for instance, in Volumnia's vision of Hector's wounded forehead—more beautiful than his mother's breasts, when it "spit forth blood / At Grecian sword contemning" (1.3.42–43); we see him also in Valeria's vision of Coriolanus's son, chasing and tearing a butterfly. Such pictures as these reinforce, rather than contradict, what we ourselves see of the hero's violent work. Immediately after the encounter with Aufidius, however, as soon as he joins the Volscian campaign, Coriolanus disappears more fully from our view. His person recedes behind a network of rumors and reports, offered both by his new allies and by his former friends and enemies in Rome. In the "news" of both sides he emerges as something ever more uncanny, something magical and daemonic. A Volscian lieutenant wonders "what witchcraft's in him" (4.7.2), to make his former enemies so flock to his command. Cominius reports that he leads the Volscians "like a thing / Made by some other deity than nature" (4.6.91–92), and Aufidius says that he "fights dragon-like, and does achieve as soon / As draw his sword" (4.7.23–24). Meninius, trying to terrorize the cowed tribunes, speaks of Coriolanus in words that recall God's descriptions of Behemoth and Leviathan in the Book of Job: "When he walks, he moves like an engine and the ground shrinks before his treading. He is able to pierce a corslet with his eye, talks like a knell, and his hum is a battery. He sits in his state as a thing made for Alexander. What he bids be done is finished with his bidding" (5.4.18–23). Coriolanus looms up in these scenes as a kind of international ghost, unresponsive to negotiation, unmoveable as death. It is at this moment, when he achieves his most frightening presence in the imagination of the world, that Coriolanus himself is most ready to have his identity disappear. His wish to transfigure himself through the desolation of praise now projects a rebirth that is even more extreme than the one which took place at Corioles. Hence, as Cominius reports of their meeting before the gates of Rome:

> "Coriolanus"
> He would not answer to; forbad all names:
> He was a kind of nothing, titleless,
> Till he had forg'd himself a name o'th'fire
> Of burning Rome.
> (5.1.11–15)

The idea that he will forge himself "a name o'th'fire / Of burning Rome" suggests that his attack on his native city will recapitulate the battle at Corioles—where, cut off from his armies, facing almost certain death, out of our sight, he reemerged reborn, covered with blood, having found a new name. Now it is a second catastrophe, actively aimed against his place of origins, his devouring mother, that must gain him—if we follow the analogy—a title which can carry only the extremest irony, the name *Romanus*.[47]

When we finally see Coriolanus himself, awaiting a Roman embassy, he is fashioning himself into someone invulnerable to all human need, closing himself off to any private appeals; he desires to act as if he could cut himself off from all influences of nature and history, which have up to this point so readily betrayed him. The danger is not from swords now, but from whatever voices might appeal to that place in himself where honor and humanity are at odds. We see him preparing not his physical weapons but his ears and eyes. At the moment when the ladies approach to beg for mercy, he says (whether to himself or to Aufidius is not clear), "I'll never / Be such a gosling to obey instinct, but stand / As if a man were author of himself / And knew no other kin" (5.3.34–37). He throws himself into the posture of sculptor and statue at once, becoming an autochthonous object unable to "sweat compassion." Many critics take his image of self-sufficiency as a final delusion: enraged by his dependence on the matrix of social and political speech that always betrays him, disgusted by his simple kinship with other humans and their language, he attempts to unknow what he cannot help but know. But accusing Coriolanus of philosophical error or infantile resentment misses the point. His insistent "as if," at least, suggests that he is aware of the merely ideal, hypothetical status of being author of oneself. But it is the only stance left to him in the face of a world he knows too well and cannot bear.[48]

The undoing of Coriolanus's hardness is the great crisis of the play, a moment of triumph for Volumnia, a moment of humanizing pity and bitter knowledge for Coriolanus. Volumnia's influence has been a theme throughout the play, but she looms up in this scene with special force, as if, at the end of the things, she must reassume that largeness of presence which we imagine her having had for Coriolanus in his childhood. She is, or tries to become, his "instinct." Stripped of all means but her words and her knowledge of her son, she indeed acquires something of the uncanny persuasiveness of the ghost in *Hamlet,* or of Lady Macbeth, but with the difference that Volumnia compels peace rather than violence. How is it that Coriolanus knows, with immediate conviction, that Volumnia's having "prevail'd" with him to make peace cannot be anything but "most mortal" (5.3.188–89) to him?

Throughout the play, Volumnia has represented a kind of full emptiness, a joining of desolation and absoluteness. She contains and tallies heroic stories, wounds, blood, and scars. She stands for an economy of substitutions whereby, had her son himself died, "his good report should have been my son" (1.3.20). Her "nursing" of her son involves, as Adelman makes clear, a kind of heroic famishing; sending him away, she gives him, instead of milk, his own spilt blood, blood which nourishes her in turn, since it becomes a sign of his wished-for heroism, a token of her son's contempt for his enemies. To quote that remarkable text yet again: "The breasts of Hecuba / When she did suckle Hector, look'd not lovelier / Than Hector's forehead when it spit forth blood / At Grecian sword contemning" (1.3.40–43). In the middle scenes of the play, we also see Volumnia as an explicitly Machiavellian stage manager, ready to have her son use his scars as theater, urging him to sacrifice even his sovereign contempt if it will palliate the anger of the mob and secure his consulship. When he continually resists her persuasions, she turns from maternal praise to maternal taunts, even disowning the angry part of him: "At thy choice then: . . . Come all to ruin. . . . Do as thou list. / Thy valiantness was mine, thou suck'st it from me, / But owe thy pride thyself" (3.2.123–30).

After Coriolanus's exile from Rome, Volumnia becomes herself the hunger artist: "Anger's my meat: I sup upon myself / And so shall starve with feeding" (4.2.50–51). Indeed, she takes upon herself some of her banished son's rage and becomes herself the chief mad person in the city of Rome. Reappearing before her son at the end, Volumnia seems ready to devour all words, all postures, all space, all nobility, all alternative forms of fame or futurity in which Coriolanus might act as "author of himself." Aufidius had said that a man's virtues "lie in th'interpretation of the time" (4.7.50). Speaking to Coriolanus in act 5, Volumnia seems to assume the mantle of time itself, or of Spenser's Nature, warning rebellious Mutabilitie, "thy decay thou seekst by thy desire," interpreting to Coriolanus the full madness of the situation he has created.[49] She shows him her own and her family's desolations in the present, their baffled love and hope. With oracular certainty she promises him answering desolations in the future, should he fulfill his purpose, especially "such a name / Whose repetition will be dogg'd with curses" (5.3.143–44). In stunning contrast to her earliest teaching, she denies the virtues of a militant posture, the nourishing loveliness of a "contemning" blood, praising instead the making of peace as the best means to honor—retrospectively emptying out Coriolanus's own voice of war, making it seem bloodless, even cowardly. During all of this, Coriolanus stands silent.

Volumnia has devoured a lot of Plutarch as well, from whose text come her depictions of loss, her appeals to Coriolanus's love and honor, her recommendations of peace, and her promises of curses. What we have seen of her earlier advice to Coriolanus, and perhaps the mere fact that this long speech unfolds in dramatic verse, can make Volumnia's words here seem calculated and self-dramatizing. Shakespeare's additions to the scene only increase this feeling, in particular the lines where she taunts her son for his refusal to break his silence and respond to her pleas. Here, Volumnia reduces Coriolanus's complex silence to nothing but a peevish game. She shames her son by staging her own shame, imputing to Coriolanus the desire to humiliate her by his silence, challenging that silence with the image of herself as an abused mother prating in the stocks: "Thou hast never in thy life / Show'd thy dear mother any courtesy" (160–61). In a remarkable parting shot— this is a play full of parting shots, as *Hamlet* is full of eerie good nights— Volumnia as Mother Time strips Coriolanus of his family, gives him a new nativity, and by implication makes even his heroic "surname" a mere place-name rather than something won in a miraculous fight. The only voice she allows him is the voice to dismiss them. At the end, she faces him with the surmise of a small, violent sound breaking the silence, preempting the noise of any "name o'th fire" he might make in burning Rome:

> Come, let us go:
> This fellow had a Volscian to his mother;
> His wife is in Corioles, and his child
> Like him by chance. Yet give us our dispatch:
> I am husht until our city be afire,
> And then I'll speak a little.
> [*He holds her by the hand silent*]
> (177–82)

One can be moved by that famous stage direction, which shifts the silence from one body to two; one knows how much weight such silences can carry in the theater. But in a play in which Aufidius tells Coriolanus, after his mother's speech, "I was mov'd withal" (194), nothing about being "moved" is certain, either for the audience or for the characters. This is how Coriolanus breaks out after his long silence onstage—with the knowledge of his mother's "victory" and the mortal danger he now inhabits:

> O mother, mother!
> What have you done? Behold, the heavens do ope,
> The gods look down, and this unnatural scene
> They laugh at. O my mother, mother! O!
> You have won a happy victory to Rome;
> But for your son, believe it, O, believe it,
> Most dangerously you have with him prevail'd,
> If not most mortal to him. But let it come.
> (182–89)

There is something primal, even infantile suggested by the text's "O my mother, mother! O!" It is not quite like Othello's animal-like howlings—

"O, Desdemona, dead," or Lear's "Howl, howl, howl, howl," or Posthumus's "O Imogen, Imogen"——but still one hears a tone of naked mournfulness pointedly in contrast to his trimphant reassurances to his mother about "happy" victories, or his earlier comment about theirs being a meeting unnatural enough for gods to "laugh at." He is here cut off completely from his mother, even as he yields to her. Tellingly, uncannily, Coriolanus's astonished cry takes its shape from the cry of his own enemy:

> O Martius, Martius!
> Each word thou hast spoke hath weeded from my heart
> A root of ancient envy. If Jupiter
> Should from yond cloud speak divine things
> And say " 'Tis true," I'd not believe them more
> Than thee, all-noble Martius.

Aufidius's "O" is a little like the apostrophe of a love sonnet, something rapturous that redeems a memory of loathing and hatred; it changes past encounters into lyric dream, even as it promises a shared, triumphal future. Coriolanus's "O," by contrast, turns the surprise of his own words against himself. In the cry to his mother, rapture is a mockery, and both past and future shut down. The notes of protest and mourning in his words mix with the certain knowledge that his resolve can only cut him off further; his sudden "pity" toward Rome is a sign of defeat. Even to call it pity, or sympathy, perhaps, is too much. The state of Coriolanus's heart receives no report. No utterance lets us in on the state of his ancient envy or love, his past dreams. Coriolanus desires mostly that we believe the unlikely certainty of his death: "But for your son, *believe it, O, believe it,* / Most dangerously you have with him prevail'd, / If not most mortal to him."[50]

Coriolanus's sweat of tears, his decision to "make peace" instead of war, should mark the emergence of some more human feeling. This is a moment when the violent, nameless statue should, as it were, become flesh and return to a shared communal life. Yet the life of statues is equivocal here, and not for the same reasons that Plutarch indicates. As with the awakening of the statue of Hermione, Coriolanus's "melting" is a test of both our faith and our skepticism. It is not that we don't recognize some breaking out of pathos, vulnerability, and pity, some return to humanity; one can hear a terrible gentleness in Coriolanus's tone. Still, Coriolanus's knowledge of his situation is stark; this statue cannot come to life without dying. There is no speech, no posture available to him which can restore the earlier motions of his raging life. Aufidius and Coriolanus's mother say nothing to deny his intuition that he will die. As we shall see, his tears all too quickly become the matter of insult, accusation, and shame. His resolve to work a treaty feels brittle, unselving: "Aufidius, though I cannot make true wars, / I'll frame convenient peace" (5.3.190–91). The word "convenient" can only sound contemptuous in the mouth of this past master of inconvenience, one whose principal form of making was of the violent truth of war, who framed his acts only in *unframing* things. From the bare text, of course, it is hard to say what jointure of bitter knowledge and treacherous optimism an actor might find in these words. The point is that there is nothing in the words of the text to reassure us. The loss of the power to make war is, for Coriolanus, the loss of almost everything.

---

What has it meant for Coriolanus to make war instead of peace? What in this shows us Coriolanus's art of drama? Here we must go back to the name-giving moment in act 1—the fight at Corioles—which seems to loom throughout through the play as his freest moment of self-realizing violence. At the height of the siege, running offstage in a burst of anger at his cowardly soldiers, Caius Martius enters the gate of the alien city. It looks like madness to his troops, a kind of self-destructive bravado. During this interval, Titus Lartius enters and, hearing what has happened, offers a speech of astonished praise. In this he converts Martius into a miracle of daring, of standing, a monstrous jewel that makes a terrifying noise. Moving quickly from present to past tense, Lartius's words become, in fact, an elegy for a hero who must, by all reason, be dead:

> Oh noble fellow!
> Who sensibly outdares his senseless sword,
> And when it bows, stand'st up. Thou art left, Martius:
> A carbuncle entire, as big as thou art,
> Were not so rich a jewel. Thou wast a soldier
> Even to Cato's wish, not fierce and terrible
> Only in strokes, but with thy grim looks and
> The thunder-like percussion of thy sounds
> Thou mad'st thine enemies shake, as if the world
> Were feverous and did tremble.
> (1.4.52–61)

Despite the fact that Martius has been left "alone to answer all the city," cut off, and surrounded by enemies, he somehow kills the Volscian guards and opens the gates again. Having fled away in a rage, he reenters covered in blood, "as he were flay'd," silent, almost like a ghost. Without words, he draws reinforcements back in and takes the city for Rome.

What happens within the gates of Corioles remains a blank, a black hole into which our wonder and speculation vanish. It is an image at once bright and dark, black and red, voiceless, but full of surmised clamor; it suggests a violence that is mortal, impossible to survive, so that surviving it is a testimony to something preternatural in Coriolanus himself. As a moment of offstage killing, the fight within the gates might recall the unseen murders committed by tragic heroes like Medea or Orestes, even the self-destructive violence of Oedipus and Milton's Samson. It is scarcely a tragic climax, however; rather, it is a fresh beginning. This unreadable, almost miraculous event fixes a new public identity for Caius Martius, wins him the honorific title "Coriolanus." But within the scope of the play as a whole, within Martius's own memory, it acquires a stranger glamour. Reemerging covered with the blood of alien soldiers, he is like an unwashed, newborn child, at once pristine and painted, waiting to be rebaptized with a name we do not yet know. This becomes, indeed, the image of an event which Coriolanus's career aims at or projects, but at which he never arrives. Memories of that fight hover around him at the gates of Rome, as he imagines making for himself "a name o'th'fire" in burning the city that exiled him (giving himself over to the fire of his own rage). And he conjures up those memories again at the moment of his murder by Volscian soldiers, in a last attempt to recover his powers of making war, his transfiguring contempt, his theater of noise.

After making an equivocal peace with Rome, Coriolanus returns to Antium with proclamations of triumph. When Coriolanus enters the council chamber, however, Aufidius tries to turn the hero's very bravado and charisma against him. He seeks to change Coriolanus's triumphal reentry into a scene of accusation and shaming, eerily recapitulating the public abuse that had driven him out of Rome. Aufidius knows his man—as if he had studied with the tribunes. In response to the taunts of "traitor" and "boy of tears," Coriolanus pauses for a moment; angry as he is, he seems ready to trust the "grave judgements" of the Volscian senators, to put himself to the justification of a public trial. "'Boy'! O slave! / Pardon me, lords, 'tis the first time that ever / I was forc'd to scold. Your judgements, my grave lords, / Must give this cur the lie" (5.6.104–7). But suddenly Coriolanus's ear catches the pleading words of a Volscian senator: "Peace, both, and hear me speak" (110). "Boy" he might have put up with. But the demand for silence and civil speech tears at him. The very word "peace" has become anathema, the cipher of his self-betrayal and the false motives of the world. Hence, Coriolanus ironically transforms the word into the key of his heroic self-immolation. His ear takes the word in and his tongue spits it back out with an energy that is at once vicious, self-destructive, and prophetic—a transfiguring vision of violence that recalls Aufidius's earlier image of the moon "scarred with splinters":

> Lord.          Peace, both, and hear me speak.
> Coriolanus.  Cut me to pieces, Volsces, men and lads,
>              Stain all your edges on me. Boy! False hound!
>              If you have writ your annals true, 'tis there,
>              That like an eagle in a dove-cote, I
>              Flutter'd your Volscians in Corioles.
>              Alone I did it. Boy!
>
> (5.6.110–16)

Coriolanus makes his death—so passively suffered—into a taunt to answer Aufidius. The substance of that taunt is his own body opened by swords, a shedding of blood that turns those swords into so many clamoring, condemning tongues, a community of stained edges. It is a sudden revelation of what Coriolanus's position in the world has been all along. Here, the blood which he spills will recuperate his impossible heroism, even as it makes grotesque the unity of the Volscian city. Epic history, prophetic indignation, and schoolboy bravado ("I'm rubber and you're glue") all intertwine.

One of the senators, insisting that Coriolanus deserves a formal, public trial, cries out: "The man is noble, and his fame folds in / This orb o'th'earth" (124–25). But Coriolanus's cry for the Volscians to kill him flatly rejects both any claims on legal justice and any privileges that fame affords him in the larger world, as if they cost him too much. Coriolanus in effect rejects "this orb o'th'earth," insofar as that orb presents itself as a gigantic fame machine, a thing that can be "folded in" by the tongue of a fame that belongs to others rather than himself. He will not accept in Antium what he repudiated in Rome. So he turns the courtroom into a version of a battlefield. The strangest moment is when he suddenly, at the end, thinks of how he is regarded by Volscian historians:

> If you have writ your annals true, 'tis there,
> That like an eagle in dove-cote, I
> Flutter'd your Volscians in Corioles.
> Alone I did it. Boy!

Here, his wish to be dismembered by Volscian assassins takes on a contemptuous substance; that wish props itself fancifully on the memory of his solitary, invisible triumph at Corioles. He has a vision of himself that recalls
Shakespeare's Phoenix, surrounded by the clamor of lesser birds (especially
haunting insofar as he turns the bird's or butterfly's "flutter" into a heroic
transitive, a form of aggression).[51] In one sense, this evocation of his earlier
victory is intended to provoke his assassins to even greater violence. But in a
subtler way, that utterance makes suddenly visible what was at stake in that
triumph itself (in that fight which had, in Rome, gained him a new name):
his isolated power to challenge his enemies. Challenging the truth of Volscian history, Coriolanus for the first and only time ferociously embraces his
own public fame. He is content to be written down, as long as it is as a
shameful memory inscribed in an alien history, within such "annals" as are,
indeed, more clearly lost to the English audience than any Roman history.

The lines above are the play's final testimony to Coriolanus's verbal gifts,
his ironic consciousness of the words that will provoke other hearers or
"shake [their] hearts." The image of self-begotten, self-risking violence has
its resonance, and Milton would remember these words when he came to
describe how Samson "as an evening dragon came, / Assailant on the
perched roosts, / And nests in order ranged / Of tame villatic fowl; but
as an eagle / His cloudless thunder bolted on their heads."[52] The peculiar
force of Coriolanus's claim on Volscian texts comes through more clearly,
however, if we contrast Shakespeare's lines with the staider, more conventional boast in James Thomson's neoclassical adaptation of the play, *Coriolanus, or The Roman Matron* (1755):

> Whate'er her blots, whate'er her giddy factions,
> There is more virtue in one single page
> Of Roman story, than your Volscian annals
> Can boast thro' all your creeping dark duration.[53]

Shakespeare's Coriolanus, who emerges so much in the shadow of Plutarch,
is by contrast given a voice that all but rejects the Roman story whose memory made him famous; it is as if a fictive character could turn not only against
the play he is in, but against the history that keeps him alive. With a self-
consciousness that seems unbearably strange, he asks that the memory of his
lone fight be recorded in annals which neither we nor Coriolanus could possess. It is as if the Volscians, in cutting up his person, were simultaneously
writing down his name, his blood the ink on their scattered pens. This version of fame is the only one he can bear.

*chapter six*

# «KING LEAR»
# AND THE REGISTER
# OF CURSE

To answer . . . this
extremity of the skies.

*King Lear*

I now understand what
Pasternak felt when he
wrote that *Lear* is inter-
preted "too noisily."

GRIGORI KOZINTSEV

man walks and walks. He wants to escape, in these
mountains, the shadow of his enemy. That shadow
comes upon him like a storm of rain. Walking, he
runs, tries not to run, not to be seen to run, lest running make him seem afraid. His baited hurry makes
him grotesque. He moves mechanically, like a scare-
crow. The wind catches him before the falling water
does. He draws his coat around him and pulls his hat
over his eyes, but the wind and rain pour through un-
stopped. He cannot see. Mud clogs his feet, stains his
clothing and hands. Falling, in flight, he yells, and
finds in that alien sound a way to outwit what he cannot outrun. He screams again and again, and then
turns the scream to a laugh. He turns his face to the
weather, opening it to the rain. When the water
makes him wince, he makes his wince a smirk. He flourishes spray around
with his arms, kicks up fresh mud, catches water in his hat and tosses it back
into the laden air, or pours it over his own head. He throws shreds of hair
into the wind or hurls up soaked paper from his pockets. His mouth tastes of
earth. He shuts his eyes to increase the darkness, pressing his palms to his eyes
to make flashes that mirror the lightning. He makes of the rain a dancing

partner or a puppet. The air is full of water drops, full of children, statues, palaces, and eyes. The storm is full of noises that amplify his speech; it answers his calls and drives other sounds from his ear. "People are afraid of noises, of words, they are afraid of their own thoughts," writes Kozintsev.[1]

This man faces the storm in the same way that Lear faces a curse. What he cannot outrun he tries to outwit, or out-jest; he tries to mock, co-opt, or steal the curse, make it over into a home or a kingdom. Lear is himself a source of the curse that overtakes him, even as it assumes forms that he cannot control. Curses acquire a frightening life in this play. They fly in the air, arrive on the rain and wind; they slip behind eyes, echo in the unreadable laughter of fools or the demented babble of demoniacs. They are scattered like seeds on a barren landscape. They conceal themselves within gifts and benedictions, becoming parts of a world in which even common words like "love," "daughter," or "king" are taken "for a reproche, and for a proverbe, for a commune talke, and for a cursse" (Jeremiah 24:9).

To understand the transformations of curse in *King Lear,* we need to remember that the word "curse" can refer to both an utterance and a habitation. On the one hand, it is a certain way of speaking, a violent species of human *cry*. A curse is a word backed by a wish to harm, something flung angrily out against a person or a world, an act of will. In this form it is, as Dostoevsky writes, a human privilege, a cipher of freedom.[2] But curse is also a state of being; it is something mysterious, an inescapable burden built into the world itself, its history, and the state of being human. Curse in this sense refers to something "general," a thing we inherit with our human gifts; *a* curse becomes *the* curse. That curse may be open to the eye or hidden away, its source in nature as hard to find as the cause of thunder or hard hearts. These two senses—curse as a contingent utterance and curse as an inescapable truth—*King Lear* holds together in frightening ways. That double valence will help us make sense of the play's imagination of suffering, its mysterious pictures of human and natural agency, and its equivocal pictures of divinity. It also helps us understand the simultaneous presence of an archaic, almost magical logic and of a more homely, ironic realism in the play.[3] Thinking about curse in this sense may clarify as well one's feeling of buried forces emerging in this play, of new worlds opening up as old ones break apart; it gives us a way to discuss the running together of human and natural catastrophe, to see what it means to *imagine* catastrophe.

Earlier plays of Shakespeare also explore the dramatic uses of curse. In *2 Henry VI,* for example, Queen Margaret has made of curse a vehicle for both her desperate love and bitter hatred; she has understood its equivocal potency, its volatility, its way of infecting both curser and cursed.[4] In

*Richard III,* this same queen, older, exiled, abject, turns her curses against Richard, a creature who himself, in his "crooked figure," represents the body of a curse within English history. The play reminds us of how human beings make curses up, even as curses make up human beings, creating a tragic order within history larger than any apparent human intention.[5] In returning to this more archaic substratum in his later tragedy, however, Shakespeare makes the workings of curse even more complex.[6] Curse assumes, for one thing, some of the labile freedom that the playwright discovers in the workings of rumor and slander. The noise of curse now mutates as strangely as these do, creeping between words, into silences, into nonsense; it demands our attention in its fragility and polymorphousness as much as in its more explicit violence. We need to listen harder, therefore, to the shifting of register of curse, if we are to understand its work in this play.

I have suggested that, in *Lear,* curse can go about in disguise; it often seems to wander about homeless, without clear aim; it finds only irregular answers and profit. By an eerie, punning logic, both curses and those who curse join the ranks of the persons whom the Elizabethans called "cursitors," that uncertain population of poor men and women who wandered about the countryside without homes, land, employment, or masters. (A "cursitor" could also be a courier, of which there are many sorts in this play as well.) The word comes from the Latin *cursitor,* or runner, rather than the Anglo-Saxon *curs,* so there is no necessary etymological connection.[7] Yet the title and condemnatory tone of Thomas Harman's *Caveat or Warening for Commen Cursetors* (1566), which describes such wanderers as a "peevish, perverse, and pestilant people," a race wandering and fugitive like Cain, suggest that a punning link might have been just audible for contemporaries.[8] Harman's pamphlet is a telling document, for while it acknowledges the need for charity, this study of wanderers is also a machine for stopping tears, insisting that the appearance of human need is often a conspiracy, a "deep dissimulation" worthy of contempt and fear. Thus, alongside the deserving poor, he catalogs the vast supply of fake madmen, demoniacs, epileptics, gypsies, and fake victims of disease, fire, flood, and war who fill the English countryside, many having given over more lawful professions. To warn the innocent, he exposes the cursitors' dodges, their con games and disguises, their violation of social taboos, their ways of extorting both pity and money, their tricky thefts, their unsettling mixture of real and fake poverty, their forged patents and licenses; he also probes their disturbingly obscure, even "unlawful" language, a mingle-mangle of English, Latin, and incomprehensible slang.[9] Earthly enough, such creatures provoke in Harman fascination as well as doubt; they are half wandering players, half spirits who take the place of any more native faeries (like the impish Robin Goodfellow). They make exile it-self a more troubled category. *King Lear* absorbs the cursitor into its own drama of curse, its own struggles with charity; through figures like Mad Tom and blinded Gloucester, it explores our fascination with those who suffer— our often fantastic, even self-wounding attachment to those we help and those we refuse to help.[10] The theater of curse ties itself to the theater of pity; that is part of the tragic experiment.

AS A DRAMA OF CURSE and the answering of curse, *King Lear* has two great rivals. The first is a crucial precursor text, the Book of Job. Here the patri-arch is tested by sufferings which constitute the classic substance of a curse—loss of possessions, family, health, love, honor, and blessings, even a kind of exile.[11] Yet Job rightly refuses to allow either that he is cursed or that he deserves curse; indeed, he curses those men who slander both him and God with the dogmatic presumption that his suffering implies his guilt. Like Lear, he anatomizes both his own desolation and that of a world apparently stripped of justice; in his bitterness he reproves and even curses the God who hides himself, yet seeks his life.[12] His pain lets him challenge God to answer and explain himself. A voice from a tempest finally answers Job; it is a voice from beyond the world that yet presents the created world as a mir-ror of God's gifts and his mystery, a mouthpiece of God's terror as well as his justice—facing Job, especially in the visions of Behemoth and Leviathan, with a power behind the created world that is unanswerable, beyond covenant, at once enemy, revised blessing, and conceptual limit. It is a power beyond curse as well.

The second text is Percy Bysshe Shelley's *Prometheus Unbound*. This verse drama opens with the Titan's attempt to recall, and call back, the curse he once uttered against the divinity who has bound him to a frozen mountain, where he is torn by ice and fire, wild storms, and his own tormenting thoughts. He cries, in words that eerily echo Shakespeare's aged king: "I gave [Jupiter] all / He has, and in return he chains me here . . . / Whilst my beloved race is trampled down / By his thought-executing ministers."[13] Prometheus's curse, which promised to Jupiter agony, weakness, and self-torment, once caused tremors in all of nature. But Prometheus himself has forgotten it. Indeed, the curse is now buried, ghostly, inaudible, a rumor murmured in a language known only to the dead. Treasured as a "spell" by Jupiter's enemies, a guarantee of the oppressor's eventual fall, this curse also threatens to assimilate the bound Titan to the cruelty of his tormentor.[14] Indeed, Shelley suggests, Prometheus's curse against the father-god has helped to sustain a history in which even the image of a suffering savior has only caused harm, impaling believers on their own cruel hopes and lending power to superstition. "Thy name I will not speak, / It hath become a curse," Prometheus says when faced with a phantasm of Christ crucified, conjured by the Furies to drive him to despair.[15] Shelley's poem is driven by the desire to undo the curse and the patterns of resentment that sustain it, and to find an answer to oppression beyond curse.[16]

Of course, even as *King Lear* explores the grammar of cursing, it does not believe in curses any more than it believes in a pure thing called "nature" or a fixed population of "gods." Like Shelley's poem, it exposes the moral and conceptual cruelty built into too simple an economy of curse and blessing; it shows us curse's equivocal genealogy in human need and fantasy. The play also explores the fate of those banished from clear systems of curse and blessing, such as the blinded Gloucester at Dover; Gloucester walks here along a flat, earthly stage, despite the improvisations of his disguised son Edgar, who comforts him with a universe of heights and depths, of moon-eyed demons who tempt mortals to sin and "clearest gods, who make them honours / Of men's impossibilities" (4.6.73–74).[17] *King Lear,* we might say, seeks not to lift or expiate a curse, but tries rather to end the cursing game entirely.[18]

---

He shall be accursed whoever does not keep his hands off this monument in this spot and the image which is set thereon, but shall dishonour it or shift some of its boundary stones, or wantonly defile it or damage it. . . . May God smite him with helplessness and fever and shivering and irritation and blasting and partial paralysis and sightlessness and derangement of his wits, and may his possessions melt away, and let him not be able to walk upon the earth or sail upon the sea, let him beget no children. . . . But let him have the Erinyes watching over him. (Hellenistic inscription found in Turkey, ca. third century A.D.)[19]

Good frend for Jesus sake forbeare,
To digg the dust enclosed heare:
Blese be the man that spares thes stones,
And curst be he that moves my bones.
(Epitaph, Holy Trinity Church, Stratford-upon-Avon [1616])

Curses crystallize around moments of violation, real or imaginary; they are provoked by breakings of law, by damage done to bodies and wishes, to forms of happiness and blessing. Curses mark a breach, and risk a breach in turn. They answer to traumas with a trauma of their own, a violence that is at once inchoate and highly structured. Curse is a reactive mode. As John Kerrigan suggests, it projects a miniature revenge tragedy, calling down violent judgement in the face of unnatural loss.[20] The formal curse is the shriek of pain at injustice, argues another scholar, and the revenging Furies, the Erinyes, are "curses personified"—something that some revengers claim to be (Aeschylus's Clytemnestra, for example, who takes on the mask of a curse Fury to justify her murder of Agamemnon).[21] Yet curses also belong to speakers who are themselves under prohibition. The great cursers of classical tradition are victims who are themselves criminal, deluded, and cursed, both sinned against and sinning. In epic, for example, the archetype is the blinded Polyphemus cursing Odysseus.[22] In tragedy, especially those Senecan plays which help shape Renaissance drama, the pattern shows itself in Thyestes cursing his hideous brother, who has tricked him into eating his own children; in the infanticide Medea calling down demonic poison on Jason and his bride; and in Oedipus, eyeless and taboo, cursing his own sons for rejecting him. These figures fall into a cursed reality, and turn their own cries against it. The very utterance of a curse creates its own victims. Cathartic as they may be, curses expose their speakers to a reflex of harm redounding from their own words, as happens in the case of Theseus's curses against his falsely accused son Hippolytus. Calling on powers over which he has little control, the curser indeed makes himself taboo, *sacer,* cursed; he becomes, as Giambattista Vico writes in *The New Science,* both altar and victim.[23] A sense of the dangerous circularity of cursing comes through in Psalm 109, even given the text's vociferous contempt for the impotence of merely human curse: "As he clothed him self with cursing like a raiment, so shal it come into his bowels like water, and like oyle into his bones" (18). Or, to cite an old proverb: curses like chickens always come home to roost.[24]

   Those curses we find written into epitaphs, guarding the dead against people who still possess life, have a kind of typical force. They suggest how curse works to help turn back a death, reaching beyond human limits to impose suffering, exile, and loss on those who would violate this last fragile defense against oblivion.[25] Epitaphic curses keep the dead alive in time, reinforcing mere fame by the power of taboo. The typical form of the epitaph curse—which puts the curse into the mouth of the grave's inhabitant—may suggest that the one who curses is, as it were, already dead, at least insofar as he or she must call on a language spoken *by* the dead. This surmise is given some historical support by what we know of the ancient Greek practice of secretly burying curse tablets or *defixiones*—maledictory spells intended to harm the living—in the graves of those already dead; such curses clearly drew on the power of the dead, and of the gods of the underworld, even at the expense of violating the grave itself.[26] This suggests that the curser puts himself in a place beyond ordinary speech, crosses a thresh-old to a realm of utterance from which it may be hard to return, risks be-coming a god or a ghost himself—entangled in a chain of malice that passes from the dead to the living. Shelley picks up this implication in *Prometheus Unbound*, I think, though in a more disenchanted, humanistic vein, when the Titan is told that the gods and daemons cannot repeat to him his forgotten curse against Jupiter, because it is stored up in a language known only to those who die.[27]

From a rhetorical point of view, cursing calls attention to itself; it is a sub-lime mode, at once extravagant and ritualized—one reason for its interest to dramatists. There is nothing discreet about curse, though it may be ut-tered in secret. Rather, the imagination of curse tends to heap up sufferings, trying to catalog and exhaust all possible forms of pain and all sources of power to inflict such pain. All these punishments, the curse says, shall pur-sue the violator: sickness, blindness, nakedness, shame, false accusation, loss of children, loss of fame, exile, slavery, cannibalism, torment by demons. Such catalogings can run to fanatic detail, but however heterogenous, they have their logic. The pains promised by curses commonly entail an anatomy of essential needs; they point to forms of pleasure and dependence, to es-sential blessings; they mark their victims' embeddedness in larger systems of relation, the very things that sustain a victim making him or her that much more vulnerable. This logic shows itself, for example, in a remarkable curs-ing litany from ancient Egypt, which begins with the call, "Mayest thou never exist, may thy *ka* never exist, may thy body never exist," and repeats the formula at length, aiming successively at its victim's limbs, bones, hair, words, children, parents, possessions, emissions, paths, doorways, and hon-ors, ending with the magical optative, "Thou art smitten, O enemy, Thou shalt die, thou shalt die."[28] Such details ground the curse in the real, even as they tie that reality to something latent, as yet unaccomplished. There is of-ten a certain speculative or promissory character in curse; it creates a "po-tential fact."[29] Curse texts often catalog pains that have not yet occurred, losses that have not yet been experienced; they are visions of what the curser wishes to happen, rather than what is sure to happen. Many formal curses, in fact, remain in the subjunctive mood, held in suspension by an "if" or a "may." Consider the catalog of curses promised in Deuteronomy 28 to those who fail in their covenant with God:

> The Lord shal smite thee with a consumption, and with the fever, and with a burning ague, and with a fervent heat, and with the sword, and with blasting, and with the mildewe, and they shal pursue thee until thou perish. And thine heaven that is over thine head shal be brasse, and the earth that is under thee,

yron. The Lord shal give thee for the raine of thy land, dust and ashes: even from heaven shal it come downe upon thee, until thou be destroyed. And the Lord shall cause thee to fall before thine enemies. . . . And thy carkeis shal be meat unto all foules of the ayre, and unto the beastes of the earth, and none shall fray them away. . . . The Lord shal smite thee with madnes, and with blindnes, & with astonying of heart. Thou shalt also grope at noondaies, as the blinde gropeth in darckness. . . . The frute of thy land & all thy labours shal a people, which thou knowest not, eat, and thou shalt never but suffer wrong, and violence alway: So that thou shalt be mad for the sight which thine eies shal se. (22–34)

The very latency of curse here is part of what makes its work as a speech act at once so powerful and so equivocal, even phantasmic. Curse puts itself beyond the domain of immediate proof (even if history or testimony proves its power in the end). At the threshold between magic and prayer, it seems always to call on some power above or beyond the human, to invoke a daemonic or divine agent to back its promise of damage. At times the invocation is direct, a cataloging of names of power, gods and demons, or (as in medieval ecclesiastical curses) a crowd of powerful saints. Yet the invocation can also be indirect, as in some biblical curses; reticent as that text is about the possibilities of idolatry, it often suggests that the power of a curse inheres in the spoken word itself.[30]

As Deuteronomy 28 also makes obvious, curses are not just for the powerless or the criminal. There are curses that exist to sustain established laws and customs. Among the most ancient surviving curse texts, in fact, are those found on legal documents or public inscriptions, promising harm to those who betray an oath, violate a treaty, disobey a commandment, or break a covenant.[31] They curse those who threaten a ruler and his symbols, who dare to damage a boundary stone, a temple, a statue, a tomb, an inscription. Curses are indeed often seen as the prerogatives of a priesthood or a judiciary. In the ancient Near East, Greece, and Rome, curses were regularly employed as weapons of war. Curses may thus both protect private wishes and underwrite systems of civil and divine law. Systems of law may in turn seek to underwrite a particular curse. Law, indeed, often seeks to appropriate the power or at least the potent posture of curse, to identify with the divine presence behind it, even as the law seeks to control curse's wilder, more anarchic employments. Hence, for example, in Aeschylus's *Eumenides,* Athena persuades the angered Furies to dwell in her city, so that their archaic energies may nourish, even bless, the work of a more rational justice system.

Strong as they may sound, official curses also carry about them a taint of weakness. Juridical curses, for example, inevitably aim at punishing violators beyond the scope of more secular authorities, just as parental curses—which are always assumed to have a peculiar power—punish children who have slipped out of lesser bonds of discipline. The utterance of a curse can offer, as it were, an excuse, a story that frames its own failure, even as it expresses a contempt for any common means of redress. One needs the curse because the violator of a law may be too large or too small to be caught, too strong, too obscure, too distant in time or space; the criminal may be, in fact, as yet unknown, acting in secret; he may not even have acted at all, or be yet unborn. The use of curses thus points not only to the resentment of the disenfranchised, but to an uncertainty haunting the wishes of authority itself. Such curses are a little like those grinning, staring Gorgon masks fixed to the fronts of ancient temples. These monstrous faces—in which Jean-Pierre Vernant sees the visual translation of voices of human terror, rage, and derision—keep at bay an entire world of undefined threat, including whatever natural or unnatural forces one particular god may not be sufficient to control.[32] Teaching us to hear the anxiety underlying the curses of those in authority is one aim, I think, of Shakespeare's *Tempest*. There the wonderfully histrionic curses of Caliban show themselves as more than a victim's spontaneous cries for revenge against his oppressor. If we attend to the text, what's clear is that Caliban's curses ironically "play back" the prior curses and complaints of Prospero, curses which are saturated with the doubt, fear, frustrated love, and impatience that the princely magician feels toward any of his recalcitrant subordinates, even devoted ones like Ariel and Miranda. This explains, in part, how the utterance of a curse can strip a person naked, as Lear is stripped naked.

Curses stick around (and stick), often in hidden and furtive ways. "A curse is written / On the under side of things," writes T. S. Eliot in *The Family Reunion*.[33] It may be set in motion without intention; it may lurk within blessings, within gifts granted in love or honor, or what seem merely innocent mistakes. That is part of what makes curses so unpredictable and intractable (like the gods we imagine behind them). There is indeed a crucial doubleness to the way we imagine the work of curse in time and in history. In things like epitaphs, curses reach outward defensively in the direction of a vulnerable, unknown future. But we also tend to posit curses shaping the past and present. We use curses, that is, to construct our genealogies of the given world, the world into which we find ourselves thrown. So the story goes: a long time ago, whether by accident or will, somebody killed someone, stole something, saw or touched something forbidden, failed to follow a rule or thank a god. Ever afterward, their descendants pay for this crime; that ancient error strips them of blessing, or places them under the aegis of powers they cannot manage, which exact a continual revenge. Curse thus becomes a foundation for terrors that are otherwise inexplicable. It helps rationalize the pains of childbirth, the need to labor, the inescapability of death, the evil nature of a place or a name, the failure of a quest, the sense of being in exile. An ancient curse accounts for the fact that one language cannot automatically answer another, that we must speak to each other through networks of babble. We thus make curses central to our systems of value; they become crucial to our way of reading nature and history, reading human luck as much as human work. To know ourselves and the world is to know where the curse lies, how far back in time, of what it accuses us, how it may be answered or borne, and what remains of the blessing it killed. It is also to know whether the curse itself could become a blessing.

———

For all its ironic distance, the Book of Job keeps vividly present the drama of curse. Job in his suffering readily sees blasphemous curses surrounding him. In chapter 31, he asks for even greater curses to fall upon him, should his guilt be proved. This is partly to show his conviction of his own virtue, but also to make himself responsible for his own desolation, even at the risk of breaking a taboo.[34] It is also a means by which to suggest that the curse which has fallen on his life remains unreadable, as blank and uncontrollable as the vision of the created world that God presents in answer to Job's protests. Job's freedom to play with curses, even to invoke curses on his enemies in God's name, is remarkable enough to have caused intense worry to Protestant theologians like John Calvin. Hence Calvin's attempt, in his *Sermons on Job,* to rein in and make almost invisible the power and demand latent in Job's curses. Such curses provoke that sacred doubt which Calvin directs at any idolatrous claims on behalf of human works—efficacious prayer, the Mass, the sacrament of the confessional, oaths sworn by the saints, not to mention the established church's own institutional curses and anathemas. The danger is that, in giving vent to human rage—especially calling upon God to punish one's enemies—human curses also preempt a divine prerogative. Calvin thus insists that Job's curses against the powerful and wicked are not curses at all, but acknowledgments of weakness, tacit yieldings up of power. He argues that when God, in Scripture, invites human beings to curse their enemies and oppressors (especially those whom the world thinks of as blessed), he in fact invites us to say that they mean nothing to us: "Wee must curse them: that is to say, we must bee fully resolved with our selves that all this is nothing."[35] God has already cursed them out of his own mouth, though that curse may show itself only over time (hence the necessity of faith).[36] We must not answer pain by turning pain back on our enemies, but rather read our pain as a test, even a blessing. Similarly, John Donne, addressing a text in Psalms, empties curse of its magic, arguing that many of the most vicious Old Testament maledictions against enemies, such as those of David, are "alwaies conditionall" and "prophetical" in their vehemence; their certainty lies in the power of God, not at all in the human speaker. This sort of malediction is indeed "Medicinall, and had *Rationem boni,* a charitable tincture, and nature in it," since it works by warning rather than menace.[37] If these texts try humanely to assuage human resentment, they equally suggest a fear of the way human curses may encroach on a strictly divine privilege or debase the currency of official oaths by too promiscuous employment. Such a fear also underlies prohibitions like the Jacobean statute of 1606 against the swearing of oaths or the naming of God, Christ, or Jesus on the public stage—a law that some critics consider to have provoked, as if in answer, the elaborate conjuring of the pagan gods in *King Lear.*[38]

It is just this equivocal status of curse at this historical moment—stripped of any real magical efficacy, yet dangerous enough to be policed—that may have opened it up more fully as a vehicle for profane, literary invention. Here I am thinking not just of the grand, bombastic cursing of Renaissance Senecan tragedies (one clear source for Lear's curses), but of lyrics like "The Curse," by the younger John Donne. This poem explores curse's origins in erotic paranoia, resentment, and impotence, reminding us of how its fanatic conceits are conjured out of nothing, even as it reduces its victim to nothing:

> Whoever guesses, thinks, or dreams he knows
> Who is my mistress, wither by this curse . . .
> . . . . . . . . . . . . . . . . . . . . . . . . . . . . . .
> Madness his sorrow, gout his cramps, may he
> Make, by but thinking, who hath made him such . . .
> . . . . . . . . . . . . . . . . . . . . . . . . . . . . . .
> May he dream treason, and believe that he
> Meant to perform it, and confess, and die,
>     And no record tell why . . .
> . . . . . . . . . . . . . . . . . . . . . . . . . . . . . .
> The venom of all stepdames, gamesters' gall,
> What tyrants, and their subjects interwish,
>     What plants, mines, beasts, fowl, fish,
>     Can contribute, all ill which all

Prophets, or poets spake; and all which shall
    Be annexed in schedules unto this by me,
    Fall on that man; for if it be a she
    Nature before hand hath out-cursed me.[39]

Shakespeare's play, too, restores the speech act to all of its dramatic ferocity, its impotence and inventiveness, its power to evade and entrap. Curses in *King Lear* open the heart to its own rage, fear, and appetite, and in a less neat, self-consuming fashion than Donne's lyric does. (Lear, for one thing, allows no mere Nature to out-curse him.) Part of Lear's dilemma is that he is a king who has undone his own juridical power to curse. Or, perhaps, he is a king who has left himself only curse in lieu of command, obedience, or love. His curses thus become parts of a demented ritual; they exhaust as much as they sustain the image of his kingship. The violent words don't "take" in any direct way, even in the elusive manner that old Queen Margaret's curses seem to take in *Richard III*. Indeed, it may seem that it is the hollowness of Lear's curses which helps catch him up in the world, in the catastrophic history he lets loose. More violently than Donne's speaker, Lear tries by his curses to command, or at least outrun and out-curse, the disorder of a human and natural world, to remake the world in a way that responds to his desire and pain. But curse is something that saturates and inhabits the world; it can never be caught up with or outrun. Lear's flood of curses cannot cure the scandal or monstrosity, the deep wound, that he discovers at the center of his world. His curses and accusations cannot probe the empty or ordinary depth of human hearts. They cannot undo an indignity which they help to shape—partly from his having cursed the wrong objects, partly from his need to resort to curse at all, to use curses to drive out other cries, memories, and gestures.

———

I fool about with my night,
we capture
all
that tore loose here,

your darkness too
load on to
my halved, voyaging
eyes,

it too is to hear it
from every direction,
the incontrovertible echo
of every eclipse.
(Paul Celan)

The register of Lear's calls and curses shifts violently through the play. We hear signs of his shame and resentment, his deep self-doubt and concealed remorse. The shape of Lear's rage is not fixed or given; it attacks him. He cannot find it fully or command its final shape. Indeed, his curses are as much a way of throwing his rage from him as of giving it voice, finding for it new objects, lest it turn back on himself or expose him to himself too clearly. Lear's curses measure his deafness as much as his hearing. He curses, at times, because he does not want to weep.[40]

I will be extending the range of the word "curse" in what follows, but we can begin with a terribly explicit instance: Lear's parting curse against his daughter Goneril. This condemnation responds most fundamentally to her free contempt for Lear, his followers, and his fool, to her shameless treatment of her father as someone old and impotent, unable to control his household, given only to "unsightly tricks" that mock his own dignity. As if chorusing with his own invocations of himself ("O Lear, Lear, Lear! / Beat at this gate that let thy folly in" [1.4.262–63]), the kneeling king addresses Nature:

Hear, Nature, hear, dear goddess, hear:
Suspend thy purpose if thou didst intend
To make this creature fruitful.
Into her womb convey sterility,
Dry up in her the organs of increase,
And from her derogate body never spring
A babe to honour her. If she must teem,
Create her child of spleen, that it may live
And be a thwart disnatured torment to her.
Let it stamp wrinkles in her brow of youth,
With cadent tears fret channels in her cheeks,
Turn all her mother's pains and benefits
To laughter and contempt . . .
(267–79)

Shamed that his own "hot tears . . . should make thee worth them," he continues,

> Blasts and fogs upon thee!
> Th'untented woundings of a father's curse
> Pierce every sense about thee. Old fond eyes,
> Beweep this cause again, I'll pluck ye out,
> And cast you with the waters that you loose
> To temper clay.
> (291–96)

Lear, unlike Job, does not curse nature or the day of his birth; rather, he turns to nature to underwrite a curse against his daughter's powers of generation. Nature must accomplish the wounding of nature, whether by sterility or monstrosity. Lear's mode of curse here starts to show its peculiarly mimetic qualities: he curses his child in his own image, in the guise of one himself bitten and forced to weep by a treacherous child, made by that child an object of contempt and laughter, one who has furthermore been cursed in unjustly cursing another daughter. Curse infects all relation. Of the phrase "th'untented woundings of a father's curse,"William Empson writes, "the *wounds* may be the cause or effect of the *curse* uttered by a *father;* independently of this, they may reside in the *father* or his child."[41] If his tears spring from the curses that should dry them, he tries by infectious magic to transfer them to his daughter. (Tears are part of the curse of being human.) As if he remembered Goneril's early offer of a love "dearer than eyesight, space and liberty," Lear asks the weather to "pierce every sense" about her— conjuring the very storm that will later absorb him. Nature, the source of curse, starts to show its cursed face. In a way that recalls Job, Lear's demented threat against his own eyes suggests the self-destructive logic of the sufferer's curse: it turns her "black looks" against his own eyeballs—though this curse will eventually fall out on different victim, the earl of Gloucester.

Lear carries these curses with him as he flees to Regan, like parts of his diminished entourage. They become his greeting to her; he repeats them on arrival as if they could keep him a king and a father, as if they could put off the evidence of this second daughter's even more shameless contempt, including her refusal to receive him and her stocking of Lear's messenger, the disguised Kent:

> O, are you free?
> Some other time for that.—Beloved Regan,
> Thy sister's naught . . .
> . . . . . . . . . . . . . . . . . . . . . . . . . . . . . . . . .
> My curses on her . . .
> . . . . . . . . . . . . . . . . . . . . . . . . . . . . . . . . .

> She hath abated me of half my train,
> Looked black upon me, struck me with her tongue
> Most serpent-like, upon the very heart.
> All the stored vengeances of heaven fall
> On her ingrateful top! Strike her young bones,
> You taking airs, with lameness! . . .
> You nimble lightnings, dart your blinding flames
> Into her scornful eyes! Infect her beauty,
> You fen-sucked fogs, drawn by the powerful sun,
> To fall and blister!
> (2.2.321–57)

At the very moment he speaks this, he denies what, given the evidence, he cannot truly believe: "No, Regan thou shalt never have my curse. / Thy tender-hafted nature shall not give / Thee o'er to harshness. Her eyes are fierce, but thine / Do comfort and not burn" (359–62). Here again, Lear's curses are the mirror of what he both fears and knows, even as they evade these things. The curses conjure images of the very storm into which he flees—which is thus a kind of literalization of his suffering, his wished-for revenge, as well as another evasion. As if merely human, more shameful forms of passion were likely to attack him, he asks the gods to "touch me with noble anger"—which is to say, let me curse like a character in a Senecan tragedy, though Senecan curses are equivocal enough.[42]

As he runs offstage and into the storm, Lear knows one thing: "I shall go mad." (Is that his fear, or his determination?) For a moment, his curses lose their amazing volubility; he starts to stammer: "I will have such revenges on you both / That all the world shall—I will do such things— / What they are yet I know not, but they shall be / The terrors of the earth!" (468–71) But soon his curses expose their more wildly speculative quality, also a kind of madly copious superfluity—like that of beggars, perhaps, who are, Lear insists, "in poorest thing superfluous" (454). Here, Lear's rage against his daughters extends to nature and humanity as a whole, even as it calls on powers both within and beyond nature to do his bidding:

> Blow winds and crack your cheeks! Rage, blow!
> You cataracts and hurricanoes, spout
> Till you have drenched our steeples, drowned the cocks!
> You sulphurous and thought-executing fires,
> Vaunt-couriers of oak-cleaving thunderbolts,
> Singe my white head! And thou, all-shaking thunder,
> Strike flat the thick rotundity o'the world,

Crack Nature's moulds, all germens spill at once
That make ingrateful man!
(3.2.1–9)

Stripped of all companions but the fool, faced with the barren landscape, with the noise, rain, and wind of the storm, Lear becomes by turns competitive, domineering, dependent, and contemptuous; the torn air shapes itself as a mouthpiece, a mirror, and an enemy. The storm is a traitor and a perjurer, but also a servant. ("Wil he make a covenant with thee? and wilt thou take him as a servant for ever?" God asks Job about Leviathan.) Lear asks the storm to second his private, self-wounding rage, even as it also annihilates the signs of that fury: he "tears his white hair, / Which the impetuous blasts with eyeless rage / Catch in their fury and make nothing of" (3.1.7–9). God in the Book of Job takes the form of the suddenness, terror, and unpredictability of the created world, its weather, its animals. In Shakespeare's play, it is Lear who lends himself to the storm—or rather, he lends himself to what he *makes* of the storm; he becomes one of the fretful elements, himself a kind of storm god. His words animate and steal the noise of the storm gods, as if he wants to expose himself to the power of his own words— words which have lost their currency in the world, lost their power to command response rather than just express a wish, which to Lear may seem as if they had lost any sense at all. ("'Inform'd them?'" Lear screams at Gloucester, who has carried Lear's orders to Regan and Cornwall. "Dost thou understand me, man?" [2.2.288]). Lear tries to identify his own curses with the storm's destructive noises, to find a new source of power in the storm's own echoes of his loss. It is a way of making his damaged authority bear fruit. The music or rumor of Lear's betrayal fills the air of the stage, all the more strongly for being played against the crying human wit of the fool.

Lear's curses are filled with the shreds and ghosts of his abused kingship. The storm is an anatomy, a fragmented map of his lost sovereignty. Wandering through it are bastard fantasies of Lear's ideologically sanctioned role as divine master over a sovereign nation, as parental source of a fruitful people, as ruler over nature, as "top" of a political hierarchy, and as the "eye" that finds out hidden error and crime. (Are these pictures seen as bastard in themselves, or bastardly insofar as they offer masks and refuges for Lear's private error? Are they a beggar's curse or a king's, or the curse of a king who doesn't recognize himself as a beggar?) Authority is not only brought down in the storm; it reveals itself as the source of catastrophe, desolation, civil and international warfare. In Lear's fantasy, the storm becomes a quasi-divine curse, a second flood which wipes out all landmarks, all signs of place and power such as he had foolishly taken upon himself to give away. With a ferocity that recalls Marlowe's imperious destroyer Tamburlaine, this deposed king unnames the national landscape, obliterates the map of the state, even as he destroys all sources of generation.[43] Authority violently spills its "germens," spills itself in the storm, in a kind of abortive attempt at generation, though it only generates more loss. It is no accident that, in an earlier scene, the gentleman's news of Lear's scattering rage is answered by Kent's insistence that there "comes a power / Into this scattered kingdome" (3.1.30–31).[44] The curse that Lear invokes all too obviously plays out his initial, self-destructive act of dividing the kingdom, splitting the gift of a fruitful landscape. During the storm, Lear runs to overtake and command a process that he set loose himself but cannot now control. One wishes to think that Lear is learning about suffering: "Expose thyself to feel what wretches feel" (3.4.34). Yet his democratic identification of "houseless poverty" continues to feel at once self-deceptive and opportunistic.

The metaphysical drama at work here is more daunting and fragile than the political one. Lear at once adopts and disowns the storm that is the sign of his exile. He tries to invent a world for his cries within that noise. As a god within a cosmos, he strives to make himself at home within the tempest, to make it something that he knows and that knows him. (Think of how Lear might answer God's questions to Job: "Who is the father of the rain? or who hathe begotten the droppes of the dewe? . . . Canst thou lift up thy voyce to the cloudes, that abundance of waters may cover thee?" [38:28, 34].) This means making a home for himself within a creation that contains its own destruction, clothing himself in what strips him. Isolated onstage, barely hearing those who speak to him, Lear utters curses that collapse together cosmological beginnings and ends; his cries reach back toward the creative word of Genesis and forward toward the depredations of the apocalypse: he "bids what will take all" (3.1.14). Lear's words are more than a display of blasphemy or cranky presumption. The eerie drama of the scene depends on the fact that Lear curses a world already under curse, under a "general" or prior curse. In his crying out for a punitive catastrophe, he takes his cue from a desolation already sifted through creation, inherent in the weather, in his visions of bestial and human cruelty; it is a desolation which he tries to catch up with, even surpass. One may recall here Spenser's visions of the world in *The Mutabilitie Cantos* or Donne's in the *Anniversaries,* where the life energies built into the world also ruin it, where birth is wrapped up with death and change, and where human desire lives to seek its own decay. But there is something even more heterodox in Lear's utterances; they suggest an almost Gnostic cosmogony, a story of origins in which the Fall and Creation are all but identified.[45] For Lear, it is the creation of the world that embeds the world's violence. Creation is a curse by which nature speaks of the loss of justice, without a ready sense of any cure or answer but further catastrophe.[46]

Describing Job's situation, Calvin writes that "God muste bee fayne too create newe worldes for us, if he mynde to satisfie us"—to satisfy, that is, either our hunger for worldly blessings or our demand for justice.[47] Calvin's warning implicitly admits that no answer which God gives to Job will be sufficient. God in the Book of Job can only make a myth of that frustration, facing Job with a more astonishing vision of the created world he thought he knew, showing him at once its alienness, divine power, and wonder. Lear, however, tries to help the gods along, lending them exactly that unreal wish to create new worlds for men. Indeed, as if he could be both Job and Job's God at once, Lear projects a world that carries his frustration as much as it answers his need, a world in which he identifies with the gods that make him suffer. Taking his cue, perhaps, from the stargazers whom Gloucester consults, Lear emerges as an ironic prophet and revisionary theologian, even a kind of demented demiurge. In his traumatic storm cosmogony, the world takes its origins in a curse; hence, in their violence and negation, Lear's curses become themselves a kind of *logos,* rather than aspects of a chaos that a divine *logos* would defeat.

None of this makes the storm vision any less earthly or the gods and demons any less "man-made." For all one's sense of some hidden structure of violence sifting through Lear's world, we cannot pry it apart from the world of animals and plants and weather, the domain of ordinary mortals that includes fake kings, wise fools, and cruel daughters. That is its natural supernaturalism. (God asks Job, "Out of whose wombe came the yce?" [38:29].) Lear asks himself, and the world, "Is there any cause in nature that make these hard hearts?" (3.6.74–75).) If there is a purgatorial logic to the suffering that unfolds in *King Lear,* it must emerge through the orders that human beings make for themselves onstage, rather than from any divine intervention.

---

Some other sound hides in the circles of this storm. It is a sound less immediately audible than Lear's cries for judgment, exposure, and damage, but it nonetheless gives to these cries their motive and occasion. Lear's savage assuagements fail to cohere or satisfy, in part because no external world will answer them, in part because no single shape of curse can contain his rage. A deeper reason is that Lear's cries seek to drive away this other sound—call it a cry, a voice, a gesture, an attitude. This voice sifts through the cacophony of the storm, choruses with the noise, yet remains distinct, if we have ears to hear. It is perhaps just a murmur, neither song nor sense, yet it speaks for a need which cannot be put off, even by so endlessly evasive a stormer. Lear seeks by his calls to push away a thought more shameful to him than that of being his cruel daughters' dog, more painful than his grief and shame at the loss of his loving daughter. What this exiled king hears is different from the harrowing demand that he acknowledge Cordelia's love, which Stanley Cavell so powerfully intuits.[48] The frantic energy of Lear's curses suggests to me a different kind of challenge; they are driven by an eerie, concealed, and endlessly thwarted game of competition. His cries wrestle with a speech whose strength, ironically, renews itself with each fresh challenge he makes to it. It is a speech he cannot master, because his very desire to master it exposes his weakness, his need. He cannot bear even to acknowledge that competition, because it is an agon moved more by desire than resentment—the chief reason, I think, why the rage of this foolish old man continues to move us.

What Lear wants both to drive from his ear and to find in his own voice is the strength of Cordelia's "nothing," a gesture of negation more unshakable than any of Lear's curses (if not a curse itself).[49] That "nothing" is the founding Word that turns Lear's world upside down; it sees through the world's lies more clearly than any of his wild vituperations. Its nonsense works more absolutely to expose the nonsense of others. In responding as she does, Cordelia opens herself to violence more absolutely than Lear with his "uncovered head." Hers is a nothing that cannot be shunted away, even by bidding "what will take *all.*" It is her nothing that he wants, the shameless, savage strength she has to utter it, without regret, without resentment, almost without need. It is a nothing that yet seeks everything, a nothing that seeks knowingly to keep us from falling, in our desolation, through a hole at the bottom of the world.

In Jean-Luc Godard's collage-like film of *King Lear,* a grave, measured voice-over describes the power of that nothing thus:

A violent silence: the silence of Cordelia. To the question of a king, a gangster, her father, she answers "nothing." He demands the essential: to be loved, desired, from where he is loved. He has power, he is king, he wants to be wanted. Who wants him? Nothing, no thing—not will, not intelligence, no sex, but all the same a body, a little bit of flesh. Because for Lear, to hear is to see: "A man may see how this world goes with no eyes . . . look with thine ears." This is what he tries to do, the king who calls himself Lear, e-a-r, in listening to his daughters: he hopes to see their entire bodies stretched out across their voices. What he wants is not what he desires. What he wants is to forget this desire that he cannot stand, the nothing of Cordelia. So that he can silence the silence, he listens as if he's watching television; but Cordelia, what she shows in speaking is not nothing but her very presence, her exactitude.[50]

Cordelia's nothing represents an exiled point of origin, the contingent beginning of Lear's rage, an "exactitude" which he can, necessarily, never recover, though he tries to recuperate it. Lear's ironic *logos* in the storm is keyed to this word.

> *Cordelia.* Nothing, my lord.
> *Lear.*      Nothing?
> *Cordelia.* Nothing.
> *Lear.*      Nothing will come of nothing. Speak again.
> (1.1.87–90)[51]

That nothing makes her silence an activity; Cordelia's silence is transitive, as if "nothing" were not a noun, but a gerund (derived from an imaginary verb, "to noth"). Her silence silences. It refuses Lear's desire to hear his daughters give themselves up in their voices; it exposes her to his wrath, but also exposes Lear himself to an answer that he cannot bear to hear. This answer opens up a hole into which all other answers fall. It matches his demand for speech in a way that undoes that demand, and exposes its peculiar emptiness. This is why the storm echoes her nothing, her transitive silence and silencing. (She speaks again, and again.) On the heath, Lear engages in a kind of singing contest, not with the fool or Mad Tom, or even with gods of the rain, but with the memory of his youngest daughter's nothing. He tries to answer the extremity of that "low" utterance which so rigorously trumped his royal game, denied his parceled gift, exposed his folly, and provoked his first curse. Lear's storm noise competes with Cordelia's more severe knowledge, her more risky gesture of love, her cooler rage. Cordelia's nothing shows itself more capable than Lear's demand ("Which of you shall we say doth love us most") of remaking the world. That nothing freshly marks the power of what appears to be alien or bastard (linking her, strangely, to the usurping Edmund). That nothing continues to occupy a space within a world which he has so neatly divided up, and whose measures so quickly escape his calculations. The memory of her voice sharpens and torments his ears in the storm, as he becomes a less poised version of Wallace Stevens's "Snow Man," "the listener, who listens in the snow, / And, nothing himself, beholds / Nothing that is not there and the nothing that is."[52]

Lear, one might say, wants to be Cordelia since he cannot have her or escape her, or even kill her—to be Cordelia with a white beard, a storm beard full of those venerable strands that he gives over to the weather, as when he "tears his white hair, / Which the impetuous blasts with eyeless rage / Catch in their fury and make nothing of" (3.1.7—9).[53] Lear can never quite say "nothing" as Cordelia says it, yet neither can he drive the word from his ear. For her delicate word has already imprinted itself on the desolate noises of the wasteland. He, after all, helps to imprint it. If Cordelia's word cannot "redeem nature from the general curse," it is because, in Lear's echo chamber, her word weaves itself into the forms of curse. That is partly how Lear finds a home for that nothing in the storm. He demands that his own words echo that nothing which had caught him by surprise, which had moved at first only a baffled, weakly ironic repetition: "Nothing will come of nothing." Lear's relentless, if also thwarted, attachment to this word, his attempts to find a version of it in his mouth, is one reason why the storm scenes are touched at once by so desolate a sense of the real and by so sustained a feeling of hallucination. The curse or blessing of the world in *King Lear* is that no one can ever become nothing, any more than one can finally *say* nothing; no one can die when he wants to, or fully alienate an inalienable humanity.

If Lear cannot forget or repress Cordelia's "nothing," or the catastrophic loss of "all" which falls out from that word, it is partly because the fool has been replaying the opening scene throughout his early conversations with Lear. He faces Lear with a vision of the desolation he has taken upon himself and continues to inherit; like an ironic Leporello, he keeps a tally of Lear's losses, his nonentity, his reduction to crust and crumb, to a shadow, an eggshell, a pea pod, an empty codpiece, "an O without a figure" (1.4.183—84).[54] Keeping Cordelia's nothing in play, he makes it partly his own, native to the "low" language of the clown, someone who sticks to his master out of love, even if he continues to harass him and turn his apocalyptic harangues to mocking prophecies. The fool thus shows us a wilder companionability with nothing. By the time Lear runs through the storm, however, he has all but outrun the fool's explicit jesting and exhausted his frenetic powers of reduction. As Lear invokes the gods of thunder, the fool's words command no direct attention. They have lost their prior purchase on his recognitions. The fool has no answers left, no riddles he can provoke Lear to answer or that can translate the candor of his daughter's voice. Lear now converses only with himself, with the sky, with the shape of his own curses, and with the gods that his own words imprint on the air.

The sky gods themselves are silent, apart from whatever sound effects eke out the storm noise, echoing with Lear's own shouts. Without transcendental warrant, the gods exist here as elsewhere in the play only in the varying styles by which a human being speaks of them, invoking them as vengeful, just, cruel, playful, apathetic, kind, or charitable.[55] They have no ears to receive either blessing or curse from those onstage—unless it is the audience who is meant to take the place of the gods.[56] If there remains anyone onstage to answer Lear or give new form to his curses, and to the nothings he cannot capture or evade, it is Edgar in the guise of Mad Tom—that creature who astonishingly emerges in the storm as the precipitate of its violence, speaking for a desolation and a madness more impersonal than that to which even this exiled king can give voice.[57]

Tom is himself a "cursitor," a demoniac who has been compelled by the fiend "to course his own shadow for a traitor" (3.4.56). Tom's world is a more demotic reimagining of Lear's sublime storm, full of dangerous magic, foul fiends, taking airs, walking fires, and infectious blasts. Here all aggression or resentment, all curse, has turned more directly back on the self. Curse is not uttered directly. Yet in the words of this demonic list maker we find animated the shapes of a cursed world, its pains, its betrayals, and its vanities. The air and earth now carry seductions to lust, provocations to suicide, temptations to horrible appetite. "Didst thou give all to thy daughters?" Lear asks. Tom's answer breaks out into a wider world:

> Who gives anything to Poor Tom? Whom the foul fiend hath led through fire and through flame, through ford and whirlpool, o'er bog and quagmire; that hath laid knives under his pillow and halters in his pew; set ratsbane by his porridge, made him proud of heart, to ride on a bay trotting horse over four-inched bridges, to course his own shadow for a traitor. (50–56)

Sunk out of the air into the landscape, covered by its dirt, hidden in its rotted hollows, torn by its thorns and leaves, Tom devours the world's most abject vermin (vermin that represent at once revenge and suffering, appetite and repulsion). Like Coriolanus, he is something of a hunger artist, consuming only food that starves him or feeds his melancholia.[58] It is a vision which recalls the biblical idea of madness itself as a curse from God, in which Tom out-Nebuchadnezzars Nebuchadnezzar:

> Poor Tom, that eats the swimming frog, the toad, the tod-pole, the wall-newt and the water—; that in the fury of his heart, when the foul fiend rages, eats cow-dung for salads; swallows the old rat and the ditch-dog; drinks the green mantle of the standing pool. (125–29)

If not horrible food, the world's creatures have become emblems of abased moral life, a reflex of the demonic character of humanity that Lear would show us.[59]

> false of heart, light of ear, bloody of hand; hog in sloth, fox in stealth, wolf in greediness, dog in madness, lion in prey. Let not the creaking of shoes, nor the rustling of silks, betray thy poor heart to woman. Keep thy foot out of brothels, thy hand out of plackets, thy pen from lenders' books, and defy the foul fiend. (90–96)

This is the storm of the world which Tom has been walking or coursing through for his entire career. This landscape is archaic, yet full of contemporary detritus, things reified, accumulated, and dispersed all at once— soaked and decayed in the aftermath of the storm, like the contents of a drowned man's pockets. Boudoir and swamp, court and wilderness marry; the world of fops and prostitutes runs together with the world of rats and dung. This is what survives of the world of ample streams and fertile meadows promised by Lear to each of his daughters in act 1, parts of a world that can neither be destroyed nor purified in the storm. In Tom's language, the moral wisdom of a Christian culture survives as fragments of Aesopian allegory or as emptied shards of biblical commandments. These admonitions have themselves *become* curses, rather than—as in their original context— being underwritten by curses.

Tom's list of past professions echoes Edgar's own history of exile and abjection, even as it mirrors his false reputation for riot and treachery (those rumors which Edmund perpetuates). Tom's memories also suggest fragments of a picaresque romance, a story like that of Thomas Nashe's "unfortunate traveller," who thinks of travel itself as a primal curse.[60] Yet it is not the phantom memory of past quests and losses that strikes me in these catalogs; rather, it is how his language strikes at and creates Tom's present life. That life, that animation, lies in the very words that Tom "courses" through, words that are trotted over bridges and devoured as we listen.[61] His "fiends" and "furies" are the fears, regrets, shames, and resentments that are still alive, subject to fresh fantasy, still able to wound—yet no more than rags of language he carries into the wilderness, coverings of an invisible wound that might, if we saw it, shame us more than we know.[62]

One scholar asks that we listen with subtler ears to the way that Tom's language echoes the very sounds of the storm, that we listen also to how the storm itself picks up from Tom the sounds of the human world's seduction and betrayal—especially the cries, moans, hissing, creaking, and rustling noises that he evokes in his fragmentary narratives of his past life.[63] In so listening, we will understand how his mad talk sets up a strange dialectic. For his words at once catch the inhuman character of even human noises, their materiality and automatism, and show us the odd humanness of natural sounds, which includes their human-seeming indifference to other speakers and hearers. In Tom's language, reason and nonsense show their troubling but also redemptive complicity, if we have ears to hear. A strange, homeless babble presses up from within Tom's lists, in their jamming up and disjunctions of sense, their isolation of bits of language, and their near echolalia (toad / tod-pole, salads / swallows, wall-newt / water, etc.). These lists contain, as it were, a beggar's superfluity, an impoverishing excess that turns itself against any more orderly grammar of words or things in the world.[64] Tom's nonsense is, as it were, an activity, almost as baffling to our sense as Cordelia's aggressive, blankly resistant "nothing." Each demonic name—Hoppedance, Smulkin, Flibbertigibbet, Frateretto—is a wound laid down upon the skin of air. The names are also games, a relief from other more coercive or frustrated vocatives in this play. Tom's rhythmic murmurings are the cut-off refrains of some song or nursery rhyme: Hey no nonny, fa la la. They conjure a nonexistent or lost childishness. Yet if we listen, their nonsense works because it transforms the sense of other words that fill the air. Each bit of nonsense is a way of hearing experience, naming its troubled parts. The nonsense translates words whose own meanings are themselves desperate, lewd, infantile, residual, and mad, words whose implicit nonsense may simply be less evident. Thus, Lear's self-wounding picture of his "pelican daughters" becomes "Pillicock sat on Pillicock hill"; the madman's prayer "Do Poor Tom some charity" becomes "O do de do de do de," and his terrified warning "the foul fiend follows me" is mocked by "Fie, foh and fum" (mutterings of a murderous giant). At the end of act 3, scene 1, Kent urges that he and the gentleman who has told him of Lear "holla" to each other when they have found the king; as if obscured by the storm, that greeting echoes in Tom's "alow, alow, loo, loo," even as those words also ironically repeat that "low" voice which "reverbs no hollowness."

The resolute "joycing" of language in Tom's mad speech—like the dream language of *Finnegans Wake*—suggests something more than mere linguistic chaos. How does this hollowing out of words achieve a hallowing or healing, as Geoffrey Hartman might ask?[65] One answer comes if we think more broadly about Tom's place in these scenes. Mad Tom offers the audience an image of what it looks like to be cursed; he shows us the image of a cursed, fallen world, answering "with thy uncovered body this extremity of the skies" (3.4.100). He shows us, moreover, the madness of one who believes curses, who takes on himself the hollow fiction of supernatural agency which Lear's invocations presume. But there is one crucial thing: whatever rage and terror or protest we might hear behind his cries, Tom himself never utters a curse. Despite Edgar's early comment on the mad beggar's "lunatic bans," no bans fall from his lips, lunatic or otherwise. Tom will name the fiends that pursue him, point to them, call to them, catalog their powers, warn others away from them. He may address them with companionable fondness ("Dauphin my boy, my boy"), or bid them pass by with gentle courtesy. Indeed, we could imagine that these illusory fiends are the beggar's own curses, fallen back upon their speaker as Caliban's do. Yet Tom's spells seek to exorcise rather than attack: "Avaunt, you curs"; "Aroint thee, witch"; "Croak not, black angel"; "Peace Smulkin, peace thou fiend"; "Beware my follower." His magic, if we can call it that, is the magic of a shaman, rather than that of a witch or a witch's victim. Like a shaman, Edgar by impersonating a madman takes upon himself and bears away the infections of cursed world. Tom bears for others the burden of a world's curse. It is the demoniac, here, who exorcises, rather than himself being exorcised.

In lieu of ban or curse, what emerges in Tom's speeches, heartrendingly, is blessing. Tom places for us the power to bless in this world. "Bless thee from spells, star-blasting, and taking. . . . Bless thy five wits. . . . Bless thee, master. . . . Bless thee, goodman's son. . . . Bless thy sweet eyes, they bleed." Some of Tom's blessings may seem absurd or empty, not answering to particular evils or sufferings (in contrast with Cordelia's "All blest secrets, / All you unpublished virtues of the earth, / Spring with my tears" [4.4.15–17]—a prayer focused on her father). He has no "blessed gods" to back his blessings; indeed, those blessings remain indebted mostly to what curses him, his madness (or to Edgar's performance of madness). Furthermore, those blessings are scarcely heard, save by us; there is nothing in the text to suggest that his companions onstage take them in at all, other than as facets of his dementia. His blessings have, after all, no power against the coarser, blunter violence of Lear's daughters. If anything, they carry an edge of satire and abuse, since they so often bless what is already irrevocably wounded, already lost, such as old men's wits and bleeding eyes, or the faith of young men.[66] These are the residues of blessing, strained, fragile, even spectral.[67] They survive in a world which makes horrible use of blessing, in which blessing and curse enter into a coercive economy, benediction being offered only in return for lies, or keyed to despair. Late in the play, Cordelia and Edgar both ask their parents for blessings which are never returned (perhaps *that* is a blessing). If there is any blessing on Tom's blessings, indeed, it is that they are not traded for land or offered under the threat of pa-

ternal curse. Whether or not they are comprehended, Tom's benedictions
cannot be bargained for or banked.

---

After the storm, after Tom has vanished, the voice of curse seems to have
been consumed, scattered. Some characters in the play keep desperate faith
with the grammar of curse and blessing. One is a nameless gentleman, a servant of Cordelia, who, seeing the mad king, improvises a remarkable revision of the history of the Fall and Redemption, bringing it within the
precincts of the story of Lear himself:

> A sight most pitiful in the meanest wretch,
> Past speaking of in a king. Thou hast one daughter
> Who redeems nature from the general curse
> Which twain have brought her to.
> (4.6.200–203)[68]

Edgar, quite self-consciously I think, prompts him to recall a more secular
noise:

> Edgar.                                        Hail, gentle sir.
> Gentleman.  Sir, speed you. What's your will?
> Edgar.                                        Do you hear aught,
>          Sir, of a battle toward?
> Gentleman.                        Most sure and vulgar.
>          Every one hears that, which can distinguish sound.
> (203–6)

The magical logic of curse cannot begin to answer to a world that contains
Cornwall's and Regan's contempt, or that "sure and vulgar" noise of war.
Nor does curse make sense of the sublime grotesque of flower-crowned
Lear meeting blinded Gloucester on that imaginary beach below the
precipice of Dover.

This is horrific daylight, without the wind, darkness, and lightning of the
storm. Some of Lear's self-wounding rage against his children finds echo
here. But in large part Lear has abandoned curse. His desolation rather
emerges in a satirical register at once homely and apocalyptic. It echoes Mad
Tom's frenetic reductions and the fool's vision of a world turned upside
down; it also recalls Job's starker vision of a world in which the poor are oppressed by justice itself, though without Job's demand for a god to set things

right. Here there is no divinity except Lear himself to sort out good and evil, reward and punishment. His is like the voice of a ruined god stranded in time, combined with the voice of an old, smirking mountebank, composing a commedia dell'arte skit or magic show for his fellow exiles out of the scattered relics of his kingdom—a vision of the world in which thief and judge, whore and beadle, whipped and whipper, each metamorphose into the other, the latter of each pair being the worse mostly for pretending to be different.[69]

Gloucester sees in Lear an emblem of eschatological decay: "O ruined piece of nature, this great world / Shall so wear out to naught" (4.6.130–31). What has always astonished me most is the grotesque animation and fullness of the desolate world that Lear projects within the space of that "naught." It has the air of mad experiment. Its forms of play and exchange are counterfeit coins, dead or imaginary eyes, real and imaginary flowers plucked from white hair. There are strange substitutions of scale, species, and substance. An old woman "whose face between her forks presages snow" (117) shows the appetite of an insect or bird. A pygmy's straws acquire the power of strong lances. A troupe of military horse is shod with felt instead of iron (to keep murder silent). Lear stands pitiless before the stripped, pitiable, eyeless Gloucester. This king who has been in flight from eyes—from the determined gaze of Cordelia, the black looks of his daughters, the glare of imaginary fiends, the pitying glances of servants, even threatening to pluck out his own weeping eyes—with kingly dispatch now fills Gloucester's empty sockets with all the degraded, rejected eyes of the world. He makes the earl's blind, bleeding rings the squinting eyes of Cupid. He suggests that Gloucester get himself the glass eyes of scurvy politicians, and so "seem / To see the things thou dost not" (167–68). Lear even lends him his own eyes—as if to give up both his mourning and self-pity: "If thou wilt weep my fortunes, take my eyes" (173). Blindness here is not a loss to be wept, but a "naught" to be subjected to fantastic substitutions. Lear finds for Gloucester not just new eyes, but new ears to hear the world's sounds under the aspect of his satire: "A man may see how this world goes with no eyes. Look with thine ears" (146–47). In the storm, Lear had imagined himself pitiably set upon by barking lapdogs; now he asks that Gloucester hear the truth of authority's voice in the barking of a beggar's cur: "a dog's obeyed in office" (154–55). The whining or protest of an accused thief echoes the "railing" of the justice against the criminal. And in the wailing of a newborn child he hears not hunger, fear, need, frustration, or sorrow, but the stark echo of his own mockery: "When we are born we cry that we are come / To this great stage of fools" (178–79). Nature is made to lament the comic desolation of history.[70]

The blind man says of Lear when he arrives, "The trick of that voice I do well remember: / Is't not the king?" (105–6). One wonders what note in the voice survives as audible to this previously dull-eared courtier. Is it Lear's contempt, command, humor, rage, or self-pity? Is it like that "authority" which the disguised Kent sees, or says he sees, in Lear's face? What painful memory of voice is Lear himself trying to transform? Lear, the suffering king, invents a voice whose authority binds itself to the trenchant mockery of authority; he has found a place to utter "nothing" or "none" that silences the world of judgment and accusation. It is neither curse nor blessing, yet keeps a strange generosity:

> None does offend, none, I say none. I'll able 'em;
> Take that of me, my friend, who have the power
> To seal th'accuser's lips . . .
> . . . . . . . . . . . . . . . . . . . . . . . . . . . . . . . .
>                   Now, now, now, now,
> pull off my boots; harder, harder, so.
> (164–69)[71]

This is not a world to be washed away by a storm. It is, perhaps, a world in which the exiled king tries to be at home, an idea which Empson finds implied by Lear's desire to have his boots pulled off.[72] Lear's words imply a making as much as an unmaking of justice; he is, for a moment, the demiurge of a world at once ancient and newly built. But so eerily leveled a vision cannot be sustained. The war itself encroaches. And crazed, if strangely exhilarating, violences of Lear's own break out through the quiet: "And when I have stolen upon these son-in-laws, / Then kill, kill, kill, kill, kill, kill!" (182–83). It may grow upon us that Lear's words continue to evade looking at particular occasions of injustice, as well as concrete sources of brokenheartedness in his own history. Looking at the blinded earl, Lear says with astonishing plainness: "I know thee well enough, thy name is Gloucester" (174). What is "well enough" in this play which cannot take the measure of "enough" or "too little"? Lear's manic consolations turn away from Gloucester's horrible face; as he reinvents Gloucester's eyes, he puts off not only pity, but any more concrete investigation of who tore them out, or why, as if that demanded imagining something more horrible.

———

And yet nothing has been changed except what is
Unreal, as if nothing had been changed at all.
(Wallace Stevens)

The magical turns of plot that end Shakespeare's late romances stake a remarkable claim on the nonmagical. Though they obey the logic of dream, those turns also restore, or bring forth, an intense sense of candor—using that word here to mean brightness, transparency, and presence as much as truth. A candid uncanniness, call it, an impossible life in a possible world, or a possible life in an impossible world. Because the wish for magic that shapes our experience is exposed so nakedly at such moments, it is less likely merely to distort that experience; we see rather how the magic gives experience form, disenchanting as well as charming us. Magic becomes part of nature as much or as little as human beings are part of nature. Thus, at the end of *The Tempest,* we sense that Prospero's magic has forced all of his victims—as well as the magician himself—to show forth the truth of their characters, their powers of love, their cowardice, wisdom, and rage, even if this threatens the pious fictions that keep an old world intact, leaving any deeper reconciliation with life as a terribly open question. In *Cymbeline,* lost children, wronged lovers, foolish husbands, and rulers all gather together at the end; here the magical accidents by which they meet serve mostly to put away the kind of compulsive, hallucinatory dream work— fed by jealousy, fear, and suspicion—which had driven the play from its first moments and made Cymbeline ruler primarily over a kingdom of nightmare. The passions visible in the last scene are anything but calm; rage, coercion, and shame are clearly at work, along with remorse and forgiveness. But these darker emotions are now present in themselves, rather than disguised as forms of love or care or honor; they thus allow the characters to invite the world back in and be astonished as much by its plainness as its wonder. Likewise, the statue that comes at the end of *The Winter's Tale* undoes the nightmare world of violence and loss that Leontes had built on "nothing."

A similar candor shows itself in the closing act of *Lear,* refining further the candor of the king's grand constructions on that imaginary beach. This candor shows itself not in the raw violence of the war, the death of Lear's daughters, or the unraveling of Edmund's plots, but in Lear's own words. Consider the moment when he wakes up in the presence of Cordelia, after the storm. At almost all earlier moments in the play, Lear seems to be in a world other than the one he is in. Here he finds himself, for a moment, in place, even "in his own kingdom" (though he thinks this expression mocks him). He continues to oscillate between what looks like clear knowledge and what feels like denial, or hallucination. But the radical sense of flight or evasion that marks so many of Lear's utterances has disappeared. His mythic recognitions cannot be disillusioned by his literal ones.

Thou art a soul in bliss, but I am bound
Upon a wheel of fire that mine own tears
Do scald like molten lead. . . .
You are a spirit, I know; where did you die?
. . . . . . . . . . . . . . . . . . . . . . . . . . . . . . .
                    I know not what to say.
I will not swear these are my hands: let's see—
I feel this pinprick. . . .

. . . . . . . . . . . . . . . . . . . . . . . . . . . . . . .
I fear I am not in my perfect mind.
Methinks I should know you and know this man,
Yet I am doubtful. . . .

. . . . . . . . . . . . . . . . . . . . . . . . . . . . . . .
Be your tears wet? Yes, faith; I pray weep not.
If you have poison for me, I will drink it.
I know you do not love me.
(4.7.46–73)

There is a challenging immediacy in what he falsely knows—"You are a spirit, I know," "I know you do not love me." Such statements feel eerily balanced with, rather than violently contrasting, his saying about what he knows he does not know: "I fear I am not in my perfect mind," "I will not swear these are my hands." To say "I am bound / Upon a wheel of fire" does not try to cancel the world in which he says "I am a very foolish fond old man. . . . I think this lady / To be my child Cordelia" (69–70). That wheel is no elegant metaphysical machine that can "come full circle," rounding out all human injustice. Hallucinatory as it is, it yet short-circuits the more volatile and evasive style of imagery by which he had previously transfigured his own and others' suffering. His eyes are his own because his tears are his own, not those of nature, the weather, or the gods, not to be given up to others. Even his way of voicing doubt about the reality of Cordelia's tears—"Be your tears wet?"—feels like a return to the world. Or, rather, it entertains the possibility of a new world that is still this world. This is an aesthetic judgment rather than a philosophical one. What I hear, or imagine, is an eerie leveling of tone here, as if illusion and disillusionment occupied one space, danced with each other—both placing Lear in the world and shamelessly challenging its power to accommodate him (a little as Cordelia had once done).

The idealizations that proliferate as the play winds to its slow catastrophe—invocations of divine sacrifice, assertions of divine revenge—can seem by turns pathetic and obscene. (To their weird credit, Regan and Goneril remain generally impervious to this idealizing habit; they know that their cruelty is never anything other than human and scarcely bother to mask their viciousness until they both fall in love with the Machiavellian Edmund.) So I do not want to evoke this candor as some guarantee of blessing, some substitute for grace. It is not conversion, much less clear inner truth. Candor is not the same as acknowledgment, either; I think Cavell is right to say that Lear is still in flight at the end, as in his "Let's away to prison" speech, and that Cordelia's tears there may express mostly her sorrow at his continued failure to understand himself and her.[73] It is risky to ask that Lear bear, scapegoat-like, our wishes for an inward change that may not be there, or for some atonement with God or the world. Notwithstanding all these doubts, I find that I want some language to describe the lines quoted above as stark as that of Stevens in the closing lines of "A Discovery of Thought":

> The accent of deviation in the living thing
> That is its life preserved, the effort to be born
> Surviving being born, the event of life.[74]

The blessing in King Lear is of a life without blessing, also without curse, or a life whose blessing and curse together lie in their plain presentness.

When they see Lear emerge howling, carrying his dead daughter in his arms, Edgar, Kent, and Albany imagine they are living under the shadow of time's closure: Kent: "Is this the promised end?" Edgar: "Or image of that horror?" (5.3.261–62). I wonder, then, why in the closing acts of the play I can never keep from my mind those Stevensian images of an early brightness reached at the zero point of winter—images whose distance from any notion of transcendental rebirth is as great in Shakespeare as it is in Stevens. Job, at the end of his trials, gets three new daughters, together with the weight of those things that mark God's blessing: strength to live, honor, family, land, friends, servants, and wealth. Lear's daughters die all three around him, as if in answer to his first question to them.

What has become in this scene of Lear's mode of speaking in the storm, his invocations of violent judgment, his evasive self-abasements, his twistings of space, his conjurings of wind and rain to destroy life, to mar, defile, and break apart all human orders? "Blow winds" has become "Howl, howl, howl, howl." It is a human cry to human speakers, still imperious in its demand, yet expecting no answer, supplying its own lack, present to its own impotence. Of the wind and rain he so ardently transfigured, nothing is left but what Lear imagines he sees breaking from the lips of his dead daughter. It is an eerie, dying gift. Her mouth breathes forth only enough air to stir a feather. The moisture that remains is only sufficient to stain the surface of a polished stone. These are now the storm of Cordelia's life, or all Lear can hold onto of that life, solid, fragile, entirely of the earth, the nearest emblems of the "nothing" or silence by which she had, at first, responded to her father's question. They are the storm of his demand for the world's response to his need. It is all still a lie, an evasion. He sees and hears what is not there—and without the knowing *ironia* or *illusio* of his sleights of hand at Dover. He still wants to put words in his daughter's mouth. But it is the nakedness of the cry for traces of life that counts here, the knowledge of how much that chance of nothing might pay back "all sorrows / That ever I have felt" (264–65); what counts is the final relentlessness of his demand to the world, the survivors of war, the dead, the audience, and the gods: "Look on her: look, her lips, / Look there, look there!" (309–10). This call is no more or less suffused with illusion than the certainty of "I know when one is dead and when one lives; / She's dead as earth" (258–59).

Despite some surviving habits of idealization, those left onstage do *not* try to imagine a procession, a grave, a monument, prayers, or praise, as so frequently happens at the end of the other tragedies. Nobody thinks about interment. Could one stage a funeral or build a monument around that stone and that feather, that stillness and that motion? Yet is their absence blessed?

# AN IMAGINARY THEATER

 small, wild-looking woman—a peasant named Lucie Cabrol—walks through a crowd of actors crouching or supine on the stage, their arms stretched up with outspread fingers. They are clumps of tall blackberry bushes, from whose wavering stems the woman, with a quick, deliberate motion, plucks the fruits one by one. The invisible berries become real as her hands move over those other hands. Yet what I see is not an illusion of visible nature. It is nature as a form of a human gesture, a form of human gift and theft. What I see is how the illusory fruit is supplied by the collaboration of the actors in the task of creating a world. It not a world without treachery, or menace; that imagined reality seems ready to disappear at every moment, sustained as it is by nothing more than the uncanny complicity of these actors. Yet that world is reborn as readily, as the players stop being bushes and assume new forms that fill the stage—pigs, horses, children, peasants, the dead, the very land itself. These beings alternately threaten and help that woman, worker, mocker, smuggler, and survivor that she is—a woman who in this story is always isolated, who when she speaks (in a voice that rings and pierces) refuses any names for the world but the one she gives it; who squats repeatedly, unblushingly, on the stage, as if to defecate, in order to claim that space more fully for herself, to show us what it means to be at home there, invulnerable, yet exposed to our eyes. Lucie's nickname, given to her in both hate and love, is "the cocadrille"—a basilisk, bred of dung, that kills by looking.

Hanging in the darkness at a height above human height is an isolated, il-
luminated mouth, with brightly painted lips. From that mouth pours a relentless, often incomprehensible flood of words. The tone is eerily flat, with
an occasional laugh or scream. The mouth's words begin in a low murmur,
but one slowly gathers pieces of a narrative. It recounts the history of a
nameless woman from her orphaned childhood to purgatorial old age. This
woman "never quite born" spends her days in silence, feeling always a dull
roar in her skull, a buzzing in the ear that might be thought—save at unpredictable moments when words break out of her, so suddenly that she hardly
recognizes them as her own. She does not know what story they tell or
prayer they offer to an uncomprehending world. In general, the mouth's
story unfolds without protest or complaint. Four times, however, the
mouth reaches a crisis in storytelling, when it is challenged, as if by an invisible questioner, to identify itself with the subject of its story, that strange old
woman—challenged, that is, to say "I": " . . . straining to hear . . . the odd
word . . . make some sense of it . . . whole body like gone . . . just the
mouth . . . like maddened . . . and can't stop . . . no stopping it . . . something she—. . . something she had to—. . . what? . . who? . . no! . . she!
[Pause]."[1] The mouth is narrating its own history of wild speaking, at once
enacting and describing its life amid dead, buzzing words, caught as the author says "by a vehement refusal to relinquish the third person."[2] Listening
to the words of this mouth, I hear at one moment the noise of speech and the
noise of what goes on behind speech, the babble out of which speech
emerges. The visible mouth is not quite a mask or even a gesture. It is more
like a wound fixed in the thick dark of the stage; it is both ear and mouth at
once. The mouth we see belongs to that hearsay woman. But it also marks
the terrible exposure and the terrible stamina of the hidden actress from
whom those words pour with such impersonal speed.[3]

On the bare, unrestored stage of an old vaudeville theater in Paris, a
group of seven actors is gathered together. They are shoeless, in casual clothing, like actors at a rehearsal, yet also with the air of refugees camping in the
ruins. Under the high plaster arches they perform, as if for their own grave
amusement, a collage of scenes from *Hamlet,* in French translation. The
piece, entitled *Qui est là,* extracts many moments of soliloquy, but it also selects many scenes of embedded performance, occasions when one group of
characters becomes an audience to the others. Complicating the collage is
the fact that these scenes are punctuated by recitations of brief passages
from great visionaries of the theater—Zeami Motokiyo, Konstantin Stani-
slavsky, Vsevolod Meyerhold, E. Gordon Craig, Bertolt Brecht, and Antonin
Artaud—passages that speak mainly about the presence of the actor on-

stage. Often, these fragments of wisdom are placed so as to spur, or give an impulse to, some action in Shakespeare's play. So, for example, an actor who repeats Brecht's account of a theater that allows for detached analysis becomes Rosencrantz vainly questioning the mad prince; Meyerhold describing how actors "playing dead" must be hidden from sight becomes Polonius stuck behind the arras; Craig describing the ghostly quality of Shakespearean characters becomes Claudius unable to pray; Artaud attacking the deceptions of naturalism becomes mad Ophelia, alone onstage, hanging invisible flowers on the air. The piece thus requires the actors continually to slide between different worlds, different scales of attention and self-consciousness. The result is not merely fracture. Rather, each scene from *Hamlet* feels like a fresh improvisation. Each has the quality of something unforeseen, newly hatched, even as it resonates with a larger history. One begins to feel, weirdly enough, as if each famous director is himself a character already imagined by Shakespeare, occupying the place of a pedantic father, a secretive king, a demanding ghost, or a guilty mother. What we see onstage is saturated with many different dreams of the theater, different dreams of the actor.

This version of *Hamlet* has no final duel. In the last scene we instead see the actors sprawled about on the stage, among overturned chairs, listening as the actor playing Hamlet says, with immense and insistent calm, "If it be now, 'tis not to come; if it be not to come, it will be now; if it be not now, yet it will come. The readiness is all." In their original context, these words invite one to speculate about secret plots, hidden enemies, and poisoned swords; they frame Hamlet's preternaturally calm attention in the face of a dangerous, temporal world. On this occasion, what blazes out is that Hamlet's ambiguous "now" refers most pressingly to the now of performance itself. The word plucks at the real time of the actor's playing, which is also the time of our watching and listening to their work. It is that now which by eerie pact has become so full, so capable of tearing at us, so undetermined in its presences and interruptions; inevitably passing, it is yet terribly hard to leave hold of. The readiness which is all becomes the readiness of these particular actors, open to so many changing impulses. It is also the real or wished-for readiness of the audience who listens to them.

THE IMAGINARY THEATER is the real theater. If theater transfigures the real with such tearing immediacy, it is by transfiguring itself—transforming our sense of the actor's presence, our understanding of the technology of illusion, our feeling for what it means to be an audience member. Different as they were, the productions I have described above—*The Three Lives of Lucie Cabrol,* a play based on a story of John Berger, performed by the British Theatre de Complicite (1996); Samuel Beckett's *Not I,* performed by Dublin's Gate Theater (1996); and *Qui est là,* "une recherche théâtrale" by Peter Brook (1997)—all shared something basic: in each piece one felt a new world being conjured up onstage, even as one was caught by the gravitational pull of the stage work itself.[4] One felt what Bert O. States calls the "shudder of [the play's] refusal to settle into the illusion."[5] Mere disenchantment, or a *mis-en-abîme* of self-reference, was not the point here. Rather, the refusal of illusion made the most ordinary facets of the stage work reveal themselves as ever stranger things, even in their very nakedness. As mysterious as any closed fictive world conjured up onstage were the actors themselves: one wondered about what drove their work, about their commitment to a space and to an ensemble, or to the rigor and mutability of certain gestures. One wondered about the mere weight of their bodies. The stage space revealed itself as at once generative and dangerous. It fed on contradictory pressures. It was the source of something immediately present, but also something "*not yet here,* a thing without a history, or rather a thing whose history is about to be revised."[6] There was no escape from time or accident—not for the actors and not for the audience. Here even the most established stage conventions were held within a space subject to continual metamorphosis, where nothing was guaranteed in advance. The most contingent gesture could thus gain a curious objectivity.

Each piece sought after more radical forms of theatrical gesture; each explored the paradoxical nakedness of theatrical masks, and the strange compulsiveness of role-playing; each was ready to break with any continuous illusion of reality onstage. All of this marked them as works in a modernist or postmodernist tradition. But even as such they can open up some more general reflections about the nature of theater. For many of the effects on which they depended—an intense awareness of the theatrical moment, a double consciousness of actor and character, a sense of the radiance of individual gestures, a feeling for the mutability of fictive spaces—can be found as readily in the theater of Shakespeare, Molière, Ibsen, and Chekhov. If I speak less at first about issues of dramatic speech, or about the play of hearing and noise on stage, that is strategic. We need to start with broader issues, in order to see better why the matter of language counts so much, both for Shakespeare and for the life of performance at large.

AT ITS STRONGEST, live theater has for me the force of a wound, the wound of a presence. That wound depends on the pressure of the stage's illusions against a world whose larger illusions have become invisible. What wounds is the stage's power to create its demands almost out of nothing, out of the most ordinary objects or gestures. What wounds is the actors themselves, the metaphysical shock to their presence onstage, the way their mere entrances and exits can so suddenly transform the space around them. I am struck by the actors' freedom or privilege—the fact that they are invulnerable yet wholly exposed to the audience's unstable appetites; that their creation depends on graceful and clumsy bodies, subject to time, yet able to give form to what is out of time.[7] What wounds is the actors' commitment to an order of words that is their own and not their own, their desire to transform themselves for the sake of what Hamlet calls "a dream of passion," something Hamlet himself thinks of as "monstrous." Actors brave their own shame and ours and yet remain present on the platform, full of risk, unwounded by what might most wound us. They yield themselves by their discipline to impulses that might shatter them but that in fact keep them alive, that keep them *onstage* rather than running away.[8]

I think here of the almost shamanistic power that masks can have for some actors. For the actor to put on an alien, immobile face, however plain or grotesque, strips away any more habitual masks, including the mask of the natural face. The actor is invisible, yet more exposed to himself. If the moment is right, improvising with that mask will open him up to less familiar, less socializable forces within, a process which lends an uncannier animation to the dead mask as well.[9] It works by a law of echo, as Peter Brook writes, sending a message in and projecting a message out.[10] Unexpected movements, sounds, expressions, characters, and creatures emerge, forms of nobility and violence that may frighten the actor as much as the audience. Theater depends on the dream of a community able to absorb and sustain such uncommon forces, to make them a means of survival, a source of increased life. Such a freeing up of things can be a cure, a catharsis; it can also "cut to the brain." It produces a wound capable of communicating itself to the world, like a plague, a wound whose strength binds audience and actor to the shared space of the theater. In the wound lies a salient wonder; there is a blessing in the *blessure*.[11] This is why, as Michael Goldman argues, so many central creations of the dramatic tradition—from Oedipus and Hamlet to Woyzeck and Winnie—offer dramatic parables of the actor's survival through role-playing.[12] They are vehicles for a role-playing that continually risks delusion and self-destruction but which thereby maintains the energy of the actor's uncanny life—a life that, as it draws us in, may help suspend our attachment to more conventional, more self-limiting theatricalizations of ourselves and the world.

   What I sense onstage is a struggle with death. It is a fight conducted not
with magical weaponry but with mortal bodies and voices that risk their
own quickness, need, and depth. The struggle is more absorbing to watch,
given that one knows how easily actors themselves can bring death onto the
stage, how quickly stage work can become lifeless, a matter of bloodless
posturing and automatism. It can happen through a failure of intelligence or
honesty, a closing off of impulse, or a yielding to mere effects. It can come
simply from a desire for repetition, or rather, since repetition is inevitable,
from failure to make each repetition a fresh occasion for risk.[13] There is
nothing deader than dead acting, and bad theater is bad in a way that bad poetry or even bad cinema cannot be. What Brook calls "the deadly theater"
sticks like pitch, especially because of one's inescapable complicity as an audience member.[14] (The space and time of performance include me, my
breath and body, my impatience, embarrassment, disgust, and delight, even
as that time and space is transformed, made fuller or more precarious.
Boundaries remain in place, but I am made responsible for keeping my distance as I am not, say, when I watch a film.) There are moments when to sit
through a bad play and to leave in the middle feel equally humiliating.

   The paradox of this struggle with death is that there remains something
necessarily ghostlike in actors onstage, caught between those alien forces
they might want to tap into and the heartless posturing they may end up
with. Stage ghosts interest us as masks for the actors' ghostliness, Goldman
writes. A theory of ghosts could help us frame a theory of drama: "Ghosts
are dramatic because they make for action. By their very nature they stimu-
late the flow of aggression on which all drama depends. Ghosts haunt us;
that is, they bring aggression to bear on us in an especially volatile way—a
way that penetrates with particular intensity to our psyche and encourages
imitation, encourages us to haunt as we are haunted. . . . The haunting
transmits itself through us to a wider world."[15] The point of theater, insists
Jean Cocteau, "is not to put life onto the stage but to make the stage live."[16]
Sometimes this means putting death onstage. These ghosts are not always of
one sort. "In any historical period, drama must find its proper ghosts,
sources for haunting that an audience can accept as both meaningful and
mysterious."[17] This suggests a useful critical exercise. While reading or
watching any play one should ask, as often as necessary: Where is the ghost?
Who is the most ghostlike? Who is becoming a ghost? It is a step toward understanding what kind of theater one is sitting in, and also a step toward seeing how a given play understands both human beings in general and actors in
particular. What kinds of ghosts, or actors, are these: in Ibsen, the frightened
woman who mimes bravery, toys murderously with her father's guns, and

burns books alive; in Shakespeare, the fat man who rises up from being killed and then starts to stab at a corpse; in Büchner, the abused soldier continually in motion, rushing through the world "like an open razor," given to strange visions of corpses and light; or, in the scene so crucial to medieval theater, the angel sitting by an empty tomb who asks the three women that approach him, "Why seek ye the living among the dead?"

WHAT I HAVE CALLED theater's wounding presence depends on acts of translation, moments of metamorphosis when the stage becomes what Artaud calls "a site of passage."[18] It is a matter of how an actor takes up a word or an object, charging it with fresh meaning or throwing it into a new relation, lending it an eccentric destiny. A conventional gesture gets animated by a new possibility, something on which the actor will seem to stake everything. The simplest things may most catch us most: an actor's way of picking up a shoe, taking off a glove, sitting on the floor, reaching for a hand, turning a head. Small movements may indeed shift a world on its axis or reinterpret an entire family history. I recall in *Qui est là,* for example, the way that Brook's Hamlet, in the battlement scene, drew around his own shoulders the arms of the trembling ghost, as if to invent the possibility of extending comfort across a metaphysical threshold. Or, in *The Three Lives of Lucie Cabrol,* I recall how that strange woman's urgent gesture of plucking kept echoing with other gestures of theft and love in the play, other forms of holding, reaching, and beckoning. Such gestures acquired their own weird momentum. Shifting as they were, the gestures had a way of sticking for a moment in the air; shared out among the group, they lived a life beyond the individual actors who made them, and for that reason these motions were things the actors themselves could either trust or betray. (Part of the power in the actors' movements was that they reminded one of how many other possible gestures filled the air—like a cloud of insects or web of rumors—even as they devoured those alternative gestures.) Watching such movements—especially in the work of a highly trained ensemble like Theatre de Complicite, where each actor is so alive to the others' impulses—can have an uncanny effect. What one ordinarily knows about a face, a hand, or a voice gets left behind: a hand can become a voice, or a tongue a hand. One person's arm becomes another's arm, a living body becomes a ghost's body; a noise can become an eye, empty space can acquire ears; a table can become a breast, a wall a mouth, the floor an erection. The very stillness of a body can become the disguise for another life. The points of contact between separate bodies can become things with individual life, as Rainer Maria Rilke said of certain sculptures of Rodin.[19] One feels, to quote Artaud again, "a perpetual play of mirrors in which the parts of the human body seem to send each other echoes."[20] New wholes are supplied in the face of what is lacking or sacrificed, as when that isolated mouth in *Not I* also became an ear and eye emerging from the dark. If such emergences onstage also make one conscious of how quickly they may be lost, that itself is part of their power. In another production of Complicite, a remarkable rendering of Bruno Schulz's *Street of Crocodiles*—a show full of the terrors of creation, the fright of ordinary objects suddenly coming to life—the clownish father continually repeats: "The migration of forms is the essence of life. . . . In the wink of an eye we may no longer be who we think we are."

Physical gesture can devour the spoken word onstage, subjecting words to an entirely visual or bodily idiom—something that Artaud hoped would create a revolution in Western theater, too much bound, he thought, by the dead authority of texts. But the opposition between gesture and word feels false to the degree that the word itself lives onstage as a gesture, a site of passage and translation, exposure and secrecy. It is here that I can return to what has been the central theme of this book: the wounding presence of the word. In Shakespeare's plays, after all, the spoken word often carries dramatic weight just through becoming an entity in its own right. Launched into the air, the spoken word can be fought over, marred, remade, juggled with, or buried, thrown back at speakers with changed force. For a dark wit like Hamlet, any word (say, "son" or "king") becomes a prop, a tool, a weapon. Words bind the actors together through forms of violence or contamination. Individual words and phrases wander, often taking up a habitation in speakers who know little of their history; each character is made to speak for many others, even in their isolation. Words hide their sense, or get caught up by darker systems of noise and murmur, like Cordelia's "nothing." What must have been unsettling as well as compelling for Renaissance audiences, even in plays by writers other than Shakespeare, was the spectacle of an actor's ability to make himself up onstage exactly out of such ungrounded words, words subject to such a conflict of employments. Fed by ever more complex and self-sustaining forms of dramatic poetry and prose, the actor could use these words as the frame or armor of a self. Such words were the means by which a self could devour and transform the world outside, even as they were also the very things which made the self vulnerable to other tongues and ears, vulnerable to its own words as well. In Shakespeare, especially, they become the key to a volatile, interior music.

Shakespeare's way of making the dramatic word both thing and creature, however rich, is not unique. Consider, for a moment, some of the longest-lived conventions of dramatic speech in Western theater: the rhythmical,

compulsive exchanges of speech in stichomythia; the use of verbal duels animated by the aggressive, shifting patterns of pun and wordplay; the use of
asides to the audience, or the presence onstage of multiple, sometimes silent
listeners; the rambling, nonsensical babble of stage clowns and madmen; the
use of offstage noises or cries; the intrusion of messengers bearing strange
stories and rumors. These devices survive, transformed and often concealed, even in a theater that strives to banish the unreal conventions of theatrical speech, such as that of Ibsen and Chekhov. The conventions work in
part because they reinforce a sense of human words gaining a richer, more
unsettling life apart from the command of any single speaker or hearer. They
create multiple levels of attention, heightening the tension between what is
heard and unheard, spoken and unspoken. They create a situation in which
mere noise, words of rumor or suspicion or surmise, gains a power to penetrate the world onstage, to reshape both atmosphere and action. Such devices work because they challenge the actor onstage to be alive to, and
changed by, the sudden gestural event of speech. How else is it that even
nonverbal sounds breaking forth on a stage—water drops, footfalls, a clock
ticking, wind, a knock—can become a call or a promise?

One ancient example may suffice here, since it points to resources in human theater that are still alive for us. Consider how, in *Oedipus the King,* the
hero's words continually open up possibilities over which he has no control.
His words become at once more and less powerful than he is prepared to allow. From the play's beginning, Oedipus wants words that will bear his
power and his promise. He looks for words that will undo curses, cure a
plague, and solve mortal riddles, words that speak from a glowing core of
truth. "Your fate looms in my words," he says to the chorus.[21] Yet the words
that Oedipus speaks carry him into conflict; they expose him to others and
round fresh riddles and curses back upon him. As the play unfolds, Oedipus's utterances are increasingly challenged by other words—old stories,
forgotten rumors, prophecies, reports, calls, and accusations. These flood
his ear and transform his speech, even though he tries to silence, distort, and
mock them; they become a storm that mirrors the storm of plague infecting
the city. In the process, he falls into ever more self-wounding utterances.
Oedipus blinds himself, one might say, precisely to mark the mortal opening
of his ears and of his language in the play.

I think here of a power or presence in the voices of certain actors that often catches me, as much a matter of technique as of natural gift. The actor's
words are put forth into external space, and yet they hover in his mouth or
around his body. The word becomes at once manifest and enigmatic, a small
part of something unseen. This is more than resonance. The word again

becomes more thinglike, takes up a life separate from the speaker and yet tied to him. Silence can grow around such a word; we sense in it traces of an unacknowledged history. The word may become a little noisy, so that we hear in it other impulses and overtones. It is visceral speech, full of a demand or desire that the speaker cannot entirely control. It colors the air with traces of lymph, blood, and bone. If such a voice is the signature of a particular actor, it may also become a mark of the character the actor plays. (I think of the vulnerable upper register in Laurence Olivier's Lear, as opposed to Paul Scofield's low, material growl.) The one who speaks, as much as the ones who hear, is exposed to the eccentric force latent in what is spoken. The word indeed seems to drop back down inside the actor as it is spoken, though perhaps only for an instant, before calling forth an answer or joining a larger rhythm. The aim is to keep the word from shutting itself up, turning mute. At such moments, the actor's voice shows itself to be an ear as much as a tongue. ("As actors, we learn to speak so that we can hear better," I heard a remarkable voice teacher, Isobel Kirk, once say.) The spoken word invites other possibilities, both physical and verbal. This is perhaps why actors whose speech has too fixed or articulate a "character" can give pain: they seem deaf.

In Shakespeare's plays, it is the written words that crucially sustain this sense of a mutable, generative presence in the actor's speech, give it shape and force. How the actor's words become gestures is, or should be, conditioned by the rhythms, echoes, ambiguities, and silences that are present in the text itself. But it is worth considering how the powers of the actor can enter into conspiracy with the text. The actor gives the text's words voice; ideally, he lends them whatever range of expression or motion are in his power to give. But his powers will also be tested, stretched, fed, and exposed by the words of the text. The text should not let the actor go. The pressure of the text's words opens up possibilities of voice more extreme than the ordinary—subtler modulations, starker contradictions. It fetches up an order of speech otherwise unavailable, or not guaranteed in advance. The actor's ability to sustain and live within such discoveries, to lend himself to them, will be one measure of his mastery.[22] There is thus a theatrically pragmatic reason why Shakespeare's texts put in the actors' mouths words that echo the voices of ghosts or reverberate with the noise of storms, or words that so strangely repeat and transform those of other speakers. By means of such patterns the words an actor speaks can become the substance of what his or her character suffers and re-creates onstage.

The drama of listening is subject to fantastic invention in such a theater. Consider this situation from *King Lear:* a disguised son leads his horribly blinded father to an imaginary precipice; he asks him to hear the screams of birds that are not heard, to see ships that cannot be seen, to believe that they stand on a cliff whose height makes crashing waves inaudible. The son's words create a world of vast distances in which everything dizzyingly shrinks. Or consider this from *Cymbeline:* a wife who has fled from court to search for her exiled husband finds herself in a forest, reading first silently, and then out loud, a letter from that husband to his servant. She repeats in her own voice her husband's insane conviction that she has been unfaithful to their marriage bed; she reads out to that servant—who himself stands listening to what he knows is a lie—her husband's command that he kill her. Or yet a third moment from *The Tempest:* on a desert island, weird music breaks around a pair of shipwrecked clowns. Their companion, a monster, tells them not to worry; he reassures them that the island is full of magical noises, "sounds and sweet airs, that give delight and hurt not." The story can feel like an improvisation, a way of keeping his new companions from fear, so that they will help him to murder his old master. But the news of those noises is also a token of some power of hearing in the monster that the master never knows. In each of these scenes the ordinary act of listening is transformed by the fiction; it becomes something frightening, as well as more absolutely uncanny. We feel a disturbing charm in the way that characters are invited to hear what is not or may not be audible, or are made to listen to words that must wound them beyond words. The very muteness of a given character makes me more interested in what it means for him or her to listen to certain words. These scenes put me in a position to identify with both father and son, mistress and servant, monster and clown, even as I am drawn in by questions that none of them can ask or answer.

LET ME RETURN IN CLOSING to Brook's *Qui est là.* This piece explored the presence of the actor exactly by thickening the drama of translation onstage; it thus made one better understand how *Hamlet* itself works as a play about translation and mistranslation, about the passage of words that can invade the ear and unsettle the world. This came through at an obvious level by the fact that one was hearing Shakespeare's text in French, in a lucid, spare translation by Brook's collaborator, Jean-Claude Carrière. The drama of listening was also given weight by the astonishing ensemble work of the seven actors, each of whom was always poised to respond to whatever impulses of sound or motion might arrive on the air from his or her companions. Also, as I have said, the actors moved between Shakespeare's text and the fragments of Brecht or Artaud, finding in such movement the motive to start or break off a given scene. But the issue of translation was given its starkest form by the presence in the play of more literally foreign languages.

One instance of this was work of a tall, gaunt actor from Upper Volta, So-
tigui Kouyate, who played both Claudius and ghost. As the usurping uncle,
he spoke in clear, if strongly accented French. But when he took on the
ghost's role, clad in a vast red mantle, he spoke in his native tongue—half
chanting, half trembling, filled with such anxiety that Brook's Hamlet
(Bakary Sangaré) pulled the ghost's arm around his shoulders. The device insisted that the urgent, opaque music of the ghost's speech belonged to the
actor as well as the character. Brook could depend on our remembering the
drift of the original text, yet it was more than a showman's clever trick
(though it was that). The speech made the ghost more uncanny by not letting
hearers take too literally the fiction of his ghostliness. (It was, in part, the ordinary ghostliness of languages we do not understand.) The device made
equally strange the fiction of Hamlet's listening to this ghost—a phantasm
who in Shakespeare's play at once withholds awful tales of purgatory and
blurts out harrowing rumors about the bloody world of the present. It made
one more aware of the ghostliness of the actor's words; one felt more
strongly the paradoxical dimension from which any actor speaks and in
which he listens. The audience was also reminded of its own vexed need to
listen to words spoken onstage. Brook made one feel the essential ghostliness of a theater in which words survive only when lent to the ears of an audience who may misinterpret or mishear them, drawn in by a music that
often exceeds the ordinary sense.

Brook used a similar device later, in the scene where Hamlet greets the
traveling players and the head player recites lines describing how "bloody
Pyrrhus" murders Priam and the "mobbled Queen" Hecuba runs up and
down with grief. One of the veterans of Brook's theater, Yoshi Oida, took on
the role of the head player. Clad in a simple kimono, he spoke the lines in
Japanese, at the same time conveying the images of violence and mourning
using the hieratic motions of Noh theater. It was a kind of audible dumb
show, combining the most primitive and most sophisticated styles of mumming; tied to the surprise of the moment, it was also full of ancient preci-
sions. The player's speech, remember, is for Hamlet the great example of
what is monstrous in the actor's work—monstrous in the willing self-
violence by which the actor forces his soul and body "so to his own conceit,"
for the sake of nothing but "a fiction . . . a dream of passion," a dream that
yet becomes visibly true in performance. In Brook, the player's monstrosity
was more mediated, but no less unsettling. The use of Japanese words and
Noh gestures made the actor's strangeness into a kind of open secret. At the
same time the performance showed the capacity of the text, and of the actor
in the text, to span worlds, to negotiate heterodox realities.

The traveling player and the paternal ghost were tied together by their use of foreign tongues. Their ways of telling stories and shaping a world were thus parts of a shared spectrum of being. Speaking in languages that signified most literally to their own ears, yet were able to strike us so immediately, both players reanimated the text's reflections on theater; the two spoke to the uncanniness but also the universality of the actor's speech, the dream of a life within or below the spoken word, something held in suspension, harking back to hidden sources. These scenes also raised with immediacy the question of what an actor's solitude amounts to, what privacy is allowed him in a mode that must expose so much.

I should add that when Brook's Ophelia, Giovanna Mezzogiorno, emerged onto the platform—standing alone, hanging her invisible flowers on the empty air—she spoke her mad songs to us in the plainest French prose. By this her songs became at once an intensely private ritual and the simplest news she could give to the theater space. Ophelia's questions became the actor's questions to the audience—not, in her case, "Who's there?" but, say, "How should I your true love know / From another one?"

Brook made *Hamlet* into something of a chamber piece. He gentled the atmosphere of menace in the play and muted its voices of rage and contempt. There was nothing in Brook's Hamlet of G. Wilson Knight's "embassy of death." Indeed, it was as if this Hamlet's grace and reflectiveness had diffused itself throughout the entire ensemble. Yet *Qui est là* also sought after something quite elemental (an aim marked by the extraordinary fact that Brook's title dropped the question mark from *Hamlet*'s opening question). The piece depended so much on moments of transformation and exposure; it kept alive the immediacy of all emergencies and emergences onstage. It staked everything on a dream of complicity between actor and actor, between actor and text, and between actor and audience. It made present a theater unsupported onstage save by the most basic of means, such that a real and an imaginary theater emerged together and continually reshaped one another.

At the very opening of Brook's piece, the young actor playing Barnardo, the watchman on the battlement, ran onto the stage crying out with great exuberance, "Qui est là?" An older actor watched critically from stage right, and stopped him. "Non," he said, "ce n'est pas ça." The young actor walked slowly back into the wings and emerged again, repeating the question with intenser energy. He was halted again, and again sent back. "That's not it, yet." The third time, however, speaking more plainly to the audience and to the space of the stage, he got it; the audience heard him, and he heard himself, asking a question, not speaking a line; and he spoke it with all of the weight which that question entails for character and actor and listener. "Qui est là?" After that, the play could begin, offering all its myriad answers to the question. The rehearsal slid magically into the performance. It was a carefully staged trick. But it was a trick of the moment, performed without a net.

———

The great noise or *fama* that makes up the afterlife of Shakespeare's plays is the subject of a different book. The playwright, often his mere name, survives as the shadowy ruler over something like Ovid's House of Rumor—a place at the crossing point of sea, sky, and land, no temple of pristine marble statues but the gathering place of all the world's clamors, murmurs, cries, tales, stories, wishes, and news, "filled with presences that shift and wander, / Rumors in thousands, lies and truth together, / Confused, confusing."[23] The world's sounds are endlessly reflected in this space, begetting and re-begetting each other. There are so many competing versions of Shakespeare, so many translations, adaptations, thefts, ventriloquisms, mishearings, such a chaos of revisionary echoes, countless forms of praise which can sound subtly like calumny. Even in their first entry into print, Shakespeare's words are often dogged by error, by suspicion of mishearing or distortion. Some cases we may rationalize, such as those curious flattenings found in the First Quarto of *Hamlet* (1603)—"Stand: who is that?" "To be, or not to be, I there's the point"—which seem to the misremembrances or simplifications of actors adapting the play for performance in the provinces. Others, like that unyielding crux in the Second Quarto (1604)—"the dram of eale / Doth all the noble substance of a doubt, / To his own scandale"—point to opacities that no theory about authorial second thoughts, playhouse revision, memorial contamination, or the errors of copyists and compositors is likely ever to explain completely.[24] The truly scandalous thing is that the poet's words, notwithstanding the confusions of their origin and reception, keep their authority, their precision, their signature strangeness, their power to penetrate the soul; that they are able to survive millions of repetitions without exhaustion and without yielding up the heart of their mystery. The texts form a labyrinth of mirrors and ghostly passages, a maze folded up within itself, moreover a maze that keeps moving about "as swyft as thought," like Chaucer's "Domus Dedaly," itself a version of Ovid's House of Rumor.[25] Yet that maze remains open to the ordinary world. The words of the plays, even in their very opacity, give us the confidence to walk on the plainest ground of earth, to speak to ourselves and to others more humanely, more urgently, eking out our experience by their "spontaneous particulars of sound." The words are always there to be renewed, even if, as Brook's actor-sentinel reminds us, it takes work and luck to make them carry, to make them afflict us again.

One reason for such a power of survival lies in the very phenomena I describe in this book; it lies in the plays' ability to keep faith with their own noise, the hard grit of sound, and yet to give that noise a gestural shape, a face, to make something generative as well as destructive out of opacities and confusions of speaking and hearing. It is something like what Milton's Satan tries to find as he moves through Chaos:

> At length a universal hubbub wild
> Of stunning sounds and voices all confused
> Borne through the hollow dark assaults his ear
> With loudest vehemence: thither he plies,
> Undaunted to meet there what ever power
> Or spirit of the nethermost abyss
> Might in that noise reside.[26]

The rumors at work in Shakespeare's plays are no vague muddle of sense, but possibilities sharp enough to penetrate the mind and lodge themselves inescapably within memory, even if only half understood, carrying as they do echoes of our most primitive cries. The plays show us what it means to build so many selves, so many sensuous worlds, precisely out of speech that troubles hearing and out of hearing that transforms what is spoken, making it speak in a different voice, making sense out of what is not heard, or heard wrongly. They teach us that even our most distorted slanders of fame carry a potential knowledge; such slanders establish a precarious bridge between persons unknown, even as they open up chasms within those persons otherwise unheard of, unseen. It is such dynamics of noise that help the plays to survive the clamor of time and history. Such a play of noise is part of Shakespeare's gift to time.

# NOTES

INTRODUCTION

1. For earlier uses of "noise" as public outcry, quarrel, or scandal, see *The Oxford English Dictionary (OED)*, s.v. "noise," 1.a, 1.c, and 2.a. "Noise" could also mean musical sound in sixteenth and seventeenth century usage, a sense dominant in Caliban's "The isle is full of noises / Sounds and sweet airs, that give delight and hurt not" (*The Tempest*, 3.2.136–37). A "noise" could also be a company of musicians, as in Falstaff's demand, "See if thou canst find out Sneak's noise" (*2 Henry IV*, 2.4.11). For other examples, see *OED*, s.v. "noise," 5.a and 5.b. The English word derives from archaic French *noise*, "discord," "din," or "quarrel," a word in use through the seventeenth century but obsolete in modern French, save in certain proverbial phrases, for example, *chercher noise*, "to pick a quarrel." *Le Grand Robert*, 9 vols. (Paris: Le Robert, 1985), s.v. "noise," derives it from the Latin *nausea*, "seasickness," but acknowledges that the semantic connection is obscure.

2. Elias Canetti, *Earwitness: Fifty Characters*, trans. Joachim Neugroschel (New York: Seabury Press, 1979).

3. See *OED*, s.v. "slander" and "scandal." "Slander" enters English by way of the Old French *esclandre*, "to defame" or "discredit," derived from the Latin *scandalum*, "scandal," which itself harks back to the Greek *skandalon*, "stumbling block." The French source is audible in older English spellings of the word such as "sclaunder" or "sclaundre," which give way to the more modern spelling by the late sixteenth or early seventeenth century. "Scandal" starts being used in English only during the sixteenth century, readopted directly from the Latin, perhaps because of the continued presence of the word in legal terminology, such as the crime of *scandalum magnatum*, "the slander of great persons." In Shakespeare's time, "to scandalize" could mean to slander a person, or to make that person scandalous. See also below, n. 13.

4. For one thing, the play of rumor and defamation crucially animates the network of hints and approximations, the mobile and contradictory patterns of suggestion, that A. D. Nuttall takes as central to Shakespeare's way of presenting the world. See *A New Mimesis: Shakespeare and the Representation of Reality* (London: Methuen, 1983), especially 163–93. Nuttall argues that it is just such combative patterns of suggestion, often built on cliché and commonplace, that give Shakespeare's characters their distinct, cognitive life, conveying the implication "that there is a reality other than the expressions, to which they more or less successfully approximate" (178).

5. Stanley Cavell's discussions of the dramatization of doubt in Shakespeare, especially the essays gathered in *Disowning Knowledge in Six Plays of Shakespeare* (Cambridge: Cambridge University Press, 1987), have been crucially illuminating to me in regard to these matters. Similarly, I gained much from the account by Harry Berger, Jr., of what he calls "interior audition" in Shakespeare—a process that often ends up by impaling the self on its own contradictions, even as it dangerously fills the world with the self's projections, its own abandoned or degraded powers. See Berger, *Imaginary Audition: Shakespeare on Stage and Page* (Berkeley: University of California Press, 1989), and *Making Trifles of Terrors: Redistributing Complicities in Shakespeare* (Stanford: Stanford University Press, 1997).

6. Michel Serres, *The Parasite,* trans. Lawrence R. Schehr (Baltimore: Johns Hopkins University Press, 1982), 126, and *Genesis,* trans. Geneviève James and James Nielson (Ann Arbor: University of Michigan Press, 1995), 72. These two books, especially *Genesis,* explore an idea of noise closely related to that which I want to evoke in Shakespeare. Serres describes a noise that is fundamental to our experience of the world. It is at once a form of knowing (noise is gnosis) and a way of being. For Serres, "space is assailed, as a whole, by the murmur; we are utterly taken over by this same murmuring. This restlessness is within hearing, just shy of definite signals, just shy of silence" (*Genesis,* 13). Such noise surrounds us, places us in space and time, at once separating us and driving us together. It can be terrifying enough, we know, a signature of violence, faction, and furor, predatory and parasitic, a mask of idiocy, a storm that entraps us and eats up our voices. (One of Serres's major source texts, I should say here, is Beaumarchais's great description of the sly, invasive, and finally explosive power of calumny in act 2 of *Le barbier de Seville,* turned into a great crescendo aria by Rossini.) Yet noise is also a signature of freedom and change, a liberation from the very forms into which the noise itself can freeze. "Noise destroys and horrifies. But order and flat repetition are in the vicinity of death. Noise nourishes a new order" (*Parasite,* 127). The idea of such noise makes of our hearing a heroic opening, apprehending in what assaults it more idiosyncratic forms of order and lost sources of strength, even in what appear to be interference and static (*son parasite*).

A "philosophy of noise," Serres insists, involves tuning one's ear to apprehend what is otherwise abandoned, invisible, or suppressed in human talk and human history; noise becomes a category that tests the terms of other ways of knowing, philosophical, anthropological, historical, and literary. As may be clear, Serres radically extends the rather restricted use of "noise" as a technical term or dead metaphor in information theory, where it refers to that quantity of any verbal message which cannot be resolved into meaning, an excess in signification that yet may be repossessed by other signifying systems. (See William R. Paulson, *The Noise of Culture: Literary Texts in a World of Information* [Ithaca: Cornell University Press, 1988], 53–100.) Another useful analogy (though again more limited in its scope than Serres's arguments) appears in Jacques Attali's *Noise: The Political Economy of Music,* trans. Brian Massumi (Minneapolis: University of Minnesota Press, 1985). For Attali, "noise" is crucially a threshold term. On the one hand, it is a word used by the enemy: it is the ideologically conditioned label for any new or marginalized sounds which an established musical idiom cannot recognize as "music." On the other, "noise" can become a true, if brazen, rubric for the subversive force of that slandered sound.

7.  On the noise level in London theaters, see Bruce R. Smith, *The Acoustic World of Early Modern England: Attending to the O-Factor* (Chicago: University of Chicago Press, 1999), 60. Smith's book more generally, especially pages 206–45 and 269–84, offers an ambitious and absorbing description of the forms of sound and hearing that shaped English Renaissance theater. Combining technical speculations about the acoustics of Shakespeare's theaters (both the Globe and Blackfriars) with more sociohistorical, phenomenological, and dramaturgical analysis, Smith creates a convincing account of the richness, range, precision, and complexity with which human voice, musical sound, and signifying noise worked together on the English Renaissance stage. In a world of terribly embodied voices, a world more dominated than ours by the authority of the spoken word, stage plays, Smith shows, worked by variously capturing, penetrating, decentering, and transporting the ears of their audience, testing their limits. This richness of sound was part of what gave Renaissance English theater the ability to "engender a more exciting and liberating subjectivity" (270) than that available in schoolroom, pulpit, or court, even if, as he argues, the promiscuous play of sound in the theater found its ultimate ground in the "bass line" of the adult male voice. Smith is right, I think, to show how in this period dramatic structures could be built around conflicts of different registers of sound—voice, music, noise—each with its own complex social and symbolic identity. But I do not think that this somehow obviates the reality of "character" on the stage. At least in the case of Shakespeare's drama, it is exactly the ambiguous play of "noise," and the play of hearing against hearing, that individuates characters, gives them their psychological density. Smith is persuasive in his account of the complexity of sounds that an *audience* would have heard in the Globe or Blackfriars. His findings also suggest something just as important, that is, that actors on stage would have heard their own voices, as well those of their fellow actors, with similar immediacy and subtlety.

8.  I cannot enter fully here into debates about the relative authority of the page and stage in Shakespeare. Nor do I want to take a stand on one side rather than an-

other. Such debates have become all too often divisive, even literalistic, posing useful questions in the wrong way. Harry Berger, Jr., draws the battle lines most
sharply in his discussion of "the new histrionicism" in *Imaginary Audition,* 3–42, and
passim, where he insists that only by reading Shakespeare's texts can we discern
their deeper, more anarchic play of irony, ambiguity, and self-reference. I share
Berger's deep impatience with the way that performance-oriented critics invoke
the contingencies of live performance, often in an entirely speculative fashion, to
render such readerly sophistications irrelevant or merely academic. But Berger, describing the limiting choices required by performance, himself underestimates the
volatile force of the actor's word onstage, which has various means to make present
the ambiguities that he sees at work in Shakespearean writing, even as it provokes
ambiguities of a different order. Our present engagements with Shakespeare share
in the dilemma so penetratingly described by Benjamin Bennett in *Theater as Problem: Modern Drama and Its Place in Literature* (Ithaca: Cornell University Press, 1990),
wherein even our understanding of drama as a literary form, as indeed "the church
of literature," is linked to a sense of its incompleteness, its often vexed and imaginary dependence on the material institutions of theater. In Shakespeare, especially,
both stage and page are necessarily incomplete, and yet each necessarily translates
the other. This creates a situation in which an iconoclastic drama can seem to play itself out in opposing directions. Berger, for instance, sees live performance as an in-
herently reifying, reductive activity, something to be cured by a more strenuous
and flexible work of reading. Stephen Orgel, by contrast, in "Shakespeare Imagines
a Theater," *Poetics Today* 5 (1984): 549–61, focuses on the power of performance to
bring in ambiguity, play, accident, materiality, and mutability, suggesting that it is
often the reader's desire "to fix the text, to transform it into a book" (558), that
makes the play into a dead, reductive idol. Our task might be to see how these two
positions form part of a larger dialectic. We would need for this (as Francis Bacon
might make clear) a better discrimination of idols.

9.  See M. Lindsay Kaplan, *The Culture of Slander in Early Modern England* (Cambridge: Cambridge University Press, 1997).

10.  See my *Spenserian Poetics: Idolatry, Iconoclasm, and Magic* (Ithaca: Cornell University Press, 1985), 224–34, and "Reflections on the Blatant Beast," *Spenser Studies*
13 (1999): 101–23.

11.  *State Papers of Elizabeth I, Domestic,* vol. 274, no. 138. Public Records Office,
Kew, United Kingdom.

12.  Michel de Montaigne, "Of Glory," in *Essays,* trans. John Florio, 3 vols. (London: Dent, 1910), 2:347. I discuss this and the other sources mentioned in this
paragraph in more detail in chapter 2.

13.  For an absorbing and detailed account of the virulent exchanges of abuse
between fifteenth-, sixteenth-, and seventeenth-century textual scholars—in particular between Poggio Bracciolini and Lorenzo Valla, Desiderius Erasmus and
Julius Caesar Scaliger, and Joseph Scaliger and Gaspard Scoppius—see Charles
Nisard, *Les gladiateurs de la republique des lettres,* 2 vols. (Paris, 1860). Jacob Burck-

hardt remarks in regard to the netherworld of Italian humanist scholarship that "the general culture of the time had educated a poisonous brood of impotent wits, of born critics and railers, whose envy called for hecatombs of victims; and to all this was added the envy of the famous men among themselves" (*The Civilization of the Renaissance in Italy,* trans. S. G. C. Middlemore, 2 vols. [New York: Harper and Row, 1958], 1:168).

14. For these senses of "scan," all current in the sixteenth century, see *OED,* s.v. "scan," 2-5. The etymological links of "scandal" and "scan" remain a bit speculative. "Scan" derives from the Latin *scandare,* "to climb" or "scan a verse," "in reference to the movements of the foot raised and lowered to mark the metre" (Eric Partridge, *Origins: A Short Etymological Dictionary of Modern English* [London: Routledge and Kegan Paul, 1958], s.v. "ascend," paragraph 1). Partridge goes on to link *scandare* to the Sanskrit *skan,* "he leapt," and *skándati,* "he leaps," as well as to Middle Irish *scendim,* "I leap," Old Irish *sescaind,* "he leapt," and Welsh *cy-chwynnu,* "to rise" or "climb," suggesting that these forms are themselves linked to the Greek *skandalon,* "stumbling block" (paragraph 2). Calvert Watkins's glossary of Indo-European roots in *The American Heritage Dictionary,* ed. William Morris (Boston: Houghton Mifflin, 1978), 1539, posits the Indo-European *skand-* as the root of both *skandalon* and *scandere.*

15. It would be useful to map out the post-Shakespearean history of "noise" and "news" in literary texts. One resource is Patricia Meyer Spacks's *Gossip* (New York: Alfred A. Knopf, 1985), which argues for the crucial importance of gossip and rumor as models for the form of the novel, especially as they give scope to a more diffusive appetite for knowledge and storytelling, at once pastoral and densely social, more open and polymorphous than traditional genres of narrative allow. See also Alexander Welsh's fascinating *George Eliot and Blackmail* (Cambridge, Mass.: Harvard University Press, 1985), which examines how the increasingly volatile energies of public news, information, and scandal in the nineteenth century affect both the inner and outer shape of Victorian fiction. We would need even more complex literary histories, I think, in order accurately to map the idea and romance of noise in contemporary writers such as John Ashbery, Thomas Pynchon, and Don DeLillo.

CHAPTER ONE

1. Baldassare Castiglione, *The Book of the Courtier,* trans. Charles S. Singleton (Garden City: Doubleday, 1959), 179.

2. George Puttenham's English nicknames for Greek rhetorical figures, cataloged in book 3 of *The Arte of English Poesie* (1589), ed. Edward Arber (London: Constable, 1906), suggest a similarly combative context for the deployment of verbal art. Consider, for example, "*Eclipsis,* or the figure of default" (175), "*Hiberbaton,* or the Trespasser" (180), "*Metonimia,* or the Misnamer" (191), "*Ironia,* or the Drie

mock" (199), "*Sarcasmus,* or the Bitter taunt" (200), "*Micterismus,* or the Fleering frumpe" (201), "*Charientismus,* or the privy nippe" (201), "*Meiosis,* or the Disabler" (195), "*Tapinosis,* or the Abbaser" (195), "*Dialisis,* or the Dismemberer" (230). For more on the deployment of "blame and slander" in courtly contexts, see Frank Whigham, *Ambition and Privilege: The Social Tropes of Elizabethan Courtesy Theory* (Berkeley: University of California Press, 1984), 137–84.

3.  M. M. Mahood, *Shakespeare's Wordplay* (London: Methuen, 1957), 111–29, speaks shrewdly about Hamlet's "defensive-aggressive quibbles," at once masks of truth and points of breakthrough for his bitter knowledge of the world. Her account is complemented by Margaret Ferguson's analysis of the literalizing and anarchic trajectory of Hamlet's puns in "*Hamlet:* Letters and Spirits," in *Shakespeare and the Question of Theory,* ed. Patricia Parker and Geoffrey Hartman (New York: Methuen, 1985), 292–309. Sigurd Burckhardt, *Shakespearean Meanings* (Princeton: Princeton University Press, 1968), 22–46, 269–72, also unpacks Hamlet's puns, and Shakespearean wordplay in general, with exemplary care. See also Robert Weimann, *Shakespeare and the Popular Tradition in Theater: Studies in the Social Dimension of Dramatic Form and Function,* ed. Robert Schwartz (Baltimore: Johns Hopkins University Press, 1978), 230–37, who connects Hamlet's language to the tradition of subversive, antimoralizing wordplay and nonsense speech we find in the Elizabethan stage fool or clown.

4.  Consider also Hamlet's final rhetorical question, as he attacks his stepfather, "Drink off this potion. Is thy union here? / Follow my mother" (5.2.331–32), in which the poisoned pearl or "union" is also a figure for incestuous marriage. Of this A. C. Bradley observes, "What rage there is in the words, and what a strange lightning of the mind!" (*Shakespearean Tragedy,* 2d ed. [London: Macmillan, 1905], 151).

5.  Thomas M. Greene, "*Il Cortegiano* and the Choice of Game," in *The Vulnerable Text: Essays on Renaissance Literature* (New York: Columbia University Press, 1986), 46–60, offers a nuanced account of how the games played in the dialogue at once conjure and contain embarrassing truths about the courtier's position. In such games we see "the doubts [Castiglione's book] flirts with, the embarrassments it skirts, the social and political and moral abysses it almost stumbles into, the dark underside of authorized truth it sometimes seems about to reveal" (53). *Hamlet* makes us feel more acutely the *disprezzo* or disdain in the courtier's *sprezzatura.*

6.  See G. Wilson Knight, *The Wheel of Fire: Interpretations of Shakespearian Tragedy,* 4th ed., rev. (London: Methuen, 1949), 17–46.

7.  Thomas Cooper, *Thesaurus Linguae Romanae et Brittannicae* (London, 1565), s.v. "fama."

8.  Randle Cotgrave, *A Dictionarie of the French and English Tongues* (London, 1611), s.v. "bruit."

9.  For broader comments on theatrical sound play in *Hamlet,* see Frances Ann Shirley, *Shakespeare's Use of Off-Stage Sounds* (Lincoln: University of Nebraska Press, 1963), 142–68.

10. Grigori Kozintsev, *Shakespeare: Time and Conscience,* trans. Joyce Vining (New York: Hill and Wang, 1966), 242.

11. In *Hamlet,* "listening speaks"—to borrow a formula from Roland Barthes's essay "Listening," in *The Responsibility of Forms: Critical Essays on Music, Art, and Representation,* trans. Richard Howard (New York: Hill and Wang, 1985), 252.

12. Michel de Montaigne, "Of Glory," in *Essays,* trans. John Florio, 3 vols. (London: Dent, 1910), 2:347.

13. Fulke Greville, "An Inquisition upon Fame and Honour," in *Poems and Dramas of Fulke Greville,* ed. Geoffrey Bullough, 2 vols. (Edinburgh: Oliver and Boyd, n.d.), 1:196. Martin Dodsworth, *Hamlet Closely Observed* (London: Athlone, 1985), passim, considers with particular tact the troubled, mutable, manipulative, skeptical, but still fascinated, even spiritualized quality of honor talk in *Hamlet.* It provides him a powerful key to Hamlet's self-dramatizations and self-mystifications.

14. See William Kerrigan's subtly Freudian meditation *Hamlet's Perfection* (Baltimore: Johns Hopkins University Press, 1994), which traces the hidden course of Hamlet's "idealism" or "perfectionism" in the play—its worm- or molelike "progress" through vicious deformity, parody, splitting, and projection, to its final reconstitution in a form that fuses rashness, revenge, and readiness. There is, for Kerrigan, an odd kind of purity in Hamlet's belated rashness, freed as it is of the muddy dithering and spoiling of doubt. Rash acts, for Hamlet, finally free him from the coil of his own and others' whorish, impotent words, and also, I would assume, from the "blots" of ill fame.

15. Harold Jenkins, in the Arden edition of *Hamlet,* emends the first three lines of the passage as follows: "The dram of evil / Doth all the noble substance often dout / To his own scandal" (1.4.36–38)—a fairly common solution. He also offers a useful account of earlier attempts at making sense of the text (449–52), supplementing the extensive history of emendations in the New Variorum Edition of *Hamlet,* ed. Horace Howard Furness, 2 vols. (Philadelphia: Lippincott, 1918), 1:82–89. It is a remarkable story. One could make a telling parable, in fact, out of this history of attempts to correct a scandalously blotted text about scandalous blots. I will not venture my own emendation here, but one point is important in the context of this study. The Second Quarto's "eale" is indeed obscure, and perhaps truly a corruption. "Evil" is a plausible enough emendation, though the word seems a bit abstract, given Hamlet's own concrete metaphors in this speech. (Construing "eale" as leaven or even vinegar, as has been done [Variorum, 1.87], might seem more fitting.) But I resist the often inevitable assumption that the quarto's phrase, "the noble substance of a doubt," is a corruption. Jenkins, like many editors, assumes that the "noble substance" refers to the entity which is attacked by that "dram" of corruption or evil. Hence his rendering of line 37 as "Doth all the noble substance often dout," where "dout" is construed as meaning "to put out," or "extinguish." But we should remember that doubt itself quite often assumes a "noble substance" in *Hamlet*—never more so than in the person of that stately, mournful ghost who appears just as these words are spoken.

16. Harold Bloom cites in regard to Hamlet an apothegm of Nietzsche's from *The Twilight of the Idols:* "We can find words only for what is already dead in our hearts, so that necessarily there is a kind of contempt in every act of speaking" (*Shakespeare: The Invention of the Human* [New York: Penguin Putnam, 1998], 400). Hamlet lends to such contempt a complex particularity, since it is something that the prince at once suffers, owns, and deploys.

17. Janet Adelman, *Suffocating Mothers: Fantasies of Maternal Origin in Shakespeare's Plays, "Hamlet" to "The Tempest"* (London: Routledge, 1992), 28.

18. Hamlet's greetings are indeed as noble and vexed as his "good-nights," on which see Adelman, *Suffocating Mothers,* 33—34; and Kerrigan, *Hamlet's Perfection,* 55—62.

19. If such names are obscene, it may be partly because they too readily collapse together into confusion, or make distinctions that reveal themselves as horribly arbitrary; the desires and fantasies let loose in the world of the play suggest that we cannot clearly know fathers from uncles, wives from mothers, brothers from friends, or sisters from lovers. On this and related questions in *Hamlet,* see Marc Shell, *Children of the Earth: Literature, Politics, and Nationhood* (New York: Oxford University Press, 1993), 96—123, and passim. Shell sees *Hamlet* as being crossed throughout by an extreme fantasy of "universal siblinghood," thus universal incest—something that Shell understands as a crucial aspect of our modernity, in which we become aware of the "free-floating conditionality" of kinship relations. Through reading of texts such as Elizabeth I's "Glass of a Sinful Soul," Jean Racine's *Brittanicus,* and Herman Melville's *Pierre,* in addition to wide-ranging meditations on twinship, anti-Semitism, religious toleration, even the history of our relation with animals and pets, Shell shows how this fantasy, by turns utopian and catastrophic, points to inevitable contaminations within our Western ideas of both nation and self. In *Hamlet,* Shell argues, it helps to account for the play's continual oscillation between images of holy liberty and profane transgression, between the twin temptations of saintliness and shamelessness.

20. See Jacques Lacan's remarks on the pattern of interrupted mourning in the tragedy, in "Desire and the Interpretation of Desire in *Hamlet,"* in *Literature and Psychoanalysis: The Question of Reading: Otherwise,* ed. Shoshana Felman (Baltimore: Johns Hopkins University Press, 1982), 39—41. Hamlet's baffled mourning is also tacitly the subject of Freud's "Mourning and Melancholia," in *The Standard Edition of the Psychoanalytic Works of Sigmund Freud,* ed. James Strachey, 24 vols. (London: Hogarth Press, 1955), 14:239—58.

21. The variety of terms for defamation in this period may itself indicate the scope of contemporary concern with such matters. Each word has its own rather complex history, often inflected by shifting relations to the jargon of the law. "Libel," for instance, is not yet, in Shakespeare's time, clearly distinguished from "slander" (for further comments see chap. 2, n. 67). Indeed, it is sometimes used in legal texts to refer not to defamation but to legal indictments—a usage which depends on its derivation from the Latin *libellus,* "small book, pamphlet," a term used in Ro-

man law to refer to almost any formal accusation or complaint brought before a magistrate. Our modern use of the word to refer to injurious words descends from the specifically criminalized category of *libellus famosus,* referring to lampoons, satires, or malicious accusations addressed to those in power (Adolph Berger, *Encyclopedic Dictionary of Roman Law* [Philadelphia: American Philosophical Society, 1952], s.v. "libellus"). A similar legal background may shape certain uses of the word "calumny," since in Roman and ecclesiastical law *calumnia* refers specifically to the willful abuse of a legal process—indictment or prosecution, say—to vex or defame a citizen (on which see Berger, *Encyclopedic Dictionary,* s.v. "calumnia"), though in Elizabethan usage this background is only faintly visible, if at all.

22. A particularly subtle version of such an etiology for slander can be found in the account of the twin hags Envie and Detraction, who lead out the Blatant Beast at the end of book 5 of *The Faerie Queene* (ed. J. C. Smith, 2 vols. [Oxford: Oxford University Press, 1909], 5.12.28 – 36), to attack the name and fame of Arthegall.

23. Richard Allestree, *The Government of the Tongue* (Oxford, 1674), 68.

24. Thomas Elyot, for example, speaks of detraction as "breath pestilential [that] infects the wits of them that nothing mistrusts" (*Book named The Governor,* ed. S. E. Lehmberg [London: Dent, 1962], 234). The anonymous pamphlet *A Plaine description of the Auncient Petigree of Dame Slaunder* (London, 1573), sigs. C4v–C5r, also stresses the peculiar damage done to the person who hears another person slandered: "For sclaunder undermindeth and casteth downe the foundation of true judgment in the outward parts, and within, trayterous confederate with their enemies, helpeth them when they breake in and receive them, and open the gates, and so endevour themselves that Madame Sclaunder may make the hearer of the tale to be her servant."

25. See Kenneth Burke, *A Rhetoric of Motives* (New York: Prentice-Hall, 1952), 221–33.

26. The language of the Marian statute "against Sedityous Woordes and Rumours" (reconfirmed and somewhat enlarged by Elizabeth in 1559) is typical, condemning those who "maliciouslye sediciouslye rebellyouslye and unnaturally, contrary to the Dutie of their Fidelytees and Allegiances, have now of late not onely *ymagined invented practised spoken and spredd abroade dyvers and sundry false sedicious and sclaunderous Newes Rumours Sayenges and Tales,* ageynst our most dreadd Sovereigne Lorde and King, and ageynst our most naturall Sovereygne Ladye and Quene," along with those who have "devised made written printed publyshed and set forthe dyvers heynous sedicious and sclanderous Writinges Rimes Ballades Letters Papers and Bookes, intending and practising thereby to move and stir sedicious Discorde Disention And Rebellyon within this Realme" (*The Statutes of the Realm* [London, 1819–22], 4:240; my emphasis). See also Paul L. Hughes and James F. Larkin, eds., *Tudor Royal Proclamations,* 3 vols. (New Haven: Yale University Press, 1964–69), 2:4, 57–60, 347–48.

27. Stefano Guazzo, *The Civile Conversation,* trans. George Pettie and Bartholomew Young (London, 1581–86), ed. Edward Sullivan, 2 vols. (New York: AMS Press, 1967), 1:70–71.

28.  See *Aeneid,* 4.173–95, in *Virgil,* ed. H. R. Fairclough, 2 vols. (London: Heinemann, 1924). Spawned in part by Dido's brazen lie about her marriage to Aeneas, Virgil's *Fama* can be seen as a kind of counterspirit, a counternarrator, within the poet's work of epic praise. Interestingly, Virgil's description of the many-eared and many-eyed *Fama* ("monstrum horrendum, ingens" [4.181]) echoes the earlier account of the blinded, one-eyed Polyphemus ("monstrum horrendum, informe, ingens" [3.658]).

29.  Spenser, *The Faerie Queene,* 4.1.21–22.

30.  Cf. *A Plaine Description of Slaunder,* sig. C3r. This partly imaginary or projected power of rumor thus ironically helps to sustain the network of secret accusations, "privy spyings," and "informations" that, as Patricia Parker argues, stitches together the political world of a play like *Hamlet*—even as the picture of rumor suggests the fragility and opacity of intention that may underlie the covert "delations" of those in power, or of their agents. See Parker, "*Othello* and *Hamlet:* Spying, Discovery, Secret Faults," in *Shakespeare from the Margins: Language, Culture, Context* (Chicago: University of Chicago Press, 1996), 229–52.

31.  Shakespeare's play on the blackened and blackening power of desire is especially prominent in sonnets 127, 131, 132, 140, and 147. The ironies I am pointing to here are congruent with the complex patterns of self-division and self-violence in Shakespeare's sonnets examined in Joel Fineman's book *Shakespeare's Perjured Eye: The Invention of Poetic Subjectivity in the Sonnets* (Berkeley: University of California Press, 1986). As far as I can recall, Fineman never addresses the idea of defamation or slander in the sonnets or links the lover's "blackness" to the idea of denigration. Nonetheless, Shakespeare's "perjured eye" and his "slanderous ear" influence each other in strange ways.

32.  L. C. Knights, *An Approach to "Hamlet"* (Stanford: Stanford University Press, 1961), argues that "what we have to take note of is not only what he says but a particular vibration in the saying" (59). Hamlet's disgusted judgments are "used to shock and damage," to drive a wedge into another's consciousness, so that it too must inevitably suffer (60–61). He is "fascinated by what he condemns," possessed by a way of knowing the world that cannot break out of the closed circle of "disgust, revulsion, and self-contempt" (65–68).

33.  "Here is the most devastating twist of all: that Hamlet's foul imaginings are correct" (Graham Bradshaw, *Shakespeare's Scepticism* [Brighton: Harvester, 1987], 117). There is a curious parallel here with earlier versions of the Hamlet story in the *Historiae danicae* of Saxo Grammaticus or Belleforest's *Histoires tragiques.* In both of these texts the hero shows an uncanny power of divination—as when, at a feast given him by the English king, he obliquely but accurately points to traces of blood, violence, decay, and shame in both his food and his hosts, and so turns away in contempt. See *Narrative and Dramatic Sources of Shakespeare,* ed. Geoffrey Bullough, 8 vols. (London: Routledge and Kegan Paul, 1957–75), 7:68–69, 102–7. In Saxo's version of this story, for example, Amleth smells human blood in his bread, human corruption in his meat, and rotten iron in his beer, even as he glimpses traces of ig-

noble birth in the English king. All of these turn out be truly observed: the bread was made from wheat grown in a field of dead warriors, the meat carved from pigs that had fed on a decaying carcase, and the beer made out of water taken from a well full of rusting weapons; the king turns out to be the son of a slave. Belleforest adds the remarkable speculation that the prince may have been learned in natural magic or, in his melancholy, been receptive to the information of demonic spirits—appending a lengthy commentary on the dangers of divination in general.

34. See Edmund Spenser, "Letter to Sir Walter Ralegh," in *The Faerie Queene,* 2:485.

35. Ben Jonson, *Poetaster,* ed. Tom Cain (Manchester: Manchester University Press, 1995), induction, lines 38—40, 25. For more on this text, see below, 64—66. The dedications and inductions of many of Ben Jonson's plays, including *Epicoene,Volpone, Sejanus, Bartholomew Fair,* and *The Staple of News,* project similar fears of unjust audience misprision and defamation of both the poet and his text. Such worries are also articulated in prefatory texts to works byThomas Nashe,Thomas Dekker, Robert Armin, John Marston, George Chapman, Francis Beaumont, and John Fletcher (to mention only Shakespeare's contemporaries). Marston, for example, in his epistle to the reader in *The Malcontent,* attacks those who say that his satire unjustly libels individual victims: "I understand, some have been most unadvisedly over-cunning in misinterpreting me, and with subtlety (as deep as hell) have maliciously spread ill rumours, which springing from themselves, might to themselves have heavily returned" (*The Malcontent,* ed. Bernard Harris [London: A and C Black, 1987], 5). Such proleptic attacks were common to books of the period, of course.

36. Hamlet's strategy reflects what Katherine Eisaman Maus characterizes as the vulnerable and improvisatory nature of inwardness in Renaissance writing, and its way of being deployed in conditions of political or spiritual danger. See her *Inwardness andTheater in the English Renaissance* (Chicago: University of Chicago Press, 1995), 1—6, and passim. What Maus's arguments do not quite account for is why Hamlet's peculiar way of eliciting his interiority has become so seductive and harassing for modern readers.

37. Dodsworth, *Hamlet Closely Observed,* 65.

38. See Avital Ronnell, "StreetTalk," in *Benjamin's Ground: New Readings of Walter Benjamin,* ed. Rainer Nägele (Detroit:Wayne State University Press, 1988), 134—35.

39. On Falstaff as "the body of rumor," see Harry Berger, Jr., "Sneak's Noise, or, Rumor and Detextualization in *2 Henry IV,*" in *Making Trifles of Terrors: Redistributing Complicities in Shakespeare* (Stanford: Stanford University Press, 1997), 126—47; and Richard Abrahms, "Rumour's Reign in *2 Henry IV:* The Scope of a Personification," *English Literary Renaissance* 16, no. 3 (1986): 467—95.

40. Something of the opposite is suggested by Avi Erlich, *Hamlet's Absent Father* (Princeton: Princeton University Press, 1977), who theorizes forcefully that Hamlet's paranoia is directed toward a world that is not just alien, but has been endowed with his *own* vitality and power. "He perceives himself as a machine run by the very

impulses he had to jettison and that are now externalized and unrecognizable" (255). Hamlet's paralysis or passivity in relation to the powers that surround him changes by the end of the play, when he manages to rewrite the official letter which had inscribed his death, even as he turns turn against his enemies the sword and the poison with which they had meant to kill him.

41. *Complete State Trials,* ed. T. B. Howell, 21 vols. (London, 1816), 2.1027. I have, I should say, emended the last phrase of the quoted passage as printed in Howell, which there speaks of an "imprisonment of the king's ear." That wording is suggestive (cf. *Hamlet,* 2.2.472–73: "a hideous crash / Takes prisoner Pyrrhus's ear"), but I can't help thinking that it represents an error in transcription at some stage. Bacon's parenthesis clearly suggests that he means to play figuratively on the idea of "impoisonment"—a word used throughout the text of the trial to refer to the act of poisoning. On the urgent need for kings to weigh true and false reports, see also James I's comments in *Basilicon Doron:* "Although it bee true, that a Prince can never without secrecie doe great things, yet it is better ofttimes to try reports, then by credulitie to foster suspicion vpon an honest man . . . since suspition is the Tyrants sickness, as the fruites of an evill conscience" (James VI and I, *Political Writings,* ed. Johann P. Sommerville [Cambridge: Cambridge University Press, 1994], 48–49).

42. Bullough, *Narrative and Dramatic Sources,* 7:172–73, points to a more literal case of ear poisoning as a source for the ghost's story: the murder of Francesco Maria I della Rovere, duke of Urbino, poisoned in 1538 by a lotion poured in his ears by his barber. But the issue of slander creeps in here as well. Bullough also quotes a fascinating letter of Pietro Aretino to Luigi Gonzaga, in which the satirist protests his innocence of any slanderous accusations against Gonzaga for complicity in the murder, even as he acknowledges the propensity of the human tongue to "talk scandal" in the face of "terrible things" (173).

43. John Webster, echoing this text in *The Duchess of Malfi,* makes the allegory more apparent: "The opinion of wisdom is a foul tetter, / That runs all over a man's body" (*The Duchess of Malfi,* ed. Elizabeth M. Brennan, 2d ed. [New York: Norton, 1983], 2.1.80–81).

44. Quicksilver here is both mercurial thought and a medicine for venereal disease.

45. G. R. Elton, *Policy and Police: The Enforcement of the Reformation in the Age of Thomas Cromwell* (Cambridge: Cambridge University Press, 1972), 46–83.

46. John Harvey, *A Discoursive Probleme* (London, 1588), quoted by Keith Thomas, *Religion and the Decline of Magic* (New York: Scribner's, 1971), 419.

47. In a chapter entitled "Wanton and Whore," in *"The Heart and Stomach of a King": Elizabeth I and the Politics of Sex and Power* (Philadelphia: University of Pennsylvania Press, 1994), 65–90, Carole Levin surveys the broad range of such stories, suggesting that they not only were repeated at the English court, in the city of London, and in the English countryside, but gained international currency as well.

48. Robert Greene, for example, writes that "the Moule deprived of sight, hath woonderful hearing," a testimony to the "secreet iudgement" of nature (in *Complete Works,* ed. Alexander B. Grosart, 10 vols. [London, 1881–83], 2.62). Pliny's *Natural History,* trans. H. Rackham, 10 vols. (London: Heinemann, 1938–63), 3:415, provides one classical source for this notion, adding the curious detail that if moles hear people speaking about them, they run away (presumably by burrowing deeper into the earth). See also the texts from Thomas Lodge and John Lyly cited in William Carroll, *Animal Conventions in English Non-Religious Prose (1550–1600)* (New York: Bookman, 1954), 110.

49. On the textual difficulties, see above, n. 15.

50. The mole-ghost thus becomes a trope of memory's contaminated and dependent state. I am indebted to Ned Lukacher's discussion of this pun in his chapter on *Hamlet* in *Primal Scenes: Literature, Philosophy, Psychoanalysis* (Ithaca: Cornell University Press, 1986), 211–22, which discusses the mole as a trope for the unconscious spaces of language, associated with the presence of feminine sexuality—a figure which returns in later images of worms inside corpses or the bodies of kings inside worms, and in Hamlet's image of himself as a loathsome fellow "crawling between earth and heaven" (3.1.128–29). Lukacher argues that the mole-ghost also represents a scandalous blot on any consistent economy of dramatic representation, and hence a token of the problematics of the "primal scene," in Freud's sense. (Here I might recall that our word "larva," referring to the immature or grublike stage of insects and other organisms, comes from the Latin *larva,* which can mean both ghost or specter and mask. See *OED,* s.v. "larva," 1 and 2. It is perhaps not an accident that Françoise Reumaux's remarkable study *Toute la ville en parle: Equisse d'une théorie des rumeurs* [Paris: Editions L'Harmattan, 1994], 8–9, uses the technical entomological terms for the developmental stages of certain insects—"larva," "nymph," and "imago"—to describe the different phases of a rumor's metamorphosis.) Marjorie Garber, *Shakespeare's Ghost Writers: Literature as Uncanny Causality* (London: Methuen, 1987), 124–76, describes the spectral authority of the ghost in a fashion that enlarges Lukacher's reading, focusing on the specter's way of marking both the mournful place of desire and the uncanny claims of literary language in general.

51. "This accrescence of Objectivity in a Ghost that yet retains all its ghostly attributes & fearful Subjectivity, is truly wonderful," wrote Coleridge; "Hume himself could not but have faith in *this* Ghost dramatically, let his anti-ghostism be as strong as Samson against Ghosts less powerfully raised" (*Lectures 1808–1819: On Literature,* ed. R. A. Foakes, vol. 5, in 2 vols., of *The Collected Works* [Princeton: Princeton University Press, 1987—], 2:299, 296). The ghost compels conviction in part because it compels a wish for human response, compels a need to compel human response where that is possible: "O answer me . . . let me not burst in ignorance." The ghost makes our doubt revolve, in Wittgenstein's phrase, around the fixed axis of our real need.

CHAPTER TWO

1. Consider Psalms 12, 15, 22, 52, 57, 59, 64, 73, 109, 120, and 140. Both the anonymous *Plaine description of the Auncient Petigree of Dame Slaunder* (London, 1573), sigs. F2v–F7v, and William Vaughan's *Spirit of Detraction Coniured and Convicted in Seven Circles* (London, 1611), 133–36, dwell at length on the example of David's trial by slander and false accusation, and his answering words of protest, lament, and indictment. See also Anne Lake Prescott, "Evil Tongues at the Court of Saul: The Renaissance David as a Slandered Courtier," *Journal of Medieval and Renaissance Studies* 21, no. 2 (1991): 163–86.

2. See Edmund Spenser, *The Faerie Queene*, 6.12.27. All quotations are from the edition of J. C. Smith, 2 vols. (Oxford: Oxford University Press, 1909).

3. Richard Allestree, *The Government of the Tongue* (Oxford, 1674); and Desiderius Erasmus, *Lingua,* trans. Elaine Fantham, in *Collected Works of Erasmus,* vol. 29, ed. Elaine Fantham and Erika Rummel (Toronto: University of Toronto Press, 1989), 268.

4. François Rabelais, *Gargantua and Pantagruel,* trans. Thomas Urquhart and Peter Le Motteux, 3 vols. (Oxford: Oxford University Press, 1934), 3:224 (bk. 5, chap. 31).

5. Nicholas Breton, *A Murmurer* (London, 1607). Breton's description of his monster deserves to be reproduced in its entirety: "Behold his Eyes, like a hogge, ever bent downewards as if he were looking unto Hell: his cheekes like an Anathomie, where the fleshe from the bones doth fall, with fretting; his browes ever wrinckled with frownes, to shew the distemper of his unquiet Braine; his lippes ever puld inward, as if Envie would speake, and durst not; his tongue, like the sting of a Serpent, which uttereth nothing but poison; his voice, like the hissing of an Adder, which maketh musique but for hell; his necke, like a weake piller, whereon his head stands tottering, and readie to fall; his breast like an impostume, that is ready to burst with corruption; & his heart, the Anvile wheron the devill frames his fireworke; his body a Trunk where Sinne hath layed up her store; his handes like clawes, that catch at the world; and his feete like winges that make hast unto hell: Now, doest thou behold this ougly sight? and doest not feare to bee such a monster?" (sigs. D3v–D4r).

6. Cf. Stefano Guazzo, *The Civile Conversation,* trans. George Pettie and Bartholomew Young (London, 1581–86), ed. Edward Sullivan, 2 vols. (New York: AMS Press, 1967), 1:66.

7. See, for example, Andrea Alciati, emblem CLXXXI, "Eloquentia fortitudine praesentior," in *Emblemata,* ed. Claude Mignault (Rome, 1621), 751; and Jean Bodin, *The Six Bookes of a Common-Weale,* trans. Richard Knolles (London, 1606), 543–44, bk. 4, chap. 7.

8. Allestree, *The Government of the Tongue,* 110.

9. Spenser, *The Faerie Queene,* 2.4.4–5.

10. *A Plaine description of Slaunder,* sig. C3r.

11.  Vaughan, *The Spirit of Detraction,* 349.

12.  See Vaughan, *The Spirit of Detraction,* 209; and *A Plaine description of Slaunder,* sigs. C4r–C5r. See also Guazzo, *The Civile Conversation,* 1:70–71. Lucian's "Slander, a Warning," in *The Works of Lucian of Samosata,* trans. H. W. Fowler and F. G. Fowler, 4 vols. (Oxford: Clarendon Press, 1905), 4:3, is one classical source for this triadic anatomy of slander.

13.  See Vaughan, *The Spirit of Detraction,* 85, 119, 143.

14.  Think of Hippolytus, Phaedra, and Theseus as a tragic version of this triad, as is suggested by *A Plaine description of Slaunder,* sig. C7r.

15.  See Vaughan, *The Spirit of Detraction,* 3.

16.  See Lucian, "Slander, a Warning," 4:2–3. Lucian writes that Apelles himself had been falsely accused by a rival painter of having taken part in a conspiracy against Ptolemy; having been acquitted by the information of a fellow prisoner, he made his painting as a memorial and a warning. Lucian's description, which I have much condensed, was well known to humanists and inspired commentary by Alberti, as well as paintings and drawings by Mantegna, Botticelli, Breughel, Dürer, and Raphael, among others. For further discussion, see David Cast, *The Calumny of Apelles: A Study in the Humanist Tradition* (New Haven: Yale University Press, 1981).

17.  This text can be found in R. H. Helmholz, *Select Cases on Defamation to 1600* (London: Selden Society, 1985), 56.

18.  As Helmholz notes in *Select Cases on Defamation,* lxxxiii–lxxxiv, while the language of such writs was for the most part formulaic, "in the parts of the plaintiff's declarations which described the good name of the plaintiff and the evil intent of the defendant . . . prolixity and invention held sway. The searcher cannot but regard with a kind of wonder the imagination which hit upon the phrase *venenossime evomuit* to describe the defendant's speaking of the slanderous words. The phrase is only one of many such efforts."

19.  Guazzo, *The Civile Conversation,* 1:61. This common sense of ill fame as an infectious disease connects to the curious fact that, in common law, the list of those utterances which were actionable in themselves, without proof of "special damage," included not only imputations of criminality and professional incapacity but also imputations of having "the pox." See S. F. C. Milsom, *Historical Foundations of the Common Law* (London: Butterworths, 1969), 339.

20.  John March, *Action for Slander* (London, 1647), 34.

21.  This danger is hinted at obscurely in the plaintiff's remarks about "the labours and expenses for clearing himself in this matter."

22.  Vaughan, *The Spirit of Detraction,* 100–101.

23.  Vaughan writes for the most part as a moderate Anglican, ready to attack both Catholic and Puritan positions in a theological language that would be acceptable, say, to Richard Hooker. His elaborate citations of Edward Coke in the later sections of his book also suggest Vaughan's wish to ground his argument in well-established legal terms. Still, his pictures of slander always verge on something more extreme, even heterodox, as when he hints at a revisionary demonology in which the "spirit of De-

traction" becomes the chief form by which Satan and his servants manifest their presence in the world. Hence, for example, this spirit is present in the serpent who tempts Eve (55), the dragon and the seven-headed beast of Revelation (70), the lying spirit that God sends to dwell in King Ahab's prophets (57), the leviathan (76), and the evil spirit that possesses Saul (58). Ultimately, the "spirit of Detraction" refers to whatever abuses the Holy Spirit of love and charity, that manifestation of divine power which secretly holds the human world together. It is anything that "takes away" (de-tracts) or steals sense, power, or fame from their proper owners, especially what belies or limits the power of God. The Mass, the doctrine of purgatory, and the radical Protestant doctrine of predestination are all detractions in this sense.

In his prefatory epistle, and later in "Circle 6" (275—79), Vaughan makes clear the very personal spur to his obsession with detraction—not direct attacks on himself, but rumors spread abroad after a stroke of lightning killed his wife. These implied that her death was a judgment against her for unchastity, or indirectly against her husband for spiritual presumption and heresy. The detractions against both man and God implicit in this interpretation occasion some of the author's most passionate arguments about how mortals distort the truth for their own ends, even to the point of stealing events ambiguously natural and supernatural to underwrite what is, in effect, a lie. He himself speaks of that lightning as a mystery, a test of his spiritual patience, and in that form a gift; he also deploys the image of "divine lightning" throughout the book in his animus against the spirit of Detraction. For more on Vaughan (who is no relative of brothers Thomas and Henry, as far as I can tell), see the *Dictionary of National Biography,* 21 vols. (Oxford: Oxford University Press, 1921—22), 20:183—85.

24. John Donne, *Devotions,* 12, Meditation, in *Selected Prose,* ed. Neil Rhodes (Harmondsworth: Penguin, 1987), 119.

25. Contemporary texts often warn victims of slander about the danger of becoming themselves evil tongued in response to false accusation. Hence, for example, *A Plaine description of Slaunder,* sig. F6r—F6v, asks readers to consider David's request in Psalm 141 that God set a watch over his mouth and lips, lest in venting his rage against evil tongues he fall into a mirroring malice and melancholy. Such responses become a particular danger, the author writes, in a context of religious controversy, where writers justifiably cherish "the libertie of the scoffes, the bitter tauntes, and sharpe dealings, even to the quicke" (sig. B4r).

26. Lacey Baldwin Smith, *Treason in Tudor England: Politics and Paranoia* (Princeton: Princeton University Press, 1986), 137—42 especially.

27. Allestree, *The Government of the Tongue,* 53—54.

28. See also Ben Jonson, in the "apologetical dialogue" appended to *Poetaster.* Reading his enemies' attacks on his poetry (especially those which see his satire only as abusive and self-serving libel), Jonson finds "not a crime there taxed but is their own, / Or what their own foul thoughts suggested to them" (50—51). See *Poetaster,* ed. Tom Cain (Manchester: Manchester University Press, 1995), 264. Allestree, *The Government of the Tongue,* 105, asks, "What are all our accusations and bitter censures, but indictments and condemnatory sentences against our selves?"

29. Prescott, "Evil Tongues at the Court of Saul," 166.

30. Leo Braudy, in *The Frenzy of Renown: Fame and Its History* (New York: Oxford University Press, 1986), suggests that the view of fame we find in Renaissance authors "is that of an elaborate pageant that they half discover and half create themselves—looking simultaneously back in time toward the great figures of the past and forward into posterity to glimpse the fame of themselves and their works" (252). In this light, see also Nancy S. Struever, *Theory as Practice: Ethical Inquiry in the Renaissance* (Chicago: University of Chicago Press, 1992), 3–56, and passim, for a discussion of humanist writing as a mode of ethical speculation, something that develops a freer, riskier, more interlocutory means for examining and testing the truth of classical exempla of virtue, especially by probing how moral theory plays itself out in human practice. In Petrarch, Montaigne, and Machiavelli, she finds that praise and blame become relatively unfixed, dialectical entities; analyzing historical models of virtue, such authors frame a mode of inquiry that "not only tolerates but takes advantage of inconsistencies, discomfitures, qualifications, failures of reception, and disjunction between production and reception" (33–34).

31. "Fame" and "fate" in fact both share a common root. The words' Latin sources, *fama,* "rumor" or "common talk," and *fatum,* "that which has been spoken," are both forms of the verb *fari,* "to speak," also the source of *fabula,* "fable" or "story." This etymological family is subtly explored in Piero Boitani, *Chaucer and the Imaginary World of Fame* (Cambridge: D. S. Brewer, 1984), 72–73 and 174–81. The links between *fama, fatum,* and *fabula* are a crucial facet of Boitani's larger account of the *imaginaire* of poetic fame in classical, medieval, and early Renaissance writing, and its way of providing poets with an increasingly complex means of articulating their literary, ethical, and philosophical ambitions. Particularly suggestive is Boitani's research into the shifting imagery of *fama* as breath, wind, wings, shadow, dream, and maze.

32. Ben Jonson, "The Masque of Queens," in *The Complete Masques,* ed. Stephen Orgel (New Haven: Yale University Press, 1969), 135, line 351. Jonson most probably derives this reading from Fulgentius's allegorical account of the myth of Perseus and the Gorgons in the first book of his *Mythologiae.* See *Fulgentius the Mythographer,* trans. Leslie George Whitbread (Columbus: Ohio State University Press, 1971), 61–62.

33. Fulke Greville, "An Inquisition upon Fame and Honour," in *Poems and Dramas of Fulke Greville,* ed. Geoffrey Bullough, 2 vols. (Edinburgh: Oliver and Boyd, n.d.), 1:195.

34. Rabelais, as I have mentioned already, shows his grotesque, multieared monster Oüi-dire, Hearsay, keeping a school for historians as well as judicial witnesses. In fact, "forty cart-loads" of historians, both ancient and modern, remain forever crowded behind a curtain at the back of Hearsay's schoolroom, peeking out, dependent on truths that are always debased and secondhand (*Gargantua and Pantagruel,* 3:224). The implication is that it is hearsay that gives the world a history; this is the form which the world's memory takes. Each state, church, or family feeds on its own precious inheritance of gossip; each nation treasures its own shadowy

myths of origin—those vague tales about heroes, places, or institutions—that other nations steal, trade, mock, or transform for the sake of shame and glory and use to justify war, coercion, and law. "It is therefore, that most of them have such fabulous grounds and trifling beginnings, and enriched with supernatural mistyries," writes Montaigne (*Essays,* 2.353–54). Worrying as he does the whole project of Renaissance humanism, Rabelais indeed suggests that even the more critical, philologically sophisticated history writing of authors such as Valla, Guicciardini, Machiavelli, and Bodin remains tied to the domain of Oüi-dire.

35. Montaigne, *Essays,* 2:350.

36. "But I wot not how, we are double in our selves, which is the cause, that what we beleeve, we beleeve it not, and cannot rid our selves of that, which we condemne" (ibid., 2:342).

37. Ibid., 2:341.

38. Braudy, *Frenzy of Renown,* 139–40, makes this useful comparison between Ovid's Erysichthon and the desire for fame.

39. *State Papers of Elizabeth I, Domestic,* vol. 274, no. 138. Public Records Office, Kew, United Kingdom. I am indebted to Malcolm Smuts for bringing this remarkable text to my attention.

40. In a similar vein, the captured queen of Egypt laments, "Antony / Shall be brought drunken forth, and I shall see / Some squeaking Cleopatra boy my greatness / I' th' posture of a whore" (*Antony and Cleopatra,* 5.2.218–21).

41. Alciati, emblem CLIIII, in *Emblemata,* 654. The full text of the glossing verses reads as follows:

> Aeacidae moriens percussu cuspidis Hector,
> Qui toties hostes vicerat ante suos;
> Comprimere haud potuit vocem, insultantibus illis,
> Dum curru & pedibus nectere vincla parant.
> Distrahite ut libitum est: sic cassi luce leonis
> Convellunt barbam vel timidi lepores.

[Struck by the spear of Aeacides (i.e., Achilles), dying Hector, who had so often before overcome his enemies, could not hold back his cries while his insulters prepared chains to bind his feet to the chariot: tear me to pieces as you will—so even cowardly hares pluck the beard of dead lions (lit. "lions without light").] (My translation)

42. Montaigne, *Essays,* 2:350.

43. As Peter Burke suggests in "Insult and Blasphemy in Early Modern Italy," in *The Historical Anthropology of Early Modern Italy* (Cambridge: Cambridge University Press, 1987), defamatory signs or *cartelli infamanti* posted anonymously on the doorways of houses in Renaissance Rome often parodied the rhetoric of epitaphs—libels being, he surmises, both a way of killing a reputation and an ironic memorial to a reputation already dead (105).

44. Edward Coke, *De libellis famosis,* in *The English Reports,* 176 vols. (Edinburgh, 1907), 77:250–52. A fuller account of official judgments against Pyckering, including pieces of the offending ballad, is contained in John Hawarde, *Les reportes del Cases in Camera Stellata, 1593–1609,* ed. William Baildon (London: privately printed, 1894), 222–30.

45. Hawarde, *Les reportes del Cases,* 223, 227.

46. Coke, *De libellis famosis,* 251. James I, in *Basilicon Doron,* defending the sempiternal institution of kingship, also makes it clear that past calumnies against the throne do not die either; rather, they live as it were by metempsychosis. Hence, he advises his son to prevent the publication even of older histories like George Buchanan's *Rerum Scotiarum Historia* (1582) and John Knox's *Historie of the Reformation* (1587), because of their calumnies against earlier Scottish kings: "and if any of these infamous libels remaine untill your dayes, use the Law upon the keepers thereof: For in that point I would have you a Pythagorist, to thinke that the very spirits of these archibellouses of rebellion, have made transition in them that hoardes their bookes, or maintaines their opinions; punishing them, even as it were their authours risen againe" (in James VI and I, *Political Writings,* ed. Johann P. Sommerville [Cambridge: Cambridge University Press, 1994], 46).

47. Julien Gracq, *The Opposing Shore,* trans. Richard Howard (New York: Columbia University Press, 1986), 286.

48. Vaughan, *The Spirit of Detraction,* 108.

49. Guazzo, in *The Civile Conversation,* 1:67–73, offers a complex figurative catalog of the different types of privy slanderers and abusers that poison the life of the court. The list includes "Maskers," who reprehend someone unnamed, but always in a way that makes his or her identity completely clear; "Rethoricians" who, using the trope of *occupatio,* abuse another by carefully listing all the faults they say they will not name; "Poets," who speak by antiphrasis, calling foul things fair and dishonest things honest; "Hypocrites," who elaborately lament misfortunes they lovingly gloat over; "Forgers," who accuse people of things they have neither done nor thought; "Traytors," who convey private complaints to persons in authority; "Byters," who can never resist scorning and scoff at what is said, and so "pearce the heart" of their victims; and finally "the unknowne," who spread their slanders by sending anonymous letters or, unseen, hang up some degrading image of their victims. He includes among these "all talebearers, and al spies, all coyners and sowers of discord, and al those which bewray other men's secrets" (70). Given the paranoia implied here, it is not entirely a joke when Guazzo's speaker ends his lengthy analysis of such creatures by saying, "I feare mee you will counte mee yll tongued, to speake so muche yll of the yll tongued" (73).

50. Virtue turns calumy back against the calumniator (Geffrey Whitney, *A Choice of Emblemes and Other Devices* [Leyden, 1586], 138; my translation).

51. See Gordon Braden, *Renaissance Tragedy and the Senecan Tradition: Anger's Privilege* (New Haven: Yale University Press, 1985), 63–98.

52. See William Bouwsma, "The Two Faces of Humanism: Stoicism and Augustinianism in Renaissance Thought," in *A Usable Past: Essays in European Cultural History*

(Berkeley: University of California Press, 1990), 19–73.

53. Francesco Petrarca, *Physicke against Fortune,* an English translation of *De remediis utriusque fortunae* (London, 1579), 200r–200v.

54. Montaigne, *Essays,* 2.346.

55. John Calvin, *Sermons on Job,* trans. Arthur Golding (London, 1574), 509.

56. "As soon as religion is internalized, what is plumbed by listening is intimacy, the heart's secret: Sin. A history and a phenomenology of interiority (which we perhaps lack) should here join a history and a phenomenology of listening" (Roland Barthes, *The Responsibility of Forms: Critical Essays on Music, Art, and Representation,* trans. Richard Howard [New York: Hill and Wang, 1985], 250).

57. Ned Lukacher's meditations in *Daemonic Figures: Shakespeare and the Question of Conscience* (Ithaca: Cornell University Press, 1994), 141–47 and passim, have been helpful in clarifying the stakes of conscience at this historical moment. See also Lowell Gallagher, *Medusa's Gaze: Casuistry and Conscience in the Renaissance* (Stanford: Stanford University Press, 1991); and John Wilks, *The Idea of Conscience in Renaissance Tragedy* (London: Routledge, 1990).

58. Robert Burton, *The Anatomy of Melancholy,* ed. Thomas C. Faulkner, Nicholas Kiessling, and Rhonda L. Blair, 4 vols. (Oxford: Oxford University Press, 1989), 3:339 (part 1, sec. 2, mem. 4, subs. 4). Burton complains that "we study to misuse each other, how to sting and gaule, like two fighting bores, bending all our force and wit, friends, fortune, to crucifie one anothers soules; by meanes of which, there is little content and charity, much virulency, hatred, malice, and disquietnesse among us" (3:341).

59. Allestree, *The Government of the Tongue,* 68.

60. Françoise Reumaux, *Toute la ville en parle: Equisse d'une théorie des rumeurs* (Paris: Editions L'Harmattan, 1994), 25 (my translation). Reumaux's examples are drawn from urban communities in twentieth-century France, but her conceptualizations can be applied to many Renaissance examples I have found. In the present context one passage commenting on the ritualized and melodramatic character of certain sorts of rumor deserves quoting: "Les rumeurs hystériques ont-elles, dans leur démesure, quelque chose de shakespearien. Elles sont dramatiques, gesticulent, se contorsionnent et se convulsent sur la scène devant les yeux des spectateurs médusés" (24).

61. See Ferdinando Pulton, *An Abstract of all the penall Statutes which be generall, in force and use* (London, 1577), 241r–242r. Later editions of this work appeared in 1579, 1581, 1606, and 1608.

62. Aside from the few licensed printed newssheets (containing strictly foreign news), the exchange of what we would call "news" in Shakespeare's London was predominantly oral, or effected through letters and ephemeral printed materials like ballads. Handwritten pages containing domestic news (parliamentary debates, state trials, military actions, etc.) did start being sold in London during the 1620s—a commodification of information which forms the basis for Ben Jonson's remarkable comedy *The Staple of News* (1626)—but otherwise something resem-

bling the modern printed newspaper emerged only after 1642, when licensing laws were suspended. For more, see Richard Cust, "News and Politics in Early Seventeenth-Century England," *Past and Present* 112 (1986): 60—90. One danger of "news" is suggested in Cust's arguments that early, handwritten newssheets, however accurate, tended both to focus on scandalous events and to promote a view of domestic politics as more disorderly, more factional in character than the official rhetoric of consensus allowed.

63. Hawarde, *Les reportes del Cases,* 39—40.

64. See Joel Samaha, "Gleanings from Local Criminal-Court Records: Sedition amongst the 'Inarticulate' in Elizabethan Essex," *Journal of Social History* 8 (1975): 61—79.

65. Burke, "Insult and Blasphemy in Early Modern Italy," speaks of the tacit acceptance of slander, and fear of slander, as a mode of social solidarity and social control in Renaissance Rome—one reason why authority might turn a blind eye (or deaf ear) to many instances of defamation. Slanders seek to present themselves as the voice of *fama comune,* working like charivaris or other forms of festive abuse (108). Only in later periods, he suggests, does the state seek to banish the competition from these alternative modes of controlling deviance (103). Burke also notes that early modern libels combine a primitive, colloquial style of abuse (including such visual signs as the smearing of doorways with animal blood, ink, or excrement) with a more bureaucratic register, a parody of the official language of judgment (105).

66. *A Plaine description of Slaunder,* sig. H3r; Sir Henry Yelverton, attorney general, "Proceedings against Mr. Wraynham, in the Star-Chamber, for Slandering the Lord-Chancellor Bacon of Injustice, Pasch. 16 James I. A. D. 1618," in *A Complete Collection of State Trials,* ed. T. B. Howell, 21 vols. (London, 1816), 2:1065; Allestree, *The Government of the Tongue,* 83—84. In the second of these texts the "libels" in question were set forth in a privately printed pamphlet sent to the king himself, accusing both the living chancellor and a dead master of the roles of handing down a knowingly false, unjust, and oppressive sentence against Wraynham in a Chancery case. The council's analysis of the "poison" inherent in the defendant's argument and rhetoric repays study, especially in the attempt to distinguish a just petition from a slanderous complaint.

67. Fernando Pulton, *De pace regis et regni* (London, 1609), 2r. William Hudson, "A Treatise on the Court of Star Chamber" (c. 1609, published in *Collecteana Juridica,* 2 vols. [London, 1791—92]), notes an instance where the truth of a slander may only add to its trouble: "Libelling against a common strumpet is as great an offence as against an honest woman, and perhaps more dangerous to the breach of the peace: for as the woman said she would never grieve to have been told of her red nose if she had not had one indeed" (2:102—3). Milsom, *Historical Foundations,* suggests that it was because of the law's concern with breaches of civic peace that Elizabethan legal texts seem to emphasize the "peculiar malice" of written or printed words, especially given their power to work diffusely, anonymously, and in secret.

Hence, he speculates, it was in the court of Star Chamber, which was most concerned with adjudicating threats to the authority of the state, that the modern distinction between written "libel" and spoken "slander" began to acquire legal force, shaping different standards of proof for either alternative—in particular the idea that whereas spoken words could be justified, "truth was no defense if the libel was written" (342). In most sixteenth- and early seventeenth-century texts, however, "libel" does not necessarily refer to written defamation. It is, in fact, not always easy to see a distinct legal category at this period for threats arising from the written or printed word. Elizabeth L. Eisenstein, *The Printing Press as an Agent of Change: Communications and Cultural Transformations in Early Modern Europe,* 2 vols. (Cambridge: Cambridge University Press, 1979), is no doubt right in suggesting that the print revolution, even as it created a more dispersed and individualized reading public, also provided stronger tools for factional propaganda; "riots, rebellions, and seditions acquired more threatening dimensions when boosted by partisan presses" (1:133). Yet while one can find in various official statutes and royal proclamations language decrying the secret and malicious power of seditious or heretical books to spread error, derogate the crown, and stir up disobedience and disorder, an equally extreme language occurs in legal texts directed against seditious rumors, heretical preaching, libelous songs, defamatory pictures, and suspect stage plays. All of these together seem parts of a more polymorphous danger.

68. See Helmholz, *Select Cases on Defamation,* xiv—xlvii; and Martin Ingram, *Church Courts, Sex, and Marriage in England, 1570—1640* (Cambridge: Cambridge University Press, 1987), 292—320.

69. See Helmholz, *Select Cases on Defamation,* lxvi—cxi, for more general discussion of slander in the common law courts. See also Milsom, *Historical Foundations,* 332—44; and J. H. Baker, *Introduction to English Legal History* (London: Butterworths, 1979), 364—68.

70. See Pulton, *De pace regis et regni,* 2r.

71. Baker, *Introduction to English Legal History,* writes that "What is said in the course of judicial proceedings has always been privileged; the reason being that the public interest requires witnesses and counsel and judges to be unfettered by fear of actions being brought against them. The recognition of this privilege accounts for the origin of the tort of malicious prosecution in the 1540s to provide a remedy in cases where the privilege was abused" (373). See also Milsom, *Historical Foundations,* 338—41. On *infamia,* see Helmholz, *Select Cases on Defamation,* xx—xxiv; and Ian MacLean, *Interpretation and Meaning in the Renaissance: The Case of Law* (Cambridge: Cambridge University Press, 1992), 187—88. Ingram, *Church Courts, Sex, and Marriage,* notes a number of cases in the church courts where slanders involved "what may be described as quasi-judicial accusations, virtually formal charges but not exempt from prosecution as slanders because they did not actually emanate from churchwardens making presentments in due legal form" (304—5).

M. Lindsay Kaplan, in *The Culture of Slander in Early Modern England* (Cambridge: Cambridge University Press, 1997), 12—34, focuses very closely on the many "legal" uses of "infamy" or "scandal" in this period, including the use of paid "delators" to bring accusations against a defendant, the acceptance of *infamia* as grounds for accusation itself, and the deployment of public shame to punish a criminal once he or she was convicted. Such a situation suggests to her the reversibility as well as the self-reflexivity of the category of slander at this time. Kaplan sees the English Renaissance justice system as itself deploying ideologically sanctioned forms of defamation in order to keep certain crimes and disorders, including defamation, under control. This is a tempting and in many ways illuminating irony. Kaplan limits the scope of her argument, however, by reading the law as little more than a tool of state ideology, something that conceals its own arbitrariness, violence, and coercion. That the law itself may work at times like slander is true enough. (That is what Essex clearly feels, justly or unjustly, in the passage quoted above.) But that slander itself tries to work like the law is a rather different issue and requires a different order of analysis. This is something to which Renaissance jurists themselves gave a great deal of thought.

72. See Milsom, *Historical Foundations*, 339; and MacLean, *Interpretation and Meaning*, 196—202.

73. March, *Action for Slander*, 23.

74. Such a flood of slander litigation in the courts could be seen as an ironic testimony to the success of a state policy which wanted a shared respect for law and legal process to maintain social order—though one Elizabethan justice saw the mass of slander cases merely as proof that "the intemperance and malice of men had increased" over time ( J. H. Baker and S. F. C. Milsom, eds., *Sources of English Legal History: Private Law to 1750* [London: Butterworths, 1986], 641). Two examples of the *mitior sensus* rule in action may suffice here. In one example cited by March, the words "Thou art a thief, though hast robbed the church" were judged not actionable as slander, because "the church" might refer to the "Church Militant," which could not be robbed (*Action for Slander*, 35). Then there is the case of a man tried in 1607 for uttering the following words: "Sir Thomas Holt struck his cook on the head with a cleaver, and cleaved his head; the one part lay on the one shoulder and another part on the other." The accused acknowledged that he said this, but the court, taking them *in mitiori sensu*, judged "that these words were not actionable: for it is not averred that the cook was killed, but argumentative" (Baker and Milsom, *Sources of English Legal History*, 643). For further discussion, see Helmholz, *Select Cases on Defamation*, xcii—xcv; and Milsom, *Historical Foundations*, 338.

75. As Donald Kelley shows well in *The Human Measure: Social Thought in the Western Legal Tradition* (Cambridge, Mass: Harvard University Press, 1990), 128—86, Renaissance legal scholars were increasingly aware of the historical and social roots of legal institutions; by their own training and tradition, they had to be pragmatists, secularizers, cultural relativists of a sort, deploying the most sophisticated tools of humanist philology in their researches, and acutely aware of how the legal rules must struggle to preserve any ideal demands for justice within the shifting orders of history and of how readily the institutions of law themselves may fail to sus-

tain those demands. This helps to account for the fact so much that was revisionary in Renaissance historiography was the product of those trained in the law. On this matter, see also Julian Franklin, *Jean Bodin and the Sixteenth-Century Revolution in the Methodology of Law and History* (New York: Columbia University Press, 1963); and William Bouwsma, "Lawyers and Early Modern Culture," in *A Usable Past,* 129–53. J. G. A. Pocock argues in *The Ancient Constitution and the Feudal Law: A Study of English Historical Thought in the Seventeenth Century* (Cambridge: Cambridge University Press, 1957), 1–69, that the thought of English practioners and scholars of the common law, like Edward Coke, remained more essentially conservative than that of their French and Italian counterparts (figures like Cino da Pistoia, Bartolus de Sassoferrato, and Andrea Alciati), since English legal practice remained bound to the idea of a timeless "ancient constitution." Still, as Bouwsma notes (141–42), Coke's close attention to the myriad particular forms of English law constituted its own brand of "local history."

76. Robert Cover, "Violence and the Word," in *Narrative, Violence, and the Law: The Essays of Robert Cover,* ed. Martha Minow, Michael Ryan, and Austin Sarat (Ann Arbor: University of Michigan Press, 1993), 203–38.

77. Cover argues that any legal culture depends on forms of *nomos* that are multiple and sometimes unpredictable, on foundational acts of judgment that can wander, go underground, or be appealed to for their renewing, prophetic force. The social order is created by what Cover calls "exiled narratives" that can always return in dangerous or recreative ways. "Every legal order must conceive of itself in one way or another as emerging out of that which is itself unlawful. . . . Revelation and (to a lesser extent) prophecy are the revolutionary challenges to an order founded on revelation. Secession is the revolutionary response to an order founded on consent or social contract. *The return of foundational acts can never be prevented or entirely domesticated*" ("Nomos and Narrative," in Minow, Ryan, and Sarat, *Narrative, Violence, and the Law,* 118–19; my emphasis). Cover suggests how a "forensic" drama may remind the law of its more ambivalent origins, including the spectacle of seeing or hearing *others* accused, and the security, the liberty of conscience this allows, even if this ends up looking rather like an ignorant parody of the established work of law—as at a soccer match where team members violated the rules, made judgments based on ad hoc standards, came and went at will, forgot why or where to kick the ball, or decided to carry it in their hands.

78. George Steiner, *Antigones* (Oxford: Oxford University Press, 1986), 257.

79. The Latin *causa,* meaning "cause," "reason," "motive," and (in legal contexts) "case," "legal process," or "faction," is indeed the source of the verb *accusare* (from *ad causam*), "to reproach," "blame," "accuse," "call to account," "indict." See Charleton T. Lewis and Charles Short, eds., *A Latin Dictionary* (Oxford: Oxford University Press, 1963), s.v. "accusō" and "causa."

80. Gregory Nagy, *The Best of the Achaeans: Concepts of the Hero in Archaic Greek Poetry* (Baltimore: Johns Hopkins University Press, 1979), 222–64.

81. Pindar, Nemean Odes, 7.61–63. I adapt Nagy's translation in *The Best of the Achaeans,* 223.

82. See Paul Ricoeur, *The Symbolism of Evil,* trans. Emerson Buchanan (Boston: Beacon Press, 1967), 29–33, and 25–157 more generally.

83. I have suggested that the myth of the Fall gives a mythic ground to this sense of being accused, under condemnation. Yet I often feel as if the impulse to accusation were itself one form of the Fall, a founding, necessary poison in our way of knowing and being known. I am reminded of a passage in Coleridge's notebooks, where he records—in order to exorcize—what he calls "One of the strangest and most painful Peculiarities of my Nature (unless others have the same, & like me, hide it from the same inexplicable feeling of causeless shame & sense of a sort of guilt, joined with the apprehension of being feared and shrunk from as a something transnatural). . . . It consists in a sudden second sight of some hidden Vice, past, present, or to come, of the person or persons with whom I am about to form a close intimacy—which never deters me but rather (as all these transnaturals) urge me on, just like the feeling of an Eddy-Torrent to a swimmer / . I see it as a Vision, feel it as a Prophecy—not as one *given* me by any other Being, but as an act of my own Spirit, of the absolute Noumenon / which in doing so seems to have offended against some Law of its Being. . . . These occasional acts of the Εγο νουμενος [spiritual Self] = repetitions or semblances of the original *Fall* of Man—hence shame & power—to leave the appointed Station and become Δαιμων [daemon] . . . and perhaps invading the free will & rightful secrecy of a fellow-spirit" (*The Notebooks of Samuel Taylor Coleridge,* ed. Kathleen Coburn, 4 vols. [Princeton: Princeton University Press, 1957–90], text vol. 3, entry 4166).

84. Franz Kafka, *The Trial,* trans. Breon Mitchell (New York: Schocken, 1998), 3. An earlier English translation by Willa and Edwin Muir has "Someone must have been telling lies about Josef K." (*The Trial* [New York: Schocken, 1937], 3), but the verb *verleumden* in the German text—"Jemand muste Josef K. verleumden haben" (*Der Process,* ed. Malcolm Pasley [Frankfurt am Main: Fischer, 1990], 3)—means more precisely to slander or calumniate.

85. Jacobus Revius, "Achterclap" (Slander), from *Jacobus Revius: Dutch Metaphysical Poet,* trans. Henrietta Ten Harmsel (Detroit: Wayne State University Press, 1968), 67. The epigram appeared in a collection of Revius's poems published in 1630.

86. Alan Macfarlane, *Witchcraft in Tudor and Stuart England: A Regional and Comparative Study* (New York: Harper and Row, 1970), 270. As records make clear enough, of course, not all accused witches were punished, nor were all witnesses believed. Many English witch pamphlets, in fact, make a point of displaying jurists' wisely skeptical handling of the evidence, their exclusion of dubious testimony—even if they never question the basic fact of witchcraft or the centrality of its prosecution to the system of law. See, for example, the pamphlets describing trials of witches from Chelmsford, Windsor, St. Oyseth, and Northamptonshire, reprinted in *Witchcraft in England: 1558–1618,* ed. Barbara Rosen (Amherst: University of Massachusetts Press, 1991), 72–102, 103–57, 344–56. Church court records also show numerous instances of people themselves prosecuted for slander by those whom they called "witch." Cf. Helmholz, *Select Cases on Defamation,* 61–63; Mac-

farlane, *Witchcraft in Tudor and Stuart England,* 68–79; and F. G. Emmison, *Elizabethan Life: Morals and the Church Courts* (Chelmsford: Essex County Council, 1973), 49, 66.

87. This is very much the focus of historians like Macfarlane, *Witchcraft in Tudor and Stuart England;* Keith Thomas, *Religion and the Decline of Magic* (New York: Scribner's, 1971), 535–70; and Robin Briggs, *Witches and Neighbours: The Social and Cultural Context of European Witchcraft* (New York: Viking, 1996).

88. On the forms of proof employed in English witch trials, see Rosen, *Witchcraft in England,* 17–19; and Alan Macfarlane, "Witchcraft in Tudor and Stuart Essex," in *Crime in England: 1550–1800,* ed. J. S. Cockburn (London: Methuen, 1977), 72–75. English law did not allow confessions extracted by torture to serve as evidence in a court of law, as was common in continental witch trials.

89. Norman Cohn, *Europe's Inner Demons: An Enquiry Inspired by the Great Witch-Hunt* (New York: Basic Books, 1975).

90. In *Ecstasies: Deciphering the Witches' Sabbath,* trans. Raymond Rosenthal (Harmondsworth: Penguin, 1991), Carlo Ginzburg works painstakingly to recover traces of the actual ritual and shamanistic practices hidden beneath reports and confessions of magical activity by witches in medieval and postmedieval Europe—stories, for example, about witches's ecstatic nocturnal flights, their disembodied battles with demonic enemies to secure the fertility of the land, and their animal metamorphoses. This requires him to strip away, as much as possible, "the interpretive categories of demonologists, the judges, or witnesses against the accused" (13). These are, Ginzburg insists, (slanderous) categories which the accused witches themselves are liable to "introject," destroying their own cultural identities in the process. They are also categories which he argues have been implicitly adopted by social-functionalist historians like Alan Macfarlane and Keith Thomas, whose work he submits to a sharp critique (*Ecstasies,* 2–7). Ginzburg's work, oddly enough, makes me understand the peculiar fascination and conceptual power that still remains in works like Jules Michelet's *La sorcière* (1862), despite some of the errors catalogued by Cohn (*Europe's Inner Demons,* 105–7), since Michelet writes so nakedly about witches from inside the myth of the witch, giving dramatic conviction to the witch's reality even as he shows us the personal fears and ideological engines that sustain it.

91. A discussion of the play and its source pamphlet—*The wonderful discoverie of Elizabeth Sawyer, a Witch* (1621)—can be found in the introductory essay to Peter Corbin and Douglas Sedge, eds., *Three Jacobean Witchcraft Plays* (Manchester: Manchester University Press, 1986), 20–28, from which I quote below.

92. The dog is a strange combination of Marlowe's Mephistopheles and Ariel and Caliban.

93. Phillip Stubbes, *The Anatomie of Abuses* (London, 1583), sig. L5r, thus derides plays based on the gospel: "The word of our Salvation, the price of Christ his bloud, & the merits of his passion, were not given to be derided and iested at, as they be in these filthie playes and enterluds on stages & scaffolds, or to be mixt and interlaced

with bawdry, wanton shewes, & uncomely gestures, as is used (every Man knoweth) in these playes and enterludes." Stephen Gosson, *Playes Confuted in five Actions* (London, 1582), sigs. C3r–E5v, similarly argues that stage plays distort stories of heroic virtue by using them to display a poet's skill, cutting and mangling the story to fill out a curious plot, mingling in discourses of love or the antics of clowns, and so on. On the sources and scope of such attacks on the stage, see Jonas Barish, *The Antitheatrical Prejudice* (Berkeley: University of California Press, 1981), 80–190.

94. Cf. William Rankins, *A Mirrour of Monsters* (London, 1587); and Stephen Gosson, *The Schoole of Abuse* (London, 1579). On the dark lessons to be learned in the theater, see also John Northbrooke, *A Treatise wherein Dicing, Dauncing, Vaine playes, or Enterluds, with other idle pastimes . . . are reproued by the Authoritie of the word of God and auntient writers* (London, 1577), 67: "If you will learne howe to bee false and deceyue your husbandes, or husbandes their wyues, howe to playe the harlottes, to obtayne one's loue, howe to rauishe, howe to beguyle, howe to betraye, to flatter, lye, sweare, forsweare, how to allure to whoredome, howe to murther, howe to poyson, howe to disobey and rebell against princes, to consume treasures prodigally, to mooue to lustes, to ransacke and spoyle cities and townes, to bee ydle, to blaspheme, to sing filthie songs of love, to speake filthily, to be prowde, how to mocke, scoffe, and deryde any nation . . . shall not you learne, then, at such enterludes howe to practice them?"

95. Geoffrey Fenton, *A Forme of Christian Pollicie* (London, 1574), bk. 3, chap. 7. I quote from an excerpt printed in E. K. Chambers, ed., *The Elizabethan Stage,* 4 vols. (Oxford: Oxford University Press, 1923), 4:195.

96. See Michael Goldman, *The Actor's Freedom: Toward a Theory of Drama* (New York: Viking, 1975).

97. Plays like Shakespeare's *Much Ado about Nothing* and *Merchant of Venice* (to cite two obvious examples) put accusation itself on trial; they implicitly test the wishes of the audience to possess and judge the world through accusation and the forms of law that structure it. Though not intended for the stage, Elizabeth Cary's *Tragedy of Mariam, the Fair Queen of Jewry* (1613) also catches at this central energy of the public theater. One central fascination of this drama lies in watching how the risky accusations and pained protests of Herod's queen—themselves set loose by the false rumor of her husband's death—are suddenly caught by the costly attention of so many equivocal and "prejudicate" ears, particularly those of Herod and his former wife, but also the ears of the vacillating chorus. It is against these opponents that the play stakes its often desperate vision of its heroine's purity, integrity, and freedom.

98. On the workings of censorship in Elizabethan and Jacobean theater, see G. E. Bentley, *The Profession of the Dramatist in Shakespeare's Time, 1590–1642* (Princeton: Princeton University Press, 1971), 145–96; Richard Burt, *Licensed by Authority: Ben Jonson and the Discourses of Censorship* (Ithaca: Cornell University Press, 1993); Janet Clare, *"Art Made Tongue-Tied by Authority": Elizabethan and Jacobean Dramatic Censorship* (Manchester: Manchester University Press, 1990); Richard Dut-

ton, *Mastering the Revels: The Regulation and Censorship of English Renaissance Drama* (Iowa City: University of Iowa Press, 1991); and Annabel Patterson, *Censorship and Interpretation:The Conditions of Writing and Reading in Early Modern England* (Madison: University of Wisconsin Press, 1984), especially 49-92. Patterson's account of the means by which playwrights make dramatic capital out of their own evasions of the censor is suggestive, even if some of her conclusions are highly speculative. Burt usefully stresses the diffused, often contradictory nature of censors and licensing controls at work on the Renaissance English stage, emphasizing the participation of authors themselves in the work of what we tend to call censorship. See also Kaplan, *Culture of Slander,* 1–11, for a pointed reflection on how (and at what cost) recent work on censorship neglects the pressing questions raised at this time by the problem of slander. I should add that I very rarely find that invoking the strictly political category of censorship helps get at any of the deeper questions about the opacities, gaps, and apparent evasions in Shakespeare's texts.

99.  Jonson, *Poetaster,* 71–73.

100.  See Tom Cain, introduction to Jonson, *Poetaster,* 30– 36, for a discussion of how Jonson's play enters into "the war of the theaters."

101.  From Jonson's letter to Robert Cecil, earl of Salisbury, answering charges that *Eastward Ho!* written by Jonson, Chapman, and Marston, contained seditious abuse (reprinted in an appendix to George Chapman, Ben Jonson, and John Marston, *Eastward Ho!* ed. R. W. Van Fossen [Manchester: University of Manchester Press, 1979], 221).

102.  Envy calls out to those obsessive, hungry talkers such as Jonson satirizes in so many plays; he encourages the kind of speaker who by his monomaniacal noise tries to silence the freer conversation of the human world, to "empty the world of all sounds but that of his own voice, and create a silence of sameness" (Alvin Kernan, *The Cankered Muse: Satire of the English Renaissance* [New Haven: Yale University Press, 1959], 174).

103.  J. M. Coetzee, in *Giving Offense: Essays on Censorship* (Chicago: University of Chicago Press, 1996), writes that "in the personal records of writers who have operated under censorship we find eloquent and despairing descriptions of how the censor-figure is involuntarily incorporated into the interior, psychic life, bringing with it humiliation, self-disgust, and shame. In unwilling fantasies of this kind, the censor is typically experienced as a parasite, a pathogenic invader of the body-self, repudiated with visceral intensity but never wholly expelled" (10). Jonson, however, cannot be said simply to have incorporated the censor figure in an entirely involuntary fashion. It is native to him.

104.  Cf. the description of aeromancy in Henry Cornelius Agrippa of Nettesheim, *Three Books of Occult Philosophy,* trans. James Freake (1642; German original, 1531), ed. Donald Tyson (St. Paul: Llewellyn, 1993), 17, bk. 1, chap. 6.

105.  *The Bible,* trans. John Wycliffe, ed. J. Forshall and F. Madden, 4 vols. (Oxford: Oxford University Press, 1850), 4:340.

106.  *A Plaine description of Slaunder,* sigs. D1r–D2v. Calvin's thoughts about

scandals in religion and religious communities—one clear source for this pamphlet—are set forth in *Concerning Scandals* (1550), trans. John W. Fraser (Grand Rapids: William B. Eerdmans Publishing, 1978).

CHAPTER THREE

1. William Hazlitt, *Characters of Shakespeare's Plays* (Oxford: Oxford University Press, 1916), 251.

2. See Northrop Frye, *A Natural Perspective: The Development of Shakespearean Comedy and Romance* (New York: Columbia University Press, 1965), 11–13, on the logic of romance in *Measure for Measure*. E. A. J. Honigman, *Myriad-Minded Shakespeare: Essays, Chiefly on the Tragedies and Problem Comedies* (New York: St. Martin's, 1989), 147–68, argues that the play in fact intentionally mixes up its generic signals, keeping them off balance, in part to show us an actor-like or playwright-like Duke who improvises the play as he goes.

3. A. P. Rossiter, *Angels with Horns and Other Shakespeare Lectures,* ed. Graham Storey (London: Longmans, 1961), 152–70; and Richard P. Wheeler, *Shakespeare's Development and the Problem Comedies: Turn and Counter-Turn* (Berkeley: University of California Press, 1981), 92–153, describe particularly well the baffled sense of conflict that characterizes this play, the relentless awareness of moral or emotional pressures that remain at once looming and unpurged throughout the action, that become the object of fear and repulsion, evasion, and projection.

4. In Shakespeare's time, the noun "quest" could refer to an inquest or judicial inquiry, and a search or pursuit more generally, but as a verb, "to quest" seems to have had a strong primary reference to hunting dogs, meaning "to search for game," also "to break out into a peculiar bark at the sight of game; to give tongue; to bark or yelp." See *OED,* s.v. "quest," *v.,* 1 and 2.

5. An obsession with bastardy, and its defamatory quality, haunts many of the Duke's speeches. Janet Adelman's sense of "the ease with which the distinction between legitimate and illegitimate sexuality breaks down in this play" (*Suffocating Mothers: Fantasies of Maternal Origin in Shakespeare's Plays, "Hamlet" to "The Tempest"* [London: Routledge, 1992], 98) is mirrored in the breakdown of distinctions between legitimate and illegitimate children. The universality of bastardy is also congruent with Marc Shell's idea that the play explores the universality of incest, in *The End of Kinship: "Measure for Measure," Incest, and the Ideal of Universal Siblinghood* (Stanford: Stanford University Press, 1988).

6. This picture of the Duke as crowded out by rumors which are themselves of his own making mirrors Angelo's image of being dispossessed of his rational powers by his desire for Isabella: "So play the foolish throngs with one that swounds, / Come all to help him, and so stop the air / By which he should revive; and even so / The general subject to a well-wish'd king / Quit their own part, and in obsequious fondness / Crowd to his presence, where their untaught love / Must needs appear offence" (2.4.24–30).

7. J. W. Lever, introduction to his Arden edition of *Measure for Measure* (London: Methuen, 1965), xx–xxii, thinks that the patching in of these lines about "escapes of wit" in act 4, scene 1, is too stark a solution to be the result of either scribal error or that somewhat mythic entity, "memorial reconstruction." Following a suggestion of William Warburton, he surmises that a bookkeeper or some other member of the company noticed a gap and filled it in, using six lines from an earlier speech which appears, now in shorter form, at 3.2.179–82. Lever himself finds it hard to explain the original gap, however. "Whether Shakespeare here showed an unusual degree of neglect, or whether he wrote a speech for the Duke which his colleagues or the censor found unacceptable, there is no way of knowing today" (xxii).

8. Harry Berger, Jr., *Making Trifles of Terrors: Redistributing Complicities in Shakespeare* (Stanford: Stanford University Press, 1997), 363, also notes that the bed trick can be seen as the Duke's way of testing and tempting the purity of Isabella: "The information about Angelo that the Duke overhears gives him a chance to test the rigor of Isabella's commitment to the high standard of purity she holds up to Claudio. He immediately, abruptly, begins his own seduction, his own attempt to 'raze the sanctuary' of her cloistered virtue—but not in the crudely sexual mode depicted by Shell and exploited by Angelo. Rather, he pulls Mariana and the bed trick out of his hood in a much subtler form of temptation, the seductive promise of which is that by a single act of deception Isabella will solve all problems—Mariana's, Claudio's, and her own—with no moral cost to herself. In fact, although the project this panacea implicates her in may preserve her chastity, it compromises her integrity and entangles her in a web of intrigue that neutralizes her ability to represent herself as 'a thing enskied and sainted.'" See also David Sundelson, *Shakespeare's Restorations of the Father* (New Brunswick: Rutgers University Press, 1983), 34–36, on the Duke's obsession with maintaining his own appearance of purity.

9. Anne (Righter) Barton, *Shakespeare and the Idea of the Play* (London: Chatto and Windus, 1962), 179: "He haunts the disguised Duke like a devoted spirit, breathing into his ear all the calumny and gossip which this temporary abdication of power, this resort to disguise, has made possible. Lucio is like an unruly extempore actor crept without permission into the Duke's tidy morality drama."

10. See August Wilhelm Schlegel, *Course of Lectures on Dramatic Art and Literature,* trans. John Black, 2 vols. (London, 1840), 2:173–74.

11. Berger, *Making Trifles of Terrors,* 364.

12. My sense of Lucio as "shadow" owes much to a 1995 Royal Shakespeare Company Production of *Measure for Measure,* directed by Steven Plimlott, which strikingly caught the relentless, if often impersonal, logic of Lucio's relation to the Duke. The actor cast to play Lucio was almost a double of the one playing the Duke; both men were dark, small, and wiry, with cropped hair and bony faces, possessed by a nervous energy that differentiated them both from the more stolid (and much taller) Angelo. Lucio, the Duke's twin, told his tales without malice, but also without clownishness or gaiety. Indeed, a similar "trick of the voice"—a deliberateness, a slightly weary precision—characterized both of them. The main difference was

that Lucio never lost control, whereas the Duke was perennially stopping, stammering, and getting embarrassed as the play unfolded. It was Lucio himself, breaking into an interview with Isabella or delaying some new intrigue, who most often kept the Duke off guard. The mirroring physique and voice meant that the Duke could not escape Lucio's images of himself as fantastical, foolish, lecherous, and liberal. Lucio's ludic stories found him out, calling the bluff of the Duke's confident narrations, even suggesting that the Duke himself was producing the slanders he could not bear to hear. The uncanniness of the situation lay partly in Lucio's very solidity and literalness. One felt, because of this, the immediacy of the verbal sparring between the actors, rather than something more dreamlike. Lucio's presence onstage composed a kind of embodied taunt that the Duke could neither mistake nor leave alone.

13. The idea that Lucio is the product of the Duke's fear about how he is talked about and mocked by others anticipates the logic of Fyodor Dostoevsky's novel *The Double*. This book's abject hero, a government clerk named Golyadkin, sees a double of himself working in his own department. He eventually becomes convinced that the arrival of this double (whose resemblance to himself no one else acknowledges) is part of a complex plot to replace him. The crucial thing, in relation to *Measure for Measure,* is that part of this supposed plot is an attempt to convince Golyadkin's fellow workers that he, the real clerk, is identical with the worst public rumors about his own incompetence and irrationality, in order that his more efficient double can usurp his position at work. The connection of the slander theme to the double theme is also central to Philip Roth's consciously Shakespearean novel, *Operation Shylock* (New York: Simon and Schuster, 1993), in which the author is harassed by a tricky, obsessive (in ways Lucio-like) doppelgänger named Philip Roth, who is obsessed with attacks on the true Philip Roth's reputation and undertakes, in his disguise, a mad and scandalous ideological crusade in order to defend the author's name from scandal. Also interesting in the present context is the last chapter of Roth's book, in which an Israeli spymaster describes to the narrator the nature of rabbinic discussions about the problem of *loshon hora,* the evil tongue. He reflects on the difficulty of purifying human speech of "ridicule and insult and accusation and anger" (335), not only among anti-Semites, but among the Jews themselves, whom he describes as possessing a wild, even tragic genius for *loshon hora.*

14. John Marston, *The Malcontent,* ed. Bernard Harris (London: A and C Black, 1987). Malevole's presence is signaled at the very opening of the play, when "the vilest out-of-tune music" is heard on the empty stage, music we soon learn is provided by Malevole himself. This noise is Malevole's signature, the emblem of his wish to mar decorum, to "build Babylon." The malcontent's speech further unfolds its quality in such exchanges as the following: "*Pietro:* How dost thou live nowadays, Malevole? *Malevole:* Why, like the knight, Sir Patrick Penlolians, with killing o' spiders for my lady's monkey. *Pietro:* How dost spend the night, I hear thou never sleep'st? *Malevole:* O no, but dream the most fantastical. O Heaven! O fubbery, fubbery! . . . dreams, dreams, visions, fantasies, chimeras, imaginations, conceits"

(1.3.39—53).This melancholiac's words indeed carry the trace of a pathological interiority.Yet it is not an interiority ablc to penetrate others—as, say, MadTom's lunatic ramblings seem to penetrate King Lear, or Lucio's the Duke.

15.  If Shakespeare's Duke more resembles Pietro than Altofronto, it is because like Marston's usurper he is a little afraid of having his own uncontrolled speech overheard. At one point in act 4 of *The Malcontent,* in the midst of a hunt, Pietro lies down to rest. In his single really humanizing moment onstage, the Duke sends his pages away, lest they hear the uncontrolled murmurings which he knows he puts forth in his sleep.

16.  The range of ambiguities in "trick" comes through when Isabella, attacking Angelo's legalism, speaks of the "fantastic tricks" that humans play before heaven (2.2.122), and when Claudio asks Isabella in regard to Angelo's indecent proposal, "If it were damnable, he being so wise, / Why would he for the momentary trick / Be perdurably fin'd?" (3.1.112—14).The word is a particularly rich one in this period, capable of meaning, according to the *OED,* s.v. "trick," "a crafty or fraudulent device of a mean or base kind" (I.1.a); "an illusory or deceptive appearance" (I.1.c); "a freakish or mischievous act; a roguish prank; a frolic" (I.2.a); "a capricious, foolish or stupid act" (I.2.b); and "a particular habit, way, or mode of acting, a characteristic quality, trait, practice or custom. (Usually a bad or unpleasant habit.)" (II.7).

17.  Cf. Rosalind and Celia's jests about "burrs" in *AsYou Like It,* 1.3.12—17.

18.  See Samuel Schoenbaum, *William Shakespeare: A Compact Documentary Life* (NewYork: Oxford University Press, 1977), 151.

19.  Henry Chettle, the bookseller who published Greene's posthumous pamphlet in 1592, included an apology for this attack in a pamphlet of his own composition published a year later, *Kind-Heart's Dream,* where he acknowledges Shakespeare's civility, "uprightness of dealing," and dramatic skill (see Schoenbaum, *William Shakespeare,* 154). Schoenbaum surmises that Shakespeare or his aristocratic patrons may have made some kind of protest, though he also suggests that Chettle's apology was itself a way of stretching out the controversy, in order to exploit it as a way of selling more books.

20.  See Honigman's account in *Myriad-Minded Shakespeare* of the Duke as an image of Shakespeare's own self-dramatizing and improvisational impulses, cited above, n. 2.

21.  This sense of a guilt or shame inherent in the wielding of power—and of power's need to displace this burden through self-dividing, self-emptying gestures—runs through all of Shakespeare's plays. It is a signature of almost all Shakespeare's rulers and political villains, sharply contrasting with the shamelessness with which power is wielded by Marlowe's violent heroes—whether that power is acting purely or impurely, in public or in secret, by natural or unnatural means.

22.  Jonathan Goldberg, *James I and the Politics of Literature: Jonson, Shakespeare, Donne, andTheir Contemporaries* (Baltimore: Johns Hopkins University Press, 1983), 231—39, sees the Duke's use of substitutes as a tacit, often satirical commentary on

James's strategies of absolutist rule, focusing especially on the king's desire for "presence-in-absence."

23. More psychoanalytically inclined critics such as Adelman, *Suffocating Mothers,* 98—99, Sundelson, *Shakespeare's Restorations of the Father,* 89—93, and Wheeler, *Shakespeare's Development,* 92—139, also see the Duke as allowing Angelo, through substitution, to give a home to aspects of his desire that he is afraid to put into play in the world but that he wants to watch and manipulate; he projects, or drains off from himself, not only the cruelty and pleasure of wielding power, but also what Angelo calls the "strong and swelling evil / Of my conception" (2.4.6—7), that infectious sexuality, ambivalently male and female, which rises up before the other principal characters of the play.

24. Aristotle, *Nicomachean Ethics,* bk. 5, chap. 10. For more general background, see Henry Maine, *Ancient Law* (1861; reprint, New York: Dorset, 1986), 21—24, 36—59; and F. W. Maitland, *Equity* (Cambridge: Cambridge University Press, 1929). Kathy Eden, *Poetic and Legal Fiction in the Aristotelian Tradition* (Princeton: Princeton University Press, 1986), 25—61, explores the links in Aristotelian thought between the work of legal equity, which probes the often unknowable intentions behind human laws and human actions, and the writing of tragic fictions. For Aristotle, the paradoxes of circumstance and motive that are the subject of tragedy demand the sort of nuanced ethical analysis and historical speculation characteristic of equity. The work of equity seems also to elicit a play of fear and pity that resembles the emotions provoked by a tragedy.

25. Edward Hake, *Epieikeia* (1601), ed. D. E. C. Yale (New Haven: Yale University Press, 1953), 28. Many English jurists insisted that equity was implicit in any true law, a part of its hidden strength. Christopher Saint German, *Doctor and Student* (1523), ed. T. F. T. Plucknett and J. L. Barton (London: Selden Society, 1974), writes that such exceptions to a law as are observed by equity are "secretely understande in every generall rewle of every posytyve lawe" (97). Hake follows Saint German in insisting that equity is something inherent in the law itself, part of its original intent, rather than an alien or extralegal entity, something to be contributed by the act of a judge. Rather, he says, the law itself thinks and persuades ("*cogit et suadet*") through equity (*Epieikeia,* 15). Opposing the opinion of Plowden's *Commentaries,* as well as that of many civil lawyers, that equity is "no parte of the lawe, but a morall vertue which reformeth the lawe" (9), Hake insists that it is rather the "secreat righteousnes of the lawe" (49), and that "if the lawe we speake of be goode lawe and well grounded, then the *Equity* that must used to the correction" of an injustice "cannot be said to be the *Equitye* of the judge, but of the lawe, for otherwise the lawe muste be . . . no lawe but a meare tyranicall constytution" (11).

26. It is this double ability to challenge and refurbish the law's claims to justice that helps lend to equity what Angus Fletcher calls its "prophetic" aspect. See Fletcher, *The Prophetic Moment: An Essay on Spenser* (Chicago: University of Chicago Press, 1971), 276—87. Angelo's "awakened law," which looks both to past and fu-

ture, is by contrast a grotesque parody of that equity which shows law its truly prophetic character.

27. William Lambarde, *Archeion, or, a Discourse upon the High Courts of Justice in England* (1591), ed. Charles H. McIlwain and Paul L. Ward (Cambridge, Mass.: Harvard University Press, 1957), describes equity in the Court of Chancery—the "court of conscience"—as aiming to correct those injustices created when petitioners were accidentally (or maliciously) trapped by the letter of the common law. Thus, he writes, Chancery "doth so *cancell* and *shut up* the *rigour* of the generall *Law,* that it shall not breake forth to the hurt of some one singular Case and person" (31–32). Lambarde goes on to associate such an exercise of equity with the justice of the sovereign himself, rather than the law in general, adding that "such as then sought reliefe by Equitie, were suitors to the King himselfe, who being assisted with his *Chancellor* and Concell, did mitigate the severitie of the *Law* in his owne person, when it pleased him to be present; and did (in absence) either referre the same to the *Chancellor* alone, or to him and some other of the Councell" (37–38).

28. In Elizabeth's time, and even more in James's, supporters of the authority of common law complained that the appeal to equity, especially in the courts of Chancery and Star Chamber, could justify the arbitrary exercise of the royal power, ungrounded by the gravitational pull of the "ancient constitution." Hence the urgency of the idea that true equity was already implicit in the common law itself. For further discussion, see Louis A. Knafla, *Law and Politics in Jacobean England* (Cambridge: Cambridge University Press, 1977), 155–82; and Donald Kelley, *The Human Measure: Social Thought in the Western Legal Tradition* (Cambridge, Mass.: Harvard University Press, 1990), 174–80.

29. The Duke's maskings, for instance, curiously intertwine the three sorts of "Princely" concealment distinguished by Francis Bacon: (1) *secrecy,* or the absolute masking of what one is (the "vertue of a confessour," as well as a spy); (2) *dissimulation,* "the Skirts or Traine of *Secrecy,*" when one gives signs that he is not what he is; and (3) *simulation,* when he "industriously, and expressely, faigns, and pretends to be, that he is not." See Bacon, "Simulation and Dissimulation," in *The Essayes or Counsels, Civill and Moral,* ed. Michael Kiernan (Oxford: Oxford University Press, 1985), 20–23. Each of these types of secrecy, Bacon argues, has its proper time and place for the true ruler. But in the Duke's case, the forms of secrecy, dissimulation, and simulation splinter and harass each other in ways that point to motives other than ones which seem strictly political. Despite their improvisational skill, the Duke's games also lack that eerily impersonal, superemotional, and "purely" political character that for Machiavelli marks the frauds and games of the true Prince.

30. In this reading of Nietzsche, I am drawing on Alexander Nehemas's argument in *Nietzsche: Life as Literature* (Cambridge, Mass.: Harvard University Press, 1985), especially 74–105. If the Duke evades either being affected by others or translating himself into his own effects on them, it is partly because this process is dangerous in itself. As Nehemas writes, "Nietzsche thinks that increase in what he describes as power does not necessarily lead to increase in strength; on the con-

trary, it often makes one more susceptible to harm and injury. Power, at its basis, is the proliferation of effects that can be associated with a particular thing, and in the process of this proliferation the 'thing' can easily fall apart" (92).

31. One might ask, Of what is Barnardine's refusal a parable? Hazlitt, in *Characters of Shakespeare's Plays,* 252, thought that Barnardine was "Caliban transported from Prospero's wizard island" to the jails of Vienna; he stands in place, half asleep and drunk, refusing to be called out, a piece of intransigent, muddy stuff blocking the Duke's theater of magical justice, calling into doubt all postures of virtue, even his own. Harold C. Goddard, *The Meaning of Shakespeare* (Chicago: University of Chicago Press, 1951), 451–53, goes even further, making Barnardine into a "vast symbol," an intimation of what it might look like for people to refuse the secretly corrupting terms of state power.

32. See Harold Bloom, *The Western Canon* (New York: Harcourt Brace, 1994), 70.

33. Hazlitt, *Characters of Shakespeare's Plays,* 251.

34. Given the title of this chapter, I should say that what I have called the Duke's not hearing is rather different from the tricks of the psyche described by Freud in his late essay "A Disturbance of Memory on the Acropolis," in *Collected Psychoanalytic Works,* ed. James Strachey, 24 vols. (London: Hogarth Press, 1955), 22:239–48. Freud takes as his subject certain strange disturbances of thought, moments of derealization or skepticism when the material world loses its substance or emotional claims, arguing that, in many such cases, an apparently intellectual repudiation of reality can also serve as a means for the mind to repress feelings of guilt or ambivalence. Intellectual skepticism thus becomes, in its own fashion, a "royal road" to the unconscious (and to the *science* of the unconscious). What is striking about the Duke is that he seems to have no unconscious of his own to ward off, even if there is something peculiarly compulsive in his actions; what his deafness repudiates is rather evidence of dangerous ambivalences and revelations in the minds of other people.

35. See above, 26.

36. See James VI and I, *Political Writings,* ed. Johann P. Sommerville (Cambridge: Cambridge University Press, 1994), 26–27.

37. Wheeler, *Shakespeare's Development,* 121, speaks well about the anomalous character of the Duke's eloquence here, its way of contradicting the regenerative impulses that seem to drive his plots. See also Rossiter, *Angels with Horns,* 166.

38. For example, Goddard, *The Meaning of Shakespeare,* 442–43, sees a deep moral cowardice feeding Isabella's turn against her brother. Berger, *Making Trifles of Terrors,* 361, speaks of Isabella's "full-throated, operatic pleasure" in embracing her own purity, and her brother's contamination. Somewhat more sympathetically, Lever, introduction to *Measure for Measure,* lxxxi, hears in the speeches of brother and sister the signs of an illusory moral impasse, one that only a higher justice can sort out. Shell, *The End of Kinship,* 139, sees no divine promise, but rather a veiled threat emerging from the paradoxical, if also potentially redemptive, idea of uni-

versal incest, a possibility that haunts all idealized pictures of marriage and justice in this play—indeed all forms of social exchange.

39. Such ambivalences and contradictions are entirely characteristic of the wide array of literary and mythic stories about statues that come to life. For more, see my *Dream of the Moving Statue* (Ithaca: Cornell University Press, 1992).

40. Darryl J. Gless, *"Measure for Measure," the Law, and the Convent* (Princeton: Princeton University Press, 1979), 126, suggests that Isabella is required, in sacrificing her virginity to Angelo, to undergo a kind of parodic *imitatio Christi*. This is part of a pattern throughout the play, whereby images that might suggest rebirth or regeneration turn more troubling, often by aggressively mingling a sexual and a religious meaning.

41. Wheeler, *Shakespeare's Development,* 121.

42. See Leonardo Sciascia, *Todo Modo* (Turin: Einaudi, 1974), 91.

43. The agon of pieties indeed recalls the central struggle of Sophocles' *Antigone,* with its violent competition between opposed pictures of law and justice and the dramatic exposure of the passions that sustain them. Isabella, too, is a threatened sister pleading for mercy on behalf of her brother. Of course, for all her ferocious, even ecstatic intelligence, Isabella's acts never pose so extreme or mysterious a threat to the authority of law as Antigone's do. And despite Isabella's imagining of her own martyrdom, she never inhabits so mortal or so frighteningly solitary an ethical position as Antigone. It is also hard to imagine a Creon awakened to criminal desire by Antigone's rapt "sayings" against his authority as Angelo is by Isabella's words. No cosmic forces invade the stage of *Measure for Measure,* save as transparently human fictions. Yet the comparison is not, I think, outlandish; it can help us weigh better what is at stake in the play, especially its way of evoking and containing more tragic possibilities.

44. William Empson, *The Structure of Complex Words* (Ann Arbor: University of Michigan Press, 1967), 274. Empson says well that "the only touching side of Angelo is that he is genuinely astonished by his desires."

45. Adelman, *Suffocating Mothers,* argues that Angelo's fantasy of his desire as a defilement of Isabella's purity looks at once like the essential motive force of his desire and like the retroactive revenge against her for having betrayed him into desire. "Confronting his own sexuality . . . he experiences the secular equivalent of original sin and the fall into death" (92). This would also make a parody of all of his attempts to redeem himself.

46. We might recall that this ruler who so frequently assumes the mask of a confessor is never shy about betraying to others the secrets he has been given in confession; nor does he ever take the measure of the consciences which he wants visibly to test, cure, and remake.

47. Lever, introduction to *Measure for Measure,* lxxxi.

48. Ruth Nevo, *"Measure for Measure:* Mirror for Mirror," *Shakespeare Survey* 40 (1988): 120, observes beautifully that "though they are dialectically opposed to any expansive, liberating 'green world,' the prison scenes function similarly, as the alembic of unconscious and contradictory impulses . . . a positive saturnalia of the

unconscious, an oneiric carnival of condensations and displacements . . . whereby the dreaming consciousness—of friar and nun, of Duke and daughter—finds ways of being both punisher and punished."

49. Berger, *Making Trifles of Terrors,* 400—401.

50. Julien Gracq, *The Opposing Shore,* trans. Richard Howard (New York: Columbia University Press, 1986), 287.

51. M. Lindsay Kaplan, *The Culture of Slander in Early Modern England* (Cambridge: Cambridge University Press, 1997), 104, sees this speech as the clearest revelation of the strange process by which the forces of law assimilate to themselves the powers of the slanderer.

52. Speaking about the ends of Shakespeare's tragedies in words that could equally apply to *Measure for Measure,* A. C. Bradley, *Shakespearean Tragedy,* 2d ed. (London: Macmillan, 1905), writes: "Any theological interpretation of the world on the author's part is excluded from [these plays], and their effect would be disordered or destroyed equally by the ideas of righteous or of unrighteous omnipotence. Nor, in reading them, do we think of 'justice' or 'equity' in the sense of a strict requital or such an adjustment of merit and prosperity as our moral sense is said to demand; and there never was vainer labour than that of critics who try to make out that the persons in these dramas meet with 'justice' or their 'deserts'" (279).

53. Shell, *The End of Kinship,* 97—138.

54. Berger, *Making Trifles of Terrors,* 364.

55. Philip C. McGuire, in *Speechless Dialect: Shakespeare's Open Silences* (Berkeley: University of California Press, 1985), 63—96, describes with great tact and care the ways in which the networks of silence in the last scene are managed in five different modern productions of *Measure for Measure,* both British and American.

56. Coleridge writes in a note that "the pardon and marriage of Angelo not merely baffles the strong indignant claim of justice—(for cruelty, with lust and damnable baseness, cannot be forgiven because we cannot conceive them as being *morally* repented of), but it is likewise degrading to the character of woman" (Samuel Taylor Coleridge, *Coleridge's Shakespeare Criticism,* ed. Thomas Middleton Raysor, 2 vols. [Cambridge, Mass.: Harvard University Press, 1930], 1:113—14).

57. Shell, *The End of Kinship,* 140—45.

58. Cf. sonnet 124, where the poet surmises, "If my dear love were but the child of state, / It might for Fortune's bastard be unfather'd," calling policy "that heretic, / Which works on leases of short-numb'red hours, / But all alone stands hugely politic."

CHAPTER FOUR

1. *Desdemonum* is reprinted in *This Grotesque Essence: Plays from the American Minstrel Stage,* ed. Gary D. Engle (Baton Rouge: Lousiana State University Press, 1978), 62—67.

2.  Robert C. Toll, *Blacking Up: The Minstrel Show in Nineteenth-Century America* (New York: Oxford University Press, 1974), 43–44, points out that many early white minstrels in fact consciously studied the dances of southern blacks, like the famous "Jump Jim Crow" of Thomas D. Rice, and made this "authenticity" part of their claim on the audience's interest.

3.  See Marvin Rosenberg, *The Masks of Othello* (Berkeley: University of California Press, 1961), 55–60, on nineteenth-century bowdlerizings of *Othello,* and 61–119 more generally on period styles of performing the role of the moor.

4.  See *The Critical Works of Thomas Rymer,* ed. Curt A. Zimansky (New Haven: Yale University Press, 1956), 131–64. With decidedly less irony, Michael D. Bristol also excavates carnivalesque patterns of grotesquery and abjection at work in the play, in *Big-Time Shakespeare* (London: Routledge, 1996), 175–202. My sense of the power of minstrel show parodies to recuperate the ironic force of Shakespearean theater is indebted especially to Leslie Katz, "Independence Day in Blackface: *Julius the Snoozer,*" *Theatre History Studies* 13, no. 1 (1993): 17–32.

5.  Ralph Ellison's analysis of blackface in his essay, "Change the Joke and Slip the Yoke," in *Shadow and Act* (New York: Random House, 1964), is salient here: "This mask, this willful stylization and modification of the natural face and hands, was imperative for the evocation of that atmosphere in which the fascination of blackness could be enjoyed, the comic catharsis achieved. The racial identity of the performer was unimportant, the mask was the thing (the 'thing' in more ways than one) and its function was to veil the humanity of Negroes thus reduced to a sign, and to repress the white audience's awareness of its moral identification with its own acts and with the human ambiguities pushed behind the mask. . . . When the white man steps behind the mask of the trickster his freedom is circumscribed by the fear that he is not simply miming a personification of his disorder and chaos but that he will become in fact that which he only intends to symbolize; that he will be trapped somewhere in the mystery of hell (for there is a mystery in the whiteness of blackness, the innocence of evil and the evil of innocence, though, being initiates, Negroes express the joke of it in the blues) and thus lose that freedom which, in the fluid, 'traditionless,' 'classless' and rapidly changing society, he would recognize as the white man's alone" (49, 53).

6.  See Ellison, *Shadow and Act,* 48.

7.  Linda Woodbridge, *The Scythe of Saturn: Shakespeare and Magical Thinking* (Urbana and Chicago: University of Illinois Press, 1994), 234–36, reminds us that blackface (as well as the reddening and whitening of faces) was common in Renaissance mumming, morris dances, and May games. She associates such carnivalesque disguises with ancient fertility rituals, popular rites of death and rebirth, and shamanistic encounters with the spirit world. She also notes that folkloric magicians often have blackened faces, as do miners who delve in the earth. "Another ancient technology, writing, blackens adepts, and the Renaissance knew those black-faced technicians, printer's devils" (236). All of this leads her to wonder whether blackface itself may not be a badge of the work of human culture in general.

8. G. K. Hunter's 1968 essay "Othello and Colour Prejudice," reprinted in his collection *Dramatic Identities and Cultural Tradition: Studies in Shakespeare and His Contemporaries* (New York: Barnes and Noble, 1978), 31–59, still seems to me the most balanced account of the cultural associations of Othello's blackness with inhumanity, exoticism, monstrosity, demonic malice, and evil, but see also Michael Neill, "Unproper Beds: Race, Adultery, and the Hideous in *Othello*," *Shakespeare Quarterly* 40, no. 3 (1989): 383–412, especially on how, in *Othello*, ideas of human monstrosity are tied to more general ambivalences about things visible and invisible. Neill's account of the generic contaminations of melodrama are also important. Besides these essays, I have also benefited from Karen Newman, "'And Wash the Ethiop White': Femininity and the Monstrous in *Othello*," in *Fashioning Femininity and Renaissance Drama* (Chicago: University of Chicago Press, 1991), 71–94; Martin Orkin, "Othello and the 'Plain Face' of Racism," *Shakespeare Quarterly* 38, no. 2 (1987): 166–88; and Arthur L. Little, Jr., "'An Essence That's Not Seen': The Primal Scene of Racism in *Othello*," *Shakespeare Quarterly* 44, no. 3 (1993): 304–24.

9. Shakespeare's language calls attention to the almost inevitable smudging of the makeup worn by the actor playing Othello. There has been much debate among scholars about the peculiar shade of black or brown appropriate to Othello's makeup, but I would suspect that its relative fixity on the actor's face (and hands) has been an equally pressing concern of actors and directors. Something like the willful smearing of the moor's makeup onto other actors which I propose above seems to have been a part of a 1991 Austrian production of *Othello*, though working to more comic, even farcical ends than I have imagined it. See Marvin Carlson, "*Othello* in Vienna, 1991," *Shakespeare Quarterly* 44, no, 2 (1993): 228–30.

10. Wynkyn de Worde, *Pilgrimage* (London, 1531), 93.

11. Phillip Stubbes, *The Anatomie of Abuses* (London, 1583), sig. G1r.

12. See above, chap. 2, 53–54.

13. Francis Bacon, "Of Revenge," in *The Essayes or Counsels, Civill and Morall*, ed. Michael Kiernan (Oxford: Oxford University Press, 1985), 16.

14. Katherine Eisaman Maus, *Inwardness and Theater in the English Renaissance* (Chicago: University of Chicago Press, 1995), 104–27, argues that Othello's jealous conviction of Desdemona's imagined adultery is fed by increasingly tenuous forms of quasi-legal "proof." In the end, Maus argues, Othello collapses together suspicion, accusation, proof, judgment, and execution, as if each inevitably implied the others.

15. Patricia Parker, "*Othello* and *Hamlet*: Spying, Discovery, Secret Faults," in *Shakespeare from the Margins: Language, Culture, Context* (Chicago: University of Chicago Press, 1996), 229–52, describes the different early modern discourses of secrecy and proof that intersect in *Othello*. In particular, the play "trains the domestic *political* activity of the delator, privy informer, and accusor, on the domestic *private* sphere of a hidden chamber and female secret place, in ways that invoke not just the language of a crime or fault to be uncovered but a simultaneously prurient and deeply ambivalent fascination with the close or privy locus of female sexuality, opened, unfolded, brought forth to show" (245).

16. J. H. Baker, *An Introduction to English Legal History* (London: Butterworths, 1979), 371, comments that the English law of libel assumes that "a man could not lose credit as a result of words which reached no one's ears but his own." One of the paradoxes of *Othello* is that this is exactly what happens.

17. See S. F. C. Milsom, *Historical Foundations of the Common Law* (London: Butterworths, 1969), 339; and Ian Mclean, *Interpretation and Meaning in the Renaissance: The Case of Law* (Cambridge: Cambridge University Press, 1992), 195–202.

18. Curiously, Iago shows little interest in plotting against or controlling the words of his own wife, an oversight that betrays him in the end.

19. Samuel Taylor Coleridge, *Lectures 1808–1819: On Literature,* ed. R. A. Foakes, vol. 5, in 2 vols., of *The Collected Works* (Princeton: Princeton University Press, 1987–), 2:315.

20. A. C. Bradley, *Shakespearean Tragedy,* 2d ed. (London: Macmillan, 1905), 225. Bradley's account of Iago—stressing his shifting explanations of his own motives, and more generally his vanity, restlessness, contempt, self-delighting artistry, and imaginative narrowness—is still tremendously suggestive. Bradley is particularly useful insofar as he refuses any narrowly metaphysical or theatrical accounts of Iago's evil.

21. August Strindberg, *Open Letters to the Intimate Theater,* trans. Walter Johnson (Seattle: University of Washington Press, n.d.), 182.

22. Bradley, *Shakespearean Tragedy,* 212–13.

23. The self-betrayals of envy and the self-betrayals of jealousy are distinctly different, although it seems right to me to say that jealousy somehow props itself upon or grows out of envy. The most compelling psychoanalytic account of envy's place in the early formation of the psyche is that of Melanie Klein, for whom infantile and pre-Oedipal feelings of envy take the place of Freud's death instinct. See Klein, *Envy and Gratitude: A Study of Unconscious Sources* (London: Tavistock, 1957).

24. One might contrast A. D. Nuttall's suggestion in *A New Mimesis: Shakespeare and the Representation of Reality* (London: Methuen, 1983), 142, that the character of Iago anticipates a yet-to-be-born modern world of existentialist reasonings about the arbitrary grounds of human identity, even as Othello seems to inhabit the more archaic logic of a shame culture.

25. See William Empson, "Honest in *Othello,*" in *The Structure of Complex Words* (Ann Arbor: University of Michigan Press, 1967), 218–49.

26. William Hazlitt, *Characters of Shakespeare's Plays* (Oxford: Oxford University Press, 1916), 44.

27. See Joel Fineman, "The Sound of *O* in *Othello:* The Real of the Tragedy of Desire," in *The Subjectivity Effect in Western Literary Tradition: Essays toward the Release of Shakespeare's Will* (Cambridge, Mass.: MIT Press, 1991), 143–64.

28. John Hollander, *The Figure of Echo: A Mode of Allusion in Milton and After* (Berkeley: University of California Press, 1981), defines the "strict-form" of echo song as that in which "questions are asked of, or propositions addressed to, Echo, in successive lines of verse; either she completes the line by echoing the last syllable or

two, or her response makes up a separate short line. Whenever possible, her fragmentary response involves a pun or other alteration of sense" (26). Classical examples include poems by Callimachus and Bion. English Renaissance poets who tried
their hand at the form include Philip Sidney, Michael Drayton, and George Herbert. As Hollander suggests, such poems often lend a mocking, disenchanting, de-
mythologizing power to Echo's responses, though they also use repetition to
amplify, seduce, or haunt. Iago's echoes show touches of all of these qualities.

29. Ludwig Wittgenstein, *Philosophical Investigations,* trans. G. E. M. Anscombe
(New York: Macmillan, 1953), 214e.

30. *The Letters of John Keats, 1814–21,* ed. Hyder Edward Rollins, 2 vols. (Cambridge, Mass.: Harvard University Press, 1958), 1:193.

31. Othello's demand for "the ocular proof" looks to many critics like the token of a degraded empiricism or legalism; it suggests how, for this devoted husband, a will to moral and sexual capture can disguise itself as a desire for specious
certainties about a wife's sexual desire, a demand at once to objectify her body and
to probe secret or interior feminine spaces. (Cf. Maus, *Inwardness and Theater;*
Parker, "*Othello* and *Hamlet*"; and the comments of Kenneth Burke, quoted above,
p. 115.) The violence in the scene lies not just in Iago's tempting Othello with the
possession of what he can never and should never have. Rather, Iago's stories manage to infect something that Othello *already* has; they steal from him a possession or
gift that perhaps he was never aware of, putting in its place a gift that keeps open a
wound and a need. Again, Iago's suggestions do offer a kind of proof (though not ocular proof), that is, proof of Desdemona's "betrayal" of the moor's brittle assump-
tions about the nature of his relationship to her. Stanley Cavell's picture of the play
is crucial here. In pages that originally formed the conclusion to his early master-
work *The Claim of Reason: Wittgenstein, Skepticism, Morality, and Tragedy* (Oxford: Oxford University Press, 1979), 481–96, reprinted in *Disowning Knowledge in Six Plays
of Shakespeare* (Cambridge: Cambridge University Press, 1987), 125–42, Cavell
argues that Othello's jealousy is fed by the sudden horror at finding Desdemona's
body, mind, and history beyond his absolute knowledge or mastery, finding these
things more elusive, intractable, and yet also more vulnerable than he had needed
them to be. In Cavell's analysis—where the moor becomes not merely a jealous
husband but an emblem for the sovereign errors of philosophical skepticism—
Othello cannot help but read vulnerability as impurity. The brave moor has made
Desdemona into his world, the measure of his heroism, the place in which he lives
his life. Given his need for evidences of his own stainlessness, for absolutes of speech,
Othello feels himself wounded or stained by his own doubt, his own perceptions of
wounds, gaps, or fissures beyond his control—whether this comes from a fear that
sexual love with his wife must inevitably produce a scar or stain (Desdemona has a
body) or that an unbridgeable gap inhibits his perfect knowledge of his bride's desires and intentions (Desdemona has a body with a mind). Othello takes upon himself *as a stain* that shared humanity which should be the very ground of their
marriage. He is harrowed by the knowledge of that doubt, by the knowledge, as

Cavell argues, that Desdemona's love is given to him in spite of all that he discovers is uncertain—indeed, that it is an uncertainty or wildness in the idea of joining with Othello which provokes Desdemona's desire. I discuss Cavell's arguments in more detail in "Slander and Skepticism in *Othello,*" *ELH* 86 (1989): 819—52.

32. Cf. Cavell, *Claim of Reason,* 485—86.

33. Cassio's complaint about the dangers of drink applies almost as well to speech in this play: "O God, that men should put an enemy in their mouths, to steal away their brains!" (2.3.285—87).

34. See Giorgio Agamben, *Stanze: La parola e il fantasma nella cultura occidentale* (Turin: Einaudi, 1977), 5—23 and passim. On the connection of melancholia and slander, see also above, 39, 49.

35. Cf. Joel Fineman, *Shakespeare's Perjured Eye: The Invention of Poetic Subjectivity in the Sonnets* (Berkeley: University of California Press, 1986).

36. See, for example, Andrea Alciati, emblem LIX, "Impossible," in *Emblemata,* ed. Claude Mignault (Rome, 1621), 273.

37. Cf. Cavell, *Claim of Reason,* 487.

38. Harold C. Goddard, *The Meaning of Shakespeare* (Chicago: University of Chicago Press, 1951), 471—72, makes the crucial point that Othello himself causes the loss of the handkerchief, brushing it from him when Desdemona tries to wrap his forehead (so as to cure what she thinks is a headache but is in fact the pain of his imaginary horns). Desdemona's carelessness of the mere token should here be taken as a sign of her faith.

39. Kenneth Burke, "Othello: An Essay to Illustrate a Method," in *Perspectives by Incongruity,* ed. Stanley Edgar Hyman (Bloomington: Indiana University Press, 1964), 190.

40. Patricia Parker, "Shakespeare and Rhetoric: 'Dilation' and 'Delation' in *Othello,*" in *Shakespeare and the Question of Theory,* ed. Patricia Parker and Geoffrey Hartman (New York: Methuen, 1985), 54—74, examines the moor's expansive, recursive mode of storytelling and suggests that his dependence on such speech helps subject him to the more contagious fabling of Iago. James Calderwood, "Speech and Self in *Othello,*" *Shakespeare Quarterly* 38, no. 3 (1987): 293—303, also offers a useful account of how Othello creates himself through a form of narration whose solid, defensive structure and illusions of "fullness" at once lend him power and make him paradoxically vulnerable to Iago's corrosive, subtly meaningless play with language.

41. Othello's single speech combines within it the possibilities that Giuseppe Verdi distributed among three voices in a wonderful moment of ensemble singing in *Otello,* where Cassio describes the handkerchief as a "miracolo vago" (a beautiful or roving wonder), while Iago, speaking to himself, converts it into "una ragna" (spider's web), and Otello, hidden off to one side, sees it as a token of "tradimento" (treachery). See *Otello,* libretto by Arrigo Boito (New York: Riverrun Press, 1981), 62.

42. Othello, for example, will later mutter of Cassio, as he watches him from a place of concealment, "O, I see that nose of yours, but not that dog I shall throw it to" (4.1.141—42).

43. Cf. Cavell, *Claim of Reason,* 483, and passim. Stephen Greenblatt, *Renaissance Self-Fashioning* (Chicago: University of Chicago Press, 1980), 247–49, makes a similar argument, suggesting that Othello's language is influenced by orthodox Christian warnings on the dangers of excessive sexual desire in marriage. He quotes John Calvin to the effect that the "man who shows no modesty or comeliness in conjugal intercourse is committing adultery with his wife" (248), turning her, by implication, into a whore.

44. The phrase "slow unmoving finger" here is taken from the quarto text of 1622. E. A. J. Honigman, whose Arden edition I otherwise use in the chapter, cites it as a variant, but in his text prefers the wording in the First Folio (1623), which speaks of scorn's "slow and moving finger." While this wording sets up a more obvious contrast between scorn's moving finger and the *"fixed* figure" of the shamed Othello, the idea of two "unmoving" entities facing each other feels closer to the uncanny quality of Othello's fixations at this point.

45. Lisa Jardine, "'Why Should He Call Her Whore?': Defamation and Desdemona's Case," in *Reading Shakespeare Historically* (London: Routledge, 1996), 19–34, argues that in a culture where women's social reputation was so vulnerable a commodity, merely to raise suspicions about a woman's dishonor was enough to confirm that she was indeed dishonorable. For Jardine, the brothel scene suggests how quickly, in early modern societies, a private fantasy about women's infidelity can become a public truth (especially given Emilia's furious rage in spreading news of the slander itself, though only to her husband). The broader question which Jardine does not seek to answer—more psychological and ethical than ideological— involves why Othello himself takes that corrosive public lie within himself and feeds it with the nourishment of his own self-doubt.

46. On the commonness of "whore" as a term of abuse for women in Shakespeare's time (at least as represented in the records of slander trials), see J. A. Sharpe, *Defamation and Sexual Slander in Early Modern England: The Church Courts at York,* Borthwick Papers, No. 58, 1980, 9–11; and Martin Ingram, *Church Courts, Sex, and Marriage in England, 1570–1640* (Cambridge: Cambridge University Press, 1987), 292–319. William Kerrigan, *Hamlet's Perfection* (Baltimore: Johns Hopkins University Press, 1994), 83–84, comments on the deployment of "whore" as a more general term of abuse for the seductions of theater or religious superstition.

47. G. Wilson Knight, *The Wheel of Fire: Interpretations of Shakespearian Tragedy,* 4th ed., rev. (London: Methuen, 1949), 97–119.

48. Othello is "rude" of speech, insofar as he seems horrified by the sort of tricks and innuendos and double meanings that honest Iago can produce. Yet he is also capable of moments of immense and delicate poetry, even in moments of anger: "He that stirs next, to carve for his own rage, / Holds his soul light: he dies upon his motion" (2.3.169–70). The rudeness and eloquence marry, as it were, in many utterances that recall the overlearned, opaque, and pseudo-Latinate style of Elizabethan "fustian" (such as we also hear in the inkhorn courtliness of Osiric in *Hamlet*). This comes through when Othello speaks of "the young affects / In me de-

funct, and proper satisfaction" (1.3.264–65), or says that he will not let Cupid "seel with wanton dullness / My speculative and officed instrument, / That my disports corrupt and taint my business" (270–72), or refers to "exsufflicate and blown surmises" (3.3.185). Some editors may see such passages either as corruptions or as instances of archaism in need of glossing; to me they always seem at the edge of malapropism. Othello's attachment to the grandiose music of individual words, though appropriate to his self-regarding sense of his own heroism, is part of what betrays him to Iago's way of making words into disguised nonsense (as opposed to patent nonsense).

49. This scene suggests one answer to Wittgenstein's question, quoted above: "What would you be missing if . . . you did not feel that a word lost its meaning and became a mere sound if it was repeated ten times over?" You would be missing your sanity, and your humanity.

50. Nor does Desdemona avoid listening to Iago's bantering slanders of women. Indeed, she explicitly urges Iago to "assay" a praise of her, knowing quite well that he is "nothing if not critical" (2.1.119).

51. See Fineman, *The Subjectivity Effect,* 158. Fineman takes this argument a further step, by arguing that the willow song, which the audience would have recognized as an old ballad *not* by Shakespeare, also inscribes the author's own name, "Will," a name thus marked both by its desire and its otherness.

52. All quotations are from *Dar's de Money* (New York, 1879).

53. I am thinking here of T. S. Eliot's argument that Othello in his final speech in the play appears to be "cheering himself up," that he is "endeavouring to escape reality, he has ceased to think about Desdemona, and is thinking about himself" (*Selected Essays* [London: Faber and Faber, 1951], 130). In earlier scenes, as well, Othello also evokes what Eliot considered the self-dramatizing quality of the Senecan or Stoic hero; this does not necessarily entail a desire to escape from reality, however. As much as anything, it helps us understand Othello's way of negotiating his place in the world, and the ways that the world can keep a purchase on him. Othello in the bedchamber scene shows the chilling way in which the self-dramatizing moor has transformed himself under the influence of both Iago's slanders and his own fears. That scene also shows us, chillingly, how ready he is to inflict that changed reality upon the real and imaginary body of his wife.

54. Cavell, *Claim of Reason,* 482–83, suggests that the final scene claims our interest in part because it makes finally visible the scene of Othello's own wedding night, something that has been unseen from the very opening of the play—unseen both in its having been literally concealed from our sights and in its having been subjected to the shifting, distorting fantasies of other characters, as well as of Othello himself.

55. What Knight, *Wheel of Fire,* 98, describes as the "inward aloofness of image from image, word from word" in the play's language assumes its most concrete form here.

56. Bradley, *Shakespearean Tragedy,* 184.

CHAPTER FIVE

1. One of the sharpest reflections on this problem comes at the close of D. J. Gordon's essay "Name and Fame: Shakespeare's *Coriolanus,*" in *The Renaissance Imagination: Essays and Lectures by D. J. Gordon,* ed. Stephen Orgel (Berkeley: University of California Press, 1975), 218–19: "This great play, relentless, unremitting, misunderstood, offers us no easy comfort of confirmed anticipation or imagined identification. And not the liberating ritual comfort of tragedy. It is a show of the civil life. The city must stand and continue, for outside it there is the monstrous, or the nothing. But within the walls absolutes turn out to be instrumental; the words that identify and bind become words that debase and destroy: whoops, or hoots, curses, lies, flatteries, voices, stinking breath. Words are torn from what they signify. They pass into their antonyms. Deeds are not—deeds. Names are not—names. The absoluteness of the self, the I, cannot be maintained; but the necessary relationship of the I with name or fame destroys. In this city to speak is to be guilty."

2. On Coriolanus's iconic resemblance to Hercules and its implications, see Eugene Waith, *The Herculean Hero in Marlowe, Chapman, Shakespeare, and Dryden* (London: Chatto and Windus, 1962), 121–43.

3. The real strangeness of Coriolanus's words here was pointed out to me by Jill Kress.

4. See William Hazlitt, *Characters of Shakespeare's Plays* (Oxford: Oxford University Press, 1916), 53–57. Hazlitt associates Coriolanus's aristocratic violence with the work of the poetic imagination: "The principle of poetry is a very anti-levelling principle. It aims at effect, it exists by contrast. It admits of no medium. It is everything by excess. It rises above the ordinary standard of sufferings and crimes. It presents a dazzling appearance. It shows its head turretted, crowned, and crested. Its front is gilt and blood-stained. Before it 'it carries noise, and behind it tears'" (54).

5. Gordon, "Name and Fame," 207, notes that the use of "voice" in this context means "vote," and that the whole scene recalls the election of parliamentary representatives by such formalized public acclamations as Coriolanus must undergo. But Gordon knows that Coriolanus is not just angry about a rigged election. What Gordon hears is rather his ferocious resentment "at the power of what they say, of the uttering, and of his need of it, expressed in the ironical assumption that it is the uttering itself he is wooing and the people are their voices, their personified voice."

6. Jean-Louis Barrault, *Reflections on the Theatre,* trans. Barbara Wall (London: Rockliff Books, 1951), 117.

7. See above, n. 2.

8. Kenneth Burke, "*Coriolanus*—and the Delights of Faction," in *Language as Symbolic Action* (Berkeley: University of California Press, 1968), 93, describes invective of Coriolanus's sort as "a primary 'freedom of speech,' rooted extralinguistically in the helpless rage of an infant that states its attitude by utterances wholly unbridled. In this sense, no mode of expression could be more 'radical,' unless it be the closely allied motive of *lamentation,* undirected wailing . . . if rage is

the infantile prototype of invective, it is a kind of 'freedom' that must soon be subjected to control, once articulacy develops . . . invective most directly invites pugnacity, since it is itself a species of pugnacity." Burke compares Coriolanus to Lear,
whose "impotent senile maledictions . . . come quite close to the state of man's
equally powerless infantile beginnings."

   A. C. Bradley, in his lecture on *Coriolanus* in *Proceedings of the British Academy* 5
(1912): 465, noted long ago of Coriolanus, "Often he reminds us of a huge boy"—
in his sense of honor as well as his rage. Lawrence Danson, *Tragic Alphabet: Shakespeare's Drama of Language* (New Haven: Yale University Press, 1974), writes that "to
be a man, as Coriolanus understands it, is to be sufficient and whole in a way no man
in fact can be. But to be a 'boy' is eminently human: the boy's very incompleteness
implies the contingency of a human state. And in *Coriolanus* the boy is always present before us, contained in, or superimposed upon, the man he has become"
(153). Danson's account is especially useful insofar as it rescues the idea of a "boy"
from its more opprobrious uses in the play. It also makes a difference whether we
speak of Coriolanus as "boyish" in Danson's sense or "infantile" in Burke's or Adelman's.

   9. As Maurice Charney observes in *Shakespeare's Roman Plays: The Function of
Imagery in the Drama* (Cambridge, Mass.: Harvard University Press, 1961), 168,
Coriolanus later becomes the very butterfly his son pursues. His Volscian
soldiers, Cominius comments, "follow him / Against us brats, with no less
confidence / Than boys pursuing summer butterflies, / Or butchers killing flies"
(4.6.93–96). Charney is one of many critics who catalog the images of vengeful,
destructive, poisonous, and cannibalistic eating that fill this play, something that he
associates not only with Coriolanus's rage against the plebeians or Rome, but with
the destructive appetite of war in general (142–63).

   10. For Bradley, too, Coriolanus shows few signs of introspection or inward
conflict; his interiority, such as it is, is mute, entirely veiled from our apprehension.
Nor, he argues, are we made to feel the presence of some fatal, daemonic agency at
once larger than the hero and shaped by his own compulsions and projections—a
presence such as we find in *Hamlet, King Lear,* and *Macbeth.* It is this that limits, for
Bradley, the play's tragic effect, so that Coriolanus's death, the "instantaneous ces-
sation of enormous energy (which is like nothing else in Shakespeare) strikes us
with awe, but not with pity" (469).

   11. See Burke, "Delights of Faction," 92.

   12. Meredith Anne Skura, *Shakespeare the Actor and the Purposes of Playing*
(Chicago: University of Chicago Press, 1993), 191–95.

   13. Tracing a pattern of scriptural echoes in the play, Stanley Cavell argues that
Coriolanus might be seen as a shadowy or failed double of Christ, whose wounds
also become mouths and whose blood and words become food, sacrificial nourishment for a new and antithetical human community. Christ offers the model for a
kind of good cannibalism, where desire to eat is redemptive rather than violent or
vengeful. Cavell brings out the pathos of Coriolanus's dilemma: "The people's lack

of desert entails his lack of desert, entails that he cannot do the thing that acquires love; he is logically barred from reciprocating. . . . The logic of his situation, as well as the psychology, is that he cannot sacrifice himself" (*Disowning Knowledge in Six Plays of Shakespeare* [Cambridge: Cambridge University Press, 1987], 155, 161). The terrible secularism of *Coriolanus,* of course, allows no saving appeal to a self-sacrificing god outside the world Coriolanus inhabits. It would be useful here to set Cavell's speculation against that of Burke in "The Delights of Faction," where he argues that it is Coriolanus's fellow Romans who contrive to make him an object of a sacrifice, a pragmatic (if ultimately dangerous) means to cleanse the community of conflict. Burke's reading only deepens the irony Cavell points to.

14. We should remember that one of Plutarch's main interests in Coriolanus in his *Parallel Lives of the Greeks and Romans* is as a case study of political treachery, an instance of a civic hero turning against his own city. Hence, Plutarch pairs his account of Coriolanus with the life of the Greek soldier and traitor Alcibiades. One might argue, in fact, that Shakespeare found in the more boyish, raucous, and contemptuous manner of Plutarch's Alcibiades elements by which to leaven and transmute Plutarch's Coriolanus.

15. T. J. B. Spencer, *William Shakespeare: The Roman Plays* (London: Longmans, Green, 1963), suggests that Shakespeare's translation of this relatively obscure history is "one of the great feats of historical imagination in Renaissance Europe" (40). Shakespeare's way of transforming Plutarch's account of Coriolanus, and how the work of transformation itself becomes part of the drama, is well described by Reuben A. Brower, *Hero and Saint: Shakespeare and the Graeco-Roman Heroic Tradition* (New York: Oxford University Press, 1971), 375—81. On "dialectical imitation," see Thomas Greene, *The Light in Troy: Imitation and Discovery in Renaissance Poetry* (New Haven: Yale University Press, 1982), 45—47. Greene's general account of the self-reflexive aspect of Renaissance imitations of classical poetry finds many analogues in Shakespearean drama, though one rarely feels in the plays that sense of melancholy distance which, for Greene, characterizes attempts at recovery in the lyrics of Petrarch, DuBellay, or Wyatt. Shakespeare's way of subjecting his classical "exemplum" to dramatic analysis also has analogues with the risky, experimental interrogations of classical history that Nancy S. Struever sees as undertaken in Petrarch's *Familiari,* the treatises of Machiavelli, and the *Essays* of Montaigne. See Struever, *Theory as Practice: Ethical Inquiry in the Renaissance* (Chicago: University of Chicago Press, 1992).

I should add that Coriolanus's vexed relation to his own fame—both within the play and outside it—offers a striking example of what Linda Charnes calls "notorious identity." The phrase describes how, in plays such as *Antony and Cleopatra* or *Troilus and Cressida,* the very name and reputation of a character becomes itself an object of fascination, scandal, and desire, independent of its grounding in any historical truth. In such plays, the main characters emerge as entities belated, self-conscious, caught by the "sedimented traces" of their own intertextual linguistic history and cultural reputation; they are the diseased and symptomatic survivors of their own disseminated, reified fame, even as they continue to "express and enact a desire to be their own 'originals'" (Linda Charnes, *Notorious Identity: Materializing the Subject in Shakespeare* [Cambridge, Mass.: Harvard University Press, 1993], 9).

16. Whereas Plutarch takes Coriolanus primarily as an example of self-destructive pride leading to political treachery, Machiavelli in his *Discourses on Livy* (book 1, chap. 7) finds in Coriolanus a lesson about the strategic uses of false accusation (delation) in maintaining liberty in a republic, in particular by providing citizens with a safe outlet for their aggression. For more on this subject, see Anne Barton, "Livy, Machiavelli and Shakespeare's *Coriolanus*," in *Essays, Mainly Shakespearean* (Cambridge: Cambridge University Press, 1994), 136–60.

17. *Shakespeare's Plutarch,* ed. T. J. B. Spencer (Harmondsworth: Penguin, 1964), 359–60.

18. Ibid., 360.

19. One other supernatural story in Plutarch's life of Coriolanus that Shakespeare omits is a digression which tells how a noble citizen, during the uproar over Martius's consulship, dreamed that Jupiter commanded him to report to the Senate "that they had caused a very vile lewd dancer to go before the procession" (*Shakespeare's Plutarch,* 339). On investigating, the Senate found that another citizen had, against the law, caused a disobedient slave to be publicly whipped to death by his fellow slaves, with such violence that "he turned and writhed his body in strange and pitiful sort" (340), and furthermore that no senator had brought the master to justice. The image of that tormented slave might also find resonances in *Coriolanus*.

20. Philip Brockbank, introduction to his edition of *Coriolanus* (London: Methuen, 1976), 59.

21. Angus Fletcher, "Allegory and Compulsion: A Conceptual System for Specifying an Allegorical Dimension in Literature" (Ph.D. diss., Harvard University, 1958), 300. Fletcher sees in *Coriolanus* both an allegory of power and an account of the power of allegory. The allegorical quality of the hero comes through in his way of acting obsessively, enclosed within a fantasy, isolated in his meaning, imitating the forms of a god or daemon. For Fletcher, insofar as Coriolanus is an "unbelievable" hero, acting within an "unbelievable" play, he resembles more a romance character such as Leontes, who acts within worlds that seem no larger than the fantasies which enclose him. Yet Fletcher also acknowledges that within the play, Coriolanus is "surrounded and influenced by too many contrary demonic powers for him to have his own way" (304).

Aufidius's resonant words about the corrosive power of fame seem relevant here. Weighing the mixture of pride, austerity, and rashness that led to Coriolanus's being both feared and banished, Aufidius sees a kind of self-destructiveness built into the very machinery of commendation itself:

> He has a merit
> To choke it in the utt'rance. So our virtues

> Lie in th'interpretation of the time,
> And power, unto itself most commendable,
> Hath not a tomb so evident as a chair
> T'extol what it hath done.
> (4.7.48–53)

Here the same forces which elevate Coriolanus to the status of a demigod also destroy him, giving his virtues an inhuman fixity, even as they are exposed to the whims of time.

22. On Coriolanus as an "unsuccessful god," see Fletcher, "Allegory and Compulsion," 304.

23. See above, n. 1.

24. From *Bell's Shakespeare* (1773), 2:62. Cited by Fletcher, "Allegory and Compulsion," 377 n. 16. I should say that, in these lines, the commons are actually condemning the tribunes, rather than Coriolanus, demanding that they be thrown, as traitors, from the Tarpeian rock.

25. One might also compare with this passage the image of Queen Elizabeth I in what is called the Rainbow Portrait, where her gown has embroidered on its surface an Argus-like scattering of emblematic eyes, ears, and mouths, as if the queen were herself a less monstrous avatar of *fama,* at once its object, source, and master. The painting is reproduced in Roy Strong, *Portraits of Elizabeth I* (Oxford: Oxford University Press, 1963), pl. 100.

26. Janet Adelman, *Suffocating Mothers: Fantasies of Maternal Origin in Shakespeare's Plays, "Hamlet" to "The Tempest"* (New York: Routledge, 1992), 146–64. Adelman's haunting, though for me too narrowly drawn, account of Coriolanus's infantile, cannibalistic appetite is directly answered by Cavell's evocation of a "good" cannibalism in Coriolanus. See n. 13 above.

27. I might recall here Harold C. Goddard's unsettling idea in *The Meaning of Shakespeare* (Chicago: University of Chicago Press, 1951), 595–627, that Coriolanus is a creature whose soul was to start as noble and delicate as that of Hamlet, but who has been turned into a bloodthirsty automaton by the dangerous ministrations of his mother and the heroic culture she embodies.

28. What Coriolanus sees as the plebeian's degraded hunger for the word may be a mirror of his own hunger.

29. Cavell, *Disowning Knowledge,* 166, 159. Montaigne's cannibal taunts his captors by inviting them to eat him, saying that they will thus be eating the flesh of their own grandfathers, fathers, wives, and children, which had earlier nourished him. See Michel de Montaigne, "Of the Cannibals," in *Essays,* trans. John Florio, 3 vols. (London: Dent, 1910), 1:227.

30. Burke, "Delights of Faction," 88, notes well that "War itself, elsewhere in the play, is called 'sprightly, waking, audible, and full of vent,' an expression that could also serve to describe Coriolanus' invective."

31. Madeleine Doran, *Shakespeare's Dramatic Language* (Madison: University of Wisconsin Press, 1976), 186–87 and 217, also brings out the structural use of noise in the play, as part of a larger account of the play's consistent, if often strained and suspect, use of tropes of contrariety or contradiction, especially "antithesis, synoeciosis [a species of oxymoron], paradox, and dialysis (the figure for a dilemma)" (188). For Doran, Coriolanus doesn't just use but is himself caught within such a language of contention, torn by unstable oppositions between war and peace, honor and dishonor, pride and humility, satisfaction and hunger, the human and the inhuman.

32. Paul A. Jorgensen, *Shakespeare's Military World* (Berkeley: University of California Press, 1956), 1–34.

33. Giacomo Porcia, *The Preceptes of Warre,* trans. Peter Betham (1544), quoted in Jorgensen, *Shakespeare's Military World,* 19.

34. G. Wilson Knight, in *The Imperial Theme: Further Interpretations of Shakespeare's Tragedies, Including the Roman Plays* (London: Oxford University Press, 1931), argues that the poison of Coriolanus's violent military honor comes from its being isolated from any private or public love, or care. War for Coriolanus becomes an end in itself; he becomes a man of death, and his "virtue" turns into a virtue of destruction, "a death-phantom masquerading as life" (181). Coriolanus's pride is, for Knight, the exact projection of Volumnia's own limited, objectifying love of glory. "She has made him what he is. But she now finds she has created something beyond her control" (181). "She finds she has created a thing apparently loveless, an idiot robot, a creaking clockwork giant, a stone Colossus" (190).

35. See Georges Dumézil, *Horace et les cuiraces* (Paris: Gallimard, 1942), 11–33.

36. See "A Treatie of Warres" in *Poems and Dramas of Fulke Greville,* ed. Geoffrey Bullough, 2 vols. (Edinburgh: Oliver and Boyd, n.d.), 1:214–29.

37. Shakespeare's soldier is, in a sense, the archaic Turnus reborn within an evolved Roman state, although Coriolanus possesses a critical intelligence and an emotional complexity that one does not see in Virgil's superseded, Achillean hero. The account of Turnus shutting himself up alone within the gates of the Roman camp, slaying hordes of his enemies, for instance (*Aeneid,* Book 9), shows strong parallels to the scene of Martius at Corioles. Many other moments in the epic evoke the likeness as well. Aeneas himself, of course, is never simply "pious." He can at moments assume an aspect of daemonic violence, general savagery, and taunting rage that anticipates Coriolanus. One great difference between the epic and the play is that war in *Coriolanus* is neither animated by divine malice nor overshadowed by supernatural fatality, save in the form that human beings create for themselves in history. Shakespeare's Volumnia, however frightening in her advocacy of martial heroism, is at best a diminished shadow of Virgil's ferocious, war-maddened Juno.

38. In a fascinating essay, "On the Significant Acoustics of Ariosto's Noisy Poem," *Modern Language Notes* 103 (1988): 87–112, James V. Mirollo suggests a related mythologizing of war noise, and noise in general, in *Orlando Furioso.* "Armor

and weapons, legitimate and illegitimate, magical and legendary as well as recently manufactured, are the primary noisemakers among the movable implements that figure so prominently in the plot of the *Furioso*" (96). Particularly interesting is Mirollo's account of the shattering, disenchanting sound of Astolfo's horn, which becomes for Ariosto the chief emblem of the power, menace, suffering, and *furor* of human war—its cries of aggression and pain—even as it points to the vexed powers of human language in general. At once preternatural and wholly worldly, this horn noise represents an energy that cuts through any simple moralizations about the use of war or words in history. Something similar can be said of the war noise of Coriolanus.

39. See T. S. Eliot, *The Complete Poems and Plays, 1909–1950* (New York: Harcourt, Brace, and World, 1952), 85–87. Eliot's account of the bitter lament of a warrior to his mother in part 2 of *Coriolan,* "The Difficulties of a Statesman" (87–89), has deeper resonances with the situation of Shakespeare's hero.

40. Iago, of course, has his own reasons for making the noble moor into a comic braggart. In truth, Othello's soldierly oratory carries a stranger power, a more equivocal seductiveness, than Iago can himself bear to admit.

41. Jorgensen, *Shakespeare's Military World,* 292–314, argues that while Coriolanus shows himself a fierce and determined soldier, his dangerous individualism and incivility makes him a poor leader on the battlefield. He has the plainspoken roughness and bravado which had become a clichéd attribute of soldiers in Elizabethan writing and which characterized even aristocratic figures like Essex, a hardy fighter but no general. Not only is Coriolanus ill adapted to peace, but he has little use for the "subtil pollicie and martial discipline" which characterized the new continental forms of war recommended by Machiavelli and which can be glimpsed in both Aufidius and Volumnia. "Although to use fraud in any action is detestable, yet in the conduct of a war it is praiseworthy and glorious" (Machiavelli, *The Discourses,* trans. Bernard Crick [Harmondsworth: Penguin, 1983], 513). At another level, however, Coriolanus could be seen as thoroughly "modern," since he sums up in his single person an image of war such as Michael Murrin sees looming up in later Renaissance epic. After the invention of gunpowder, and after the experience of the wars of religion and colonialist expansion, we start to see images of a war that is faceless, total, automatic, bent on extermination and terrorism. Such war is less and less available to the idealizations of a chivalric epic such as Ariosto's, even to such tragic patterning of violence as Tasso derived from allusive parallels to Virgil. See Michael Murrin, *History and Warfare in Renaissance Epic* (Chicago: University of Chicago Press, 1994), 199–228 and passim.

42. Aristotle, *Politics,* 1253a, bk. 1, chap. 2, in *The Basic Works of Aristotle,* ed. Richard McKeon (New York: Random House, 1941), 1130.

43. R. P. Blackmur, *Language as Gesture: Essays in Poetry* (New York: Harcourt Brace Jovanovich, 1952), 419 (my emphasis).

44. See Antonin Artaud, *Selected Writings,* ed. Susan Sontag, trans. Helen Weaver (New York: Farrar, Straus, and Giroux, 1976), 256: "With that mania for

depreciating everything that we all have today, as soon as I uttered the word 'cruelty' everyone immediately took it to mean 'blood.' But *'theater of cruelty'* means a theater that is difficult and cruel first of all for myself" (256)—a theater of gestures and sounds which break through conventional words and motions, in which literal "violence and bloodshed [are] placed at the service of the violence of thought" (258–59).

45. Fletcher, "Allegory and Compulsion," 318.

46. Percy Bysshe Shelley, *Shelley's Poetry and Prose,* ed. Donald H. Reiman and Sharon B. Powers (New York: Norton, 1977), 103. Fletcher notes the echo in "Allegory and Compulsion," 318.

47. Burke makes this point in "Delights of Faction," 91.

48. As a way of remaking the world on his own terms, Coriolanus's idea of becoming his own author has less playful bravado than his earlier fantasy about Aufidius: "Were half to half the world by th'ears, and he / Upon my party, I'd revolt to make / Only my wars with him" (1.1.232–34). It is also less outrageous and less explicitly ironic a gesture than his parting taunt, "I banish you." But the fantasy of self-authoring does in this context show antithetical clarity. Measure it, say, against the Macbeth's wish to become a marble statue, so as to banish all fears about the consequences of his murders, so as not to *know* them (*Macbeth,* 3.4.20–24), and one may feel how much knowledge of the real is still included in Coriolanus's wish.

49. Edmund Spenser, *The Faerie Queene,* ed. J. C. Smith, 2 vols. (Oxford: Oxford University Press, 1909), 7.7.59.

50. Cavell, *Disowning Knowledge,* 161, suggests that by "most mortal" Coriolanus cannot be expressing any ordinary fear of physical death, which he has more often than not invited. Rather, he "must mean somehow that [Volumnia] has brought it about that he will have the wrong death, the wrong mortality, a fruitless death."

51. The First Folio's *"Flatter'd* your Volscians" suggests a more immediate and contemptuous irony in Coriolanus's speech, but most modern editors prefer the stranger evocation of *"Flutter'd* your Volscians," from the Third Folio.

52. *Samson Agonistes,* in John Milton, *Complete Shorter Poems,* ed. John Carey (London: Longman, 1971), 398, lines 1692–96. Milton's phrase "evening dragon" also echoes Coriolanus's farewell to his mother: "though I go alone, / Like to a lonely dragon that his fen / Makes fear'd and talk'd of more than seen" (4.1.29–31).

53. James Thomson, *Coriolanus, or, The Roman Matron, A Tragedy* (London, 1755), 75.

CHAPTER SIX

1. Grigori Kozintsev, *King Lear: The Space of Tragedy, The Diary of a Film Director,* trans. Mary Mackintosh (Berkeley: University of California Press, 1977), 225.

2. "They would launch curses on the world, and since man alone can utter curses (it is his privilege and the thing that chiefly distinguishes him from the other animals), perhaps through cursing alone he would attain his end, to convince himself that he was a man and not a piano-key!" (Fyodor Dostoevsky, *"Notes from the Underground" and "The Double,"* trans. Jessie Coulson [Harmondsworth: Penguin Books, 1972], 38).

3. Maynard Mack, *"King Lear" in Our Time* (Berkeley: University of California Press, 1965), 43–80, offers a pointed account of the play's way of combining an ironic realism with elements of morality play, biblical homily, and dream vision, its jointure of "epic disengagement and psychic intimacy" (78). Mack's sense of the play's balancing act leads him to see both redemptive and nihilistic readings of *Lear* as equally sentimental.

4. See in particular the great and sorrowful exchange of curses between Margaret and her lover Suffolk, *2 Henry VI,* 3.2.300–366.

5. Richard Bevington, "'Why Should Calamity be Full of Words?': The Efficacy of Cursing in *Richard III,*" *Iowa State Journal of Research* 56, no. 1 (1981): 9–21, explores well the ironic effectiveness of Margaret's curses in the play, though I do not share Bevington's secure sense of how this confirms a providential order in the play.

6. *King Lear* represents a return to this more archaic stratum in Shakespeare's work; it does this as part of a return to a native history and a native soil. The tragedies of slander and rumor mostly take place abroad, say, in Italy or Denmark; the tragedies of curse take place in Britain.

7. See *OED,* s.v. "cursitor." The *OED* also notes that Old English *curs,* the root of "curse," is of unknown origin, no similar form and sense being known in Teutonic, Romanic, or Celtic languages.

8. Thomas Harman, *A Caveat or Warening for Commen Cursetors* (London, 1566), reprinted in *The Elizabethan Underworld,* ed. A. V. Judges (London: Routledge, 1930), 63. The fact that Harman's title uses an uncommon spelling of the word— "cursetors"—may itself evoke an echo of "curse," as does the fact that, on the title page, the word runs across two lines, isolating "Curse-" at the end of a line. See *Elizabethan Underworld,* pl. 5.

9. We see the heterogeneity of this jargon even in the names by which, according to Harman, the various sorts of cursitor (both men and women) are known: Ruffler, Hooker, Rogue, Palliard, Frater, Crank, Whipjack, Clapperdudgeon, Dummerer, Swadder, Autem-Mort, Walking Mort, Doxy.

10. Harman's analysis of the cursitor's performance of victimhood has obvious connections with Samuel Harsnett's *Declaration of Egregious Popish Impostures* (London, 1603), one of Shakespeare's main sources for the demon talk of Mad Tom, which exposes the staged exorcism of counterfeit demoniacs by Catholic priests.

11. Martin Buber, *On the Bible: Eighteen Studies,* ed. Nahum N. Glatzer (New York: Schocken, 1982), 189, suggests that Job's sense of loss echoes Israel's collective experience of exile.

12. It is a central question, of course, whether Job's protests and complaints about God's justice constitute an actual curse against the deity, or a blasphemy. That

they might appear so to a Renaissance reader is implied by John Calvin's comment that "he who grudgeth against God as though he were cruel and unkynd curseth God" (*Sermons on Job,* trans. Arthur Golding [London, 1574], 32). That Job himself is worried about unspoken cursing is suggested in his habit of offering daily sacrifices for his sons, who may have "cursed God in their hearts" (1.5).

I should note that the word "curse" in the Geneva and King James texts of the Book of Job translates the Hebrew verb for "bless." Marvin Pope, in his Anchor Bible edition of Job (Garden City: Doubleday, 1965), calls this "a standard scribal euphemism" (8), suggesting that the rabbinic editors thought it dangerous even to refer to the act of cursing God.

13. Percy Bysshe Shelley, *Prometheus Unbound,* act 1, lines 380–88, in *Shelley's Poetry and Prose,* ed. Donald H. Reiman and Sharon Powers (New York: Norton, 1977), 147. How much Shakespeare's Lear shares with the ancient Greek Prometheus—creator, rebel, divine victim, and prophet—is a question I will not try to answer here.

14. Hence, when Shelley's Prometheus must call up a spirit from a secondary world to repeat the forgotten words of his curse, he asks that this be done not by his own double, but by the phantasm of his enemy, Jupiter (act 1, lines 262–301). Shelley thus shows us the tyrant-god pronouncing a curse upon himself, yet implies that even a Prometheus becomes a Jupiter through uttering such a vengeful curse.

15. Shelley, *Prometheus Unbound,* act 1, lines 603–4, in *Shelley's Poetry,* 154.

16. Shelley's play *The Cenci*—written immediately after he completed the first three acts of *Prometheus Unbound* in 1819—is also obsessed with curse, and in fact uses the story of Beatrice Cenci's murder of her father to construct a kind of nightmarish, compacted rereading of *King Lear* as a whole. Count Cenci's great parting curse against his daughter (act 4, scene 1, lines 114–36), for example—a text which directly echoes Lear's curses against both Cordelia and Goneril—reinforces the spiritual violence of his hidden, incestuous rape of Beatrice. That curse carries, indeed, a frightening certainty about his words' ability to destroy his daughter's psyche, to kill any blessings she might lend to the world, even as it translates the count's unspoken fear of being infected by her powerful will. Beatrice, in her turn, becomes at once the wronged Cordelia and the parricidal Goneril and Regan.

17. Here as elsewhere in this chapter I quote from R. A. Foakes's 1997 Arden edition of *King Lear.* This has for me the advantage of being what Foakes calls a "reader's text," one that includes within its text the principle variants between the First Quarto (1608) and First Folio (1623) versions of the play, identifying them carefully, without trying to approximate by collation some putative, lost original. Given recent controversies over the text of *King Lear,* it is worth making clear certain points of difference that are relevant to my argument in this chapter. The folio text, for example, does not contain the mock trial in act 3, scene 6, a scene which helps extend, and make more grotesque, the demented legalism implicit in Lear's curses, as well as deepening one's sense of Lear's attachment to Mad Tom. The quarto, on the other hand, does not include the fool's prophecy at the end of act 3, scene 2, a passage which more coldly ironizes the mad king's metaphysical pre-

sumptions, both indulging and mocking the desire for prophetic truth. This prophecy also suggests the paradox whereby a future of apparent civic order—"when every case in law is right . . . when slanders do not live in tongues," and so on—is taken as the forerunner of a period of curse: "Then shall the realm of Albion / Come to great confusion" (85–92). Interesting and even mysterious as these variants are, the difference remains one of local emphasis. The central paradoxes in the drama of curse hold in both texts. For myself, I cannot account for these differences by saying that the folio text represents Shakespeare's own revision of an earlier version (which may or may not be represented by the quarto), an argument pursued variously in Steven Urkowitz, *Shakespeare's Revision of "King Lear"* (Princeton: Princeton University Press, 1980); Grace Iappolo, *Revising Shakespeare* (Cambridge, Mass.: Harvard University Press, 1991), 161–88; and most of the contributors to *The Division of the Kingdoms: Shakespeare's Two Versions of "King Lear,"* ed. Gary Taylor and Michael Warren (Oxford: Oxford University Press, 1983). Many of the variants which are puzzled over in these volumes are remarkable, even harrowing, and the local differences in effect often striking. But the patterns of difference do not seem to me to have enough scope or coherence to produce, in the folio *King Lear,* a truly different or (as is often said) more economical play. See also the pointed questioning of the revision debate in Stephen Booth, *"King Lear," "Macbeth," Indefinition, and Tragedy* (New Haven: Yale University Press, 1983), 159–60.

18. Stanley Cavell, "Ending the Waiting Game: A Reading of Beckett's *Endgame,"* in *Must We Mean What We Say?* (Cambridge: Cambridge University Press, 1976), 115–62, suggests a similar end at work in Beckett's play, itself a powerful reimagining of *King Lear.*

19. From Lindsay Watson, *Arae: The Curse Poetry of Antiquity,* Arca Classical and Medieval Texts, Monograph no. 26 (Sydney: Francis Cairns, 1991), 31.

20. John Kerrigan, *Revenge Tragedy: From Aeschylus to Armageddon* (New York: Oxford University Press, 1996), 128.

21. Watson, *Arae,* 38, 30, speaks of curses as the Furies personified. Clytemnestra, in *Agamemnon,* thus explains herself to the chorus: "You say I killed him / And I was his wife. / You saw better / When you saw / The curse, the hideous / Heritage / Of the house of Atreus / Standing here / In my shape" (Aeschylus, *The Oresteia,* trans. Ted Hughes [London: Faber and Faber, 1999], 75). *The Oresteia* as a whole, of course, gains much of its dramatic power from its way of dramatizing and transforming the ancient curse on the house of Atreus—which began with Thyestes' banquet—not only following its revenges from generation to generation, but questioning its scope and surprising us with its metamorphoses, allowing characters themselves to interpret the curse in often strange and opportunistic ways. For example, not only does Clytemnestra identify herself with the curse Fury of the house of Atreus, she also sees the curse as objectified in the terrible red carpet she lays out for her husband on his arrival, foreshadowing his bloody murder. The highly gestural, rhetorical, even self-deluded way in which

characters can possess the curse in this play offers some remarkable anticipations of the use of curse in *King Lear.*

22. On the afterlife of the blinded Polyphemus's curse in later classical and Renaissance epic, especially in its way of framing the pathos and politics of epic questing, see David Quint, *Epic and Empire: Politics and Generic Form from Virgil to Milton* (Princeton: Princeton University Press, 1993), 99—130.

23. "Among the Greeks *ara* [in the sense of legal curse or execration, an act which makes criminals "consecrated" or "devoted" to the Furies] remained in the senses of harmful body, vow, and fury, and among the Latins it meant both altar and victim" (Giambattista Vico, *The New Science,* trans. Thomas Goddard Bergin and Max Harold Fisch [Ithaca: Cornell University Press, 1968], paragraph 957). Cf. Plutarch's account of an episode during the wars between Caesar, Pompey, and Crassus, when the tribune Ateius set up a burning brazier at the city gate to prevent Crassus's entering. "And when Crassus came up, Ateius cast incense and libations upon it, and invoked curses which were dreadful and terrifying in themselves, and were reinforced by sundry strange and dreadful gods whom he summoned and called by name. The Romans say that these mysterious and ancient curses have such power that no one involved in them ever escapes, and misfortune falls also upon the one who utters them, wherefore they are not employed at random nor by many" (*Plutarch's Lives,* trans. Bernadette Perrin, 10 vols. [London: Heinemann, 1916], 3: 363—65).

24. For the proverb and its many variants, see *Dictionary of European Proverbs,* ed. Emanuel Strauss, 3 vols. (London: Routledge, 1994), 2:651—53.

25. See Richmond Lattimore, *Themes in Greek and Latin Epitaphs,* Studies in Language and Literature 28, nos. 1—2 (Urbana: University of Illinois Press, 1942), 108—25.

26. Hundreds of such tablets have been found at ancient Greek grave sites, dated from the early classical through the Hellenistic periods. For more see Ashley Montagu, *The Anatomy of Swearing* (New York: Macmillan, 1967), 39—40, 47—48; and E. R. Dodds, *The Greeks and the Irrational* (Berkeley: University of California Press, 1951), 194—95.

27. Shelley, *Prometheus Unbound,* act 1, lines 150—52, in *Shelly's Poetry,* 140.

28. See *Egyptian Religious Poetry,* ed. Margaret Murray (London: John Murray, 1949), 64—65, quoted in Angus Fletcher, *Allegory: The Theory of a Symbolic Mode* (Ithaca: Cornell University Press, 1965), 205—6.

29. See Jan Assmann, "Inscriptional Violence and the Art of Cursing," *Stanford Literary Review* 9, no. 1 (1992): 59.

30. See S. Gevirtz, "Curse," in *The Interpreter's Dictionary of the Bible,* 4 vols. (Louisville: Abingdon Press, 1962), 1:750. Sheldon H. Blank, "The Curse, Blasphemy, the Spell, and the Oath," *Hebrew Union College Annual* 23, no. 1 (1950/51): 73—95, notes that curses in the Hebrew Bible—whether formal or informal, whether uttered in anger or as part of a ritual oath—tend to suppress any direct mention of divine agency. He takes this as evidence of Hebraic belief that the

power of the curse came from the effective and enduring force of the words alone. This means, for one thing, that "the difference between the human and the divine curse is not a clear-cut distinction" (79).

31. The juridical oath often implies a provisional curse, even in the eviscerated modern formula "I swear to tell the truth, the whole truth, and nothing but the truth, so help me God." See Marvin Pope's article "Oaths," in *The Interpreter's Dictionary of the Bible,* 2:575–77; and Jane Harrison, *Prolegomena to the Study of Greek Religion,* 3d ed. (New York: Meridian Books, 1957), 138, 142. See also Moshe Weinfeld, *Deuteronomy and the Deuteronomic School* (Oxford: Oxford University Press, 1972), 116–29. Assmann, "Inscriptional Violence and the Art of Cursing," studies ancient Near Eastern and biblical curses against those who damage monuments on which treaties, laws, or oaths are inscribed, suggesting that such curses implicitly acknowledge the terrible fragility of written law, and of writing in general. Consider the following curse cited in Robert C. Elliott, *The Power of Satire: Magic, Ritual, Art* (Princeton: Princeton University Press, 1960), 285, taken from two fifth-century-B.C. pillars on the island of Teos. A series of juridical curses against poisoners, swindlers, and thieves concludes as follows: "Whosoever of them that hold office doth not make this cursing . . . let him be bound by an over curse . . . and whoever either breaks the stelae on which the cursing is written, or cuts out the letters or makes them illegible: 'May he perish, both he and his offspring.'" Here the inscribed curse must, as it were, protect itself.

32. See Jean-Pierre Vernant, "Death in the Eyes: Gorgo, Figure of the *Other,*" in *Mortals and Immortals: Collected Essays,* ed. Froma I. Zeitlin (Princeton: Princeton University Press, 1991), 111–38. Vernant's essay might also be called "Death in the Ears," citing numerous Greek myths, poems, and historical texts in which the power of the Gorgons' eyes is reinforced by their horrible voices—voices that are said variously to echo the cries of madmen and maenads, the derisive laughter of mimes and clowns in satirical theater, the barking of dogs, and the terrifying noises of warriors on a battlefield. All these noises, Vernant suggests, carry the echo of sounds from the underworld.

33. T. S. Eliot, *The Family Reunion* (London: Faber and Faber, 1939), 135. And earlier: "A curse comes into being / As a child is formed. / In both, the incredible / Becomes the actual / Without our intention / Knowing what is intended" (110).

34. Blank, "Curse, Blasphemy, Spell, and Oath," 92, suggests that Job's oath in chapter 31 shows an "audacious breach of the word-taboo" since he so relentlessly catalogs the curse punishments that are ordinarily concealed or evaded in the typical oath formula. Marvin Pope comments that in this passage "we see the oath in all its force as a kind of ideal and spiritual combat" ("Oaths," 577).

35. Calvin, *Sermons on Job,* 80.

36. To quote more at length: "When the despisers of God seeme to bee as Kings and Princes, so as they take theyr pleasure and glorie in their estate: yet they ceasse not to bee cursed. True it is that this cursednesse appeereth not at the first day, for it is secrete: But it must have leysure too shewe itselfe. And on the other side, we

must beholde the thing though it cannot be seene with eie: yea we must beholde it by fayth: and bicause God hath spoken it alreadie with his owne mouth, we must sticke untoo that which hee sayth. . . . Wee must curse them: that is to say, we must bee fully resolved with our selves that all this is nothing. and why so? For God hath tolde us it is so. . . . And as concerning thys worde *Curse,* let us marke that it giveth not us scope too wishe the mischiefe and confusion of the partie, (I meane through desire of vengeance, as oftentymes we bee so caryed away by our passions, as there raigneth nothing in us but hartburning and bitternesse, or at leastwise a foolishe and undiscreete zeale:) . . . A man must not presume so farre: but it belongeth to God only to curse or to blesse" (Calvin, *Sermons on Job,* 80).

37. In this sermon, Donne is commenting particularly on Psalm 6:8–10. See *The Sermons of John Donne,* ed. Evelyn M. Simpson and George R. Potter, 10 vols. (Berkeley: University of California Press, 1953–62), 6:54–55. Lester K. Little, *Benedictine Maledictions: Liturgical Cursing in Romanesque France* (Ithaca: Cornell University Press, 1993), 95–113, sets out the patristic backgrounds for such readings of biblical curses as "prophecy in the guise of imprecation." In Jerome, Augustine, Chrysostom, and Gregory, for example, sustained attacks on the blasphemous use of curses by pagans or Christians went along with a guarded justification of curses when spoken by men of peculiar sanctity or authority within the church community.

38. See "An Acte to Restraine Abuses of Players," May 1606 (3 *Jac. I,* c.21), reprinted in E. K. Chambers, *The Elizabethan Stage,* 4 vols. (Oxford: Oxford University Press, 1923), 4:338–39.

39. John Donne, *The Complete English Poems,* ed. A. J. Smith (Harmondsworth: Penguin, 1971), 50–51. Donne's lyric is a condensed but studied imitation of Ovid's curse-poem, *Ibis,* a 650-line diatribe in which the poet demands that his eponymous enemy inherit the various fates of a vast catalog of mythic victims (Hippolytus, Hercules, Cacus, Priam, Oedipus, Ixion, and a hundred more). In *Ibis* curse becomes, like metamorphosis, a category by which to arrange an anarchic mythic encyclopedia, a poetic key to all mythologies. See Ovid, *The Art of Love and Other Poems,* trans. J. H. Mozley, 2d ed. (Cambridge, Mass.: Harvard University Press, 1979), 235–92.

40. Harry Berger, Jr., *Making Trifles of Terrors: Redistributing Complicities in Shakespeare* (Stanford: Stanford University Press, 1997), 25–47, beautifully explores the intricate patterns of evasion in Lear's speeches.

41. William Empson, *Seven Types of Ambiguity,* 3d ed. (London: Chatto and Windus, 1953), 89. Empson continues: "The curse, indeed might be uttered *against* the father by the child, and certainly the king would have meant this if he had thought of it. All the meanings arrived at by permuting these versions make up one single-minded *curse;* any pains Lear has felt or is still to feel, any pains Cordelia has felt or is still to feel, as an effect or cause whether of this *curse* on Goneril or of his previous *curse* on Cordelia, or of Goneril's implied *curses* on him, all these give him good rea-

son for *cursing* Goneril with the same pains in return; and if any pains in Goneril are to be cause or effect of any of these *cursings,* so much the better, let them *pierce* her. These pains are already all that he can foresee from the *cursing of fathers;* they, therefore, mean also, 'all the curses that a father *can* impose on his child.'"

42. Kerrigan, *Revenge Tragedy,* 117–21, points out that in Renaissance plays the Senecan understanding of curse as an expression of irrational human rage can mingle, often uneasily, with a Christian idea of curse as an expression of a divine will to justice and vengeance. Hence, in taking up the posture of curse, a tragic speaker may seem ambiguously both righteous and mad.

43. On the "unnaming" aspect of the hero's dramatic rhetoric in *Tamburlaine,* see Kimberley Benston, "Beauty's Just Applause: Dramatic Form and the Tamburlainean Sublime," in *Christopher Marlowe: Modern Critical Views,* ed. Harold Bloom (New York: Chelsea House, 1985), 207–9.

44. These lines are found in the First Quarto text of Kent's speech, but not the folio. Foakes cites them only in a textual note.

45. I am recalling here the Gnostic idea of the cosmos as beginning from a disruption or crisis within the divine world itself, an event that leads to the falling away of pieces of that world into an alienated, corporeal state. This alienation of primal being is abetted, in many versions of Gnosticism, by the work of an ignorant or demented demiurge, who creates the natural cosmos as a botched imitation of a higher order of being, setting a demonic overseer to guard each of its levels. Rather than an image of divine order, the cosmos becomes a horrific cage by which to capture and torment what fragments of true being remain in the world. This picture, developed most fully in the Syrian-Egyptian strain of Gnosticism, especially the writings of Valentinus, is powerfully described in Hans Jonas, *The Gnostic Religion,* 2d ed., rev. (Boston: Beacon Press, 1963), 57–65 and 174–96. It is the comprehensiveness of Lear's vision of an alienating, monstrous creation that provokes the analogy with Gnosticism. But of course, the play's vision is at best a fraction of a complete Gnostic mythology. *King Lear* contains no higher world, no call from above, and no promise of a secret knowledge that would save both human and divine beings trapped within the fallen orders of the cosmos—all of which are part of the Gnostic story. Part of the fright of the play lies in its ardent refusal of dualism. The only demons are those imaginary ones that pursue Mad Tom, the only gods those improvised by Gloucester, Kent, Lear, or Edgar. If there is any recollection of the Gnostic demiurge it is found in Lear himself during the storm, where he becomes, as Kozintsev writes, a mad clockmaker or "collector of space" (*King Lear:The Space of Tragedy,* 119).

46. Cf. Harold Bloom, *Ruin the Sacred Truths: Poetry and Belief from the Bible to the Present* (Cambridge, Mass.: Harvard University Press, 1989), 72: "Nature, in the drama, is both origin and end, mother and catastrophe, and it ought to be Lear's function to hold and safeguard the middle ground between the daemonic world and the realm of gods. He fails, massively, and the ensuing tragedy engulfs an entire world."

47. Calvin, *Sermons on Job,* 30.

48. Stanley Cavell, "The Avoidance of Love: A Reading of *King Lear,*" in *Disowning Knowledge in Six Plays of Shakespeare* (Cambridge: Cambridge University Press, 1987), 39–124.

49. Geoffrey H. Hartman, "Words and Wounds," in *Saving the Text: Literature / Derrida / Philosophy* (Baltimore: Johns Hopkins University Press, 1981), 129, writes that "Cordelia's 'nothing' has, in its very flatness, the ring of a curse." I am indebted here to Hartman's broader meditations in this essay on our ineluctable human need to be blessed or cursed by language, and on the often traumatic consequences of our desire to be "worded."

50. Jean-Luc Godard, *King Lear* (1987); my transcription.

51. I quote the First Folio text of Lear's response in line 190. The text of the First Quarto, which Foakes chooses, has instead, "How, nothing will come of nothing."

52. Wallace Stevens, *Collected Poems* (New York: Alfred A. Knopf, 1954), 10.

53. Recall that the white hair of old men is one of the play's chief metonymies for age and authority, the thing that should command respect and pity but is instead exposed to mockery. Lear's tearing out of his beard enacts his shame; his self-violence also preempts his daughters' cruelty. Compare here Gloucester's amazing fancy, when Regan so shamelessly plucks at *his* beard (the shadow of his eyes): "These hairs which thou dost ravish from my chin / Will quicken and accuse thee" (3.7.37–38). Gloucester imagines that his hairs could become a crowd of tongues which would take his part against his tormentors. Lear, by contrast, allows his hairs to become nothing. Yet as an ironic gift to the storm, they too might inflect his curses as much as his shame. Amazed at his wife's cruelty, Albany cries, "O Goneril, / You are not worth the dust which the rude wind / Blows in your face" (4.2.30–32). What if that derogating dust included particles of her father's beard?

54. Marvin Rosenberg, *The Masks of King Lear* (Newark: University of Delaware Press, 1972), 113, suggests that the fool's words keep in play, often ironically, Lear's early willful language of more and less, less and more.

55. William R. Elton's *"King Lear" and the Gods* (1966; reprint, Lexington: University of Kentucky Press, 1988), remains the most comprehensive scholarly account of the varying styles of skepticism about divinity to which the play gives voice, and their sources in Renaissance thinking. He focuses especially on the conflict between an Epicurean tradition of doubt, which sees the gods as at best idle and disinterested, ruling over a world dominated by fortune and chance, and the skepticism of thinkers like Montaigne and Luther, who do allow the presence of a controlling providence in history but place it beyond the scope of human knowledge, an aspect of a God who remains entirely "unlike."

56. We who watch and listen are indeed among the sole residues of divine attention left in this archaic but resolutely secular theater of cruelty; we share, in a sense, the desolation of the gods, something which may ask us to reconsider our authority or lack of authority as members of an audience, our real and conventional

impotence in the face of what we see, our pleasure or sport or pain in watching human suffering. This would entail a more radical version of what Franco Moretti sees happening in much late Elizabethan and Jacobean theater. When the ideology of absolutism starts to be degraded, Moretti argues, the functions of judgment, moral reason, and political critique in the theater are taken away from the onstage chorus (as well as from a world of wise aristocrats) and relocated in a popular audience. See Franco Moretti, "'A Huge Eclipse': Tragic Form and the Deconsecration of Sovereignty," in *The Power of Forms in the English Renaissance,* ed. Stephen Greenblatt (Norman: Pilgrim Books, 1982) 7–40.

57. There is something of the sublime showstopper explicitly written into the role of Mad Tom. The title page of the First Quarto (1608) in fact calls attention to this role, as if to catch the interest of buyers who had heard rumors of the stage performance: "M. William Shak-speare: HIS True Chronicle Historie of the life and death of King LEAR and his three Daughters. *With the unfortunate life of* Edgar, *sonne* and heire to the Earle of Gloster, and his sullen and assumed humor of TOM of Bedlam: *As it was played before the Kings Maiestie at Whitehall upon S.* Stephans *night in Christmas Hollidayes.* By his Maiesties servants playing usually at the Gloabe on the Banck-side."

I imagine Lear at certain moments looking into Edgar's mouth—with as much fright as fascination—in order see what's inside it. He looks not as an exorcist, searching for an alien demon, but as one who wants to take upon himself the voice of Tom's madness. Such a gesture would anticipate the end of the play, where Lear looks into Cordelia's mouth and tries to hear from it the low sound he knows she can no longer produce. I build this thought on my recollection of an extraordinary moment in John Cassavetes's 1974 film *A Woman under the Influence,* in which a somewhat anarchic housewife (Gena Rowlands) listens with rapt attention as a guest at her table—one of a crew of ordinary laborers her husband is boss of, and has brought home to supper—starts suddenly to sing a Verdi aria. She puts her face close to his, staring into his mouth, as if intent on finding there the source of the voice or the song, to breathe in his breath, to frame her lips to repeat the song. For a moment, indeed, her mouth becomes her ear.

58. Thomas Nashe, in *The Terrors of the Night,* associates melancholy with Mad Tom's swampy landscape: "The grossest part of our blood is the melancholy humour, which in the spleen congealed whose office is to disperse it, with his thick steaming fenny vapours casteth a mist over the spirit and clean bemasketh the fantasy. And even as slime and dirt in a standing puddle engender toads and frogs and many other unsightly creatures, so this slimy melancholy humour, still thickening as it stands still, engendreth many misshapen objects in our imaginations" (*The Unfortunate Traveller and Other Works,* ed. J. B. Steane [Harmondsworth: Penguin, 1972], 217).

59. G. Wilson Knight, in *The Wheel of Fire: Interpretations of Shakespearian Tragedy,* 4th ed., rev. (London: Methuen, 1949), argues that the animal symbolism in *Lear* has a twofold relation to the "purgatorial" but still naturalistic progress undergone

by so many of the play's characters. "These numerous [animal] references serve a dual purpose, both insisting on man's kinship with nature—especially, here, nature ugly as a mongrel-cur—and also lending themselves at the same time to the extravagant and bizarre effects of madness. But madness itself is the disjointing of the mind by the tug of conflicting principles: the animal and the divine; the past and the future. Man's agony comes in the wrench of futurity from the inertia of animal life" (205)—even if that future is no less animalistic.

60. As Nashe's Jack Wilton says: "The first traveller was Cain, and he was called a vagabond runagate on the face of the earth. . . . God had no greater curse to lay upon the Israelites, than by leading them out of their own country to live as slaves in a strange land. That which was their curse, we Englishmen count our chief blessedness. He is nobody, that hath not travelled" (*The Unfortunate Traveller and Other Works,* 341).

61. If Tom recalls Nashe's unfortunate traveller, he is also like someone compelled to live inside one of Nashe's manic catalogs.

62. One wants to ask, is there a single self whose history could unite these fragments? Or does Tom strive to be the voice of all suffering?

63. Leslie S. Katz, "Robert Armin and the Audio-Structure of *King Lear*" (unpublished essay).

64. See Paolo Valesio, "The Language of Madness in the Renaissance," *Yearbook of Italian Studies* 1 (1971): 199–234, on the subversive and indecorous literariness that characterizes representations of mad speech in the period. More generally on the infectious, corrosive self-referentiality of nonsense speech, see Susan Stewart, *Nonsense: Aspects of Intertextuality in Folklore and Literature* (Baltimore: Johns Hopkins University Press, 1979); as well as Jean-Jacques Lecercle's *Philosophy through the Looking-Glass: Language, Nonsense, Desire* (La Salle: Open Court, 1985), which speaks of nonsense as *délire,* an utterance that, like a scream, returns us to the divided, incoherent, and material origins of language. Lecercle's chief examples come from Lewis Carroll, but his characterizations are resonant for the case of Mad Tom.

65. See Hartman, "Words and Wounds."

66. Lear takes his cue from the cruelty in these blessings later on: "I remember thine eyes well enough." Herbert Blau comments: "What we show prescribes. 'Bless thy sweet eyes, they bleed,' says Mad Tom to his blinded father, agape with the incredible wound. Is it a benediction, or is the blessing revolted? Bless what bleeds. Almost unbearable—but you might have to live it both ways. We see what might happen if what *is* happening weren't so palpably true" (*The Impossible Theater: A Manifesto* [New York: Collier Books, 1964], 107–8). Hartman, "Words and Wounds," 132, notes that "the etymological meaning of blessing is to mark with blood in order to hallow."

67. William Flesch's *Generosity and the Limits of Authority: Shakespeare, Herbert, Milton* (Ithaca: Cornell University Press, 1992), 146–90, offers a nuanced account of the residual blessing or gift in Lear's words, making telling use of Marcel Mauss's theory of the gift.

68. I take it that this gentleman's "twain" refers as much to Goneril and Regan as to Adam and Eve.

69. Kozintsev, *King Lear:The Space of Tragedy,* 160, writes: "It is as if the old man takes off his battered hat from his grey head and as in conjuring tricks in the circus, shakes various people out of it: a judge, a thief, a prostitute, an executioner, a money-lender, a swindler. He arranges them in pairs: For instance, he starts with the thief and the judge and covers them with his cap. One, two . . . On the count of 'three' the cap is lifted: the figures have changed places, now they are indistinguishable."

70. The dilated, often grotesque satirical play of this scene is a particularly complex instance of what Frank Kermode sees as the continual suspension of apocalypse in *King Lear:* "When the end comes it is not an end, and both suffering and the need for patience are perpetual." See *The Sense of an Ending: Studies in the Theory of Fiction* (New York: Oxford University Press, 1967), 82.

71. G. K. Hunter notes: "What we think the exact nature of *that* [in line 165] is depends on whether we suppose that Lear is more obsessed with kingship or with corruption at this point. If he is concerned with his kingship, what he gives Gloucester to *able* him will be some document of the royal prerogative. If corruption is uppermost in his mind (as I suppose) what he gives is 'money,' and what *seals th'accuser's lips* is (as in lines 165–66) a bribe. In either case his flowers would seem the only things he can give" (*King Lear,* ed. G. K. Hunter [Harmondsworth: Penguin, 1972], 290–91).

72. See William Empson, *The Structure of Complex Words* (Ann Arbor: University of Michigan Press, 1967), 145.

73. Cavell, "The Avoidance of Love," 72.

74. Wallace Stevens, *Opus Posthumous,* rev. ed., ed. Milton J. Bates (New York: Alfred A. Knopf, 1989), 123.

CODA

1. Samuel Beckett, *Not I,* in *Collected Shorter Plays* (New York: Grove Press, 1984), 221. The mouth is not entirely alone onstage. Across from and slightly below it onstage right is a still, hooded figure, "fully faintly lit," who raises and lets fall his arms after each of the mouth's refusals to say "I." It is "a gesture of helpless compassion. It lessens with each recurrence till scarcely perceptible at third" (215).

2. Ibid., 215.

3. Billie Whitelaw describes the terrible strain of mastering the part of Mouth for the first English production of *Not I* in *Billie Whitelaw . . . Who He? An Autobiography* (New York: St. Martin's Press, 1995), 116–31.

4. The Theatre de Complicite production of *The Three Lives of Lucie Cabrol,* adapted by Simon McBurney and Mark Wheatley from a story by John Berger, directed by Simon McBurney, was performed at Alice Tully Hall, Lincoln Center,

August 9, 1996. The Gate Theatre production of Beckett's *Not I,* directed by Michael Colgan, was performed at the John Jay Theater, New York, August 1, 1996. *Qui est là,* conceived and directed by Peter Brook, was performed by the actors of Le Centre International de Créations Théâtrales, at Bouffes du Nord, in Paris, on January 31, 1997.

5. Bert O. States, *Great Reckonings in Little Rooms: On the Phenomenology of the Theater* (Berkeley: University of California Press, 1985), 37.

6. Ibid., 113.

7. I am indebted here to Michael Goldman's remarkable study *The Actor's Freedom: Toward a Theory of Drama* (New York: Viking, 1975).

8. Cf. Herbert Blau, *The Impossible Theater: A Manifesto* (New York: Collier Books, 1964), 141–42: "*Thoughts beside a dark window:* There is an actor in the center of an acting area. Say all you want about exhibitionism, if I understand anything about human nature and profited from my experience in the theater, the first thing an actor in the center of an acting area wants to do is get the hell out of there. The drama . . . explores the question of what keeps him there. . . . The will to stay contests with the will to run. (As that great runner Falstaff proves, that is no small will.) The director's action consists of realizing the specific world in which this conflict is to occur, organizing its traffic, making it a figure of the conflict, and using every resource of his psychology and his stage to compel the actor back to his own tensions, rhythm summoning image and image rhythm, to make him want to run and will to stay, without letting one impulse triumph easily over the other."

9. Jean-Louis Barrault writes of such paradoxes: "A mask confers upon a given expression the maximum of intensity together with an impression of absence. A mask expresses at the same time the maximum of life and the maximum of death; it partakes of the visible and of the invisible, of the apparent and the absolute. The mask exteriorizes a deep aspects of life, and in so doing, it helps to rediscover instinct. This kind of simultaneous exteriorization of the inner and outer aspects of life, of the relative and of the absolute, of life and death, makes it possible to reach through incantation a better contact with the audience" (*The Theatre of Jean-Louis Barrault,* trans. Joseph Chiari [New York: Hill and Wang, 1961], 76–77).

10. Peter Brook, *The Shifting Point* (New York: Harper and Row, 1987), 220.

11. See Thomas Bishop, *Shakespeare and the Theatre of Wonder* (Cambridge: Cambridge University Press, 1996), 17–41, on the ambivalent, threshold quality of theatrical wonder, something that both invites and obscures knowledge, that simultaneously wounds and heals the spectator's desire to see what cannot be seen.

12. See Goldman, *The Actor's Freedom,* 53–110.

13. Wallace Stevens's thoughts about repeating things—"Perhaps, / The man-hero is not the exceptional monster, / But he that of repetition is most master"—ring deeply true for the struggles of the actor in the theater. See *Collected Poems* (New York: Alfred A. Knopf, 1954), 406. The manner in which Stevens's poetry thinks about the life and death of human gesture, and about the way we stand, and look, and listen in space, makes him one of our great, if still unrecognized, theorists of theater.

14. See Peter Brook, *The Empty Space* (New York: Atheneum, 1968), 9–41.

15. Goldman, *The Actor's Freedom,* 27. Speaking of the vexed relation of audiences to what they see onstage, Eric Bentley, *The Life of the Drama* (New York: Atheneum, 1964), 181, writes: "One begins to feel like a ghost as one tries to figure out one's own place in this scheme of things, but how much more ghostly is the actor's experience! . . . If the actor's role is a ghost, an audience is a ghost of a ghost."

16. Cocteau's words are quoted in Bentley, *The Life of the Drama,* 169.

17. Goldman, *The Actor's Freedom,* 28.

18. See Antonin Artaud, *The Theater and Its Double,* trans. Mary Caroline Richards (Grove Press: New York, 1958), 109.

19. Rainer Maria Rilke, *Rodin and Other Prose Pieces,* trans. G. Craig Houston (1954; repr. London: Quartet Books, 1986), 19.

20. Antonin Artaud, *Selected Writings,* ed. Susan Sontag, trans. Helen Weaver (New York: Farrar, Straus, and Giroux), 217.

21. Sophocles, *Oedipus the King,* trans. Stephen Berg and Diskin Clay (New York: Oxford University Press, 1978), 33.

22. Recall Marcel Proust's description of his fictive actress Berma (based partly on Sarah Bernhardt) lending body and voice to the character of Phèdre: "all these, voice, posture, gestures, veils, round this embodiment of an idea which a line of poetry is . . . were merely additional envelopes which, instead of concealing, showed up in greater splendour *the soul that had assimilated them to itself and had spread itself through them,* lava-flows of different substances, grown translucent, the superimposition of which causes only a richer refraction of the imprisoned, central ray that pierces through them, and makes more extensive, more precious and more beautiful the flame-drenched matter in which it is enshrined. So Berma's interpretation was, around Racine's work, a second work, quickened also by genius" (*In Search of Lost Time,* trans. C. K. Scott Moncrieff and Terence Kilmartin, rev. D. J. Enright, 6 vols. [New York: Modern Library, 1993], 3:56; my emphasis).

23. Ovid, *The Metamorphoses,* trans. Rolfe Humphries (Bloomington: Indiana University Press, 1955), 287, bk. 12, lines 54–56.

24. I wonder if these words, which all but announce the arrival of the ghost, are not an example of the intentionally opaque speech which Stephen Orgel examines in "The Poetics of Incomprehensibility," *Shakespeare Quarterly* 42, no. 3 (1991): 431–37.

25. Geoffrey Chaucer, *The House of Fame,* in *The Riverside Chaucer,* ed. Larry D. Benson, 3d ed. (Boston: Houghton Mifflin, 1987), 370, lines 1920–1924.

26. John Milton, *Paradise Lost,* ed. Alistair Fowler (London: Longman, 1971), 134, bk. 2, lines 951–57.

# INDEX